Making Marriage Modern

D1617565

STUDIES IN THE HISTORY OF SEXUALITY
Guido Ruggiero, General Editor

Further volumes are in preparation.

Making Marriage Modern

Women's Sexuality
from the Progressive Era
to World War II

CHRISTINA SIMMONS

OXFORD
UNIVERSITY PRESS

OXFORD
UNIVERSITY PRESS

Oxford University Press, Inc., publishes works that further
Oxford University's objective of excellence
in research, scholarship, and education.

Oxford   New York
Auckland   Cape Town   Dar es Salaam   Hong Kong   Karachi
Kuala Lumpur   Madrid   Melbourne   Mexico City   Nairobi
New Delhi   Shanghai   Taipei   Toronto

With offices in
Argentina   Austria   Brazil   Chile   Czech Republic   France   Greece
Guatemala   Hungary   Italy   Japan   Poland   Portugal   Singapore
South Korea   Switzerland   Thailand   Turkey   Ukraine   Vietnam

Published by Oxford University Press, Inc.
198 Madison Avenue, New York, New York 10016
www.oup.com

First issued as an Oxford University Press paperback, 2011

Oxford is a registered trademark of Oxford University Press.

Library of Congress Cataloging-in-Publication Data
Simmons, Christina.
Making marriage modern : women's sexuality from the Progressive Era
to World War II / Christina Simmons.
p. cm. —(Studies in the history of sexuality)
Includes bibliographical references and index.
ISBN 978-0-19-506411-7 (hardcover); 978-0-19-987403-3 (paperback)
1. Sex in marriage—United States—History—20th century.
2. Marriage—United States—History—20th century.
3. Sex customs—United States—History—20th century.
I. Title.
HQ18.U5S554 2009
646.7'80973—dc22   2008033823

Printed in the United States of America
on acid-free paper

For Bruce, Matt, and Daniel

and

in memory of Susan Porter Benson

Acknowledgments

Mari Jo Buhle's lecture on the "New Morality" in her women's history course at Brown University first drew me to the study of women's sexuality and marriage. She taught us about women's rejection of Victorian mores, their claiming of sexual rights in the 1910s and 1920s, and the proposals for companionate marriage that followed. Yet these changes seemed limited because in our time women were still denied sexual initiative and hemmed in by the double standard. But courses like Mari Jo's and the wider women's liberation movement radically opened and recast many women's visions of the world and challenged the reigning sexual images of women. These new perspectives enabled us to understand the past in new ways as well.

Therefore, my first acknowledgment is to the brave feminists of this largest of all the great social movements of the late twentieth century, and in particular to pioneer scholars like Mari Jo Buhle and Louise Lamphere, my dissertation advisers, and Nancy Cott and Estelle Freedman. Their work has been formative for my own, and their comments on my earlier work furthered the development of my thinking. I have a great debt to my own cohort as well: sisterhood inspired the wonderful model of committed scholarship of my graduate school dissertation group friends, Judith E. Smith and Barbara Melosh, and of the Providence women's history group, including Mari Jo, Judy, Barbara, the late Susan Porter Benson, Kate Dunnigan, Sonya Michel, Gail Sansbury, Sharon Hartman Strom, and Valerie Yow. Overlapping these groups was The House, 659–661 Hope St., where raucous discussions of movies and politics, outstanding meals, and the camaraderie of feminist cooperative living engaged, over my time there, Ruth Milkman, Peter Evans, Louise Lamphere, Barbara Melosh, Bruce Tucker, Susan Porter Benson, Ed Benson, Ophelia Benson, Kate Dunnigan, Frank Costigliola, and Judith Sealander. Although this book is my project, like all intellectual work, it was made possible by this wider political and intellectual world and by these and other feminist colleagues and friends.

Subsequently, over the long gestation of this book, other friends and colleagues also helped by discussing aspects of the work or reading and commenting on papers, chapters, or article manuscripts. These include Barry Adam, Susan Porter Benson, Elsa Barkley Brown, Anne Forrest, Estelle Freedman, Nancy Hewitt, Molly Ladd-Taylor, Barbara Melosh, Patricia Palmieri, Kathy Peiss, Leila Rupp, Charlene Senn, Judy Smith, and Bruce Tucker. Joanne Meyerowitz and Mari Jo Buhle commented in depth and with great insight on the entire manuscript. Thomas LeBien of Oxford University Press gave useful feedback on early chapters, and most recently Susan Ferber's acute and sensible editing greatly improved the manuscript. My deepest thanks to all these people for their comments, suggestions, and support.

I would like to acknowledge the aid of a University of Cincinnati Summer Faculty Research Fellowship and an American Council of Learned Societies Grant-in-Aid that enabled me to find more African American sources. A National Endowment for the Humanities Fellowship gave me the space to conceptualize the entire project for the first time as well as to further the research after a period of childbearing and heavy teaching. A semester of support from the University of Windsor's Humanities Research Group provided space and time to draft the second chapter and further develop the material on companionate marriage. I am most grateful for the help of all these agencies.

I wish also to thank librarians at places I have lived and worked over the time of the research, including Brown University, Dalhousie University, the University of Cincinnati, and the University of Windsor. Archivists Richard Wolfe of the Harvard Countway Library, Deborah Edel, Joan Nestle, and Judith Schwarz of the Lesbian Herstory Archive, and Shawn Wilson of the Kinsey Institute Library were of great assistance. My gratitude goes as well to research assistants Carmen Poole and Andrew Anastasovski of the University of Windsor for their excellent research and bibliographic work. Thanks also to Irene Moore, Frank Tucker, and John Thale for help with illustrations, and Jim O'Brien for excellent indexing.

I walked a very long road completing this book, and I often felt discouraged. I have been sustained by love, advice, and generosity from family and friends. Long ago my parents, Katherine Blocker Simmons and James

E. Simmons, stood behind me in the education that underpinned this work. I am sorry they did not live to see its conclusion. I am happy that my supportive baby boom siblings, Jay, Anne, Katherine, Martha, Sarah, John, and stepbrother Dan, are here to see it. Encouragement and ongoing friendship from Susan Porter Benson, Marian Geyer Williams, Anita Kerbeshian McPherson, Barbara Melosh, Joanne Meyerowitz, Judy Smith, and Sharon Strom especially revived me in the difficult moments. Fun and incisive feminist discussions with my Windsor feminist "reading/dinner" group, including Janice Drakich, Anne Forrest, Rena Isenberg, Ramona Lumpkin, Pam Milne, Veronika Mogyorody, Lynne Phillips, Charlene Senn, and Meredith Smye, have kept me going. Paula Merideth provided vital support during my long struggle with chronic fatigue syndrome. And "my guys"—my partner, Bruce Tucker, and our sons, Matthew and Daniel Tucker-Simmons—have borne with me and even been enthusiastic about this project. Bruce is the world's best listener. He has offered his wonderful, careful, and insightful reflections on the questions in this study, on history generally, and on the writing process. He has also shared the demands and the joys of household, parenting, and professional work as we moved from Providence to Halifax to Cincinnati to Windsor and has often done more than his half. Matt and Daniel have diverted me with their growing up, with Scouts, soccer, hockey, and their excellent cooking. I am more grateful than I can say to this marvelous circle of friends and family who upheld me over many years and believed in the importance of this work.

Portions of pp. 21–25 and 49–54 were originally published as "African Americans and Sexual Victorianism in the Social Hygiene Movement, 1910–1940," by Christina Simmons, *Journal of the History of Sexuality* 4 (1): 51–75. Copyright © 1993 by the University of Texas Press. All rights reserved.

Portions of pp. 58–104 were originally published as "Women's Power in Sex Radical Challenges to Marriage in the Early-Twentieth-Century United States," by Christina Simmons, *Feminist Studies* 29, 1 (Spring 2003): 169–98. Reprinted by permission of the publisher, Feminist Studies, Inc.

Portions of pp. 150–77 were originally published as " 'Modern Marriage' for African Americans, 1920–1940," by Christina Simmons, *Canadian Review of American Studies* 30 (3): 273–300. Reprinted by permission of Canadian Association for American Studies, www.utpjournals.com.

Contents

Making Marriage Modern

Introduction

Marge Piercy's striking novel *Small Changes* (1973) opens with the story of Beth Phail's wedding day in the 1960s. An ordinary, shy, working-class woman from Syracuse, New York, Beth feels lost in her huge wedding dress and swamped by the demands and criticisms of female relatives. Every conventional step in the wedding celebration seems to unfold mechanically, with no connection to her self or her emotions. She feels wrapped "like a package"; her hair is a "stiff coiled mass that smell[s] chemical." Her mother reminds her to be grateful that the family is spending money for a "real wedding" "in church with flowers and bridesmaids." Jim, her husband-to-be, "look[s] like somebody else," and she cannot "find her way into his eyes" as she comes up the aisle. Relieved when the event is over and they take off for a New Hampshire honeymoon, Beth experiences further alienation after unsatisfying lovemaking that lasts only fifteen minutes.[1]

Dramatizing the surging feminist censure of heterosexual relations and marriage, Piercy portrays the first year of Beth's unhappy marriage. As the Phails settle into the routines of married life, Jim's sense of entitlement allows him to take the car to work, after he drops Beth off at her department store job forty-five minutes early. He often watches sports on television and never wants to talk with her about her day or her thoughts. He takes her cooking and housekeeping for granted, while dropping his dirty clothes all over the apartment. When Beth tells him she, too, is tired from her job and does not want to cook a fancy meal, she experiences his anger and the threat of violence. Her mother and sister convey the cynicism of older married women as they encourage her to deflect conflict and "manage" Jim. Finally, the sex, usually pleasant during premarital petting, only goes downhill from the wedding night. When Beth speaks up about it, "[h]e calls her frigid," and she learns to fake enjoyment to evade his awakened scrutiny. Lonely and increasingly desperate after her mother and mother-in-law conspire to discipline her and urge pregnancy and Jim destroys her birth control pills, Beth finally flees to Boston, where she finds the women's movement and ultimately enters a lesbian relationship.[2]

Piercy's feminist perspective seemed revolutionary in the 1970s as second-wave feminism came to life in colleges, unions, and women's organizations and surged across the nation's television screens. Yet in fact not all of it was new. Radicals and reformers from the 1910s through the 1940s had made many similar critiques. Lawyer Crystal Eastman and novelist Helen Hull, for example, both members of the radical feminist Heterodoxy Club in Greenwich Village in the 1910s, had also lambasted the gender division of labor. Eastman called for both boys and girls to learn to do housework as well as prepare for careers. Hull depicted in her fiction the sad decline of a marriage from early sharing of domestic tasks to the wife's loss of self in home duties in the face of a stronger male ego; she compared the situation unfavorably to the more equal partnership of two women.[3] Women like birth control campaigner Margaret Sanger, feminist physician Rachelle Yarros, and marriage educator Gladys Groves also demanded sexual pleasure for women and urged men to be more sensitive.[4] These women, along with male colleagues, had criticized sexual and marital arrangements fifty years before the women's liberation movement. This book addresses that earlier moment of challenge and upheaval.

Between 1910 and World War II, a range of activists, writers, and thinkers reconceived women's sexuality and the marriage relationship in response to major social shifts. Increased female employment, higher education, and voting rights were undermining older images of women as frail and innocent. Public panic over venereal disease evoked calls for sex education for both girls and boys. And after a century of Americans' private practice of fertility control, birth control advocates were asserting publicly that contraception should be legalized. Thus began a contentious public conversation that resulted in a new vision of women's sexuality and relation to marriage in the United States, one that became the predominant, though certainly not the only, cultural ideal by the 1940s.

Centered on the East Coast, especially New York City, the people who were most visible in calling for change were predominantly middle-class whites of northern European descent, as was their intended audience. It was their social group that had promulgated and enforced the previously dominant values through churches, schools, public media, and courts. These people not only had the greatest ability to broadcast their views but also saw what was happening in their social class as most significant for society as a whole.[5] Due to culture, class, and/or religion, many recently arrived European, Mexican, and Asian Americans and their children, as well as rural and working-class African Americans, stood apart in various ways from the sexual changes this study describes. Some of these groups held significantly different understandings of womanhood and marriage based more in nonromantic economic and familial solidarity and/or in Catholic sacramental ideas of procreative marriage. The alternative views of these groups are not addressed here.[6] Depending on their separateness and the development of their own institutions (like Catholic schools), they may have been more or less able to fend off the ideas of "modern marriage." But many would have found it increasingly difficult by the mid–twentieth century not to be aware of the new views, broadcast by national media as well as organized professionals.

Yet some less powerful social groups did affect the rethinking of sexuality and marriage. Urban immigrant youth contributed indirectly by forging new patterns of heterosexual behavior, such as dating, that influenced those who were writing and publishing on the issues. Working-class immigrant radicals like anarchist Emma Goldman were important voices in the debates. It is less well known that African Americans also took part. They were an especially stigmatized population; freed from formal slavery in the mid–nineteenth century, they continued to be marked as inferior to whites and as representatives of an excessive and supposedly savage sexuality. Defending themselves against attacks on their respectability and fitness for citizenship in the post–Civil War era, the tiny African American middle class, as Protestant Christians, had generally adopted similar sexual and marital values to those of the dominant white culture.[7] In the early twentieth century an expanding black middle class joined in public discussions of sex, though they did so from a distinctive perspective shaped by their experiences of racism. This study investigates their role in these challenges.

Disseminated as part of a broad and increasingly national culture by the 1940s, the tracts, social commentary, and advice manuals examined here created new public standards for men's and women's behavior and sensibilities, but it is difficult to describe precisely how ordinary people responded to or tried to enact these ideas. One way of piecing together evidence is to use early medical and social science studies of sexual behavior, which I have done where possible. But the predominant emphasis is on the gender politics of the new formulations—what they implied about cultural expectations for women's power in heterosexual relations.

———

Women have participated in heterosexual relations most significantly by marrying. Of course, men and women engaged in much sexual activity outside marriage, notably in prostitution and in casual or long-term nonmarital relationships, which frequently came to be recognized as marriages. But legally, socially, and culturally, marriage has been a key social institution. It has organized kinship, social and economic life, and day-to-day governance in Western cultures, and it has grounded the subordinate place of women. Marriages undergirded bonds between families, most obviously in the marriages that joined European political dynasties in the Middle Ages and after. Before industrialization, marriage and the households it created were the center of much economic production, as artisans produced goods in their homes with the help of family members and apprentices.[8] These households were patriarchal ones that also served as a means of governance in early modern societies without extensive agencies of the state, as was the case when Europeans spread across the vast lands taken from aboriginal people in North America. Patriarchal families governed children, servants, and unmarried youth, and they subordinated women: a single woman's father controlled her sexual behavior because her virginity at marriage guaranteed to her husband her sexual fidelity and the legitimacy of his heirs. After marriage, husbands owned wives' labor, controlled their children, and were entitled to their sexual attentions.[9]

The revisions of marriage proposed in the 1920s were a new phase in the development of love marriage, one in which reformers sought to stress the specifically sexual component of romantic love. The idea of marrying for romantic love rather than social, economic, or political considerations had emerged in Western culture in the eighteenth century.[10] It gave greater weight to young people's preferences. It began to create higher standards for emotional compatibility in marriage, at the same time that increasing opportunities for separation and divorce in the geographically mobile society of the nineteenth century made ending difficult unions more feasible. Nevertheless, assumptions of patriarchal order within intact marriages remained very powerful long into the twentieth century.[11]

———

Sexual reformers and radicals ascribed their society's sexual crisis to outdated conventions of genteel Victorian culture, with a special emphasis on women's experience. They especially condemned what they considered Victorianism's dysfunctional sexual repressiveness and created what I have termed the myth of Victorian repression. It was a myth in the sense that it strategically created a broad generalization about Victorian culture that advocates of change used rhetorically to distance themselves from the past and present themselves as pioneers of a modern way. Yet the myth did point to some powerful elements of Victorian culture and society that rested increasingly uneasily with modern urban people after 1900, in particular, intrusive moral policing, including denial of free speech for alternative sexual views; the illegality of contraception; and constraints on women, based on the double standard of moral judgment. These interrelated problems stemmed from the large historical changes connected with industrial capitalism.

The need for moral policing that bourgeois groups felt in Victorian America arose from political and economic shifts that were eroding older hierarchies of authority, including the patriarchal family. The factory system began to replace household economic production, pulling young people out of immediate family supervision. Growing cities enticed some to seek fortunes in the volatile business economy, while others escaped traditional family and community authority by moving west.[12] Culturally and psychologically, these transformations were related to a developing concept of individual self, with a sense of the sexual at its center. This sense of self became a new means for surveillance and control that relied on individuals' inner consciousness and self-discipline, partially displacing the external, often bodily, controls of traditional authority. For example, child-rearing practices focused more on self-control by conscience rather than parental use of force, to produce young people who could maintain their sexual purity until marriage.[13] The notion of individuality should not be overstated, since both men and women also remained deeply embedded in often coercive social and economic relations with family and community. Nevertheless, women always had much less personal freedom and remained more tied to and defined by family relationships than men did.

The growth of individual freedom led to social tensions over sexual expression versus restraint that were both powerful and different for women and men. On the one hand, the growth of the market allowed and relied on the cultivation of individual desire. In the growing cities, where families and religious communities were less able to oversee the behavior of youth and where large numbers of single men and women were drawn for work, sex was commercialized. Erotica, sexual acts, abortion, contraceptives, and scientific and speculative writings about sexual life were readily bought and sold. A male sporting culture developed in which men could freely indulge in sex with prostitutes. Women, in contrast, whose sexuality was valued more than their capacity for labor, could only sell their bodies on this market.[14] In a less commercial vein, radicals known as free lovers critiqued the legal rigidities of marriage and its restriction of individual freedom, especially for women; some called for divorce and others for the freedom to have multiple relationships. They emphasized loving sexual relationships, rather than conventional marriage, as the focus of personal meaning in life.[15]

On the other hand, a volatile business economy also required men with self-control, who could delay marriage, work hard, and save money. Republican political forms called for morally self-governing men, who could restrain themselves without the heavy hand of traditional hierarchy and authority; and evangelical Christianity extolled the model of the sexually upright "Christian gentleman." Thus, sexual propriety was linked to proper governance and virtue. Sexual restraint was also essential for respectable women, but they played a different role. Excluded from the public economic and political world, as wives they were to inspire men's self-control and dedication to work and family.[16]

The polarized gender roles—"separate spheres"—that upheld this Protestant culture of moral control included the idea that women were "passionless," less sexually interested or assertive than men. In the past, women had been considered just as sexual as men and feared as potential seductresses. The concept of passionlessness emerged from women's important place in evangelical Christianity—they were the majority of converts in the wave of revivals early in the century. Passionlessness gave women a moral dignity the older culture had denied them for their supposed sexual perfidiousness. Although passionlessness could coexist with romantic love, and early thinkers did not intend to deny women's sexual potential, by the late nineteenth century the culture acknowledged respectable women's sexuality primarily as maternal instinct or as a highly spiritualized romantic love, different from the aggressive passion associated with men.[17] To claim respectability and middle-class status, women had to present themselves as passionless and were judged more harshly than men in their sexual conduct.

It is worth noting that chaste public appearance did not preclude sexual feeling expressed privately within the confines of engagement or marriage. Even for the morally respectable, the psychic focus on sex within courtship and marriage was growing. Love letters between engaged and married couples about their passionate sexual feelings show one of the ways that some women found to live out their sexual selves within or in secret opposition to the public culture of passionlessness, linking sex tightly with romantic love.[18]

Yet values of sexual self-control and purity were officially very powerful. Advocates pressed their cause through both voluntary moral reform organizations and the state. Early efforts, mostly by women, were missionary and voluntaristic, aimed at saving prostitutes and shaming or converting promiscuous men. After the Civil War, both men and women were involved. Groups like the Young Women's Christian Association (YWCA) and Women's Christian Temperance Union (WCTU) and other supporters of women's rights opposed proposals by police and physicians to regulate prostitution legally for public health reasons. They objected to the recognition and acceptance of it and to the violation of the civil rights of prostitutes, who faced both sexual exploitation and compulsory health examinations. Founding the Social Purity Alliance in 1885, these activists sought legislative action, as in their successful efforts in many states to raise the age when women could legally consent to sex, from ten to sixteen or eighteen. But the social purity movement also continued voluntaristic reform, with efforts to inculcate sexual purity in young men and women through moral education.[19]

In addition, wealthy and influential white evangelical businessmen proposed to regulate the world of commercialized sex, or "vice." They sought to suppress prostitution, erotica, contraception, and abortion through legislation, judicial decisions, and private reform organizations.[20] Most notably, the Young Men's Christian Association (YMCA) of New York and its committee on vice (later the independent Society for the Suppression of Vice) obtained state and then federal obscenity legislation (in 1868 and 1873). They then underwrote the work of vice crusader Anthony Comstock, who was also appointed federal agent to enforce the 1873 law, which popularly bore his name.[21]

The Comstock law allowed prosecution not only of distributors of pornography and performers in erotic entertainments that were part of the commercial sex underworld but also of free lovers like Victoria Woodhull, an outspoken women's rights advocate who ran for president in 1872. She proclaimed the value of free sexual love and denounced hypocrisy, most notably by publicizing the adultery of popular Brooklyn minister Henry Ward Beecher. The Comstock law also defined birth control and abortion information and devices as obscene, and Comstock ruthlessly pursued abortionists and sellers of condoms.[22]

The moral policing of contraception and abortion pointed to another major transformation of the era—the declining birthrate through active fertility control. Smaller families fit better with the economic interests of the urban middle class, less reliant than farm or working-class families on the labor of children and more concerned to educate them. As the primary nurturers and child rearers, women benefited from having fewer children; intensive mothering was more feasible, and their physical health was enhanced. Books on withdrawal and douching had appeared in the 1820s and 1830s, followed by masses of pamphlets and self-help manuals advising the married on how to prevent conception. These ideas were greeted by an eager public already practicing fertility control, primarily through abortion, which in the early nineteenth century remained a woman's common-law right before "quickening," the moment when a pregnant woman can perceive fetal movement (usually in the fifth month). Traditional home remedy abortions persisted along with the increasingly visible commercial type by midcentury. In addition, a range of women from free lovers to suffragists and purity reformers promoted "voluntary motherhood," fertility control through a joint or female decision to abstain from sex. Together these methods helped reduce the U.S. white birthrate from 7 to 3.5 children per woman between 1800 and 1900. (After emancipation the African American birthrate likewise dropped by 50 percent between 1880 and 1940.) Later in the century, commercial contraceptive products, many of them unreliable, were sold on the black market.[23]

Although much contraceptive use merely contributed to smaller families and did not challenge marriage per se, the practice indirectly affected people's thinking: as couples took a more calculating approach to sex and tried to limit pregnancies, they helped to separate conceptually the reproductive and interpersonal aspects of heterosexual relations. In addition, the growing public visibility of these practices, through commercialization of contraception and publication of advice books, brought the issue into public discussion and revealed its potential to subvert the prevailing ideology. That potential lay most pointedly in reducing women's fear of pregnancy, which was a major disincentive to sex outside marriage. Evangelical Christian reformers feared that contraception and abortion, like free love and commercialized sex, would incite sexual licentiousness and destroy moral order.[24]

Thus, both women and men of the dominant white social classes in the United States worked actively to enforce conservative evangelical views of sexuality and marriage. While these efforts did not end the targeted practices, they did drive them underground and suppressed public discussion of alternatives.[25] This power of policing explains the prominence of "repression" in the complaints of twentieth-century reformers, as well as the ignorance of Margaret Sanger, for example, about the nineteenth-century pioneers of birth control and sex radicalism.[26]

—

Earlier commentators have told a story about this period that retains considerable power in popular culture. That story incorporates the myth of Victorian repression and relates the demands for sex education, birth control, and a new form of marriage as a story of escape from the "puritanical" Victorian world to a secular, scientific, and rational modernity in which women were much more equal and sex was finally and rightfully acknowledged as a positive and vital part of human life. Grounding his sexual ideals in nature and biology, erstwhile Greenwich Village radical Floyd Dell illustrated this perspective when he proclaimed grandly in 1930 that the destruction of the repressive patriarchal family "has laid the basis for a more biologically normal family life than has existed throughout the whole of the historical period."[27]

My view of this "repression-to-liberation" theory diverges. Feminism and women's history have offered a more complicated account of women's lives. Inequality has persisted in modern marriage in domestic labor, child care, and sexual activity; "repression" continued for women. In addition, "nature" or a biologically based "truth" cannot be known apart from human culture. Modern sexuality and marriage are historically conditioned and constructed, just as they were in their Victorian forms.

In the early twentieth century the dominant conservative Victorian sexual definitions and codes no longer made sense to many people, and new forms of consciousness and identity developed. Politically, the consolidation of the nation and its government after the Civil War had created many other institutions of social order besides marriage. Conventional marriage and morality no longer seemed so crucial.[28] A culture of consumption expanded and touched more Americans as leisure time increased, advertising developed, and the availability of consumer goods grew. Self-control and self-denial, including in the realm of sex, were out of step with that trend. And, as women became more visible and active in the public world, they could be seen and see themselves more as individuals like men, not passionless but sexual. In these circumstances the ideal of sexual restraint began to seem excessive and even harmful, and sexual expression claimed more cultural cachet.[29]

Conservative Victorian values retained great power in formal, official culture, but popular culture was already moving in a different direction by 1900. Urban nightlife changed as middle-class men began to take their wives and respectable girlfriends to luxurious restaurants and cabarets with sexually suggestive entertainments. Unlike the haunts of the male sporting culture in which only women of the demimonde had appeared, these new resorts were cleaned up enough for "good" women to attend, allowing men and women to dance and drink alcohol together, pleasures Victorian morality had condemned.[30] Other amusements such as movies, dance halls, and skating rinks proliferated in cities of the period, drawing not only an immigrant working-class population but, increasingly, middle-class participants. Before significant censorship started in 1910, movies portrayed respectable women as sexually interested and mocked moral reformers and "old maids." Even later, hints of sensuality in romantic movies were more open than allowed in genteel culture.[31] In this cultural environment, sophisticated urbanites scorned and ridiculed Anthony Comstock's moral surveillance even before his death in 1915.

But it was women's growing presence in the world beyond the family that most undermined Victorian bourgeois culture, because it was their roles as wives and mothers that had anchored it. A small group of college-educated white women and a few African American women gained visibility disproportionate to their numbers as they created new professional roles for themselves as charity and social settlement workers, doctors, and college professors at the end of the century. Many more middle-class women engaged with the temperance and club movements, while a small band of dedicated suffragists continued the fight for the vote. Working-class single women had customarily worked for pay, and though most gave their small wages to their families, their earning gave some leverage against parental control and allowed a few to live with peers and apart from family. Their numbers grew after 1890, and they became very noticeable to reformers, journalists, and novelists seeking to document the "New Woman." Growing numbers of middle-class women also began to take paid employment before marriage, and they, too, helped revise the image of the innocent and domestic woman.[32] When the vote was finally achieved nationally in 1920, it capped the sense that women could no longer be defined as purely domestic. Breaking out of that image of sheltered domesticity and purity, they began to assert that they were sexual beings, too.

Men's right to nurture their sexual selves was also important, but women are more central to the story. People at the time believed women's increased freedom was driving sexual and marital change. Even in colonial New England, women had formed the majority among divorce seekers, but after the 1880s they obtained more than two-thirds of American divorces, pointing to their dissatisfaction with marriage and their ability to do something about it.[33] In addition, women's independence disrupted power relations more than changes in men's lives, since the very definition of marriage in the past involved men's control of women's bodies and labor. Certainly, men played a part in these marital changes. By the end of the nineteenth century, a greater valuation of male passion helped to sexualize the new marriage of the 1920s. Sexual advice manuals also spoke to men in instructing couples about how to achieve ideal sexual relations.[34] However, by and large it was women's behavior and conceptualizations of women's nature and sexuality that lay at the heart of the cultural revisions examined here.

Women's choice of intimate relationships with other women most clearly exemplifies this point. In the nineteenth century a few working-class women obtained male wages and social freedom by passing as men, and some of them sustained relationships with other women. Earlier middle-class women had often carried on romantic friendships with other women that began in adolescence and continued alongside their domestic and marital responsibilities. After the Civil War, higher education and the option of self-support allowed some of these women to remain unmarried and to enter into "Boston marriages," where two respectable women lived together. By the late nineteenth century, some of these women considered themselves sexually different.[35] Women's failure to marry in itself made conservative social critics anxious; sexual relationships with other women epitomized the rejection of men and marriage. While these relationships are not at the center of this study, they are significant because the reshaping of women's heterosexuality was in part a response to this potential.

⸺

This book explains the vision of women's sexuality in relation to marriage that emerged to replace the dominant Victorian model, and it traces how relations of power between men and women were imagined and contested by those who helped to create modern marriage. Those creators were not a monolithic group. Some were claiming a women's sexuality that was independent and no longer a possession of men. Others, especially but not only men, accepted—or feared losing—the power that men had traditionally held. The material and cultural power that marriage represented in this period, when most women continued to need it economically and socially, undermined the possibility of a strongly egalitarian or independent sexuality for women. But modern marriage nonetheless bore the imprint of these contestations and represented some women's claims in a new form.

Chapters 1 and 2 sketch two major challenges to the dominant Victorian synthesis, while chapters 3 through 5 describe the creation of a new model for marriage. Chapter 1, "Education for Social Hygiene," examines the most conservative aspect of the movement for change.[36] Social hygiene reform developed in the 1910s from the coalescence of an earlier religious social purity movement and the more scientifically inclined anti–venereal disease movement. Like other urban reformers, social hygienists were developing sociological methods of gathering knowledge and claiming "science" rather than morality as the basis of their work and of social policies. Many physicians were involved; informed by new scientific knowledge of venereal disease and by sociological approaches to reform, they promoted scientific but conservative sex education. In this work they challenged public reticence about sexuality because they believed prostitution and venereal disease represented so great a social threat that ignorance could no longer be tolerated. They did not challenge the institution of marriage or the gender segregation and difference anchored in it. Nevertheless, by opening the fraught question of men's greater sexual freedom (and greater chance of becoming infected with venereal disease), they provided some opportunity for women to articulate and to criticize dominant sexual practices of the time.

Chapter 2, "Sex Radical Challenges to Marriage," examines individuals who in the same decade overshadowed the cautious sex educators with dramatic gestures of rebellion and violation of prevailing mores. Composed of a loose network of anarchists, feminists, and bohemian artists and intellectuals, sex radicals opposed the Victorian form of marriage and even the institution itself. They reconceived women's sexuality as more similar to men's. They drew on a humanist critique of capitalism developed in the 1880s and 1890s in both Europe and the United States that centered on its damaging effects on personal life, in particular the psychologically deadening impact of the ideals of sexual restraint and respectability.[37] They supported the cause of free speech as they experimented with modern literary and art forms that addressed sexual life.[38] Finally, left-wing women, especially Emma Goldman and Margaret Sanger, began openly to promote birth control. The secretive use of abortion and black market contraceptives that had reduced the American birthrate over the previous century was no longer enough; a determined group of radical women sought to speak publicly about more effective modern contraception and women's need for and right to it.[39] A few supported homosexual or interracial relationships, evoking outrage from defenders of the older moral order.

Chapter 3, "Companionate Marriage," and chapter 4, "Modern Marriage: Three Visions," trace the development of the concept of companionate, or modern, marriage in the 1920s, after the 1919 Red Scare had silenced many of the sex radicals. Companionate marriage was an effort to meld modern practices with legal marriage. Chapter 3 outlines the common elements of the concept, especially sexual intimacy as the cement of marriage and the necessity of birth control to it, freedom from familial control and privacy for young couples, and sexual and psychological equality for women. Chapter 4 compares three competing versions of companionate marriage—what I term "flapper marriage," which modernized male dominance; African American "partnership marriage," in which marital roles were less distinct and marriage was anchored in wider kin and community networks; and "feminist marriage," in which not only sex but also paid work and household labor involved greater equality between women and men.[40]

Finally, chapter 5, "Sexual Advice for Modern Marriage," describes the patterns of sexual advice created in the 1920s through 1940s to assist couples in finding satisfactory forms of sexual relations for the model marriage. Growing out of the birth control and marriage education movements and freed by 1930 from some of the Comstock censorship, a large body of sexual advice literature was published during these decades. Within it strains of feminist support for women's sexual pleasure contended with demands for more sexual activity in the context of ongoing male sexual initiative and control. The highly unequal partnership of marriage limited most women's ability to act on the advice, but its promotion of a new female heterosexuality and a revised form of marriage dominated American culture until the explosive challenges of the women's liberation movement.

1

Education for Social Hygiene

The wistful face of a conventionally beautiful white woman, flanked by a soldier and a sailor staring at her, graced the cover of one of the social hygiene movement's most widely distributed pamphlets on sex education. Its author, Dr. Max Exner, of the Young Men's Christian Association (YMCA), claimed that 2.7 million copies of the pamphlet, "Friend or Enemy?," had been printed by 1918. Exner explained that the potential friends or enemies of his title were a man's "primitive instincts," but he did not comment on the obvious implication of the cover—that it was woman who could be either man's friend or his enemy.[1] As in the Victorian period, such thinking projected onto women responsibility for men's attraction to proper or improper sexual behavior. Exner appealed to the soldiers' sense of loyalty and their manly duty to protect wives and sweethearts as he explained the spread of venereal infection: "[M]any innocent wives are infected with gonorrhea, to pay the penalty for the husband's selfishness with wrecked health, chronic invalidism, or mutilation. All outward symptoms of the disease having long ago disappeared, the young man thinks himself cured and marries." Social hygiene literature appealed to mother love also, as in the poem "Mother-Mine," by Ella Wheeler Wilcox, which ends, "I must be strong, I must be clean, / In mind and body, too— / My debt to all posterity/ and women such as YOU."[2]

This psychological dynamic worked for many men. Exner reported widespread and "deeply touching" responses from "thousands of soldiers" to "Friend or Enemy?" and other leaflets. More popular even than "Friend" was

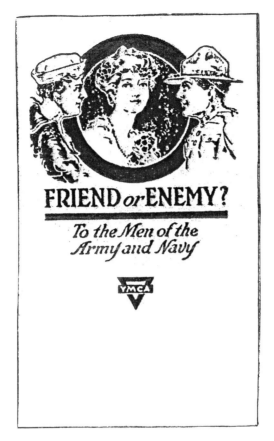

Fig. 1 "Friend or Enemy?"

Cover illustration of Max Exner's social hygiene pamphlet for World War I soldiers, with a woman representing the dual potential of a man's "primitive instincts." Exner, "Social Hygiene and the War," *Journal of Social Hygiene* 5 (1919): 285.

one called "The Nurse and the Knight" that the YMCA had initially declined as "oversentimental." However, when social hygiene workers nonetheless received some from the author and distributed them, "urgent requests came to us for these pamphlets," and they began to use it. "[N]o other pamphlet" generated as much mail, and Exner recounted the story of an officer who read it on board a ship to France and promptly threw overboard the "supplies" he had brought (presumably condoms), resolving "that he would return from France to his family and friends, the same clean man that he was when he left." Nonetheless, the YMCA later withdrew the pamphlet, to great protest, because its content did not accord with the "standardized" scientific presentations of "facts" that "governmental social hygiene agencies" had established. Although science trumped moral sentiment in this case, in fact the two approaches continued to blend uneasily in the movement's work.[3]

This highly visible war effort was part of the opening salvo that social hygienists hurled to begin an intense public debate over sexuality and marriage in the early twentieth century. Despite echoes of Victorian thinking, these reformers moved beyond the earlier social purity movement in using the language not only of morality but also of medicine and science—hence the new label "social hygiene." The movement assumed formal shape as the American Social Hygiene Association (ASHA) in 1913, as white physicians and social workers took up the sexual issues that the social purity and antiprostitution movements had addressed in the nineteenth century. In addition to their moral concerns, however, they drew on new scientific knowledge from Europe about the causes of venereal disease and its serious long-term consequences, such as paralysis, insanity, and sterility. Social hygienists hoped to eliminate venereal disease and prostitution through medical research and treatment and legal measures. In addition, relying on psychologist G. Stanley Hall's new conceptualization of adolescence as a sexually fraught stage of development, they stressed sex education—a more explicitly scientific kind than purity reformers had provided.[4]

By the 1910s, reformers were emphasizing preventive educational work. William Freeman Snow, a physician and first general director of the ASHA, argued in 1916 that social hygiene was no longer primarily a negative force, opposing the evils of venereal disease, but had become "a constructive movement for the promotion of all those conditions of living, environment, and personal conduct which will best protect the family as an institution and secure a rational sex life for the individuals of each generation."[5] Movement leaders continued to promote this "positive" approach, although in practice they had the greatest success in getting the state to institute formal policies repressing prostitution and to establish public health facilities for the treatment of venereal disease. Putting any substantial or explicit sex instruction into public schools was much less successful, although programs were more common in colleges and workplaces.[6] Nevertheless, social hygienists continued to promote sex education and remained influential voices into the 1930s.

The movement was started by white physicians and purity reformers, predominantly men, who represented the most culturally and politically influential classes in the United States. They expressed the ambivalence of reformers who both looked back to the moral conventions of the past and recognized that those conventions were no longer effective. Their decision to use scientific knowledge to inform their activism arose not only from developments in scientific research but also from concerns about the morality and well-being of their own class, especially increasing divorce rates and declining birthrates. It seemed that the independence of women was unsettling the old moral order.[7] They were motivated also by fears about the social and cultural influence of European immigrants and African American migrants in the great cities. Although most social hygienists hoped to restore the Victorian vision of sex and family, their movement opened a small venue for middle-class white women and a few African American men to speak critically about their place in the sexual order. The growth of more explicit discussion of sexual development and disease led some white women to reject their place on the sexual pedestal, while the few African American professionals who gained a foothold in the movement battled racist interpretations of black venereal disease rates. Without intending to, social hygiene reformers stimulated public debate on broader questions of gender and sexuality.

The Cultural Context of Social Hygiene among Whites

Like other Progressives, social hygienists were usually middle- or upper-class white Protestants who sought to ameliorate the social problems of industrial society. In that vein, they revered science, experts, and efficiency and often wished to control, even as they wished to help, immigrants, African Americans, and the working classes of the cities.[8] They feared the new-stock southern and eastern Europeans, Catholic and Jewish, who dominated the waves of immigration from 1890 as a threat to Protestant "civilization," including the prevailing conventions of sex, gender, and marriage. Urban anonymity, alien cultures, and industrial exploitation and poverty, they believed, undermined Victorian mores by means of institutions like the saloon and the brothel.[9] They saw popular amusements like dance halls, cheap theaters, movies, and skating rinks enjoyed by urban working-class youth as menacing. Religious reformer Josephine L. Baldwin noted, "Many of the amusements of the young people of today form a broad and straight road leading directly to dissipation because the powers which must be brought into play in wholesome recreation become atrophied through disuse."[10] The threat to "civilization," then, stemmed from an urban way of life, created by and for the immigrant and African American working classes, that undermined controls over sexual behavior customary for the Anglo-American middle class.

Social hygienists posed the sense of peril in biological as well as moral terms. President Charles W. Eliot of Harvard, for example, explained that "[p]ublic opinion has been moved strongly toward the subject of sex hygiene because of the many signs of physical deterioration among the civilized nations which suffer from the eager rush out of the country into the city, from the factory system, and from alcoholism and the sexual vices." He claimed that army recruits were physically smaller than in the past and pointed to declining family size, a (supposed) widespread inability of women to breastfeed, and infant mortality in cities. Finally, he noted "the increasing proportion in civilized communities of persons... who are practically unable to earn their own living."[11] Employing the popular eugenic thinking that merged moral and physical traits, Eliot was proclaiming a physical degeneration that led to a loss of economic productivity, and thus implicitly a decline of American greatness. He feared that this decline would also taint the nation's elite and thus end Anglo-American dominance.

The social hygiene movement included some eugenicists, who sought to limit non-Anglo populations through scientific breeding and sterilization of those they deemed "defective."[12] However, an equally significant emphasis of social hygiene was on moral and educational rather than biological or legal control. Social hygienists hoped to shore up Victorian morality among middle-class Anglo-Americans and to inculcate it in other groups and classes. As Northwestern University physiology professor Winfield Scott Hall explained, "[A] large majority of those conditions which are inimical to race welfare are the result of ignorance and of distorted mental attitude regarding the sex life.... [That] can be rectified only by education."[13] To maintain their group's social and political dominance, white social hygienists wanted to recapture control of the moral education of their youth, especially the female side.

Controlling women was central to efforts to set boundaries and maintain group purity because women both bore children and were supposed to be arbiters of sexual behavior. In 1905 Theodore Roosevelt expressed the fear of declining Anglo dominance when he warned against "race suicide" and condemned elite women for failing adequately to reproduce their group. Social hygiene writings intended simultaneously to encourage (efficient, eugenic) motherhood and the maintenance of the sexual purity symbolized by good Victorian women.[14] In addition, like the conservative Victorians, social hygienists argued that "the women of the educated classes... must ultimately set the moral standards for the masses."[15] Young middle-class women on their own in city jobs and settlement houses, as well as the unruly female factory workers who frequented dance halls, roused reformers' fears that the sexual barriers would not hold. If working-class women tempted, and middle-class women failed to inspire, middle-class men would fall prey to their "primitive instincts," and moral and physical pollution would overwhelm the group that white social hygienists believed had made America great.

The Cultural Context of Social Hygiene among African Americans

White Protestants of British descent dominated the formal social hygiene movement, but African American leaders also became actively involved with it during World War I, when the U.S. Army appointed Arthur B. Spingarn, a (white Jewish) director of the National Association for the Advancement of Colored People (NAACP), to oversee morale among "colored troops." Although whites published a few articles on African Americans, there is little evidence of sustained dialogue with them. Instead, African Americans engaged with the white movement in order to find their own way to address venereal disease and the need for sex education. They tended to support values similar to those of white reformers but with different aims. Blacks were eager to improve health, support family life, and protect black women from sexual exploitation, but they faced an especially virulent racism in this period. Both legal and extralegal aggression against African Americans intensified, and racist thought flourished between the 1890s and the 1920s. Desperate to keep blacks' labor cheap and political power minimal, southern whites freely applied the racist label of excessive, or bestial, sexuality—stamping black men as rapists and black women as whores—to justify the menial social position blacks occupied, as well as the brutal means, such as lynching, used to keep them there.[16]

Men and women suffered differently from this branding. Most lynchings were of men, who were actually attacked for assertiveness of various kinds but were often depicted in the media as raping white women. Black women, meanwhile, experienced sexual harassment and rape by employers and other white men, had no legal recourse, and lived with the stigma of sexual promiscuity. A black male witness reported in 1912 to the *Crisis*, the journal of the NAACP, that he had been awakened on a train by the cries of a young black female passenger being molested by the white conductor. To white men like this, black women were "bad women" by definition and fair game for sexual pursuit. White women shared the framework dividing their sex into good women and bad women and, labeling African American women "bad," often shunned intimate association with them. Even at Oberlin College, a liberal institution with roots in the abolitionist movement, administrators found white female students increasingly resistant to racial integration in the dormitories in the early twentieth century.[17] This racist thinking was powerful and pervasive, expressing extreme intolerance for race mixing through the intimacy of black men or women with white women while masking the reality of white male sexual aggression and extensive but nonmarital sexual relations with black women. The taint of sexual impurity imposed on blacks, then, served as a cultural undergirding for segregation and antimiscegenation laws.

Mary Church Terrell, race leader and feminist, reported that everywhere she lectured to whites, someone brought up the question of intermarriage. White men especially seemed to "believe that colored men lie awake nights trying to devise ways and means of marrying white women." She found widespread uncritical acceptance of the rape myth even among sympathetic whites, who used it to rationalize their failure to oppose segregation. Educator Nannie Helen Burroughs scathingly attacked white hypocrisy over the issue of interracial sex, exhorting whites to "[s]top making social excursions into the Negro race, depositing white offspring and then crying out against social equality."[18] The ideology and laws that sanctified these sexual arrangements served as an integral part of the subordination of African Americans in the United States, symbolically marking the entire group as inferior by implying that blacks were unfit to marry whites.

This hostile atmosphere bred adherence to Victorian morality among respectable African Americans as they sought dignity and protection for black women. In 1895, when a white editor labeled all black women "prostitutes," "thieves," and "liars," middle-class black club women, in the process of organizing nationally as the National Association of Colored Women (NACW), responded vigorously. Defending themselves against such libels, club women accepted the "duty of setting a high moral standard and living up to it," according to Terrell, and the group remained committed to this goal into the 1930s.[19] This "politics of respectability" sustained race pride as a collective resource.

Respectability could also be used as a tool to expose the sexual hypocrisy of whites. Terrell attended a number of purity conferences between 1905 and 1927 to speak "in behalf of the colored people." The only African American on the program during those years, Terrell used her speech in Battle Creek in 1907 to explain the vulnerability of black women servants to sexual advances from white employers. She overturned the stereotype of "loose" black women by shifting the blame to the white men who used economic and personal power to demand sexual favors. Terrell did not oppose the Victorian concept of respect for female purity but rather whites' failure to apply it to black women. Despite her clearly middle-class social status within the black community— she was a college graduate, ex-teacher, and wife of a federal judge—Terrell reported many incidents of personal insult when white men either threatened her or refused her ordinary courtesies on trains and trolleys. In speaking out for domestic workers, she was speaking also for herself. In this context a society that lived up to official morality represented the possibility of security for black women from constant assaults on their personal dignity and autonomy. Some whites and a few blacks perceived Terrell's 1907 speech as extremely militant. The Associated Press reported it as "Bitter, Furious Invective against the People of the South."[20] Embodying purity in her self-presentation and public commitments supported Terrell in speaking truth to power.

Relatively well-off African Americans worried about sexual morality within their own communities, as well as in relation to whites. In 1913 black ministers, teachers, and other professionals across the nation answered questions for a sociological study of "manners and morals" done by W. E. B. DuBois at Atlanta University. Sharing Anglo-Americans' Protestant heritage, the African American elite were closer in outlook to dominant Anglo-American groups than most other subcultures were.[21] Many agreed with the sentiment of a Texas respondent: "Morals in the masses are not so good." Behavior of the "enlightened and cultured" was sound, but the lower classes were characterized by "sexual looseness." Respondents blamed the influence of decadent whites and the presence of commercialized sex in black districts (which blacks could not control). They also echoed white moralists in their anxiety about losing control of young people due to the temptations of popular amusements. A writer from Illinois condemned movies, roller-skating, ragtime music, cabaret songs, and dancing clubs as "vicious." Racial segregation, which severely limited places of entertainment open to blacks, kept their young people away from the "wholesome amusements."[22]

Because middle-class African Americans lacked significant economic or political power and because whites lumped all classes of blacks together, the more respectable felt their status was threatened by behavior among the masses that might confirm white prejudice about blacks' "uncivilized" character. This was true, for example, among the northern blacks who feared the reaction of whites to the rural southern migrants streaming to northern cities in this period. Northern community leaders encouraged migrants to adopt restrained public behavior—to avoid loud talking, shabby dress, and vulgar language, and for men to show more public deference to women. Class tensions were evident in the activities of the Urban League and other groups thus assisting migrants to adjust to urban life. Like white reformers, black social workers sought to help but also to control. And for the urban black elite as for the white, the expanding and culturally different working classes and the new commercial amusements that catered to them posed a challenge to established Protestant morality. Among African Americans, however, the unifying factor of race muted internal class conflicts, by contrast with the social distance between white Anglo-Americans and European immigrants.[23]

Organization of a Movement

White reformers concerned about sexual issues began to shape a formal movement at the turn of the century as they called for new responses to venereal disease, prostitution, and the resulting economic impacts. Physicians, led by Dr. Prince A. Morrow, centered their attention on the ravages of venereal disease. Morrow was an elite Kentuckian who attended Princeton and New York University's medical school. He traveled in Europe before starting a practice in dermatology and genitourinary disease in New York in 1874 and became very engaged with the European research on venereal diseases. He translated and published some of this research in the United States. Like other physicians, he was deeply affected by his close knowledge of the physical effects of the disease, as well as its impact on family life. Systemic syphilis affected the heart, spinal cord, and brain; gonorrhea caused arthritis and other inflammations of internal organs. Physician William Freeman Snow, who had been a professor of hygiene and public health at Stanford and an epidemiologist for the California State Board of Health before becoming director of the ASHA, left an affecting account of one experience that led him into social hygiene work. As a young doctor, while assisting an eye specialist, he had met a miner who had contracted gonorrhea on a visit to San Francisco, "believing at the time...that it was necessary for his health to visit" the red light district. The man lost his sight as a result and had passed the infection on to his son, though "the ophthalmic surgeon was making a fight for the sight of the boy." Snow later began talking to other physicians about doing something to prevent these diseases. These activist physicians melded in sexual reform a bourgeois moral perspective and a commitment to science as the proper way to proceed.[24]

In 1904 Morrow published *Social Diseases and Marriage* on the prevention of venereal disease through education. He then proceeded to organize a group of doctors into the Society for Sanitary and Moral Prophylaxis, which aimed to educate both other physicians and the public to the dangers and treatment of venereal disease through explicit and scientific descriptions. The development of the Wasserman diagnostic blood test for syphilis in 1906 and the effective (though toxic) drug salvarsan in 1909 provided the cause with powerful new weapons. Similar groups joined with Morrow's New York–based one in 1910 to create the American Federation for Sex Hygiene, with Charles W. Eliot as honorary president.[25]

White purity reformers also organized campaigns against prostitution and the "white slave trade" in the first decade of the century. Numerous city vice commissions investigated and issued reports on prostitution like the New York Committee of Fifteen's *The Social Evil* (1902).[26] Several purity groups merged in 1911 to form the American Vigilance Association. These twentieth-century purity reformers had already moved away from the earlier movement's explicit evangelicalism and were influenced by the emerging profession of social work and the methods of Morrow's group.[27] They feared that urban danger would contaminate vulnerable women, even those from the rural heartland, the mythical backbone of the white nation, as illustrated in a story told by James Bronson Reynolds. Reynolds was a lawyer who became active in the antiprostitution movement after working at a settlement house in New York. There he met a gas inspector whose work had taken him into a nearby house of prostitution and who reported to Reynolds a story told by the women in the house. They said that a "flaxenhaired" "Pennsylvania farmer's daughter" with a "sunny smile" had died of venereal disease after being lured to the brothel by a false advertisement for employment.[28] The social work experience brought educated middle-class people like Reynolds close to an urban world that seemed threatening to such innocence.

African American reformers voiced similar concerns. Northern black organizations tried to assist southern migrants in locating jobs and housing, and especially to protect single women from the wiles of pimps and dishonest employment agents. The Philadelphia Association for the Protection of Colored Women's 1912 report, for example, detailed a "black slave traffic" by which naïve young women were tricked into prostitution. The association cooperated with the Travellers Aid, Children's Aid, and the City Mission and it ran a home for young female migrants and single mothers.[29]

The drive for moral order and economic efficiency also motivated social hygienists. John D. Rockefeller Jr. headed a grand jury in New York City set up after the 1909 mayoral elections to investigate the traffic in women. Deeply affected by the experience, he founded the Bureau of Social Hygiene in 1911 to fund social scientific investigations of sexual problems. Both his Baptist upbringing and his growing commitment to a rationalized and healthy society led him to oppose prostitution. As one writer explained, unhealthy workers were inefficient workers.[30] The research done under the auspices of the bureau formed an integral part of the social hygiene movement.

In 1913 these three organizational efforts, focused on venereal disease, prostitution, and the scientific investigation of sexual problems, came together to form the ASHA, which became the institutional center of the movement. Rockefeller provided substantial financial support. In 1915 the ASHA began publishing *Social Hygiene*, which printed reports of research done by Rockefeller's bureau, as well as articles on prostitution, venereal disease, and numerous projects in sex education. The ASHA and associated groups like the YMCA also broadcast their vision of proper sexual life through books, public exhibits, pamphlets, posters, lectures, university courses, and films in the period through World War I.[31]

With the coming of war the government sought to suppress prostitution near army camps and heavily emphasized disease prevention at the expense of the broader goal of "constructive" or "positive" sex education to promote healthy marriage and family life. When the United States entered the war in April 1917, the War Department established the Commission on Training Camp Activities to organize venereal disease education and provide alternative entertainment for the troops. The ASHA and the YMCA participated. Congress also created in 1918 the Venereal Disease Division of the U.S. Public Health Service and disbursed money for hygiene courses at normal schools and colleges, and occasionally for biology or social hygiene instruction in elementary or high schools. After the war, public money continued to flow most readily for disease prevention, although social hygienists came to criticize that emphasis, fearing the counterproductive effects of "negative" information, and began promoting broad and positive education about biological development.[32]

⸺

The work of the Oregon Social Hygiene Society between 1910 and 1915, as recounted by its president in *Social Hygiene* in 1916, provides a good example of the two thrusts of the movement in its early years—stimulating state regulatory action and broad educational outreach. William Trufant Foster, a native of Boston and a graduate of Harvard, headed Reed College at the time he related the history of early work in Oregon. The Oregon Social Hygiene Society had successfully obtained financial support of $35,000 from the state legislature for its education campaign, something that had not been achieved elsewhere.[33] The group both promoted more effective treatment for venereal disease and attempted to correct the public's false sexual beliefs.

In pursuit of better treatment, reformers attacked "fake doctors" who promised easy but medically unsound cures for venereal disease. They were able to get a state law passed prohibiting advertisements by such businesses in all periodicals sold in the state. Foster claimed that this campaign had led to a decline in the business of the quacks and to the removal of many from Oregon. The group received some support from druggists and drug companies in distributing notices urging people to go to medical doctors and not attempt to cure themselves with patent medicines. The state also enacted a law requiring a certificate of health (guaranteeing the absence of venereal disease) for people seeking a marriage license.[34]

Foster recounted with greatest pride the Oregon Social Hygiene Society's educational efforts. He claimed that its meetings had reached 100,000 people (out of a state population of 672,000). It showed exhibits at the state fair and held separate meetings for fathers and sons and for mothers and daughters, as well as for businessmen, from whom the society received large subscriptions. Business supported these efforts by facilitating the society's organization of programs for workers in "factories, department stores, laundries, lumber camps, mining camps, office buildings, candy stores, railroad shops, and commercial schools." More than half of these meetings, he reported, were held on company time. In its lectures and exhibits the society attacked "sex lies"—that sexual intercourse was necessary to health, that venereal disease was not dangerous, and that the double standard was acceptable—and replaced these notions with "scientific facts." Foster asserted that false beliefs were on the wane, and he estimated that Oregon's economy had gained $200,000 because the declining incidence of venereal disease meant more days per year of productive labor.[35]

The Oregon campaign represents well the mixture of concerns in the social hygiene movement—that the conspiracy of silence simultaneously encouraged immorality, commercial manipulation of the ignorant, and personal suffering and industrial inefficiency through disease. Social hygienists sought the cooperation of the state in addressing these social problems, but they looked most confidently to education to attack the root causes. In promoting a scientific approach, however, they also revealed their ambivalent relationship to Victorian gender roles.

Science, Gender, and the Myth of Victorian Repression

The social hygiene movement proclaimed its adherence to science and its consequent superiority over sexual reform movements of the past, which also entailed the superiority of male over female leadership.[36] In 1914 Foster denigrated the capacity of the older female-dominated purity reformers to teach about sex: "Some are ignorant and unaware that enthusiasm is not a satisfactory substitute for knowledge. Some are hysterical." Yet a strong tension persisted within the movement between the moralistic thinking of the older purity groups and the newer orientation toward science and efficiency. This tension was sharply exemplified, for instance, in conflicts about whether to use the newest and most effective drugs to treat venereal disease, since such treatment might undermine the status of disease as a punishment for sin. Many social hygienists were outraged when the army distributed prophylactic kits to soldiers, putting health and military efficiency above commitment to chastity.[37] The conflict between purity and science affected not only such policy considerations but also the gender composition of the movement and the nature of sex instruction. In many ways social hygiene stood halfway between the earlier female-dominated purity movement and a growing male-dominated scientific and public health establishment.

Looking ever more to science and professionals for legitimation usually meant looking to men. The authors of works on sex education and articles in *Social Hygiene* were largely doctors, educators, social workers, and medical and social scientific researchers. The movement's most comprehensive tract, *Sex-Education: A Series of Lectures Concerning Knowledge of Sex in Its Relation to Human Life* (1916), was written by Maurice A. Bigelow, a biologist who taught at Columbia Teachers College. Bigelow's graduate work had drawn the attention of Dr. Morrow, who invited him to assist in the developing movement.[38] Prominent public figures and leading authorities in social hygiene were more frequently male, since few women obtained such training. Female college deans, social workers, and physicians wrote and taught but were less visible in the leadership as well as the membership. The American Federation for Sex Hygiene's membership figures for 1913, for example, showed more than twice as many male as female members. The low proportion of women in the movement indicated both the decline of their influence in sexual reform and the tendency to make professional, scientific men rather than virtuous women the acknowledged moral leaders.[39]

Social hygienists' use of science, like that of other Progressives, constituted an effort to create a more effective source of legitimation as the authority of Victorian Protestantism waned. According to one study, students at City College in New York judged the most moralistic pamphlets, such as those produced by the YMCA, to be least effective. Gynecologist Robert L. Dickinson, who practiced in New York for many decades starting in 1882, noted that his patients called most sex education works "priggish apologies, two generations behind the times." Bigelow, who as a professor at Teachers College was always most interested in prevention through education, agreed strongly with Morrow "that biological facts were necessary for teaching young people" and were "the most satisfactory starting-point" for sex education.[40]

Social hygienists encouraged sex education that contained at least minimal biological information in addition to moral training and that asserted sexuality as both a positive and a negative force in human life, but they emphasized the need to control sexuality for the sake of social and moral order. Hoping to discourage further questions, instructors tried to mete out facts bit by bit, just enough to satisfy curiosity. A 1913 plan for instruction argued, "The less children and youth think of sex, and the later they mature sexually, the better both physiologically and ethically." Reformers cautioned against presenting isolated lectures on sexual issues, preferring to integrate sex education into existing biology or health classes with a known and respected teacher. Thus, they hoped to avoid too much attention being given to sex and to control reactions through safe and familiar authority. Laura B. Garrett, a New York City social worker active in the Federation for Sex Hygiene, gave specific instructions for seating arrangements in which members of the class faced the speaker directly and were unable to see one another's faces, thus avoiding "the danger of their becoming lost in an unfortunate personal curiosity."[41] Communication among listeners with a consciousness of sexual matters obviously threatened the fragile control of the sex hygiene lecturer venturing into alien territory.

Social hygiene writers asserted the principle of starting with the study of plants and animals, then gradually introducing information on humans. Discussing nature seemed safer, as it was removed from the urban temptations that they feared.[42] The stories about plants and animals, however, echoed Victorian sentimentality about motherhood. One talk, for example, described how plants and animals prepared "cradles" for their young.[43] Another plan of instruction was to give six-year-old boys

> *Realization that They are a Part of Mother.* That she had given birth to the egg, and that therefore they were a part of her. That she had protected the egg and given it care, food, and kept it warm and that if it had not been for this care, each of them would not have been here. That she had suffered in order to give the eggs birth— thus, that she had endured for them. Love, care, and courtesies to mother. (Wonderful results.) Sister a prospective mother. Necessary to protect.[44]

Thus the sex educationists shaped scientific descriptions to encourage Victorian moral dynamics and shied away from the details of human sexual arousal and intercourse. They upheld women's moral status as mothers despite transferring formal authority to science.

Although social hygienists neither departed as dramatically from dominant Victorian values nor relied as strongly on science as they claimed, they still appeared too liberal to some. Catholics involved in this discussion called for a purely religious approach. The Reverend Richard Tierney, a Jesuit priest who spoke at the 1913 American Federation for Sex Hygiene conference, for example, opposed giving explicit sex hygiene instruction in schools because discussing the details of sex would rouse children's imaginations. He favored teaching only general ideals such as the sacredness of marriage, motherhood, and the human body. "Christ, not hygiene, will clean the world," he argued. The near absence of identifiably Catholic figures in the movement suggests that this was a representative Catholic position, at least for the early years. In an early experiment with sex education in Chicago public schools, Catholics were prominent in the political opposition that developed.[45] Initially, however, most social hygienists felt some actual description of bodies and reproductive functions was necessary.

Social hygienists had taken a step away from the Victorian perspective and proudly portrayed themselves as pioneers. They initiated the myth of Victorian repression, exaggerating the old morality as authoritarian and sexually repressive in order to contrast it unfavorably with their own supposedly enlightened and scientific approach. They claimed that their instructional programs would no longer harshly repress but rather would safely guide children to self-government. As Oberlin College dean of women Florence Fitch declared, "[I]n our day we cannot trust machinery and external compulsions; we must make stronger the inner defences." And Max Exner condemned what he saw as an ascetic past in favor of a rational acceptance of sexuality; he said the idea that feeling sex desire is "sin or a cause for self-reproach and shame is false and pernicious. Youth must not be taught that the sex nature is to be repressed because it is shameful but that it must be controlled and refined because of its dignity and power." In fact, Exner was reiterating a very traditional idea—that the sexual impulse had "dignity and power," indeed sanctity, because when properly guided it created the family, the cornerstone of civilization. What is significant about Exner's words is not the truth of his description of the past or acceptance of sexuality but rather his need to assert new grounds upon which to base the old morality.[46]

By the 1920s many proponents of sexual reform linked Victorian repressiveness with the unnaturalness of female authority and blamed moralistic women for repressing sexuality. Social hygienists, however, continued to assert respect for women in their roles as mothers even though (or perhaps because) men dominated the movement. This continued reverence for women's maternal role as well as the marked ambivalence about explicit sexual description muted the implications of social hygienists' deference to science and professionals. The thinking of white social hygienists, then, was in transition between a Victorian framework and a modern one. The movement's supporters used scientific language and authority to reach people who had abandoned the evangelical framework of the old purity movement, but they continued to idealize the moral authority of mothers.

The movement's traditional vision of class and gender relations is most evident in the accounts of specific sexual problems and how to solve them through education. White reformers' concerns and their programs for young people differed according to the gender and the class of students. It was in classes for middle-class youth where social hygiene instruction showed its potential to disrupt women's expected modesty and deference to men.

Sex Education for Middle-Class Whites and Empowerment for Women

Social hygienists cared most deeply about forming character in middle-class youth—sexual attitudes and behavior sharply distinguished from those of the working class.[47] Reformers placed themselves metaphorically in the respectable "home," observing with anxiety the alien influences of the "street." The street represented the world beyond sheltered middle-class domesticity where the behavior of immigrant or working-class children seemed to threaten propriety and order. An Indianapolis housing law reformer wrote in 1914 that children would acquire not only physical diseases but "other things, too, from the children of the slums whom they meet on the street and in the public schools, other things that they will not come to you with, for you would not allow them to repeat the words and tales they hear."[48] Sex education workers gave their greatest energy to preserving middle-class youth from such talk.[49]

Although social hygienists believed boys were more likely to encounter bad influences than girls, their writings as a whole identified equally important but complementary problems among middle-class boys and girls. Among young men they criticized the belief in "male sexual necessity" (the notion that men's health required sexual activity) and declining chivalry, or respect for women. Among young women, on the other hand, reformers feared the potential for feminist sexual alienation from men or, alternatively, "overdeveloped" sexuality—bohemian unconventionality. Reformers' analysis reveals both the internal contradictions of their belief system and the clash between their ideas and the social behavior of middle-class young people.

The issue of male sexual necessity recurred with stubborn persistence in social hygiene writings because, as studies of the time showed, it was in fact a pervasive popular belief among men, and many women worried about it as well.[50] The idea of male sexual necessity was important because it served as the ideological foundation of the sexual double standard: if men had to have sexual intercourse to preserve their health, then it made sense for society at least tacitly to countenance men's premarital sexual activity, which reformers deeply opposed.

Social hygiene writers also observed what they called a decline of chivalry among young middle-class males. Chivalry meant politeness and respect toward women and the restraint of male sexual aggression in deference to women's vulnerability. Such deference had never held sway in the behavior of dominant-class males toward black or working-class women. The decline of chivalry as described by social hygienists meant the erosion of respectful attitudes toward middle-class women. Ill-trained boys who were not "chivalrous even to their mothers and sisters" were likely later to repel their wives as well, "for many men are positively crude in manners, coarse and vulgar in language, and disgusting in personal habits."[51] In essence, reformers accused middle-class boys of bringing the working-class culture of the streets, with its open sexual references, before respectable women.

Social hygienists were responding defensively to real phenomena—the lessening of structured or ritualized distance between the sexes. Bigelow believed that "the industrial competition and daily association of the two sexes is making young men realize that women are simply human beings and not super beings." The growth of high school attendance also extended middle-class male-female contact beyond the family. Pairing off become more popular than collective social activities. Dating replaced formal "calling" in middle-class courtship, thus approximating working-class behavior. Chaperonage declined. Mothers in Robert and Helen Lynd's 1929 sociological study *Middletown* reported their daughters were less inhibited in dress and manners than previously. Early sex studies subsequently confirmed popular perceptions that various forms of premarital sexual intimacy were increasing among respectable young women.[52] As patterns of life changed for middle-class youth, young men were simply extending to young women of their own class the sexual attention they had previously confined more to women defined as socially inferior.[53] As a result, sexual dangers threatened young middle-class women as well as their brothers.

Reformers first worried that middle-class women would be alienated from sexuality by the new mores: "Today we either teach nothing, leaving to the newspapers, the musical comedy and vaudeville unopposed their perennial task of discrediting marriage and parentage, or else we hurl a revolting mass of information on venereal disease and prostitution at our young girls before they are taught the real significance of sex and reproduction." Such knowledge might turn women against sexuality and lead to "increasing discontent and disappointment in marriage or deliberate celibacy" (and thus "race suicide"). Social hygienists voiced distress about women who "charged men with full responsibility for existing sex problems." Bigelow approvingly cited a criticism of feminists for interpreting sexuality and reproduction to mean "subjection to man," asserting instead that "the watch-cry of women's emancipation" would become not " 'Free *from* man' " but " 'Free *with* man.' "[54]

The visible presence of feminism and of single women within it in the 1910s also stimulated some of the reformers' concerns. Women who decided against marriage and motherhood in order to fight for suffrage or to enter careers were accused by social hygienists of creating a "one-sexed world" and denying the "unalterable difference" between men and women. What some of the men feared was exemplified by the unmarried Lavinia L. Dock, a nursing leader and one of the older antiprostitution reformers, who conveyed a vigorous feminist anger at men. Dock noted sarcastically that "the doctrine of 'physical necessity' has been invented for men by themselves" to support the utter injustice of the double standard. She encouraged women "to revolt against a status of political and legal inferiority which is the direct cause of their economic and social degradation."[55] Social hygienists were accurate in associating feminism with anger at prevailing sexual values.

Less politicized forms of alienation were also common. Dr. Dickinson's patients indicated how women were angered by the daily experience of male dominance in family and sexual interactions. A single woman office worker, thirty-two years old in 1924, wrote that in childhood, "I despised the whole thing and could not see anything of the 'glory of motherhood' which was being so much spoken of to me.... Woman seemed like a sort of slave." Dickinson generalized in 1930 from his forty-five-year gynecologic practice: "The wife becomes quickly chilly and disgusted because of 'vulgarity' of speech or act in coitus." Several women complained, " 'He talks about getting me down.' "[56]

Such comments suggest the deep psychological barrier many middle-class women felt between themselves and men. Men's greater sexual sophistication, ability to obtain sexual satisfaction from prostitutes, and access to the popular "street" language of sexuality constituted a real form of social dominance that women resented.

Studies done by social hygienists of the young women they were instructing showed that learning about prostitution and venereal disease angered many. A YWCA worker reported in 1915 that girls in her class refused to see "their own responsibility" for correcting evils like prostitution, which they saw as men's responsibility. Teaching "aroused resentment against the 'injustice' which puts women at a disadvantage." Psychologist Miriam Gould studied another group of fifty young students, teachers, and businesswomen about the impact of learning about prostitution and venereal disease. Nine felt they were safe because they associated only with respectable men, but "11 developed a pronounced repulsion for men" and "now avoid association with them." Eleven more said they would not marry now that they knew the realities of sex. At least one had become "an outspoken feminist and misanthrope." The researcher concluded that the emphasis of the past upon women's chastity to the neglect of men's had had an injurious effect, making women hostile to (hetero)sexuality altogether.[57]

Despite the emphasis on middle-class women's rejection of sex, social hygienists also harbored the opposite fear—that women would be attracted by men's sexual language and behavior and imitate them. Bigelow warned, "There is the widespread misunderstanding among young men that sexual hunger is as insistent in virtuous young women as in themselves and that therefore illicit gratification is a mutual gain and responsibility." Dean Fitch of Oberlin warned in 1915 that some young women thought so, too. The single standard now meant women following men "rather than the reverse"; "self-supporting business women," she reported, were "seeking pleasure when they choose in sexual relationships." Although the most common assumption in these writings was that respectable women felt less sexual desire than men and were unlikely to err except through deep affection, reformers increasingly suspected young middle-class women of illicit sexual activity.[58]

Bigelow identified two types of overly sexual middle-class girls—"one with intensive sexuality which is often modifiable by medical or surgical treatment" and "one of probably normal instincts but with radical sexual philosophy," the latter being the bohemian influenced by European ideas and radical socialism—a group increasingly visible during the 1910s. The former group was less threatening because medicine could control them (as it had done in the nineteenth century). Bigelow denied the bohemians were very numerous yet hinted at a powerful "undercurrent towards sexual freedom." He feared readers of Freud, Ellis, or Krafft-Ebing would think sexual repression was unhealthy and encourage other celibate women to be restless and dissatisfied. They might also influence naïve young men. Appropriate sex instruction would crush these errors, he hoped.[59]

Certainly more young middle-class women in the early twentieth century were stepping beyond Victorian conventions. The early studies of sexual behavior (all based on a middle-class population) showed increasing premarital heterosexual activity among women.[60] Some college students commenting on sex education pamphlets for young women illustrated the new consciousness. One wrote in the early 1920s, "It is antiquated and unfair to say that sex is solely for reproduction and home-making." Another also complained of the restriction of sex to reproduction: "Different sort of argument should be used for girls who think and act according to their own opinions. For instance, to state flatly that 'the use of sex for any other purpose is immoral' is likely to antagonize a free intellect."[61]

Sex reformers then were fearful of female independence from Victorian prescriptions, an independence that could go either toward celibacy or toward sexual libertarianism. They wished to encourage motherhood, but they did not want women to take a casual view of sex. It was difficult to achieve the proper balance: "The girl is assured that not *all* men are bad, and that it is unfair to condemn as it is silly to trust all men."[62] Sex education programs needed to guide young women between the Scylla of "sex-antagonism" and the Charybdis of sexual license.

To this end reformers denounced wrong beliefs and defensively inculcated their definition of upright behavior in opposition to popular trends. They acknowledged that sexuality involved more than procreation but still emphasized it as reproductive rather than as a source of individual pleasure or freedom. Bigelow argued that sex was exclusively reproductive for animals, "but human life at its highest has superadded psychical and social meaning to sexual relationships, and the result has been affection and the human family." Controlled sex created proper families: "The fundamental problem of sex is to secure an early and happy marriage.... Ideals of marriage are the greatest restraint against sex dissipation."[63] The answer to the dangerous social freedom of youth, then, was to move them more quickly toward marriage and childbearing—a theme that would be pursued by advocates of companionate marriage in the 1920s.

Social hygienists' belief in distinct processes of sexual development in boys and girls, however, led to gender-differentiated approaches. They understood males to experience an earlier and sharper awareness of their sexuality than females. In *Sex-Education*, Bigelow wrote that "every normal boy passes in early puberty through peculiar physiological changes...involuntary sexual tumescence and...occasional nocturnal emissions, which processes leave the boy in no doubt whatever as to the nature, source, and desirability of sexual pleasure." In contrast, "the average healthy adolescent girl does not undergo normal spontaneous changes which make her definitely conscious of the nature, source, and desirability of localized sexual pleasure. On the contrary, such consciousness commonly comes to many only as the result of stimuli arising in connection with affection." The gender difference assumed here supported an argument for divergent social training: "[I]t is probably best, as many parents urge, that in pre-adolescent years the girl's instruction in social-sexual lines be training in modest deportment and a proper reserve towards boys. This ought to be sufficient for the girl's protection until gradually in adolescent years she learns the whole story of life, probably several years later than her boy friends whose natural leadership in sexual activity makes their early information desirable as a protection to both sexes." Bigelow used his expectation (and hope) that girls blossomed later to justify male leadership and to encourage female self-restraint.[64]

Sex educators sought to train boys to protect girls by appealing to boys' loyalty to female relatives. A boy's "sacred duty" was to offer every girl "the same respect and protection which he would exact from another boy toward his own sister." This admonition was common in the pamphlet literature and was said to appeal effectively to boys. Although abstractly the rule covered all women, in practice, middle-class white boys learned that black and working-class girls were not like sisters but in different (and inferior) groups, and thus fair game for sexual pursuit. Social hygienists sought to summon up sufficient sanctions against illicit sex with these women by emphasizing the threat of venereal disease to a young man's potential fatherhood. Warnings about harm to a future wife and children—those of his own group—served as the primary means of extending the sexual taboo beyond the middle class.[65]

Sex education writers exerted themselves most strenuously in denying male sexual necessity. They claimed instead that continence, or restraint of sexual activity, was healthful and tended to conserve vital energies needed later for reproduction. Here they were reprising the nineteenth-century battle between the male sporting culture, focused on the primacy and entitlements of male sexual desire, and the evangelical commitment to chastity. An American

Social Hygiene Association pamphlet attempted to refute "mistaken beliefs which have been widely circulated," "such as the notion that the reproductive organs will not develop without exercise, and that a man will be considered a mollycoddle if he refuses to go with prostitutes. Those who by thought, word, or act, arouse the sex desire until it overcomes them, do so *not* because of physical strength and courage but because of a *lack* of *mental* strength. They are not the strong men but the weaklings."[66]

The very force of denial, however, suggests the defensive posture from which social hygienists spoke. They, too, felt that "strength" was important. Only a fine line lay between condemning the impetuous energy of adolescent male sexuality and seeing its uncontrollability as a sign of vigor and the male's "natural leadership" in sexual activity. Reformers' own understanding of male adolescence acknowledged, indeed expected, that the intense sexual consciousness of that period might lead to lapses. Most men, wrote Bigelow, were probably "loose" at some period in their lives, usually "in early manhood before marriage." Such laxity was, "though not excusable,... explainable on physiological grounds."[67] The notion of male sexual necessity, then, was not only a practical problem for sex educators but also a focus of ambivalence because it expressed in inverted form their own belief in male sexual vigor.

Social hygienists were facing a shifting balance between support of restraint and support for vigor in the model of masculine character in middle-class culture. A concern about the restrictions of "civilized" life and the need for more outlets for male aggression and energy was being sounded in a cultural preoccupation with sports and the outdoor life as well as in imperialism from the 1890s on. The ideal of restraint was paling by comparison.[68] Aware that their values were judged "sissy" by much of the male public, social hygienists attempted with difficulty to claim their position as the most manly.

Although sex educators fought the good fight for men to uphold chivalry and sexual restraint, they believed the real hope (and responsibility) for controlling male impulses still lay with women. Through all the preaching to young men, reformers were sounding an appeal to women to remain in their place, acting as inspirations of purity to men. As Bigelow claimed, "[M]any of the faults of men are largely traceable to the fact that women as a sex have not been able to hold a high standard for manhood." Mothers in particular were called upon to sustain close relationships with adolescent sons and to avoid what was considered the common practice of turning them over to their fathers. If a mother became distant, claimed Bigelow, "the sudden change of attitude... will surely impress upon the boy that there is something about sex in boys that even his mother dares not talk over with him." He will get the usual vulgar information from the street but will not discuss it before the delicate ears of mother and sisters. Hence, he will be set "adrift. If there is ever a time in a boy's life when he needs intimacy with his mother, it is in the early adolescent years."[69] Most clearly in this approach, social hygiene thinking showed its affinity with the nineteenth-century reverence for motherhood. Women, and mothers especially, were to retain the responsibility for controlling sexuality—their own and men's.

Tantalizing evidence from two studies in 1923 suggests how this cultural dynamic functioned for some men. Like the soldiers reading wartime social hygiene literature, the subjects of these studies (high school and college students and college graduates) reported being inspired by respectable women. Being with young women they knew to be of a "better class" or "decent" helped them to inhibit their sexual cravings. One young man wrote: "If with a decent girl I am O.K., but if she is indecent and tries to make me, I have to think of my ideals and use will to break and run." He wanted young women to embody the virtue of sexual restraint for him, and when they did not, desire seemed overwhelming.[70] Sex educators feared that women might decline this responsibility.

It seemed urgent that young women be properly educated about sexuality, but reformers' efforts in this direction were as laden with ambivalence as their approaches to males. Providing real sexual information to women would enable mothers to counsel their sons, but it also violated the cherished image of female innocence and need of protection. Bigelow admitted finding a lack of consensus among parents and scientific authorities on what to teach women: many preferred to keep "nice girls" ignorant. The use of scientific language served as one strategy for confronting this difficulty. The "serious impressiveness of cold scientific language" provided an effective defense against the widespread male use of "vulgar terminology."[71] The use of scientific language could sanitize the discussion of sexual matters, thus allowing for the education of middle-class women without having to teach them the popular language known to males of all classes. This approach appeared to stake out a middle ground, avoiding either total ignorance for women or their initiation into male culture. Scientific sex terminology was also intended to woo middle-class males away from vernacular language and the male street culture with which it was associated, but it is more likely that males simply acquired a dual sexual language.

Scientifically correct sex education was expected to combat the twin dangers of celibacy and bohemianism. Reformers wanted "superior" young women not to be celibate but to reproduce: the purpose of sex education "should not be to make chaste celibates, but rather efficient mothers," wrote Roswell Johnson, a eugenics supporter. To this end sex educators claimed, "frankly," as Laura Garrett put it, "that the racial or sex instinct...is good."[72] Providing information on the "normal" biology of sex first and explaining the "abnormal" facts of prostitution and venereal disease only as young women neared maturity would prevent the danger of revulsion against men and marriage. Present chastity not as an end in itself for young women (as compared to men), urged psychologist Miriam Gould, but merely as a means to an end— safe parenthood for both sexes. Reformers thereby asserted a single sexual standard and de-emphasized the divergent training of men and women that seemed to generate "sex antagonism."[73]

Yet in pursuing the other goals of sex education—combating venereal disease and bohemianism—reformers re-created that male-female sexual difference. In particular, they were unable to speak of sexual feeling in the "better class" of women. Even if postponed, teaching about venereal disease and prostitution was so essential to the aim of the social hygiene movement that even respectable young women received it. Sex educators, however, presented venereal disease to these women as a distant social problem, something that plagued men and the lower classes but never anything they themselves could acquire in any way except as victimized wives of promiscuous men. Such knowledge would help them select "clean" husbands and uphold high social standards rather than affect their personal behavior. Lecturers frequently reinforced the double standard also by advising young women to restrict flirtatious behavior in order not to "tempt" men, but they suggested that ignorance rather than sexual desire lay behind such dangerous behavior. No one intimated that middle-class women could be prostitutes. Even sexual bohemians were not described as autonomously expressing sexual feeling. Bigelow claimed that both men and women of this type were "neurotic and hysterical," the dupes of unreliable sexual radicals, or victims of naïve and "unscientific" readings of Ellis, Krafft-Ebing, or Freud. "Especially is this true of the women of this type whose introspective morbidity has led them to diagnose their own functional disturbances as the direct result of 'over-sexuality' and restraint from normal sexual expression....Such a woman is...a positive menace."[74] Hence, despite social hygienists' desire to "normalize" sex and encourage marriage for middle-class women, they remained mired in Victorian assumptions of such women's relative asexuality compared with men. They feared the sexual woman much more than the asexual woman and were willing to risk the problem of feminist "sex hostility" in order to keep women on the moral pedestal for men.

Despite this clear attachment to an older cultural dynamic, social hygien-ists were addressing a fundamental issue of male-female inequality, acknowl-edging how differently middle-class women and men were taught about sexuality, and offering sex education programs with new information that women welcomed. A fairly extensive and diverse study in 1919 of the effects of viewing an educational film about venereal diseases showed women par-ticipants overwhelmingly approved the showing and felt young girls could also see it. Even those initially offended in some way soon recovered and "stated that they were glad to have had the experience and to have been forced to face the problems squarely." Interestingly, however, the majority of men ques-tioned, though happy to have seen the film themselves, felt women should not see it. These results suggest that men felt uneasy about women's knowledge. Perhaps they liked the notion of female innocence or feared women's anger about men's role in transmitting venereal disease.[75]

An unusual female voice in a discussion of sex education in 1913 further illus-trates the potential for women's empowerment that even the modest program of social hygiene could offer. Held at the annual meeting of the American Federation for Sex Hygiene and the Fourth International Congress on School Hygiene, this discussion included physicians, schoolteachers, and social hygiene workers. One-fourth of those who spoke (of twenty-three altogether) are identifiable as women. Into this discussion a psychology teacher at the New York Training School for Teachers, Frances Isabel Davenport, injected a bold and authoritative statement based on her seven years of experience providing sex instruction. Davenport shared many assumptions and concerns common to social hygienists—about the need for "decent" sexual language; the importance of clean, healthy, and intelligent parenthood; the propriety of integrating sex information in other courses of study rather than present-ing it as a special subject; and the desire to avoid rather than stimulate what social hygienists called "sex consciousness." ("Sex consciousness" referred to the emotionally heightened awareness of sexual facts, a dangerous sensitiv-ity to the power of sexuality to direct human actions, especially in violation of convention.) Hence, Davenport appeared within the mainstream of social hygiene thinking; she was not a sexual radical.

Davenport differed startlingly from other speakers, however, in the tone with which she discussed sexuality and in her views on men and women. She was the only person to name sexual organs explicitly (vulva, penis, testicles) or to advocate teaching human reproduction even to elementary school children (where teaching only about plants and animals was most common).[76] She also confidently asserted, unlike other speakers, that she, or any well-informed teacher who lacked sex consciousness, could instruct mixed-sex classes of any age successfully. Her sense of her own authority and power gained from clear scientific knowledge led her to argue against barriers of age and gender that most social hygienists were desperately seeking to maintain. Also central to Davenport's sense of confidence was her assertion that women's sexual desires were not different in degree from men's: "[T]here is a fallacy that men are a peculiar race unto themselves as far as sex temptation and feelings are concerned. I tell you, don't believe it, men; because it is not so." She denied the basis for male sexual "leadership" and women's innocence and need of protection, undermining the double standard. "If biology and psychology teach us anything upon which we can rely, it is that the organism is fundamentally its own protector." She called for the "human" education of women to replace a socialization that determined "every habit of a woman's life" not by its value for her life "but on the sole basis of sex." She argued (like feminist thinker Charlotte Perkins Gilman) that this narrowness incited sex consciousness and thus immorality in women and men both. Much more than other sex educators, Davenport seemed convinced that explicit sexual knowledge was safe and could effectively weaken the covert sexual dynamics that led to immorality.[77] In short, she saw women and men as more similar than dissimilar sexually and asserted a single standard of conduct on that basis.

The sole response to Davenport's daring statement came from a man who argued that a female instructor "could not be sure that the lads she was instructing were aware that she was free from sex consciousness." He thought male youths could intimidate a college-educated woman because he perceived a greater power in the traditional male sexual culture than in a woman's scientific sexual knowledge. In response, Davenport reasserted her belief that lack of sex consciousness in the teacher could overcome "nasty-minded" thinking in any group. The fact that no one else even commented on Davenport's striking remarks suggests that she may have made other participants ill at ease.[78] Most male social hygienists did not want women to claim equality with men either in sexual knowledge or in sexual feeling, but Davenport's example shows that social hygienists' campaigns laid open those possibilities.

By the early 1920s, Davenport had carried out a study on her students that demonstrated their eagerness for information, especially on menstruation, intercourse, and childbearing, and also articulated her own feminist, social hygienist views. Inspired by her experiences at the 1913 conference, which were reinforced by a direct request of her students for sex instruction,

Davenport agreed to a series of meetings where she would respond to questions. Overwhelmed by the response on the first day, she closed the door when the crowd reached 161. She asked students to submit questions anonymously on slips of paper ahead of the next meeting and received more than 900; these formed the basis of her Columbia University dissertation and subsequent book. Eager to combat the "erotico-mystic conception of female sexuality," she wanted to investigate the actual knowledge and questions of young women. Her subjects, teachers in training, were drawn from middle-class and upper-working-class New York City families, aged seventeen to twenty-three; all were secondary school graduates who had studied one year of biology.[79]

Handily demonstrating the reign of ignorance and superstition even among these relatively well-educated young women, the study showed a vast hunger for basic sexual information. The largest number of questions was on menstruation (164), followed by copulation (101) and childbearing (physical aspects of pregnancy and birth) (98). Twenty-seven percent of these childbearing questions were about birth control. Seventy-seven questions addressed venereal disease, and seventy were about sexual feelings and attraction. She noted her subjects expressed significant interest in men (fifty-six questions, predominantly on their sexual organs and development) but not in companionship or courtship. She observed the "absence of proper specific terms for coitus" and the "crudity" of many terms that were used, as well as myths about determining the sex of a baby, concluding that the biology courses "had not to any great extent disturbed the even tenor of the paths of superstition as they everywhere permeate the realm of sex in the instruction of girls."[80] Finally, committed to the importance of intelligent preparation for marriage and motherhood, Davenport was disappointed at the much lesser interest in marriage (a mere fifty questions, many of them about practical matters such as whether to marry a relative or a man with venereal disease) and motherhood apart from the physical aspects (only four questions).[81]

Certainly, these results show the great eagerness for basic biological facts and their apparent inaccessibility for these young women. Davenport seems almost surprised that the students could request this instruction "without a vestige of embarrassment" and with "a somewhat unusual degree of persistence and firmness." Again, this suggests both how information was withheld from respectable women and their agency in demanding it where they could. These teachers-to-be asked about the "primitive aspects" of sex—the nitty-gritty of menstruation, sexual intercourse and contraception, birthing, and penises—rather than submitting high-minded questions on how to prepare themselves for the social roles of wifehood and motherhood. These findings suggest disinterest in the more ideologically laden aspects of marriage and parenting—"social ideals," Davenport labels them—that she wished her subjects had been interested in. Perhaps they had heard enough about ideals and just wanted some explicit sexual knowledge. Another woman psychologist, commenting on the marital ideals often presented in social hygiene pamphlets, said the pamphlets needed to offer " 'a defense of marriage as being more interesting than to the observation of most of them it seems to be! Just to settle down and have children is not an inspiring motive to either girls or boys, in the midst of joy-rides, movies, picnics, and flirting. It is dull, and nothing in most pamphlets makes it seem otherwise.' "[82] Sex, on the other hand, was exciting.

For Davenport herself, the study seems to have confirmed her in a feminist direction already apparent in the 1913 conference discussion, with her claim of women's equal ability to teach about sex. In her 1924 book, in which she ventured beyond her survey data to expatiate on broader proposals to "salvage" American girlhood, she remained firmly in the social hygienist camp. She felt that women as "potential mothers" should create the "norms for sexual life." She understood sex to have social meaning rather than to be about "personal gratification." And she echoed eugenic thought in her concern that the economically better off should be bearing more children. However, she also pressed for more equality for girls and women. Besides equal sex education, she stressed girls' equal need for physical activity and physical education (in part to make them healthier for childbearing). Most interesting, she conceived of ideal marriage as a "partnership." Citing women's historic training in "the productive industries of their day" and economic contributions to their households as wives, she argued that the modern standard of sole male support and female dependency was hindering marriage for working-class and middle-class families and should be abandoned.[83] No doubt few of her social hygiene colleagues would have gone so far, but her story suggests how the opening up of sex education, even with the primary intention of preserving marriage and motherhood, could lead in new directions for women.

————

Social hygienists believed that middle-class young people's behavior threatened their class either with pollution from without (impure sexual ideas and diseases from alien groups) or with sterility from within (through female spinsterhood). Young men seemed to be absorbing and exposing young women to attitudes from a working-class street culture; they accepted too readily the notion of male sexual necessity and thus prostitution. As their female counterparts learned of the underground male sexual world, social hygienists perceived them to be either rejecting men, sex, and marriage altogether, or imitating men. All this behavior was thought to wreak eugenic harm on their class. To curb such dangerous patterns, social hygienists proposed to instruct middle-class youth in "normal" (i.e., morally correct) sexuality and to develop a positive, purified image of sexuality through dignified scientific language. They hoped to create "better understanding and better adjustment between men and women" and to elevate sexual love to a higher spiritual plane. Young men and women did not need to be segregated totally; they could be comrades as long as they did not forget "the fundamental distinction and the reverence due each from the other."[84]

The message of white social hygienists to middle-class youth foundered on their own ambivalence. They advocated the single standard but remained committed to a Victorian understanding of sexual differences that underlay the double standard. Most social hygiene thinkers found it difficult if not impossible to consider that respectable women really had sexual impulses, and, as the example of Davenport shows, they became tongue-tied in the presence of a woman even speaking about sexuality.

The contradictions of social hygiene discourse stemmed not only from reformers' divided minds but also from the tension between the goal of sexual restraint and the social context in which middle-class women and men related to each other. The sexual expression of male dominance inevitably formed a "temptation" for young men, and cultural anxieties about "manliness" may have fueled this dynamic. For middle-class women, feminism and other public activities supported female resistance to socially imposed sexual ignorance and constraint. Urban anonymity, new cultural forms like dating, and the wider public discussion of sexuality, of which social hygiene itself was a part, also undermined the goal of sexual restraint. Sex education classes may have improved students' biological knowledge, but they were unlikely to reverse changing patterns of sexual interaction among middle-class youth.

White Working-Class Outreach

Acute as were their anxieties about middle-class youth, white social hygienists also gave attention to the working class. The literature of the movement up through the early 1920s records significant efforts to reach a working-class audience—particularly through exhibits and public lectures in workplaces, fairs, and storefronts as well as programs in settlement houses. From 1913 to 1919, private filmmakers and the government Commission on Training Camp Activities produced sex hygiene films.[85] Social hygienists promoted similar ideas about sexuality to working-class as to middle-class youth but were probably less effective in reaching working-class adolescents because of the class-bound language in their published works. They were also more likely to support coercive state action as an approach to sexual problems in relation to working-class people. Reformers, including settlement workers like Jane Addams, identified the sexual exploitation and the independence of young wage-earning women and venereal disease among working-class men as primary problems.[86] They cared less about—or felt less capable of affecting—the formation of character than they did for middle-class youth.

Both social hygienists and some working-class parents felt overpowered by the forces of industrialism, which drew youth into wage labor and commercialized recreation and subverted traditional controls over their sexual behavior. A doctor at the 1913 American Federation for Sex Hygiene conference pointed to "this awful cataract of infection that is going on among young people, especially just as they leave the elementary school and go into factory life." Jane Addams criticized the public dance halls as "a sorry substitute for the old dances on the village green in which all of the older people of the village participated. Chaperonage was not then a social duty but natural and inevitable, and the whole courtship period was guarded by the conventions and restraint which were taken as a matter of course." She feared that sexual impulses would overflow the proper channels leading to marriage and domesticity and become destructive, especially under the influence of alcohol.[87] Reformers also attacked overcrowding, and boarding in particular, as sources of immorality and physical contagion. Overcrowding, they said, "breaks down the feeling of privacy, and hence brings on loss of self-respect, of modesty, of order, of neatness" and leads ultimately to "the disintegration of the family" and "a tendency to focus life on the streets."[88] Some immigrant parents also experienced a loss of control over their children that was very distressing. Mexicans and Italians, for example, who were accustomed to chaperoning young women, faced social shame and economic burdens if unmarried daughters got pregnant. Both reformers and parents looked to the state: reformers sought laws to improve the industrial environment and to supervise recreation, while working-class parents made use of the age-of-consent laws to charge their daughters' boyfriends with statutory rape.[89] While the social hygienists were exercising their power of class, their interests sometimes intersected with those of working-class people. Both were responding to real changes in intergenerational relationships.

Young wage-earning men captured reformers' attention less than their sisters, but the few references made suggest that misinformation, venereal disease, and poor deportment toward women were working-class as well as middle-class problems in reformers' eyes. Male wage earners were said to hold as stubbornly to the belief in male sexual necessity as did high school and college youth and also to use indecent language and show inadequate respect for women. Some writers suggested working-class men might be more liable than middle-class men to acquire venereal disease, since low wages could leave them unable to marry and thus likely to patronize prostitutes, and also because working-class men lacked the "distinct ambitions" in work life that one observer associated with the ability to resist sexual temptations.[90] Reformers' greatest concerns, however, were about industrial and military efficiency rather than eugenic reproduction.[91] Educational materials addressed these problems, offering disease information, urging exercise and distractions to cope with sexual urges, and calling for respect for women ("fairness" or opposition to the double standard). And reformers vainly battled the belief in sexual necessity, arguing that continence was healthy and that health, not sexual conquest, was the true sign of "manly strength."[92]

Social hygienists attended much more closely to the sexual problems of young working-class women. Single factory and department store workers represented what reformers feared about overly sexual middle-class women—improper sexual involvement with men. Though sympathetic reformers preferred, like earlier purity reformers, to see the women as victims, some were also beginning to believe that young women were choosing a more active sexual life.[93] They did not fear the development of feminist "sex-antagonism" but, rather, expected working-class women to err by consorting with men too much.

Female wage earners could be seen as victims, but they were also making choices. They were indeed vulnerable to the power both of their bosses and of male coworkers: social work studies before 1913 found more than 50 percent of young working-class women surveyed reported that they had been solicited while looking for work, and what today is called sexual harassment was common.[94] Low wages meant they were reliant on male companions to pay for leisure activities like dancing, skating, and going to the movies, and so were exposed to men's sexual demands.[95] Yet reformers also accurately perceived a new female independence based on wage earning. Most employed women may have been poorly paid, but according to social workers' accounts, the pay envelope was still "the supreme symbol and potent instrument of newly gained power." They went to amusement resorts and sought men rather than waiting, in reformers' words, to be "sought after." They had a "sense of self-responsibility, fostered by their wage-earning."[96] They enjoyed more freedom from familial supervision in their social relations with men than would have been customary for middle- or upper-class women at the time, and their status as wage earners allowed them to alter their traditional sense of obligation and subordination to parents, struggling with parents over money, clothes, and recreation. Some also lived apart from family. Though not on a plane of equality with men, some did seem able to bargain with men on their own rather than submit to parental authority in matters of courtship.[97] Such independence disturbed reformers, as it did some of the parents.

To combat these dangers, reformers presented scientific information about puberty, sex relations, childbirth, and venereal disease, but they also taught middle-class feminine ideals as the appropriate standard of conduct. Such conduct emphasized female self-restriction and idealized marriage and homemaking. Like middle-class girls, working-class girls were taught that women should hold themselves in check to avoid arousing men's passions. Pamphlets and talks for settlement house club members urged young women to understand the stimulating effects of immodest clothes and behavior and thus the female responsibility for male responses. Dancing that seemed innocent to a girl might be a "terrible temptation" to a boy, wrote YWCA educator Margaret Eggleston. Bigelow tried to be evenhanded, asserting that "[w]hile we refuse to excuse men who allow the sexual suggestiveness of women's dress to overcome their self-control, we should at the same time recognize that women have themselves to blame for much of the existing situation."[98] But encouraging marriage and domesticity was most important in battling loose morality. Reformers sought to control the dangerous currents of sexual feeling before they became destructive by carrying young women, in Jane Addams's words, "into the safe port of domesticity." As social worker Eleanor Wembridge noted, poorly educated working-class girls "of ignorant and foreign parentage" (unlike the "sheltered" "student class") typically had physical sex knowledge, even experience, as men did. They needed sex instruction, but in "ideals" rather than biology. Exposure to high culture and middle-class ritual in the settlement houses was one means of "elevating" such young women. Staging a wedding ceremony "with a minister, a veil, a wedding march, and ice cream" in a working girls' boarding home was considered a glamorous way "to impress the...beauty of marriage upon the young guests."[99] As a whole, social hygienists' outreach to the working classes promoted middle-class values, including sexual purity before marriage and domesticity for the women as a means to control the raging sexual forces reformers perceived in the urban environment.

How effective was the sex education directed at working-class audiences? Reports of social workers and studies done by social hygienists suggest that, while many people were grateful for the information, language, class, and cultural barriers inhibited communication. The use of scientific language, important to social hygienists as a strategy of legitimation and modernity, did not help them to reach less-educated people. One study of sex education pamphlets that were meant to reach a wide audience found them totally unsuited in style and vocabulary for working-class readers. A group of Jewish and Italian continuation school students (who held jobs but attended school one day per week) were given some sex education pamphlets. Up to 30 percent of them marked as unfamiliar words such as "gonorrhea," "seminal," "fallopian tubes," "uterus," and "vagina."[100] The scientific language itself served as an assertion of the middle-class standards social hygienists wished to uphold.

More important than vocabulary were different socioeconomic and cultural environments and values. Working-class people with ambitions to improve their social class status or with powerful religious values may have been receptive to or have already agreed with social hygienists' ideas, but many felt justifiably that changing their behavior would have little impact on their lives. Others simply operated under a different set of social rules. Some men, for example, were "proud of being 'sporty,'" that is, known for "sex aggression" and "sex mastery." Among young working-class women, some sexual intimacy was a sign of having a serious relationship and also a means of holding a man. Families often showed what to reformers was an exasperating lack of indignation about their daughters' behavior: "In some homes there is only indifference, provided marriage is the outcome." Working girls ignored reformers' often very broad definition of prostitution as nearly all nonmarital sex and acted according to their own conception (that prostitution meant taking money for sex). Most of them carefully avoided such an identification. Their class position meant that observing middle-class moral strictures brought few practical rewards. As one young single mother commented, "'A real smart fellow with money wouldn't marry me anyhow, so what's the difference?'" Many were not willing to adopt a style of sexual restraint and domestic purity in the period before marriage.[101]

Social hygienists' relationship to the working class mirrored that of Progressives as a whole. Reformers saw the working class both as victims and as sources of disorder and contamination. They did not question deeply the existing class hierarchy or dominant culture. Within this framework, however, they exhibited the same differential approach to men and women as among middle-class youth: implicitly, they accepted men's wilder nature and looked to women to control men by adopting middle-class domestic and sexual values. Many probably ignored these lessons or found them impractical. Social hygienists' campaigns, however, reinforced older standards for women's sexual deportment and relations with men that were increasingly out of kilter with modern urban life.

African Americans and Social Hygiene

Only during World War I and after did the ASHA and other groups turn sustained attention to the African American population, and with a strong emphasis on combating venereal disease. As black professionals became involved, they used the ideology of social hygiene not only to fight venereal disease but also to resist the racism that they identified as a basic cause of its prevalence. Just as in the club women's early campaigns against lynching, rape, and racist sexual stereotyping, black reformers in the social hygiene movement claimed a place for the race among "civilized" people with "civilized" morality.

Concern about venereal disease rates triggered black involvement in social hygiene work. Army statistics showed much higher proportions of these diseases among black than among white troops. Because these numbers were marred by racist practices and reporting, the reality is unclear, but the reports did lead to action.[102] Anxiety about the effect of disease on military efficiency led to efforts by the wartime Commission on Training Camp Activities, the YMCA, and the ASHA to provide social hygiene instruction for black troops. Special black committees of groups like the YMCA and religious organizations were formed to provide camp activities for the segregated units.[103] The War Camp Community Service (WCCS), a voluntary agency closely allied with government that provided places of recreation for the troops in training and for local young women as well, created the Division of Colored Workers and hired Mary Church Terrell as supervisor of its female section. In 1918 she traveled through the South seeking the support of white local WCCS boards to initiate work in the black community. Segregation and the consequent lack of almost any public recreational facilities open to African Americans exacerbated the situation facing soldiers, and local black leaders often expressed concern about the lack of "protection" for young women.

Southern whites on WCCS boards, however, obstructed these recreational antiprostitution and anti–venereal disease programs for blacks. In community after community, Terrell heard the objections of whites who feared that hiring trained black social workers to organize programs for young women would give the women "hifalutin" notions and dissuade them from seeking domestic work. Terrell also visited black women in a segregated detention home and reported on the inferior facilities and more humiliating treatment they experienced by comparison to incarcerated white women.[104] Black reformers and nationally oriented whites based in the North promoted more equivalent and universal programs, but southern whites concerned enough about venereal disease to participate in preventive programs for whites opposed such work for blacks because it clashed with their interests in controlling black labor.

After the war, official government promotion of social hygiene among African Americans continued through the work of the U.S. Public Health Service, supported by the ASHA, the NACW, and the Urban League. The Public Health Service employed black physicians Roscoe C. Brown and Charles V. Roman, a former head of the black National Medical Association and professor at the Meharry Medical College in Nashville, Tennessee, to lecture on social hygiene in African American communities. In addition to his medical work, Dr. Roman was a strong believer in racial solidarity, a promoter of black history and pride, and a Bible class teacher at his African Methodist Episcopal church. He reportedly lectured to more than 22,500 people in the South in 1919. The ASHA, too, set up a program for blacks after the war and employed a black man, Franklin O. Nichols, to head it. Nichols had attended Temple University and the University of Chicago and was hired by the International Red Cross during the war to organize services for black troops in France. From there he moved to an army public health position and then to the U.S. Public Health Service before being hired by the ASHA. These men represented the small but growing African American professional class.[105]

The thinking expressed by African American social hygienists and programs for blacks resembled those of the larger white movement. Black social hygienists favored "high" moral standards, sexual continence outside marriage, and the provision of basic venereal disease information. They shared a distaste for the "artificially sexed" environment of the modern city. Black programs included sex education at normal schools and colleges in order to reach teachers in training and through them their future students. Nichols attempted in the early 1920s to gain ministers' support for social hygiene programs because these powerful institutional figures could reach black people not in schools. The ASHA offered summer institutes for black social workers and physicians to train them to recognize and deal with syphilis and in 1923 became involved with National Negro Health Week, an annual event begun in 1915 by Booker T. Washington and others to promote health education. The ASHA provided free pamphlets and posters for a "Hygiene Day" during Health Week. In 1929 the *Journal of Social Hygiene* cited research showing syphilis was getting worse among blacks and by 1932 considered it a "special health problem of Negroes."[106] An example of one program was a campaign in

New Orleans, held in November and December 1933 with the cooperation of the Flint Goodridge Hospital of Dillard University and the U.S. Public Health Service, and supervised by Nichols and Dr. Brown of the Public Health Service. Concerned with reaching an audience with literacy problems, coordinators used films and talks extensively and presented programs in a wide variety of neighborhood institutions. Organizers believed that a minimum of 8,500 people had been reached.[107]

Women of the NACW also took up the social hygiene issue after the war. They asked Dr. Brown to speak to them at their 1920 convention and sponsored lectures on venereal diseases at several other conventions through the 1930s. By 1925 at least one NACW leader, Mrs. Sallie Stewart of Evansville, Indiana, was soliciting funds to pay for the ASHA to hire a black woman doctor to carry on social hygiene education for college and high school girls for a year.[108]

Finally, the Urban League supported social hygiene work by publishing an article by Franklin Nichols in 1926 in its journal, *Opportunity*. The article addressed concerns about educating "future leaders of the race" and summarized all the dominant themes expressed in the white literature: the need to convince youth through science rather than autocratic rules; the idea that sex education concerned character and not merely health habits; the admonition to integrate sex education into all relevant parts of the curriculum rather than separating it off as a special subject; and the belief in monogamous marriage as a norm for sexual life. In addition to promoting education, the league was administering Wasserman tests and referring syphilis patients to hospitals in New York in the early 1930s.[109]

The African Americans participating in governmental and voluntary organizations' social hygiene programs shaped an argument about the causes of high venereal disease rates among blacks that addressed white racism's effects on sexual life and working-class morality. They claimed entitlement to resources for education and for treatment of the diseases in order to improve health conditions for all blacks, and they urged more involvement by black leaders in programs for the black community. Drs. Brown and Roman and social worker Nichols (as well as Spingarn of the NAACP) argued that venereal diseases among the masses of blacks were common due to a combination of racial discrimination, poverty, and a faulty sexual morality that was a heritage of slavery. Discrimination, they argued, exacerbated sexual problems: corrupt or discriminatory law enforcement allowed prostitution to flourish in black neighborhoods, surrounding children with vice. The neglect of black public schools and the "slum life of the city and the poverty and illiteracy of the country" represented "dangerous enemies to the personal purity and self-restraint of good homes." A double standard of justice and enforcement meant failure to protect black women from sexual assault or to enforce marriage and support laws when black men deserted their wives. Thus, modern racist practices as well as the "heritages of slavery," argued Roman, had "played havoc with the home life of the colored people" and, asserted Nichols, had encouraged common-law marriages, illegitimacy, and unstable families. In the view of conservative reformers, these were morally disordered conditions, which in turn produced higher rates of venereal disease.[110]

Unequal access to education and health care, black reformers and their supporters argued, also made blacks more susceptible to venereal disease. In 1932, for example, Nichols interviewed 300 black men at the Harlem Hospital syphilis clinic. In his report he strongly indicted both the educational materials being distributed and the medical professionals for their failure to teach these illiterate men about their disease. He found printed materials "unsuited to the educational level of this group" and urged shorter, simpler, illustrated leaflets be given. He suggested no one was really talking with the men, noting "that the patients seemed to need to talk to someone about their condition." He also called it "essential" that printed instructions "be supplemented by explanations" by doctors or social workers. "The interviews revealed definitely that the instruction...was not effective in impressing upon them the facts in the interest of their own welfare...or in protecting others from their disease."[111]

By showing how racial oppression affected sexual disease rates, African American analysts addressed widely accepted racist notions that blacks as a racial group were inherently susceptible to venereal disease. Nichols asserted in 1932 that "public health opinion," supported by recent progress in reducing venereal disease, attributed high rates to "environmental conditions." These thinkers accepted the same moral framework as whites, however, and, like white reformers, believed that what they considered "immorality" contributed to venereal disease. This perspective probably reinforced their sensitivity to the charges of "immorality" among blacks and their eagerness to instill officially sanctioned sexual morality in the masses. Thus, despite great sympathy for the working classes, they continued to promote middle-class morality and believed such observance was an essential part of combating venereal disease.[112]

As African American reformers claimed entitlement to education and medical treatment for their people, they gained a major role for themselves as professionals. The ASHA offered programs in the 1920s at colleges, teacher training schools, and schools of medicine and social work in order to train black professionals. This segregated approach paralleled patterns in other social welfare work, reflecting white racism. It also, however, allowed black professionals to take a limited role in the administration of programs for black people and probably to reach people whom whites would have ignored. The *Journal of Social Hygiene* itself editorialized in 1924 that the employment of "Negro personnel" was important for achieving the community-wide social hygiene education and treatment that was necessary, since diseases "do not draw color or race lines." This allusion to the fact of interracial biological community represented a rudimentary acknowledgment by white northern reformers of the new salience of African Americans in the population outside the South.[113]

African American involvement in the social hygiene movement well illustrates the complex, mediating role of the black middle class. Members of this class served race interests by presenting a historical account of sexual problems, disputing racist views of these problems, and demanding access to scientific and financial resources that they did not have themselves. At the same time their advocacy of "uplift" showed social distance from working-class African Americans, though less than most white reformers exhibited in relation to European immigrants.[114]

African American social hygienists, then, employed rhetoric similar to that of whites even though they did so from a racially distinctive standpoint and for their own ends. They differed from whites, however, in their employment of gender. Black social hygienists' published discussions never reflected the tensions over female roles so evident in the white discourse. Their support for improving "home life" did point to female purity, as among whites, but no black writer drew out the implication that women were responsible for men's sexual behavior. Indeed, in 1925, Mary Church Terrell reiterated the feminist emphasis of the earlier purity framework when she stressed male responsibility for sexual control in a speech to male students at (black) Howard University. She criticized the double standard and urged the young men to respect black women and sustain their moral reputations, especially since white men so seldom did. Black reformers, however, did not express concern about the sexual dangers of women's independence. Nichols once voiced opposition to celibacy, but he did not link it specifically to women. Dr. Roman even supported birth control, which had fearful associations with female autonomy; the ASHA did not support it.[115] And in the discussions of working-class mores, no one discussed men and women separately.

African American social hygienists shared with Anglo-American leaders the ideal of a modified Victorian order, but their concerns and analysis differed significantly.[116] Taken as a whole, this body of thought constituted a strong indictment of white racism and its effects on sexuality, from poverty and lack of sex education and medical care to the intrusions of crime into black neighborhoods. Unlike white social hygiene thinkers, however, blacks did not appear concerned about limiting women's independence in the interest of sustaining the older sexual order. Eager to establish the "civilized" character of both men and women, African American reformers supported a more egalitarian version of Victorian morality that stressed sexual restraint neutrally rather than emphasizing women's responsibility. This difference points to a distinctive African American take on gender that persisted in subsequent marriage reform.

Conclusion

Social hygienists had articulated their basic critique of prevailing sexual knowledge and practice by the 1920s. Until World War II they battled venereal disease and prostitution through public health regulations and legal measures such as mandatory premarital and prenatal testing for syphilis; they funded social investigations; and they continued their work in sex education for both whites and African Americans.

Reformers attempted to reach the working-class population in several ways but were less successful than with the middle class and professionals. Outreach to industrial workers continued both through appeals to employers' desire for healthy and efficient workers and through direct approaches to workers' groups, as when articles were placed in the magazine of the Brotherhood of Locomotive Engineers and Firemen in 1933. In the same year the Canadian Social Hygiene Council and the ASHA cooperated in an "experiment in mass education"—a dramatic movie, *Damaged Lives*, about the effects of syphilis on the family, that was shown at public theaters. Access to poorer groups also came about through the movement's increasingly close relationship with government, as when during the Great Depression the ASHA helped the Civilian Conservation Corps address issues of social hygiene.[117]

Attempts to establish sex education in public schools would have been the most effective way to speak to working-class people, but success in this area was not great. By 1920 the U.S. Public Health Service reported that about 40 percent of public high schools had "some kind" of sex education, and as of 1927 the proportion of schools providing it had reached 45 percent, but these offerings often meant single events such as a lecture or film on venereal disease rather than sustained course instruction. In the early 1940s, a survey of state boards of education revealed that only ten of forty-eight states either encouraged or mandated sex education in high school curricula, although some schools in other states did also have programs. Sex education was obstructed both by officials' fears of public hostility and by actual opposition from conservative religious groups, especially the Catholic Church. In general, although most school administrators (and the vast majority of high school–aged youth) believed sex education was needed, implementation remained limited.[118] Working-class people probably received relatively little sex education.

Educated middle-class people and their cultural values remained normative for reformers, and the heart of their efforts lay with them. When a major 1934 conference on marriage and family education (cosponsored with Columbia Teachers College and the American Home Economics Association) discussed noncollege groups (who constituted 75 percent of the population), they called for "specially adapted" programs, emphasizing the difference of less-educated people from the assumed audience of most social hygiene materials. Social hygienists had some real success getting sex education into colleges and universities, and by the mid-1930s the National Conference on College Hygiene had begun. They also targeted middle-class professional and voluntary associations, including the American Medical Association, the National Council of Parents and Teachers, the National Conference of Social Work, the League of Women Voters, the Federal Council of Churches, and the Junior League, to promote social hygiene, especially to nurses, doctors, social workers, and teachers, and to the middle-class white public.[119] Finally, between the 1920s and World War II, programs for African Americans were affected by the hard financial times of the Depression, leading to the curtailment of the college and normal school programs in 1932, which were replaced by an intensive emphasis on medical treatment and training for doctors, nurses, and social workers. The ASHA did, however, cooperate with the National Council of Health in 1934 to establish and upgrade student health services at black colleges, and by 1938 announced a "new impetus" in its college work.[120] Although reformers attempted to contact working-class audiences, in black as in white educational work, they did more to teach middle-class and professional leaders, hoping through them to reach the rest of the population. Thus, despite the growing attraction of alternative values disseminated through mass popular media, the social hygiene message probably reached a good many middle-class people, reiterating the social hygienists' values as the official moral standard.

Those values continued to include firm control of sexual impulses and the centrality of reproduction, with an increasing emphasis on the "normality" of marriage and parenthood, as opposed to the "abnormality" of celibacy or sexual relations outside marriage. In an article in the *Journal of Social Hygiene* in 1939, eugenicist Paul Popenoe quoted college students who were dissatisfied with their marriage education courses. The teacher of one was mocked as an " " "old maid" who hadn't had a date for thirty years and was always mourning over the fact that chaperones are no longer required.' " Another described a teacher " 'who was only about twelve years old emotionally. He spent a large part of the time asserting that all marriages are unhappy, and he practically advised free love.' " Popenoe called for colleges instead to hire "emotionally well-adjusted" faculty "with backgrounds of successful marriage and parenthood." Social hygiene writers maintained older expectations about women—that they would all be homemakers and mothers, that they were more vulnerable in relation to sexuality, and that they should set the standards for men in sexual restraint. Social hygienists maintained their claim to a "middle ground" between "prudery" and "abandonment" to distance themselves from more conservative, religious moralists but they were decidedly more worried about "abandonment."[121]

As a whole, the social hygiene movement expressed the conservative impulses of Anglo-Americans fearful of new immigrants and southern working-class blacks in urban life. As Max Exner noted in his pamphlet that opposed petting, "Petting means the cultivation of low tastes and ideals in love. He whose musical tastes have been fed on jazz is not likely to rise to a full appreciation or rendering of a masterful symphony." Jazz—the contribution of southern black migrants to American popular culture—represented for him the "low" passions of sexuality and dangers of disease. Reformers complained, too, about the effects of popular media. They believed that cheap magazines and movies, in addition to radical tracts such as Bertrand Russell's *Marriage and Morals* (1929), promoted "abandonment" to pleasure, the following of "natural" impulses, and the substitution of "promiscuity" for "discrimination."[122] Drawing on both science and their own class status, they attempted to beat back the barbarian influences and sustain the values of the Victorian middle class, especially for women.

Education for social hygiene demonstrates how important the role of middle-class white women was to the maintenance of a social class hierarchy and the gender order. In the early twentieth century, social hygienists' analysis of prostitution and venereal disease led them to see some dysfunctional effects of the Victorian style of male dominance. When it alienated women, male sexual privilege could lead to the destruction of the family life that reproduced Anglo-American social dominance. To renew these important women's devotion to motherhood and sexual purity, social hygienists offered sexual knowledge and tried to mitigate the effects of the double standard. In the 1920s and 1930s, as social hygiene programs turned toward the goal of "knowledge of development" (showing how sexual development led to monogamous marriage) and family life education, they hoped the knowledge conveyed would guarantee what they considered correct attitudes toward sex and marriage.[123] But the knowledge itself could not guarantee how students would receive it.

And in fact the responses of African Americans, of Frances Davenport, and of young women surveyed after exposure to sex education illustrate how the social hygiene agenda could be turned to other uses. Black social hygienists claimed their own place in civilized morality, argued the need and entitlement of blacks to venereal disease education and treatment, and articulated a historical account of the prevalence of disease that countered racist views of them as the "syphilis-soaked race." And despite using the language of purity, they did not turn it into a critique of women's independence. For Davenport, scientific knowledge and experience teaching sex education conferred a sense of authority that was unusual and perhaps unwelcome among the social hygiene men in 1913. For the female subjects of her study and others, even the veiled information on sex, the provision of some language with which to speak about it, and a limited forum in which to do so seem to have facilitated some critical consciousness about sexual relations, whether based on young women's resentment of the double standard or merely their lack of access to basic sex information. Social hygienists may have hoped in many ways to restore Victorian gender relations, but they could not control the impact of their programs.

Although social hygienists' vision clashed increasingly with newer images and norms of expressive female heterosexuality, their hold on official public cultural expression and influence within middle-class institutions probably helped sustain that vision much longer in native-born middle-class circles than in popular culture or among Americans as a whole. Their claim to "modernity" and "science" may have increased the legitimacy of their ideas for middle-class people who were turning away from the most conservative, religiously defined thinking. The actual state power that their ideas gained in wartime military programs and postwar public health projects would have enhanced that legitimacy. Certainly social hygienists offered for some time a middle way between the dominant Victorian thinking and modern understandings of sexuality and marriage. Yet theirs was a losing battle against women's growing independence, popular cultural amusements, a consumerist turn against asceticism, and the model of sex freedom proclaimed by cultural and political radicals in the 1910s.

2

Sex Radical Challenges
to Marriage

Anthony Comstock had been battling vice for forty-two years when journalist Gertrude Marvin interviewed him in 1914 for the radical magazine the *Masses* (1911–17). As special agent of the U.S. Post Office, he was still enforcing the 1873 obscenity law that bore his name, which prohibited distribution of birth control and abortion information and devices. He opposed even the reformist sex education efforts of the social hygiene movement. Marvin allowed Comstock to damn himself in the eyes of the magazine's sophisticated readers by eliciting from him the statement that "there is a personal Devil sitting in a real Hell tempting young and innocent children to look at obscene pictures and books."[1] Mocking Comstock's conservative Victorian sexual and religious beliefs, Marvin's piece exemplified the much more vociferous use of the myth of Victorian repression by sex radicals who were writing and agitating at the same time that social hygienists were active.

Social hygienists deployed the language of science to modernize but sustain the ideal of women as wives, mothers, and pillars of sexual restraint. Sex radicals, in contrast, challenged these views fundamentally. A potent interaction of socialist, feminist, and antiracist radicalism converged with new conceptions of sexuality from the 1910s to the 1930s to produce a period of openness in the United States that allowed sex radicals to convey explosive messages about the centrality of sex to human well-being, about women's sexual desire and autonomy, and about the sexual rights of African Americans and same-sex lovers. Radicals envisioned egalitarian sexual relationships that were less centered

Fig. 2 "The Public Sneak"

The birth control movement had to battle censorship as well as laws prohibiting contraception itself. This caricature of a censor, with Victorian sideburns and clothing, looks like Anthony Comstock, longtime federal agent enforcing the 1873 obscenity law bearing his name, although it was published after his death in 1915. It could refer to his successor, John S. Sumner. "The Public Sneak," *Birth Control Review* 2 (November 1918): 8.

on marriage and reproduction, more expressive of individual attractions, and more satisfying than they believed Victorian codes had allowed.

Sex radicals comprised a diverse set of people drawn from anarchists and socialists, birth controllers and feminists, bohemians, the more radical "New Negroes," and urban homosexual communities. They did not all seek the same forms of sex freedom and were not institutionally organized as such, but they all challenged key aspects of the prevailing vision of white bourgeois marriage and the codes of respectable sexual conduct associated with it. Social conservatives certainly perceived it as a serious threat to social order and stability and lumped sex radicals together as enemies of marriage and the family, while social hygienists also cited the dangers to sexual life of "the extreme feministic movement" and "radical socialism." So culturally and politically loaded was this sex radicalism that even many woman suffragists, socialists, communists, and civil rights leaders distanced themselves from it in order to avoid additional stigma on their causes.[2]

The institution of marriage against which radicals were rebelling was patriarchal, heterosexual, monogamous, procreative, intraracial, and increasingly regulated by the state. Legal prohibitions against contraception and abortion in the Comstock law and similar state laws defined marriage as officially procreative. Seduction, fornication, and adultery laws demanded monogamy and the sheltering of unmarried women from sexual activity. Antimiscegenation laws confined spouses to the same race.[3] A variety of legal and extralegal sanctions restricted people's ability to participate in the incipient same-sex subcultures of the large cities.[4] Sex radicals excoriated this form of marriage and its ways of ordering sexuality.

Instead, they confronted Victorian sexual culture and prescription with three fundamental ideas, which were enacted in several alternative practices. First, radicals rejected community and state surveillance and control of sexual relationships and activities, calling instead for individual freedom. Second, they proclaimed the goodness of sex and turned away from the prevailing culture of moderation and restraint. Third, they asserted women's sexual rights and acknowledged women's newly prominent place in the worlds of employment, politics, and public leisure. The practices that enacted these ideas included free love (the refusal of legal marriage), nonmonogamy, interracial marriage, birth control and domestic equality, and lesbianism. Male homosexual relationships also subverted Victorian sexual culture. I do not address them because men were freer than women to pursue extramarital sexual relations of any kind; it was women's potential independence from marriage, combined with same-sex attraction, that posed the greater challenge. Although the ongoing practical power of gender and racial inequality set significant limits on what proponents could achieve, these bold claims and experiments addressed many of the inequities women faced in conventional heterosexual relationships. These new ideas and practices were avowed hopefully within the liberatory context of the radicals' distinctive social, political, and racial worlds in the 1910s.[5]

Sex Radical Worlds

The first decades of the twentieth century were a period of dramatic and self-conscious cultural, political, and intellectual change in the United States, the beginning of a shift from a Victorian to a "modern" mentality, in which feminism and female public roles, the emergence of sexological science and modern psychology, and the effects of an ethnically diverse urban culture conjoined to undermine Victorian marriage and sexual codes. This change occurred especially among sophisticated and educated urbanites, artists, and intellectuals, and most publicly and intensively in major cities like New York and Chicago. In these metropolises European Jewish and Catholic immigrants in the pre–World War I era defied the reigning Protestant culture of Anglo-American elites; European Marxists sharpened American socialist thought; during the war years African American migrants from the South created an urban jazz culture; and homosexual communities and identities emerged in the anonymity of furnished room and red-light districts. Out of this dynamic mix emerged a collection of urban intellectuals who critiqued the sexual system as they shaped an American modernity.[6] These arguments, which were carried on in print, did not include Mexican, Asian, or Native Americans. Individuals from these groups, mostly located in the West, participated in changing patterns of sexual behavior, but Anglo and European ethnic groups, East Coast publishing institutions, and African Americans in the burgeoning community of Harlem dominated the written debates.

Class and Ethnic Backgrounds

Sex radicals came from both middle-class and working-class backgrounds and a variety of ethnic groups. Native-born African Americans like journalists Chandler Owen and George S. Schuyler, poet and novelist Langston Hughes, and novelists Nella Larsen and Zora Neale Hurston, as well as West Indian immigrants like Jamaican-born Claude McKay, tended to be well educated and thus middle-class culturally if not economically. Some whites, like journalists Hutchins Hapgood and Neith Boyce, socialist Max Eastman and his sister Crystal, and avant-garde editor Margaret Anderson, came from the Anglo-American middle class. Other nonblacks such as anarchist Emma Goldman, *Masses* editor Floyd Dell, birth control pioneers Margaret Sanger and Dr. William J. Robinson, and Baltimore radical V. F. Calverton (George Goetz) were immigrants or descendants of immigrants from Europe—Russian Jewish, German, or Irish.[7]

Sex radicals were fascinated and influenced by urban life and the immigrant and black working-class people who had created a vibrant popular culture of "cheap amusements" in the late nineteenth century and early twentieth century. Disreputable male (and sometimes racially mixed) working-class urban spaces such as saloons and gambling halls had always been associated with sex, but in the early twentieth century, skating rinks, dance halls, movie theaters, jazz joints, and immigrant cafés proliferated and attracted middle-class male and female patrons. Major cities developed furnished-room districts where single people could escape familial and moral scrutiny. Sex radicals looked to this working-class world to reinvigorate and reform the stultifying Victorian middle-class culture, and as they did so, they helped bring into being a new cultural and intellectual world in which more diverse groups came into conversation with one another.[8]

Yet a sharper divide remained between African Americans (U.S.- or Caribbean-born) and all others. By the 1920s a new biracial dynamic was superseding elitist beliefs in a hierarchy among white races (nationalities or ethnicities in today's terms); at the same time African American migration out of the South and growing civil rights activism made black-white divisions a national, not just a southern, phenomenon. Blacks were contrasted with a more unified "Caucasian" race, in which formerly marginal Europeans like Irish, Italians, and Jews of various nations (considered a separate cultural group) were being included. Anglo-American radicals anticipated this incorporation, engaging with non-Anglo ethnic groups, especially eastern European Jews, in the 1910s. Not until the 1920s did blacks enter this world.[9]

Egalitarian politics, however, did not inoculate white radicals against racist practices or ideas. A black cook still waited tables in Max Eastman's bohemian commune, although Eastman once admonished his lover for speaking sharply to the woman. Birth control advocate Dr. Robinson voiced overtly racist views, calling blacks "organically inferior on account of a difference in the brain structure." Many white radicals perceived African Americans as exotics more than as social equals. Yet blacks and whites did sometimes collaborate in left-wing politics and increasingly mingled in literary circles after 1920. In the 1920s Max Eastman made Claude McKay coeditor on the *Liberator* (1918–24), successor to the *Masses*, and McKay fought to get more coverage of African American issues. The prolific leftist writer V. F. Calverton worked particularly closely with African Americans. He especially promoted black writers like McKay and Hurston, who portrayed working-class characters. In his independent Marxist journal, the *Modern Quarterly* (1923–40), Calverton attacked segregation and published articles supportive of racial intermarriage.

Contributors included many black authors, such as leading black intellectual W. E. B. DuBois, sociologists Charles S. Johnson and E. Franklin Frazier, and George Schuyler. He also published writers of poetry and fiction in his *Anthology of American Negro Literature* in 1929. In addition, Calverton socialized with African Americans at the weekly intellectual gatherings at his Baltimore home.[10] While relations were neither equal nor simple, African American and white sex radicals did engage in a common discourse, though often with different emphases and intent.

Political and Intellectual Contexts

Most sex radicals had one—often more—of three broad intellectual affiliations: to the political Left, feminism, or the artistic bohemian world. They published their ideas in small radical and literary magazines and anthologies as well as in fiction; their texts grew out of their political movements and bohemian milieus in the 1910s and 1920s. Public sex radical debate (as opposed to private discussion and practice) declined after 1930, though lesbian texts continued to appear.[11] While most of their writings were not bestsellers, the sex radicals put into print radical ideas and debates about sexual issues in the culturally important metropolitan centers, especially New York, debates that more gradually filtered into the American hinterlands as part of a broader popular reportage on radical movements and practices.[12]

The 1910s and 1920s saw a burgeoning of left-wing activism in the United States, and its vibrant radical atmosphere nurtured sex radicalism. Russian Jewish-born anarchist Emma Goldman began lecturing and publishing in English after 1903, attracting native-born rebels like pioneer Chicago modernist editor and lesbian Margaret Anderson with her evocations of sexual freedom. Anarchists drew on the nineteenth-century free love tradition that had elevated individual autonomy and love as well as female equality over loyalty to permanent, reproductively centered marriage, opposing the social coercion of individuals by legal marriage and sometimes opposing monogamy.[13] Socialism influenced birth controllers William J. Robinson and Margaret Sanger and journalist and bohemian love enthusiast Floyd Dell.[14]

In Harlem's lively black community, migrant southerners and Socialist Party members A. Philip Randolph and Chandler Owen, with a number of West Indian immigrant writers, began to publish the *Messenger* (1917–28). They promoted socialism; opposed war, imperialism, and racism; supported women's rights; and integrated sexual questions into political thinking. A 1921 editorial, for example, mocked the Ku Klux Klan as a "gang of Anthony

Comstocks" who policed the conduct of others while violating their own morality. In the 1920s other black leftists contributed to sex radical thought, including *Messenger* writer Schuyler, Langston Hughes, and Claude McKay, author of the famous poem "If We Must Die" (1919), a militant paean to resistance against the white mob violence taking place across the United States that year.[15]

The massive women's movement of the 1910s formed another context for sex radicalism for both African Americans and whites. Although the defensive morality of many middle-class black club women limited their ability to address sexual questions explicitly, the Harlem literati and more prosperous women activists began to discuss birth control and other feminist issues. Grace Nail Johnson, a member of a prosperous Harlem family, was an antilynching crusader and wife of Harlem Renaissance writer and NAACP official James Weldon Johnson; she was the only black woman who belonged to the Heterodoxy Club, which was started in 1912 by a group of New York female artists, activists, and intellectuals who met to discuss feminist issues.[16] Radical white women, too, seeking much more than suffrage, shaped a new feminism involving a more psychological and social as well as political vision of women's equality. *Masses* writers like Floyd Dell and Max Eastman, the feminists of Heterodoxy, such as anthropologist Elsie Clews Parsons and novelist Helen Hull, and V. F. Calverton and his colleague Samuel Schmalhausen all linked modern women's political and economic emancipation with new sexual possibilities.[17]

The new feminist concern for sexuality blossomed particularly in the birth control movement of the 1910s, which pressed against the physical, cultural, and legal yoke of reproduction. After Margaret Sanger's dramatic resistance to obscenity charges under the Comstock law for her journal the *Woman Rebel* (1914), birth control agitation erupted powerfully in 1915; many advocates similarly ran afoul of the law, thus also becoming vanguard proponents of free speech. Through lectures and the selling of Sanger's and Dr. Robinson's birth control pamphlets, Goldman and Sanger linked a feminist vision of birth control to the momentum of working-class rebellion and pushed debate into the most powerful and widely read media.[18] Sanger's first birth control clinic was opened, raided by police, and closed in 1916, and she began to publish the *Birth Control Review* the following year. African American women in the Harlem Women's Political Association offered birth control as a lecture topic in 1918, and black writers provided articles for a special issue of the *Birth Control Review* in 1919.[19] Agitation had an impact: Goldman noted that in 1916 a judge trying a woman for theft implied that birth control might have prevented the crime by limiting the large family the defendant was trying to support.[20]

By 1919, however, increasing wartime repression and the postwar Red Scare were affecting both Left and feminist engagement with sex radicalism. Goldman was deported along with other noncitizen radicals. Sanger's shift to the right and toward the medical community as the arena for pursuing birth control has been well documented, though a concern for women's sexual pleasure and rights remained in her writings. Universally assumed as correct by feminists and political radicals, birth control was also claimed by liberals in the 1920s, no longer promoted as a tool of working-class direct action or sexual liberation but rather as an element of liberal marriage reform and social engineering.[21]

Problems of marriage and sexual repression remained on political radicals' agenda, however, and increasingly acrimonious debates took place about them. Many communists and supporters turned against sexual freedom in the 1920s, defining it as bourgeois self-indulgence. Others, appropriating psychoanalytic language and theory, argued for its importance. Some of the latter, most notably Floyd Dell, moved in a liberal direction, supporting marriage, family life, and modernized but distinct gender roles. Calverton continued to combine a Marxist politics with a psychoanalytically informed advocacy of sex freedom, including a fierce opposition to marriage and sexual repression. Marxist journals published vitriolic exchanges among Dell, Calverton, and others in 1927 about the sexual revolution. In the *Modern Quarterly*, John Collier (writing as "John Darmstadt") said the Communist *Daily Worker* was like the "Sunday School Times" in its treatment of sex, while *Daily Worker* writer H. M. Wicks accused the *Modern Quarterly* of "sex anarchism." Most Left publications then ceased discussing sexual issues.[22] Only Calverton and Samuel D. Schmalhausen, an enthusiast for psychoanalysis and a teacher who had lost his job for criticizing U.S. entry into World War I, sustained a radical debate on sexual matters for a few more years. In 1929 they sponsored a "Great Meeting on Sex and Civilization" that resulted in several anthologies of articles on the sex and woman questions.[23] Leftists continued to talk about sex privately and to act unconventionally, as did some feminists, but in the 1930s most stopped talking about it in the public domain.[24]

Bohemian communities of white and black intellectuals, writers, journalists, and artists formed a third context for sex radicalism in a number of American cities but most prominently in New York's Harlem and Greenwich Village. Urban freedom and the possibility of work in the print media drew these people to the big city; for blacks especially, northern urban life contrasted strongly with the all-encompassing racial restrictions of the South. These people's independent urban lives impelled them to seek more intense personal relationships, while urban anonymity protected them from the immediate scrutiny of moral conservatives. At the same time, they were deeply engaged with the intellectual and artistic rebellion of the day against Victorian thought and culture. Margaret Anderson, rebellious daughter of a prosperous and conventional family in Columbus, Indiana, published modernist poetry and fiction, including early excerpts of James Joyce's *Ulysses*, in her magazine, the *Little Review*, begun in Chicago in 1914. The freedom of thought and the unconventionality long associated with artists and writers readily extended to questions of sex in this period as well. Many whites debated and wrote about the new morality in institutions such as New York's Liberal Club, founded in 1913. Journalist Hutchins Hapgood, son of a midwestern manufacturing family, who wrote about marginalized groups like prostitutes and anarchists, and his wife, Neith Boyce, who had pioneered as the only woman reporter on the *New York Commercial Advertiser* staff before marriage, are well-known bohemian experimenters who also documented their sexual relationships in their writings. The younger New York writer Tess Slesinger, graduate of the Columbia School of Journalism and participant in left-wing Jewish circles, later delineated marriages and affairs among New York's Left community.[25]

An African American community of artists and writers that challenged middle-class sexual norms did not develop fully in New York until the 1920s, in the movement known as the "New Negro Movement" or later as the Harlem Renaissance. It was centered around periodicals associated with major organizations, the *Crisis* (1910–) (NAACP) and *Opportunity* (1923–) (National Urban League), as well as the *Messenger*, which had shifted in the twenties from a socialist to a more general race-advancement and pro-labor position. While older bourgeois leaders, epitomized by W. E. B. DuBois, editor of the *Crisis*, supported birth control, they were more cautious on other sexual issues. But a younger group boldly addressed sexual freedom. Harlem Renaissance writers such as Langston Hughes, Jean Toomer, Claude McKay, Nella Larsen, and Zora Neale Hurston wrote about women's equality, birth control, and the importance of a sexual life for all.[26] This younger group began as well to appreciate the working-class culture, especially jazz and blues, that the more respectable middle class had scorned and distanced themselves from. Dazzling performers like Ma Rainey, Bessie Smith, and Ida Cox modeled in their songs and lives a fractious female sexuality that celebrated both pleasure and independence from men. Both black and white bohemian and literary figures sometimes socialized with blues women, especially Bessie Smith, and saw them as part of a (desirably) "primitive" and "natural" black working-class culture (though black intellectuals, of course, held a more ambivalent relationship to this exoticizing). In this sense, the blues women's music served as a source for the sex radicals.[27]

The fiction produced in bohemian communities makes especially vivid the new sensibilities of the period. Writers of all kinds attempt to affect the swirl of cultural images and narratives in their world, but fiction writers can dramatize patterns of feeling that have not yet become part of conventional expectations. For African Americans, especially, whose cultural visibility was so obscured by racist stereotypes, fully drawn fictional characters could convey a more nuanced picture of their emotional lives. In her novel *Quicksand* (1928), for example, Nella Larsen's protagonist Helga Crane teaches at a southern black school, modeled on Booker T. Washington's Tuskegee Institute, whose Victorian rules of appearance and conduct enforce the respectability that was such a prominent part of black middle-class culture. Larsen shows Helga's restiveness under those constraints and her desire for more sensually expressive clothes and "nice things," such as middle-class white women were getting in the 1920s. Middle-class African American women in particular produced few texts directly disputing Victorian morality; their fiction, however, reveals how the sway of respectability was being shaken.[28]

In addition to journalism and fiction, bohemian intellectuals and birth controllers contributed to sex radicalism by popularizing Freudian ideas beginning in the 1910s. Max Eastman published simplified accounts of psychoanalysis in popular magazines in 1915. Dr. Robinson appreciated and used Freud's ideas in his numerous books on birth control and sex problems. He was the first English translator (in 1915) of Freud's important essay "Civilized Sexual Morality and Modern Nervousness" (1908), which critiqued sexual repression. Samuel Tannenbaum, a New York psychiatrist, analyzed Floyd Dell and also worked as coeditor with Robinson on several journals. Robinson and Tannenbaum published European psychoanalytic thinkers and helped propagate new sexual paradigms in medicine and psychology that gained increasing cultural authority in the 1920s and 1930s.[29]

The bohemian communities in Greenwich Village and Harlem were important, too, for the small space they opened for same-sex relationships. Wealthy women like Mabel Dodge, Heterodoxy member and supporter of the *Masses*, in Greenwich Village, and A'Lelia Walker, daughter of African American hair product entrepreneur, Madame C. J. Walker, in Harlem, were known for their bisexuality. As many as a fifth of Heterodoxy feminists were lesbians or possible lesbians (24 of 110 members). The atmosphere seems to have been quite accepting, at least until a meeting in 1927 where psychologist Leta Hollingworth asserted that "the perfect feminist" was "a woman happily

married and with children." Harlem was also experienced as a relatively tolerant place for same-sex couples, though that may not have been true for native
Harlemites as much as for white visitors. This somewhat freer social practice,
however, was not immediately reflected in published texts. Mentioning homosexuality in print was much less common than discussion of free love or birth
control, for example, until later in the 1920s, after publication of Radclyffe
Hall's famous lesbian novel *The Well of Loneliness* (1928), and lesbians often
did not write under their own names.[30]

The Myth of Victorian Repression

These three communities—anarchists and socialists, feminists and birth control advocates, bohemians and artists—nurtured sex radicalism as part of a
broader questioning of Victorian modes of thought as well as of social, political, and gender order. For this questioning the myth of Victorian repression
served as an important mechanism. They elaborated this rhetorical strategy
much more than social hygienists had done.

Where social hygienists had merely used the myth of Victorian repression
to criticize the lack of scientific discussion of sex, sex radicals presented themselves as rebels against the entire edifice of Victorian thinking. The idealism
of Victorian culture sat more and more uncomfortably with self-consciously
modern thinkers' sense of a complex and profoundly shifting urban industrial world. Radicals elevated individual freedom over submission to a cultural
order based on what they saw as false Victorian beliefs; thus individual freedom was linked to opening up a new truth. Radicals were among those who
initiated a "great sexual sermon" that "chastised the old order, denounced
hypocrisy, and praised the rights of the immediate and the real,"[31] which
they understood as the source of modern truths. In the 1930s Claude McKay
illustrated this perspective when he looked back with bitterness at the critical response of the respectable black leadership to his novel *Home to Harlem*
(1928): "I have never wanted to lie about life, like the preaching black prudes
wrapped up in the borrowed robes of hypocritical white respectability." Similarly, in *Quicksand*, Larsen critically described a dowdy woman reformer's
distaste for the story of "race intermingling and possibly adultery" in protagonist Helga Crane's family. "For among black people, as among white people, it
is tacitly understood that these things are not mentioned—and therefore they
do not exist."[32] Radicals scorned such denials and claimed the right to write
and speak about whatever they chose.

Radicals drew on this modernist appeal to the "real" or the "natural" to cast the "civilized" (and its sexual rules) into disrepute. Samuel Schmalhausen put it well:

> If we survey traditional civilization, we are impressed by one fact as always conspicuously present; the vast array of machinery of intimidation (physical, emotional, intellectual, spiritual) used by the authoritative elders to prevent the free and easy expression of sex desire. The times waited for a Freud to come along and make clear to a blind mankind how tragic the costs of this civilized machinery of intimidation. This exposé of sexual frustration I look upon as the ultimate important contribution of Freud. Why were the authoritative elders so concerned with preventing nature from being natural?[33]

Max Eastman illustrated this point when he recounted how his parents had whipped his elder brother for a childhood episode of sexual exploration with sister Crystal and a friend. The harrowing scene is structured to inspire appropriate horror in the reader at "religious America's deep, awful, pious, and theological zeal for saving souls from the flesh and the devil." Moral relativism was invoked to counter this type of absolutism, since scientific knowledge of the great variety of human types meant that no single and universally valid law of sex could apply to all. The search for variable, individual "truth" justified violating old rules. Journalist Hutchins Hapgood described bohemian socialite Mabel Dodge as "engaged in a strenuous effort to connect herself with the quiet reality of nature.... That accounts for her violences, for her transgressions against what seems to most of us to be morally obligatory, but it also accounts for her power of expression, and for her deep searching into life." For sex radicals traditional moral codes wrongly repressed the search for the (sexually defined) truth of individual self.[34]

By making such claims and framing sex as a fundamental need, these radical critics pointed to a more general rejection of Victorian restraint and a rising acceptance of consumption and pleasure. The value of self-control for building character was being replaced by an emphasis on self-realization of personality. Greenwich Village bohemian Edith Summers Kelley captured this sensibility well in her novel *Weeds* (1923). The novel traces the childhood and marriage years of a young and vital woman, Judith Pippinger Blackford, who resists the "stifling and oppressive aura" of a poor white farming community. The aura comes partly from repressive sexual mores but also from the community's more general ascetic values. One of the few prosperous families, the Pettits, lived in "dreary monotony," "slaves to their lifelong habit of thrift," which Kelley indicts as useless and life-denying. By the 1920s the newly prominent advertising industry was undermining such frugality and encouraging people to buy more to absorb the array of goods produced by modern industry. Psychologist A. A. Roback in Calverton and Schmalhausen's anthology *Sex in Civilization* (1929) pointed directly to the link of sex with consumption: chastity in itself, he argued, was "perhaps a useless quality, but it constitutes a great barrier...against future inroads of the whole gamut of desires which lie dormant in the breast of man." It was those very desires that advertisers sought to unlock. Roback favored a policy of "*minimum joy* in the sexual sphere" as he did a minimum wage in employment.[35]

In addition to pleasure and self-expression, the search for truth led, as with the social hygienists, toward science and medicine, but in a more iconoclastic style. Objectivity and scientific investigation, physician William J. Robinson proclaimed, not "theologic or moralistic bias," were requisite to the study of sexual continence and its effects. Havelock Ellis received credit for pioneering attacks on old superstitions, though he lacked "the rigid training and discipline of the scientist" necessary to complete the task, judged one philosopher. Freud was considered more scientific.[36] The rhetoric of repression then served as a weapon to discredit Victorian cultural authority, particularly "religion" and "superstition," in favor of "individual truth" or "science." The radicals thereby initiated a long-lived popular cultural notion about repression, echoes of which resound today in attacks on moral conservatives.

Leftists, feminists, and bohemians, then, used the myth of Victorian repression to distance themselves from the nineteenth-century intellectual world and prevailing Anglo-Protestant culture. They were iconoclastic and engaged with the modern, with its emphasis on science, individual freedom, and rejection of tradition. As avant-garde proponents of a sexualized self, they all voiced in some form, though in disparate registers, claims to new forms of sexual subjectivity and relationships that broke with those of the dominant Victorian culture. As Floyd Dell put it, intimate relationships gave place for "the enjoyment to be had in each other's separate, unique self."[37] Promoting such pleasure in individuality, sex radicals criticized marriage and its restrictive role in both bourgeois social and moral order and the subordination of women.

Gender and Race in the Moral Order

The moral order radicals confronted was centered on legal marriage and its gendered and racialized code of respectable sexual conduct (or "civilized sexual morality," as Freud labeled it). And marriage is what "makes the public order a gendered order," historian Nancy Cott has argued. Marriage law buttressed gender order by stipulating privileges and obligations of matrimony such as property control and economic provision for men and economic support and domestic and sexual service for women. That gender order was simultaneously a racial order; U.S. law has prominently included race-specific regulation of sexual and marital relations.[38] Marriage, then, was structured in ways that created and maintained inequalities.

Depending on where they stood in this unequal social structure, white men, white women, African American men, and African American women brought different experiences, protests, and aims to their project of challenging the marital and sexual system.[39] White women of the middle and upper classes in Victorian America were desexualized but served vital roles in bearing and nurturing white children. They sustained class hegemony, racial and class endogamy, and their own security through the public appearance of respectable sexual conduct, including premarital chastity and legal marriage to men of their class and race.

Men of this group were formally enjoined to the same sexual restraint as women, but in fact male and class/race privilege produced a double standard: white men of the middle and upper classes could choose between the code of the Christian gentleman and the aggressive masculine sporting culture that targeted lower-class women of all kinds outside of marriage (domestic servants, "charity girls," or prostitutes).[40] In parallel fashion African American men of high status could also exercise these prerogatives but only within their own community.

Lower-status women, subordinated by race or class, were defined as "bad" and "available" by nature. They had the role of providing sexual service to men and domestic service to women of more powerful groups but also to their own families; they also reproduced the labor force. Most whites automatically placed African American women in this category of "available" women, despite African American club women's vigorous protests.[41]

Finally, in a precise inversion of the relationship of higher-status men and lower-class women, lower-class and racialized men were denied sexual access to higher-status women, whose reproductive role for their class was jealously guarded. Laws against racial intermarriage, beginning in the late seventeenth century and continuing into the mid–twentieth century, were intended to prevent these latter relationships. Lynching and mechanisms of social ostracism also blocked them. (Laws and lynching, however, never served to prevent powerful men from pursuing relationships with lower-class or racialized women.)

Owing to their different positions in this social-reproductive system, then, creating sexual freedom meant something different for men and women in the different categories.[42] All protested barriers that kept people from pursuing love and sexual relations with partners of their choosing, but class, racial status, and gender fundamentally constrained how they could imagine freer sexual and marital alternatives. Despite their differences, however, most sex radicals sought to free sex and to free women. Some men mentioned the possibility of sex without love altogether, but most women and many men did not distinguish the terms "love," "passion," and "sex experience" and sought freedom for that sexual love from what they saw as unjust and repressive controls.

Freeing Sex and Freeing Women

In order to achieve individual freedoms, sex radicals made three critiques: they rejected repressive state, community, and familial controls over sexual relationships and activities, essentially privatizing them through a call for sexual freedom; they affirmed the inherent legitimacy, goodness, and healthfulness of sexual activity and relationships; and they promoted sexual equality for women. Women's equality was integral to the first two critiques because it was women who were most tightly confined by social controls over sexuality and women's sexuality that was most tainted with fear and disgust. In a world being transformed by industrial capitalism, the erosion of patriarchal family and community structures was creating people who felt or wished to feel more like "individuals"; as such they looked increasingly to sexual relationships to replace those more collective social structures that seemed to restrict their freedom.

First, while radicals differed about the appropriate stance toward the legal form of marriage, they were united in rejecting traditional social controls over sexual relationships and activities, looking to sexual and psychological intimacy instead of external forces to sustain relationships. Radicals claimed a wider arena of privacy for the couple, free of the prescriptions and intrusions of either government or social opinion. The couple's bond entailed, as Emma

Goldman said, a "glorious" coming together "in freedom and equality," a union incorporating "knowledge of, and respect for, each other" in place of the "insurmountable wall of superstition, custom, and habit" that traditionally separated men and women, who were so often trapped in coercive social structures that held together emotionally distant spouses.[43] Radicals sought a new, more psychologically and sexually intimate relationship that differed from the spiritualized romantic love of the nineteenth century and that broke down the separation of male and female social, intellectual, and emotional spheres to achieve greater psychological closeness. This sharing of worlds in a sphere of privacy was seen as possible due to radicals' sense of men's and women's human similarity.[44]

Building on this vision of similarity and closeness in the heterosexual bond, radicals rejected the wider social functions of sexual partnerships in favor of the personal. Hapgood and Boyce recorded stories of their own marriage in their novels *The Bond* (Boyce, 1908) and *The Story of a Lover* (Hapgood, written in 1914, published in 1919). Boyce's novel presents the old and new visions of marriage in a discussion between the female protagonist and a traditionalist male admirer. The latter argues that marriage is a social institution, for mutual assistance and bringing up children; "the personal relation is a very small part of it." The woman argues, however, that marriage is more of a private and intimate relation, and she relishes sharing full intimacy with her husband rather than occupying the socially mandated and sex-segregated roles of traditional marriage.[45] Likewise, anthropologist and Heterodoxy member Elsie Clews Parsons looked for "reciprocity in passion, emotional integrity, and mutual enhancement of life" in modern marriage—highly individualistic aims.[46]

Like Clews Parsons, African American writer Zora Neale Hurston placed reciprocal passion and love at the heart of marriage. Hurston, daughter of a Baptist preacher who was also mayor of the all-black town of Eatonville, Florida, arrived in New York in the mid-1920s and became a figure in the Harlem Renaissance, writing fiction about her southern experiences. She also studied anthropology under Franz Boas at Columbia University and collected southern African American folklore as her research project. She set her famous novel *Their Eyes Were Watching God* (1937) in the Florida world of her youth. The novel follows the life of Janie, a young black girl raised by her grandmother. Nanny understands marriage instrumentally as a social institution necessary to protect women from worse things—exploitation by white or black men. Nanny first marries Janie off to Logan Killicks, a much older but economically secure farmer who wants to exploit her labor and whom she cannot love. She leaves him and runs off with Joe Starks, a sweet-talking and ambitious traveler who settles with her in an all-black town and becomes successful; he wants to put her on a pedestal and display her as an ornament of his power. But for Janie it is only love—and love with an equal—that creates a genuine relationship, which she finds after Joe's death with a joking, gambling, piano-playing poor man named Tea Cake Woods.[47]

Men, too, looked to the personal aspects rather than collective conventions as the real substance of marriage. Hapgood wrote in his novel that "the closest personal relation" offered a "challenge" to the lack of meaning or life in the rest of society, and his protagonist obsessively sought to create "so strong a spiritual bond" that it could survive everything. An anonymous married businessman wrote in the *Masses* in 1914 about leaving his job for one that required less commuting: "I had begun to feel that the one-sexed world in which I had been living was inadequate to human needs—that life ought to be lived and shared by men and women together."[48] Floyd Dell envisioned the new intimacy in very romantic hues: "[T]he impersonal, elemental, irresponsible fire of sexual love, when given the privilege or obligation of having no fruition in children and domesticity, could become a kind of passionate friendship, a recognition of the truth that each was, beyond sex, a person."[49] Such persons were individuals who claimed privacy and did not accept society's right to dictate their intimate relationships.

The radicals' second critique of prevailing sexual and marital norms stemmed from their imagining of those intimate relationships. They affirmed the basic goodness of sex, seeking to reverse the cultural emphasis on moderation and restraint in order to allow that basic sexual goodness to nurture a more vital humanity and the passionate friendships they sought. They redefined cultivation of sexual life as the sine qua non of individual maturity, power, and well-being for both men and women. Vigorous sexuality, for example, was important to the new ideal of "strenuous" manhood that preoccupied white Americans from the 1890s onward. Memoirs of white radical men often stressed their need for the "irresponsible freedom" to have sexual relations with many women and a sense of weakness and failure for submitting to conventional rules of self-control. Post–World War I proponents of "New Negro Manhood" also valorized sexually active men, though cautiously. One example is the character Jimboy in Hughes's novel *Not without Laughter*, whose wife, Annjee, forgives his long absences and lack of money when he comes home and takes her to bed. A sexual man, Hughes implied, was more attractive than a traditionally responsible husband. White feminists such as Suzanne LaFollette extended these ideas to women, rejecting nineteenth-century passionlessness and calling it "unnatural and unworkable" to deny women's sexuality.[50]

Radicals elaborated on this theme in relation to both health and social well-being. Drawing on an increasingly medicalized discourse of "health" and "the natural," they argued that sexual repression produced poor physical and mental health, inability to work, loss of love, and lack of joy in life. Dr. Robinson wrote that abstaining from sex would "lay the foundation for irritability, weakness, nervousness, or even genuine neuroses, and a cooling or even destruction of the affections." Radicals turned away from the social hygienists' stress on moderation and increasingly promoted sexual expressiveness. They envisioned the sex drive, especially men's, as a nearly irresistible natural force that, when denied satisfaction, would burst forth destructively to create social problems such as rape and prostitution. As the *Messenger*'s Chandler Owen declared, "Man is a veritable Vesuvius, whose molten lava of sex passion, burning and boiling and seething with unrest, drives him to seek satisfaction."[51]

These two themes—rejection of repressive sexual control in favor of individual freedom and the promotion of more sexual expressiveness as positive and healthy—pervaded the writings of both male and female sex radicals. However, women and men confronted very different situations in regard to acting on these themes due to women's subordination and the sexual double standard. In the 1910s, then, when "[f]eminism was in the air," as Floyd Dell put it, the third theme—sexual equality for women—emerged in close relation to the first two.[52] White men, white women, and black women all promoted greater freedom and sexual equality for women, while the few black male radicals' concern was quite specifically focused on white women's right to choose black men as sexual partners.

In their efforts to "free sex," white radical men faced less a social restriction than a moral and psychological one that triggered their desire for women's equality and freedom. Though the double standard allowed these men the social freedom to acquire much more direct and varied sexual knowledge and experience than their female peers, they were distressed by guilt and by the unpleasant division between legitimate love with class equals and illicit sex with class subordinates. They sought to bring respectable women more equally into the world of sex, sharing the burden of moral responsibility for it, asserting its legitimacy in resistance to polite convention, and enjoying more of it. In this they were developing the more modern definitions of masculinity that valorized sexual experience.

Floyd Dell became one of the most prolific writers on this issue. Son of an Illinois butcher and antislavery Republican who had fought in the Civil War, Dell later witnessed the economic misfortunes of his father, who ended up as a factory worker. He joined the Socialist Party at age sixteen and found his own way out of the working class during the family's years in Davenport, Iowa. There his bookish ways gained him entrance into the bohemian edges of the city's intellectual circles. He was able to move into newspaper work in Davenport, then went to Chicago in 1908, where he became editor of the *Friday Literary Supplement* in 1911. He married Margery Currey, a modern woman and suffragist. They had a self-consciously egalitarian modern marriage; with her consent he had affairs with other women, but the two separated in 1913. He then moved to New York and became an editor of the *Masses* in 1914. After undergoing psychoanalysis, he got married again in 1919, to B. Marie Gage, another suffragist. In the 1920s he began to write novels and tracts on modern love and marriage. Dell was experimenting with new ways of being a man, something based less on the breadwinner model and more on sexual self-expression. He was very attracted to the new women who were breaking the Victorian mold and sought a different kind of relationship with them. As a youth he had felt caught between the obligation to respect traditional limits on sexual advances toward respectable women and shame at not being enough of a man to seduce the women. He did not want to assume the onus of seduction but rather wanted men and women to break through conventions together in an honest admission of mutual desire. Women's equality in this view was a call for women to reject their nineteenth-century role as guardians of morality and to support men in a freer sexual life, often through practices of free unions or nonmonogamy.[53]

Many radical white women agreed, but they wanted freedom not on men's account but on their own. They faced more surveillance and social barriers to sexual activity than their male peers due to their identity as prized wives and potential mothers of the dominant racial group. Thus they had to battle to gain access to the sexual knowledge and freedom of action that men had. During the courtship of Hutchins Hapgood and Neith Boyce, for example, her landlady served a chaperone-like function, reprimanding her when Hapgood slept in a hammock on the porch one night when he missed his ferry back to New York from Boyce's home on Governor's Island. This kind of respectability roused the fury of Sanger and Goldman. Sanger stood as a "woman rebel" against women's enslavement "by middle class morality, by customs, laws and superstitions." Love, not marriage, was the greatest part of life, Goldman wrote: "Can there be anything more outrageous than the idea that a healthy, grown woman, full of life and passion, must deny nature's demand, must subdue her most intense craving…abstain from the depth and glory of sex experience until a 'good' man comes along to take her unto himself as a wife?"[54] Goldman and Sanger both framed sex in intensely romantic terms and deployed that romanticism to assert publicly the legitimacy of women's desire. Enacting that desire led some radical white women to the practices of birth control or lesbian relationships.

African American men and women stood in a different relationship to the race-gender system than either white men or white women because of the racist labels of savage sexuality they faced. White authorities defined black men as most dangerous and justified lynching as retribution for supposed assaults on white women. In the 1890s antilynching crusader Ida B. Wells had been severely attacked, losing her Memphis newspaper to mob violence, for pointing to the forbidden truth that some of those white women were consensually involved with black men. In the early twentieth century some black men, especially in the freer atmosphere of the North, wanted more sexual freedom, including the right to such relationships. They rejected the intensely self-controlled masculinity that was supposed to defend them against attack and, like white men, sought a more "passionate manhood."[55] In this way a few black male radicals came also to call for white women's freedom to choose black partners as they argued the legitimacy of interracial relationships.

By contrast, interracial freedom was not a primary concern of African American women, who had suffered too much from coerced interracial sex under slavery and after. They resisted other harsh, though class-divided, constraints that impinged on their sexual lives. The taint of immorality imposed by racism made all black women potential targets of male aggression. Middle-class women, however, complained most of the social taint that undermined their respectability and class status if they exhibited the slightest hint of sexual impropriety, while the physical threat of male aggression, both white and black, was greater for poor black women.[56]

Despite the tremendous community pressure for black middle-class women to appear chaste and respectable, a few challenged the strict regulation of their lives as well as arguing for birth control. By the 1920s some black women writers articulated women's desire for sexual pleasure, though only in fiction. Nella Larsen, a mixed-race woman born in Chicago, wrote novels that captured sex as women's desire for connection as well as pleasure. Daughter of a Danish immigrant woman and a West Indian black man, whom she never knew, she took her Danish stepfather's name. She was caught between the two racial worlds and comfortable in neither. She studied in 1907–8 at the historically black Fisk University in Tennessee. Later she lived in Denmark for several years. After returning to the United States, she trained as a nurse at the black Lincoln Hospital in New York. Both her novels, *Quicksand* and *Passing*, imagine black women struggling painfully against both prudish black middle-class moralism and the exoticizing white gaze. Despite tragic endings that suggest the high social price black women had to pay for opening the issue of sexual passion, Larsen did present women as sexual beings. In the autobiographical *Quicksand*, Helga Crane, whose mother is Danish and father black West Indian, is pulled back and forth between white and black, with white representing money and physical freedom but spiritual isolation, and black representing belonging, spiritual satisfaction, and sexuality but imprisonment through racial prejudice and reproduction. Helga is repelled by her fiancé's sexual desire while teaching at the Tuskegee-like southern school. Yet later in Harlem she experiences her own desire for Robert Anderson, who is married to a close friend. He kisses her once and "[f]or days, for weeks, voluptuous visions had haunted her. Desire had burned in her flesh with uncontrollable violence." Rejected by Anderson, she seduces a black preacher, who marries her and takes her to Alabama, where she is reduced almost to death by constant childbearing, the apparent penalty for her awakened desire.[57]

Zora Neale Hurston voiced a more powerful feminist anger at women's objectification and traditional moral controls by choosing rural southern characters, already associated with peasant lustiness and strength, rather than urban middle-class ones. In *Their Eyes Were Watching God*, Janie's resistance to the stifling conventionality and emotional deadness of her first marriage specifically evokes her sexual desire. She indulges in a luxuriant fantasy of a flowering pear tree that represents sexual pleasure and fecundity. Janie tells her grandmother, "'Ah wants things sweet wid mah marriage lak when you sit under a pear tree and think.'" Soon she runs off with another man. Larsen and Hurston, however, were the only black women novelists to address sexuality so boldly. Contemporary readers may have been affected by the words of these pioneering novelists.[58]

In a different style than middle-class novelists, working-class African American women also enacted claims for women's sexual equality. Already labeled as excessively sexual, these women did not face the tight moral controls of their bourgeois sisters but instead raw male power and the oppressive stigma of sexual looseness; hence, their sexual struggle took a different form. Some of these women carried their stigmatized sexual character into performances as blues singers and made their living by playing on that image. Blues women of the 1910s and 1920s both protested patriarchal objectification of women and asserted desire directly and humorously in their songs. Ethel Waters celebrated her divorce and freedom in "No Man's Mamma Now"; Bessie Smith rejoiced in her sexual power in "Young Woman's Blues," claiming, "I'm a good woman and I can get plenty men"; and Ida Cox critiqued male sexual prowess and demanded her own pleasure in "One Hour Mama."[59] Not unlike the lively working-class European immigrant women who were creating a new sexual style on urban streets, these African American women singers inscribed the moral challenge of assertive female sexuality (both heterosexual and occasionally lesbian) in popular culture and reached a wider audience than the novelists or writers in radical magazines.[60]

Such vibrant and humorous expressions of women's sexuality were distinct from the high seriousness of Sanger, Goldman, Larsen, or even Hurston. Blues women's strength of sexual voice was also made possible by the emergence of a wider market and their ability to earn a living singing this music. Regardless of its source, their broadcast of a female sexual self became an important reference point in the contestations over sexuality in this period.[61]

Critiques of repression and support for the centrality of sex in life had been growing among sexual reformers since the nineteenth century. What was new in the early twentieth century—and often culturally explosive—was the combination of feminist claims for sexual equality with the rejection of social and institutional controls and the promotion of sex in the political demands and practices of American sex radicals. Practices such as free unions and nonmonogamy, interracial relationships, birth control and domestic equality, and lesbianism distinctly challenged the reigning conventions of heterosexual relations and marriage.

Radical Sexual Practices

No monolithic sex radicalism existed. Rather, a variety of alternatives to monogamous marital sex were envisioned by different subsets of radical thinkers attempting to live out their critique of sexual regulation and claims for individual privacy and freedom, their positive and liberatory vision of sex, and their feminist demands. Continuing nineteenth-century anarchist and free love traditions, political radicals and bohemians—whites in the 1910s and African Americans by the 1920s—made free love and nonmonogamy matters of debate. A few African Americans and whites made interracial relationships an issue of public discussion by the 1920s. Male and female radicals of both races advocated birth control, which became safer to discuss by the 1920s; a few radicals, more often women, extended the implications of birth control to address women's equality in the division of domestic labor. Very few made public claims about lesbianism before 1920; more spoke out—a few African American blues singers and white lesbian novelists and autobiographers—during the 1920s and 1930s.

Conservatives and fundamentalists considered these practices violently offensive and destructive of social order. Even radicals wondered at times about what would hold the sexual world together: Samuel Schmalhausen pondered whether "casualness in the love life [can] create profound sexual or human values.... Will love be impoverished and trivialized?"[62] Yet despite doubts and anguish, sexual radicals propounded and attempted sexual practices that they hoped would break down Victorian controls over sexuality and help them attain the sexual freedom and intensity they sought. The dialogue over these practices reveals differences of perspective, strength of voice, and costs for speaking out—differences that expose the structured tensions between women and men, blacks and whites, in the social-cultural system. While both men and women were potentially affected by the following practices, free love, nonmonogamy, and interracial relations tended to meet men's concerns more, while birth control and domestic equality and lesbian relationships spoke more directly to women's needs.

Free Love

In search of vital personal relationships, some radicals opposed legal marriage, drawing on feminist as well as leftist arguments. Feminists offered ravaging critiques of bourgeois marriage and its oppression of women as property and status symbol. In *Their Eyes Were Watching God*, Hurston writes evocatively of female resistance to marriage and shows Janie blithely leaving her first husband. Likewise, after her second husband's death, wealthy widow Janie laughs at the men who want to marry her and muses that she prefers that "freedom feeling." The novel's setting in the rural South suggests the tradition of common-law marriage among some poor blacks as one source of Janie's alternative.[63] White radicals based antimarriage positions on either anarchism or Marxism, usually combined with feminism. Anarchists argued the freedom of the individual to follow out the "natural" flow of passion and love, undeterred by state repression. Goldman denounced marriage grandly: "[H]ow can such an all-compelling force [as love] be synonymous with that poor little State and Church-begotten weed, marriage?"[64] Sanger praised and published Goldman in the six-month run of the *Woman Rebel* in 1914 and editorialized that neither church nor state should be concerned with the "personal agree-ment between a man and a woman." Max Eastman married but could not tol-erate the confinement: "[M]arriage always seemed to me a gauche intrusion on the part of the state and society into the intimacies of a private romance." Elizabeth Stuyvesant, one of the "modern women" whose stories were solic-ited for the *Nation* in 1926 and 1927, recounts the development of her belief that the "utmost measure of freedom" was essential to life; she reports having lived eleven years in a "free and uninterruptedly happy association" unsancti-fied by "lay or clerical formalities."[65]

A specifically Marxist critique of marriage, articulated in these sources only by men, echoed this concern with individual freedom but stressed mar-riage as an element of the system of property and class relations.[66] In the 1920s V. F. Calverton articulated a Marxist critique of marriage. He and fellow *Modern Quarterly* writer John Collier argued against monogamous marriage because they saw it as part of the capitalist system of property relations that subordinated and controlled women, wrongly segregated legitimate from ille-gitimate children, and blocked spontaneity and variety in the sex impulse.[67] Economist and philosopher C. E. Ayres, a contributor to one of Calverton and Schmalhausen's anthologies, argued that the marriage system and its eti-quette amounted to a method for perpetuating class endogamy by controlling who could meet and marry whom. Destroying marriage thus undermined the capitalist class system. It also freed the individuality and sexuality of both women and men. The latter, more anarchist, element of this group's thought was rejected as decadent and individualistic by more orthodox Marxists of the Communist Party.[68] Calverton cited Russian Communist Alexandra Kollontai approvingly on the goal of substituting collective support for women and chil-dren in place of reliance on the individual male breadwinner, but little fur-ther discussion is evident in these writings, perhaps due to the utopian nature of such a vision in U.S. society.[69]

Over all, relatively few of these writers—and none of them African Americans—sustained consistent opposition to legal marriage. Even in the radicals' cosmopolitan environment institutional marriage retained consider-able social power. Dominant African American race leaders like DuBois and the women of the National Association of Colored Women had considered the practice of informal unions among poor blacks a problem since the nineteenth century and continued to do so.[70] The small number of more sexually radical African Americans also mounted no campaign against marriage. In an essay contest sponsored by the *Messenger* in 1927 on the theme "Is Marriage a Fail-ure?" the prizewinning male author argued modern marriage was degraded because it made women into property; yet he opposed abolishing it, for "the [black] woman [would be] placed at the mercy of the amorous Caucasian." Hurston was unique in voicing a powerfully explicit feminist critique in the early sections of *Their Eyes Were Watching God* (and implicitly in her short stories of the 1920s). But later in the novel she shows the heroine Janie, having found an equal partnership with Tea Cake, deciding to marry as a sign of permanence and commitment.[71]

Among whites, too, sustained and consistent antimarriage positions were relatively rare in published statements. Emma Goldman was the most well-known white woman to argue the antimarriage position, and she personally never remarried (following a brief early marriage) after adopting anarchist principles. Elizabeth Gurley Flynn, an Irish American labor organizer for the Industrial Workers of the World who became known as the Rebel Girl, echoed Goldman's equation of marriage with prostitution in a 1915 essay; after an early marriage she also practiced free love all her life, though she wrote little else about it.[72] Elizabeth Stuyvesant's glowing account of free love in the *Nation* was published anonymously. Even among the men, opposition to the legal form was often less important than arguments about the oppressiveness of monogamy. Calverton, for example, stressed the need for flexibility and nonexclusivity; he did actually marry.[73]

In practice, marriage continued to bear important connotations of class status for both sexes among whites as among blacks. Dell conveys the class distinctions in Greenwich Village between mere "passing love affairs" and "something better"—"conscious and deliberate control of one's life and restraint of one's sexual impulses" expected of those who were "serious." He himself ultimately came to feel his "life would be a failure" if he could not achieve a more permanent relationship. Likewise, the more upper-class Hapgood believed a long relationship, in which a couple shared the experiences of "children, hardship, disease, and death," was a superior form; divorce had to be available but was a "lamentable failure" both morally and aesthetically.[74] Stability and permanence were associated with social value and status, even among some rebels.

But for white women marriage promised economic support or assistance as well as respectability, and rejecting it was even more difficult for them, as reports about women close to sex radical circles reveal. Floyd Dell, engaged in Freudian analysis and moving away from his earlier bohemianism, participated with leftists Mike Gold and Calverton in 1921 in public debates billed as "Freedom vs. Marriage." While Gold and Calverton argued that the "true revolutionary position of Freedom" necessitated opposition to marriage, Dell supported marriage and reported many women in the audience "pleased that I did not regard their desire to have babies, and to have the babies' father around the place, as counter-revolutionary." The many anarchist wives who were hostile to Goldman might have feared losing their husbands (and the husbands' wages) to a free (or "loose") woman.[75]

White women who themselves wrote as sex radicals tended to be self-supporting and relatively less concerned with respectability, but their evolving positions also demonstrate the pervasive social and legal power of the institution. To claim equality merely in premarital sex, for example, Elsie Clews Parsons gingerly proposed trial marriage in her textbook *The Family* (1906), but the suggestion aroused a "storm of controversy."[76] Sanger, who seemed a thorough free lover in *Woman Rebel* (1914), quickly moved to a more pragmatic position. In *Woman and the New Race* (1920) she argued for women's freedom in choosing mates and controlling their bodies but did not specifically attack marriage. After divorcing William Sanger, she married the wealthy Noah Slee in 1922, having earlier told a friend that she would marry again only for money. Psychologist Phyllis Blanchard, who had firmly rejected marriage because it denied women's independence, at age thirty finally accepted "the outward form" as long as the "inner spirit...embodied freedom" and "because it is the only way in which we can give expression to our love without interference."[77]

As clearly as these white women saw the limitations of marriage, they also saw the way its entrenched power gave married women "freedom" of another kind—from social exclusion and harassment by conventional society. Their stance parallels that of respectable black women, who also needed marriage. For a variety of reasons—racial vulnerability for African Americans, social punishment and economic need for white or black women—publicly stepping outside the protective wall of marriage was more difficult for women than for men.

Nonmonogamy

More of these writings focused on loosening the institutional rigidity of marriage than on breaking its legality. Principled nonmonogamy—called "varietism" by the nineteenth-century free lovers—could accompany either marriage or free unions; it loosened the moral grip of long-term relationships and heightened sexual intensity. This position proposed greater openness and sometimes mutuality in the extramarital freedom long relatively accessible to men. Like positions on legal marriage, views of nonmonogamy were necessarily affected by the cultural and social power differences of men and women.

White and black men who favored nonmonogamy argued both from Marxist critiques of marriage and from the new individualistic and consumerist sensibility about sex. Calverton and Collier more or less equated nonmonogamy with nonmarriage and saw both as revolutionary action against the old capitalist order, freeing wives and dissolving the property relations of marriage. In the *Messenger*, Thomas Kirksey approvingly reviewed Calverton's *Sex Expression in Literature* (1926), labeling monogamy a "vestigial social appendage" on the economic institution of marriage. He bitterly contended that "the Negro" had nothing to gain from bourgeois morality: "what, pray, has he to be puritanical about?" since white men had "dissolved" black families by making black men's wives their whores. (Despite critiques of white men and of bourgeois morality, however, Kirksey also vituperated against black women for betraying their "economically emasculated mates.")[78] Nonmonogamy from this perspective showed up the bankruptcy of the reigning class and racial order.

Men's impulse toward multiple sexual affairs could also be seen as a kind of craving for experience, a desire to "consume" (more) women and their sexuality, that was part of male privilege in the new world of urban amusement and consumption. Chandler Owen, *Messenger* coeditor, bachelor, and man-about-town, was an enthusiast for cabarets and the new morality they exemplified. His satirical articles on love, marriage, and divorce portrayed romance as the froth overlying biological urges, and he stressed the temptations of novelty in contrast to the monotony of marriage: monogamy might be "wrecked" on the "shoals of this heartless law"—that "a thing has less power to satisfy you the more it is used by you." Couples needed to "create new desires" in each other to keep marriage alive (not unlike what advertising was doing to maintain consumption). Claude McKay's bawdy *Home to Harlem* (which the respectable DuBois said made him feel like "taking a bath") drew on his experience among black working-class people in New York after immigrating in 1912. Though a well-educated man from the landowning Jamaican peasantry, McKay was no more comfortable with the American black elites than they were with him. He saw in working-class characters like his protagonist, Jake, "the primitive vitality" of the race and a less suspicious approach to sexual desire. He himself pursued affairs with both men and women. In the novel Jake imagines consuming Harlem's "Brown girls....Brown flesh....Brown lips....Brown breasts" like luscious "belonging-to-us honeycomb." Sleeping with many women but keeping his distance from them, and especially refusing to be a "sweet man" (supported by a woman), define manhood for Jake. Calverton argued that "[c]hange, variety, newness, seem to be part of the ineluctable demands of the sexual impulse—at least of the masculine impulse." The older Hapgood retained a Victorian sense of reverence about sex, but he, too, seemed unable to resist sex with many different women, all of whom he saw as a way to make contact with "the primitive, the instinctive, and the ideal."[79]

Though many male radicals (theoretically) advocated equal freedom for women, men's support for nonmonogamy in practice often meant extending and attempting to legitimize traditional male sexual privileges, to have a secure claim on one woman while also having sexual access to others. This seems especially true of Hapgood, who strongly supported the notion of marriage as part of a traditional order to which he could retreat from his engaging encounters with the bohemian world. Many men, including Hapgood and Calverton, were not comfortable granting women that freedom. They experienced strong jealousy when women took the same liberties.[80]

Often, however, women themselves did not take such liberties. Women of both races tended to write less positively than men about nonmonogamy. Blues singers like Bessie Smith could playfully assert their ability to "get plenty men," but the African American women writers primarily alluded to nonmonogamy in the traditional form of male affairs and female jealousy. Hurston's "Eatonville" short stories, for example, published in the *Messenger* in the 1920s, feature women's pain as well as violent retaliation against men for their infidelities. In "Sweat," for example, hardworking washerwoman Delia Jones supports her husband, Sykes, who both beats her and runs with other women. He torments her, playing on her fear of snakes, by bringing a caged rattlesnake into the house. Returning from church one Sunday to an empty house, Delia finds the snake loose in her laundry basket. She runs safely to the barn, where she ponders the situation in a "cold bloody rage," realizing that Sykes had let the snake out. She sleeps in the barn loft, waking up when he returns and enters the house. The snake attacks him. She hides as he calls her, then sees him through the door and turns to suppress "a surge of pity." In a rare literary case of full female revenge, Hurston ends the story with Delia standing "in the growing heat while inside she knew the cold river was creeping up and up to extinguish that eye which must know by now that she knew." Larsen does not imagine such an outcome. She is the only writer here to portray a woman's adulterous desire, in *Quicksand*, but when Anderson spurns Helga, she is deeply humiliated. In *Passing*, Larsen protagonist Irene is driven throughout the novel by the fear that her husband is having an affair.[81] These two novelists present nonmonogamy as damaging to women.

A few white women thinkers openly supported nonmonogamy based on the anarchist vision of free self-expression and nonpossessiveness. Goldman labeled monogamy a false restriction on the essential freedom of love. She argued in a lecture that two lovers always remain two, not one, and should not try to own or control one another; in cases of genuine love, an "outside attraction" would not destroy "mutual confidence and security." Publicly, she sustained a principled position, but her private letters reveal that she found her lover Ben Reitman's nonmonogamy very painful and tended to be monogamous herself when she was in an ongoing love relationship. Elizabeth Gurley Flynn likewise suffered silently over the infidelities of lover Carlo Tresca. Sanger, on the other hand, discreetly carried on affairs during her second marriage but did not argue publicly for nonmonogamy; birth control garnered enough opprobrium without added associations with "immorality."[82]

More white women expressed hesitation about nonmonogamy. Hutchins Hapgood and Neith Boyce depict extramarital liaisons, based on their own experiences, in their novels. Their portrayals situate her as the reluctant participant, him as the free-spirited experimenter, pressing her to join him, yet ultimately overcome with jealousy when she did participate. These published representations correspond to private letters in which Boyce wrote to Hapgood that "no one could maintain two complete love-relations at the same time."[83] Floyd Dell argued that modern male-female friendships could lead to extramarital affairs but that the latter need not disrupt marriage if they were dealt with as "light-hearted play." Feminist Suzanne LaFollette, on the other hand, opposed exactly such "levity" as inferior to the high spiritual seriousness that should characterize the "sexual relation," in which "passion and affection are fused."[84] In her novel *The Unpossessed* (1934), Tess Slesinger paints a withering portrait of a male philanderer (possibly based on Max Eastman) who opens repeated seduction attempts by presenting himself as pathetic and lonely. One of the women hurt by him expresses the ambivalence of the sexually modern woman: she "felt proud of herself,...of taking chances in the world, proud even if it brought her suffering."[85] White women's representations of nonmonogamy usually remained set in the framework of women's greater social and emotional vulnerability and thus seem at least implicitly negative. Some of them accepted or practiced nonmonogamy, but fewer publicly advocated it.

Those few women who supported nonmonogamy also did not ground their vision in the language of consumption, suggesting their less privileged position and their stronger affiliation with the language of love. Goldman's rhetoric, for example, drew much more on romantic conceptions of grand and selfless love than on the desire to possess men sexually (though her autobiography does report her objectifying gaze on various men). Sanger and others also swept women's desire up in "higher" meanings like love and spiritual freedom. The occasional drivenness of Larsen's character Helga resembles the consuming male's, but her desire is presented as degrading and ultimately defeating her after she seduces the preacher.[86] Thus, most women writers wrote uneasily of nonmonogamy, and the remainder had to authorize it with more elevated concepts than the desire for novelty.

In the nineteenth century, men's nonmonogamy had been partially underground, but the twentieth-century radicals brought it out and defined it more positively, whether as a political act or as the valorization of experience and variety. The result was to portray men as more evolved, while painting women as more entangled in the webs of civilized morality. As Calverton argued, "Through cultural inhibitions the feminine impulse has taken on a monogamous character that will undoubtedly disappear with the new morality of the next epoch."[87] Some men felt deprived and restive in the face of women's jealousy and urged women to separate sex and love, though such condescension belied the men's own jealousy.[88] Less powerful as black men, writers Owen and Kirksey did not condescend to women—indeed, Kirksey was openly angry at those who slept with white men. But men of both races embraced a more open freedom for themselves while looking critically at women.

Women radicals were more ambivalent. White women claimed a right to freer sexual experience but at the same time sounded more critical or stoical than enthusiastic about giving up values of exclusivity. Black women showed even less interest. Radicals who did support this kind of sexual freedom were reversing the dominant Victorian view that "good" women were models to emulate; now women were cited for their artificially constricted response to sex and urged to learn from men.[89] In the context of persistent gender inequality, nonmonogamy could reinforce male dominance.

Interracial Sex and Marriage

African Americans participated in discussion of all the issues under scrutiny here, but they had a special stake in addressing interracial relationships, informal as well as legal. With the important exception of traditional white male exploitation of black women outside marriage, such boundary crossing—marriages of white men and black women or married or unmarried relations of white women and black men—challenged the dominant race-segregated sexual codes. The greater freedom of speech and the press in northern cities allowed some black male radicals to make that challenge.

Most northern states had repealed anti-intermarriage laws following the Civil War (while southern states retained and western states developed them). As more African Americans moved north in the early twentieth century, the visibility and probability of intermarriage grew, though actual numbers remained tiny. In response, antimiscegenation laws were repeatedly introduced (though not passed) in northern states from 1890 to 1940. In practice, vigilante actions and discriminatory application of morals laws enforced the taboo in the absence of actual statutes.[90] In such a hostile environment African American political and reform leaders faced a dilemma. They recognized the laws against interracial marriage as an assault on their social and legal status and had been fighting such laws since the post–Civil War years. These laws, like segregation in public accommodations, stigmatized all persons of African descent. As the *Messenger* noted in 1919, both types of law denied the human equality of blacks and whites and imposed starkly unjust controls over individual freedom. Yet the threat of white violence as well as nationalist sentiments led W. E. B. DuBois simultaneously to "emphatically advise[ ] against race intermarriage" and yet to denounce the laws as discriminatory.[91] White hysteria made claiming even such civil equality a courageous act. The few black radicals who argued substantive support for interracial relationships thus were voicing an even more fundamental challenge to the dominant racial and sexual order.

Most white radicals left the task of questioning these codes to African Americans, although a few whites began to engage with the issue in the 1920s. Eugene O'Neill's play *All God's Chillun Got Wings* (1921) opened up discussion of consensual interracial relationships in the North. Calverton published George Schuyler's essays on interracial relationships in his *Modern Quarterly*. O'Neill and Calverton accepted interracial sex out of commitment to racial equality. Some radical whites manifested elements of the popular primitivism of the period that marked African Americans as more "natural" or "vital" than "over-civilized" whites. Claude McKay called others "faddists," especially the "precious bohemian white men" who express "love and admiration for Negro women" while remaining "shocked at the idea of intimacy between a black man and a white woman." Historian Kevin Mumford suggests that for the "artistic cultural elite, the images and discourses of interracial sex could be appropriated and employed in opposition to Victorian values." Both such discursive activity and the voyeurism involved in slumming expeditions to black clubs and bars, even by sympathetic and egalitarian whites, were shaped by the larger racial hierarchy and thus could be exploitive—whites attempting what Mumford terms the "pleasurable appropriation" of African American culture for their own purposes.[92]

African American sex radicals, on the other hand, wrote passionately of interracial sex as part of their larger claims for social equality and justice. In a 1927 cartoon, for example, *Messenger* artist Wilbert Holloway bitingly satirized the racial double standard of antimiscegenationists. The cartoon portrays "Senator Lynch of Mississippi" with his mulatto children on his knees "after a strenuous fight in the legislature for the passage of his racial integrity

Senator Lynch of Mississippi, whiles away an hour or so with his children after a strenuous fight in the legislature for the passage of his racial integrity bill.

Fig. 3 "Senator Lynch of Mississippi"

White anxieties about racial purity intensified in the 1920s, as exemplified in Virginia's Racial Integrity Act of 1924, which instituted the "one-drop rule," defining a person with any African genetic trace as Negro. The cartoonist is ridiculing white male politicians who promoted such laws though they might well have had black children of their own, such as those pictured here. Wilbert Holloway, "Senator Lynch of Mississippi," *Messenger* 9 (May 1927): 152.

bill." The cartoonist obviously delighted in uncovering the hypocrisy of white politicians who sought to forbid black-white intermarriage while practicing interracial sex themselves. *Messenger* editors attacked the cultural rationalizations of such laws: "[R]ace purity is both a myth and without any value. There is no pure race in the world." Black writers decried the evils resulting from the laws, such as mulatto children's loss of inheritance rights and the abuse of black women who could not demand marriage in affairs with white men.[93]

Unlike race moderates, African American radicals appealed to the revolutionary potential of interracial sex. George Schuyler, who married a white woman in 1929, pointed to the place of sexual controls over white women in the overall system of white domination. Paralleling Calverton's claims that nonmonogamy could undermine class endogamy, Schuyler argued that the economic and resulting sexual freedom of white women and their choice of black partners served as a progressive force in breaking down racial separateness. Schuyler stressed the class functions of "purity" in general, which became "race purity" when white and black were involved. To attack purity rules was to attack racial hierarchy and segregation and thus advance race struggle. Just as Calverton's views alarmed more conventional communists and socialists, who feared the stigma of sexuality, however, so Schuyler's ideas disturbed the leaders of the National Association of Colored Women and the NAACP.[94]

This revolutionary potential, however, had much more to do with black men and white women than with black women and white men. Chandler Owen wrote with enthusiasm, for example, that the black-and-tan (mixed-race) cabaret was "one of the most democratic institutions in America.... [It is] breaking down the color line...destroying the psychology of caste.... It is the dynamic agent of social equality." In the context of the long tradition of white men's sexual access to black women, the mingling of white women and black men—and not only black women and white men—enhanced the cabaret's value. The social equality to which the cabaret contributed, then, most centrally involved black men's equality with white men in access to white women. An editorial from the African American newspaper the *Pittsburgh American* was reprinted by the *Messenger* to illustrate this point: it expressed anger that unaccompanied white men could intrude in black social events and feel free to approach black women; the editor called this phenomenon "Spurious Social Equality." He urged black men to halt this practice by being more solicitous of black women but also proclaimed that if white men "debauch and consort" with black women, then "we must have the same right to consort with theirs." Such reciprocity (carefully omitting the right to "debauch"), the writer argued, would help to debunk "the myth of Negro inferiority." The greater provocativeness of the black man–white woman combination that Owen celebrated is evident, too, in the fact that only the more disreputable interracial "dives" made space for black male–white female couples, whereas the nightclubs established for more mainstream white slummers presented black *female* entertainers to the white gaze.[95]

These sources predominantly addressed relations between black men and white women. In some *Messenger* stories black men and white women shared intellectual and artistic interests and were depicted as far superior to the white men who competed for the women's love, highlighting the tragedy of social prejudice. Lovett Fort-Whiteman, an African American from Texas with a degree from McGill University who later joined the Communist Party, wrote a story called "Wild Flowers," in which a white southern woman has had an affair and a child with a black former butler and student of music with whom she shared literary and musical tastes. Other stories indicted deceitful, exploitive white women whose thrill seeking endangered the black men with whom they were involved. Jean Toomer's stories in *Cane* show white women as poor, crazy, and isolated or attracted by the sense of exotic difference.[96] White women could fit the stereotypes of tragic victim, dangerous temptress, or gay rebel, but the center of attention was on their meaning to black men.

The *Messenger* also published a few poems by white women celebrating their joy in the social rebelliousness of their attraction to black men. Josephine Cogdell, who later married George Schuyler, wrote a poem entitled "Temptation" in which she proclaims:

Well, I couldn't forget
That big drum's beat
And the shuffle of feet
As we stepped to the Blues
In Harlem!
. . . .
That pansy sea!
A-tossing me
all loose and free, O, lily me
In muscled arms
Of ebony!
. . . .
And that drink we mixed of rye and anisette
At dawn

In Harlem . . . .
When paler folk would fret
And scold the dawn
Outside of Harlem . . . .
And caught
Do I regret?
No, boy, not yet![97]

A white woman named Reba Cain, writing in the *Crisis* of her marriage to a black man, mixes individualist views—that differences are "temperamental," not "racial"—with the typical racial exoticizing, arguing whites need contact with blacks "to leaven [their] dull lump of respectability." Crossing race boundaries was usually dangerous, if exciting, for white women. Privileged white women in interracial relationships were excluded from conventional white society, though some rebels may have relished escaping the cultural burden of white motherhood and its restrictions. Poor and marginal ones experienced extreme ostracism for relationships with black men, often being treated as prostitutes or institutionalized as mental patients. Those who lived among what Mumford calls "the forward-thinking modernists," such as the "artists, writers, thinkers, humanitarians" with whom Cain and her husband socialized, may have been somewhat less harassed, at least in their private lives.[98] But whatever the difficulties, as whites they held some power through their status and attractiveness in the prevailing racialized norms of womanhood. Black women's resentment at that power appears indirectly in Larsen's *Passing*, where the impetus of the narrative comes from protagonist Irene Redfield's fear that her husband is attracted to the very light-skinned Clare Kendry (who is passing).[99]

These writings describe African American women's relations with white men negatively. If the relationship is based on passing, like Clare's, it is marked as dangerous if not unethical. More important, black women's relations with white men too strongly echoed for many African Americans the long and savage history of white male sexual exploitation; black men were distressed not only by black women's plight but also by their own powerlessness and a sense of betrayal by the women. In *Cane*, Jean Toomer depicts a black kitchen worker, Louisa, who feels a "warm glow" at the thought of Bob Stone, the son of her white employers. To Stone, however, Louisa is not just a beautiful "gal" but specifically a "[b]eautiful nigger gal," and "it was because she was nigger that he went to her." He imagines how in the days of slavery he could have taken her "as a master should.... Direct, honest, bold. None of this sneaking that he had to go through now. The contrast was repulsive." Toomer devotes little effort to imagining Louisa's consciousness, instead presenting her as passively caught between the pulls of Stone and her black lover, Tom Burwell, who is later lynched after he attacks Stone. *Messenger* writer Thomas Kirksey resented black women for "cuckolding" black men with whites—likewise a male perspective.[100] Clearly, black women's relations with white men had a distinct political and historical meaning from those of black men and white women and were usually not understood as progressive in the same way.

Alone among these writers, Nella Larsen in both *Quicksand* and *Passing* suggests individual choice and attraction as possible sources of interracial relationships. She describes one marriage of a white man and black woman as relatively unproblematic where passing is not involved—the couple had been high school friends. Larsen's northern metropolitan settings and personal history as a biracial woman may have made possible a more individualistic vision, but her writing also depicts the community's traditional wisdom. One woman speaks with "cold hatred" of parties where "'white men dance with colored women. Now, you know,...that can mean only one thing.'"[101]

The preponderance of sources on interracial relationships, then, addressed black men's rights and desires while also hinting at resentments and fears of betrayal among both women and men due to the power of whites. "Sexual freedom" in this context represented primarily an element of black manhood. Black men's relations with white women were transgressive against the hierarchy of power in America (for both black men and white women), while white men's relations with black women were not. The relative paucity of African American women's voices is striking, though no white male writers in these sources speak of interracial desire either. It would not be surprising if many African American women avoided white men as unappealing racial predators, feared being labeled as prostitutes, dreaded black community disapproval, or all of these, but without more women's stories, it is not possible to know.[102]

Hence, for women's power, discourse on interracial sex gave a racially divided message. White women who crossed the race line risked severe sanctions and banishment from white status, though they could also feel affirmed as rebels against a racist sexual code. The historic sexual abuse of African American women, continuing in new forms in the twentieth-century vice zones, as well as their silence on this issue, suggests their disinterest in this particular form of sexual practice.

———

These three sex radical practices were claimed for both women and men, but their meanings were in fact mixed. Free love and nonmonogamy were oriented much more to the practical realities of men's social and sexual lives than women's. The idea that spontaneous sexual desire, often detached from social bonds such as marriage and parenthood, "naturally" was—and should be—a major driving force in human life stemmed from a subjectivity more available to men, which assumed the privilege of gratifying such desire with relative impunity and little concern about disruptive consequences, which remained much more serious for women. This perspective defined women as "too repressed" or out of kilter with sexual "realities" and made men the standard of modern sexual freedom. Likewise, the demand for interracial sex was based in a male viewpoint. Black women's relations with white men unappealingly replicated the traditional exploitive power of white men over them, while black men's relations with white women dramatized black women's difference from normative white womanhood and undermined their prior claims on black men's loyalty. Thus an abstract "freedom" tended to benefit men more than women. Demands for contraception and domestic equality and the public assertion of lesbian desire, however, more unambiguously articulated women's subjectivity.

Birth Control and Domestic Equality

Birth control was the most widely known of the radical sexual practices and has been the most extensively treated by women's historians. Throughout the nineteenth century, reproduction had fundamentally defined and confined respectable (especially white) women's sexuality and social roles. Mechanical contraception had not fit into the elaborate edifice of white Victorian female passionlessness and maternal imagery and women's need to maintain sexual virtue to earn men's fidelity and support in marriage. Prostitutes knew about and used mechanical methods like condoms, but respectable Victorian women were more likely to promote abstinence to achieve "voluntary motherhood."[103] Twentieth-century white radicals, however, opposed abstinence and advocated mechanical birth control, making clear that women's sex drive went beyond motherhood. They wanted to pluck women out of the mire of reproductive duty to the (white) race and let them become individuals claiming a sexual life. Goldman and Sanger proclaimed women's right to develop their "love nature separate from and independent of [their] maternal nature."[104]

The radicalism lay less in actually limiting fertility, since middle-class Americans already extensively did so, than in publicly discussing it, challenging the legal prohibition of birth control, and raising the specter of women's sexual independence from both marriage and reproduction. Goldman and

Sanger's free love ideas intensified the controversy. While acknowledging women's sexuality had become common in sophisticated conversation by the 1910s, it remained very controversial for women to be public about it, and especially shocking to suggest that single women might be sexually active.[105] But to make pre- or extramarital heterosexual freedom viable women needed birth control, which in fact became the most prominent demand of women sex radicals in the 1910s and 1920s.[106]

In addition, demanding birth control struck at the symbolic importance of white women's reproductive role in this period of expanding U.S. imperialism and racism and evoked cries of "race suicide" from conservatives. Theodore Roosevelt famously reminded elite white women of their duty to reproduce their class and race.[107] These ideas were sustained as the power of nativist politics in the 1920s pushed birth control advocates away from the inflammatory invocation of free female sexuality and toward arguments about maternal health and (white) racial betterment.

By the late 1930s, birth control's clear value for families struggling economically during the Depression brought more statements of public support, especially from officials worried about the size of public relief rolls, and some measure of legal acceptability. In the 1936 federal court decision on an importation case that Sanger had instigated, *United States v. One Package of Japanese Pessaries*, judges ruled that the Comstock law did not apply to materials "'intelligently...employed by conscientious and competent physicians for the purpose of saving life or promoting the well-being of their patients.'"[108] Though Comstock and other anticontraceptive statutes remained on the books, in practice many of the obstacles to obtaining birth control had been removed for urban married women with knowledge and resources.

Among whites, women dominated the discourse on birth control, but men also supported it, and gender differences permeated the discussion. Dr. Robinson's voluminous writings, for example, emphasized the benefits to men as supporters of families, the importance of leisure and sex for all people, and the benefits for the working class when child spacing improved the health of mothers and children. Compared with Goldman and Sanger, he acknowledged a woman's nonreproductive sexuality only minimally: "[S]he must not be forced to be a breeding machine merely."[109]

More consequentially, white men and women differed in how they addressed the broader, more persistent questions of reproduction that lay beyond the use of mechanical contraception. However argued, birth control on some basic level empowered women by providing greater control of biology and implicitly recognizing women as more than mothers, in order to permit them sexual pleasure, better health, or paid employment. With this tool, radicals hoped to create egalitarian sexual relationships much less sharply polarized by gender, more sexually and psychologically intimate, and less defined by the socially or legally enforced goal of reproduction. But the potential for women's advantage from birth control was limited either by a narrow framing of freedom as childlessness or by the unchallenged sexual division of labor for those who bore children. Controlling births could leave women either bereft or overburdened, consequences women radicals addressed much more than men.

Though some women embraced childlessness, for others bearing children remained a deep desire, due to the ongoing cultural power of motherhood and individual women's personal investment in it. In a piece published in *Birth Control Review* in 1918, Crystal Eastman first seems to stress women's sexual rights: "Feminists are not nuns." Yet later in the paragraph she writes, "[M]ost of us want children, one or two at least." In *The Unpossessed*, Tess Slesinger movingly depicts how powerfully childbearing and family continued to serve as the basis of moral values, as images of social cohesion, and as sources of meaning for women in particular. Protagonist Margaret Flinders contemplates (though later rejects) an extramarital affair with the thought that her mother's conventional code was based on having "the sanctity of the family...to preserve. But Miles and Margaret Flinders had no such tender thing, their rooms housed nothing but each other." Later, thrilled at discovering she is pregnant, Margaret hopes to overcome Miles's fears of bringing a child into a Depression-ruled world, but she is unsuccessful. He presses her to have an abortion. The description of Margaret's hospital stay for her D & C incisively conveys Margaret's female consciousness, in which exchanging a baby for "economic freedom" or "intellectual freedom" is a refusal of life and what it means to be a man or a woman; the abortion makes them both "sterile; empty and hollow."[110]

African Americans' writings on birth control took a different tack. Unlike Sanger, they did not present childbearing per se as the central source of women's subjection. Rather, they named poverty, hard labor, sexual abuse, and racist conditions as the problems. Their writings link sexual autonomy closely to economic and physical security. For example, Mary Burrill, a teacher at Dunbar High School, a black school in Washington, D.C., published a short play, "They That Sit in Darkness," in the *Birth Control Review* in 1919. In it a mother of eight children dies in childbirth; her eldest daughter must forgo her planned education at the Tuskegee Institute in order to care for her siblings. The lack of contraception harms the mother, thus the family's well-being, and also the daughter's individual opportunity—opportunity that the name Tuskegee marks as simultaneously familial and race advancement.[111] Some black writers also suggested that birth control might be a weapon of self-defense for black women against persisting sexual exploitation by white men.[112]

Due to the ongoing sexual stigmatization of African American women, most black writers, male and female, argued the benefits of birth control for maternal health and economic improvement rather than linking it to women's sexual pleasure. In 1932 a special "Negro Number" of the *Birth Control Review* whose articles were authored by African Americans featured only one small mention (by a female social worker) of "sexual maladjustment" as a possible rationale for birth control (and that was within marriage).[113] And black women fiction writers did not connect birth control and sexual pleasure in their work. Larsen and Hurston acknowledged sexual desire but nowhere explicitly discussed birth control, while Burrill and others who wrote of birth control never mentioned sexual feeling. African Americans understood birth control as a way to liberate women, but its middle-class advocates seemed united across gender lines in stressing arguments for race advancement rather than women's sexual freedom.[114]

———

Beyond the question of freedom and the ability to prevent or space pregnancy, some sex radicals did address the question of domestic equality within heterosexual relations. Dell's egalitarian image of "passionate friendship" encapsulated the radicals' critique of the gender inequality of marriage and their construction of modern sexual relationships as flexible, empathic bonds between people who lived more in each other's worlds than Victorian men and women had. The movement to shared worlds, however, was for women to enter men's, or the public, world more than vice versa. This is apparent in the radicals' treatment of domestic gender inequality and especially their discussion of child-rearing work.

Those who did have children faced the difficulties of combining employment with the child care and family maintenance tasks that remained women's work. Both men and women condemned the economic inequities of marriage for women but achieved little consensus on how women could both bear children and be economic producers. One of the most vivid accounts of the conflict between married women and men on this front is Heterodoxy member Helen Hull's novel *Labyrinth* (1923). Strikingly modern in its perspective, this book details the struggle of Catherine, a young mother of three, to reclaim a place of pride in the world of employment, to rescue her brain, grown "mossy" from immersion in child rearing. She faces both internalized guilt about the children and powerful covert resistance from her husband, Charles, a psychology professor whom her lesbian sister, Margaret, calls "the King." Catherine recalls a perfect example of Dell's "passionate friendship"— an earlier period of marriage before children when the lovers enjoyed social evenings that ended with joint dish washing and analysis of their guests. But now Charles is caught up in workplace politics and leaves Catherine to put the children to sleep and struggle through the washing up alone. The divisions between them undermine sexual passion as well. Although the forces arrayed against Catherine are too strong to overcome, the novel articulates clearly both Catherine's desire for more than motherhood and the need for men to share equally in parental and household responsibilities.[115]

Few women and no men, however, made a full case for male sharing of domestic and child-rearing responsibilities. Later, after his turn away from radicalism, Floyd Dell acknowledged the unfairness of that position but advocated as a solution the return to men's financial support of women in marriage. Marxists Collier and Calverton alluded briefly to the ideal of superseding "individualistic modes of … rearing the young" and guaranteeing male support of women and children in divorce but did not develop the ideas extensively.[116] Hence, while white radicals of both sexes proclaimed birth control as a means of sexual liberation and other benefits for women, women spoke more than men did of the context of relationships over time in which child-bearing decisions had to be made and children cared for. White women may not have wanted to be only mothers, but the role retained tremendous power for many, and they would have liked to have some help.

Lesbian Relationships

For another group of white women writers, "freeing sex" meant the ability to escape marriage and relations with men altogether. A few, writing later in the 1920s and 1930s, claimed lesbian desire on similar grounds to heterosexual passion—asserting individual freedom to pursue sexual relations with whomever one loved. The "natural" force of sexuality demanded respect in either form; as Dr. Robinson argued, "Homosexual feelings [are] as natural to homosexuals as heterosexual feelings are to the majority." Lesbian autobiographer Diana Frederics made claims for her homosexual relationship that echoed those of heterosexual radicals: sex was a "center of mental creativity" and balance in life and an individual claim, rather than a social duty to reproduce. (Though we know of women who pursued heterosexual and lesbian relations simultaneously or sequentially, those who were publishing texts arguing for same-sex sexuality were not explicitly promoting bisexual lives.)[117] But to take this perspective and to assume a universal sexual drive in women as well as men altered the meaning of women's relationships with each other. It produced a shift from the romantic friendship model—less sexual, sometimes coexisting with marriage—to the more sexualized but also pathologized concept of lesbianism. Lesbian relations created a sexual alternative that, combined with modern women's greater capacity for self-support, challenged men's control of women through marriage.[118]

The growing gay social presence in the largest cities, especially in Greenwich Village and Harlem, as well as the popularization of psychology underlay the increasingly explicit notice of lesbianism in the press, theater, and fiction by the 1920s.[119] John Sumner, Comstock's successor as censorship agent, in 1916 raided the bookshop run by the *Masses* because it carried Auguste Forel's *Sexual Question*, which treated homosexuality. Police also closed down plays for mentioning homosexuality. But radical free speech fights bore fruit by the late 1920s. Radclyffe Hall's novel *The Well of Loneliness*, which told the story of an upper-class English lesbian during World War I, presented lesbianism as a tragic but inborn condition. Although the novel had no sexual scenes, the treatment of homosexuality itself initially led U.S. Customs to prohibit its importation when it was published in 1928. But attacks against censorship got the book released in 1929. More novels and personal stories appeared in the 1930s. Their new salience, however, brought intensified stigma. "[I]t was far easier to live with a man out of wedlock than it was to live with a woman in lesbianism," Diana Frederics wrote in 1939.[120]

Nonhomosexual sex radicals were notable primarily for openly acknowledging same-sex relationships, sometimes with ambivalence. Several of them merely mention homosexuality in the course of explaining Freudian and other modern psychology, attributing same-sex desire to polymorphous perversity or the fact that the "sexual impulse is notoriously unruly." Others like Samuel Schmalhausen argued that new historical conditions—the excitement of the jazz age—inevitably produced sexual changes: "The modern mad quest for stimulation is driving men and women into the arms of abnormality. . . . Homosexual attachment achieves increasingly a status of respectability."[121]

Relatively few of the lesbian voices were African American. Middle-class moralists like prominent Baptist minister Adam Clayton Powell in Harlem attacked homosexual "vice" as a threat to the family. Already sexually marked by white racism, African American women would have assumed an even greater stigma by risking the label of "perversion." None of the black women novelists clearly portrayed lesbian figures in their writings. Outside the respectable world, a few women blues singers were known as lesbians or bisexuals and occasionally sang openly about their desires—most notably Ma Rainey in her "Prove It on Me Blues," in which the singer proclaims: "Went out last night with a crowd of my friends / They must've been women, 'cause I don't like no men." This song expresses the same female autonomy other blues songs posited in relation to men and portrays lesbian relationships as competitive alternatives to heterosexual ones.[122]

Many more sources exist for white women. Among these writings two different frameworks for legitimating lesbian relationships appear—individualism as the basis of sex freedom and feminism as a critique of gender relations. Thinkers deeply committed to individual freedom like Goldman sometimes carried that value into support for same-sex love. For Goldman, anarchism was "a living influence to free us from inhibitions" like those suffered by same-sex lovers; she defended homosexuals as victims of social prejudice and sympathized with "their anguish and their isolation."[123] Unlike Goldman, as a lesbian Margaret Anderson wrote with anger rather than pity, offering an impassioned criticism of a 1915 Chicago lecture by Edith Ellis (also a lesbian and the wife of Havelock Ellis) in which Ellis had urged tolerance for the sexually "abnormal." Anderson condemned Ellis's meekness and shame and asserted "there is no difference between the normal and the inverted type. In my view all organisms have both homosexuality and heterosexuality." But like Goldman, Anderson employed individualist anarchist thinking to defend "special people"—she did not use the term "lesbian"—on the grounds of universal rights of self-expression.[124]

Frederics and another lesbian writer of the late 1930s, Elizabeth Craigin, likewise claimed voices as subjects who felt desire and had a right as individuals to a sexual life, although both wrote under pseudonyms. Craigin's novel *Either Is Love* (1937) compares lesbian and heterosexual love and sex, praising both but depicting lesbianism as more exciting and compelling partly because it does not follow "a pre-ordained road" like marital sex. Here she echoes the critique of community and state control of sexual relations and advocates the radically individual nature of desire and human attachment. Frederics explains the unchangeable nature of her desire for women and asserts the vital importance of a sexual life for every individual: lack of sexual response (to men) indicates she is "not a whole woman"—to become one, she needs a woman lover.[125]

But attraction to women involved more than individual freedom. For many lesbian writers it was also legitimated by a feminist critique of gender relations. An autobiographer writing under the name Mary Casal delineates a late-Victorian childhood of male sexual abuse covered up by a conspiracy of silence about sex. The force of her narrative suggests that horrible experiences with men turned her toward women. More mildly, Frederics cites the common lesbian view that male lovers err in "haste and selfishness" by comparison to respectful and sensitive lesbian ones. Novelist Helen Hull offers the most explicitly feminist portrayal of women's relationships as an alternative to heterosexual ones. Her novel *Labyrinth* features two lesbian characters, the sexual nature of whose relationship is certified by reference to reading Freud. Margaret, sister of protagonist Catherine, both snipes at Catherine's sexist husband and presents her own relationship with a woman as superior: "I know lots of women who prefer to set up an establishment with another woman. Then you go 50-50 on everything. Work and feeling and all the rest, and no King waiting around for his humble servant." Though not as explicitly critical of men, Margaret Anderson offers one of the most unambiguous declarations of female sexual independence from them in her autobiography: "I am no man's wife, no man's delightful mistress, and I will never, never, never be a mother."[126] These more gendered portrayals not only normalized lesbian relations by comparison to heterosexual ones but associated them with a criticism of men.

Lesbian writers, like heterosexual women, were haunted by the charge of "lust" and felt the need to hallow their relationships, legally and popularly associated with "vice." Novels and autobiographies usually portrayed women seeking serious romantic relationships. Craigin denies lesbian alliances are more lustful than others and calls her own love a "pure" passion in which she and her partner paid for their "unspeakable joys" (as wives do by bearing children) by living in "a rarefied atmosphere of high purpose." Casal echoes Victorian thought in asserting that relations between women were "of a higher type" than heterosexual ones.[127] Love, rather than greedy lust, remained a powerful legitimizer for them.

Male sex radicals also wrote of lesbian relations, though often with more ambivalence. The most positive comment in these sources is also the only one from an African American writer, Claude McKay, perhaps sympathetic because he was bisexual. In *Home to Harlem*, a friendly railroad waiter defends Sappho and contradicts the stereotype that all dykes are ugly. Among whites, Dr. Robinson, like Goldman, supported homosexual relationships on the grounds of humanity, personal freedom, and privacy. Whether of the same or different sexes, he argued, "the sex relations of two adults are a strictly private matter." But Robinson still labeled same-sex relations abnormal. His son Victor, also a physician, wrote condescendingly in the introduction to Diana

Frederics's book, "That charming women should be lesbians is not a crime, it is simply a pity."[128]

Other white men wrote of women's same-sex love in relation to male dominance, naming lesbianism a manifestation of women's resistance. Writing for the *Masses* in 1917, the political and cultural thinker Randolph Bourne made the classic link between lesbianism and feminism in reviewing Clemence Dane's *Regiment of Women*, a novel about a love triangle between an older woman, a younger teacher, and a student at an English girls' school. The older woman is described as a "vampire," who enslaves younger women and spreads a philosophy of "sex-antagonism" that in Bourne's view "is a little too much like the doctrines" being "inculcated" in the real world "as the gospel of true feminism." At the end of the 1920s, Samuel Schmalhausen claimed lesbianism was increasing because it gave young women a way out of the "complexity and tragic profundity of the life of the sexes," especially since men had never accepted women as equals; though outspokenly opposed to moralism and repression, he conveys anxiety about women's possible escape from heterosexuality. More extremely, Floyd Dell, who had had an affair with woman-loving poet Edna St. Vincent Millay and tried to "rescue" her from lesbianism in 1918, turned to advocacy of marriage in the 1920s; by the end of the decade his writings had moved beyond condescension to outright and obsessive hostility toward homosocial and homosexual bonds.[129]

Thus, some sex radicals followed the logic of individual freedom only into the beginnings of tolerance. Actual lesbian voices claimed legitimacy, whether through Ma Rainey's blues defiance, Anderson's individualist views, or feminist resistance to male power, as in Hull's novel and Casal's autobiography. But when lesbianism was viewed through the lens of feminist politics, some male radicals showed their skittishness at the notion of fully freeing women's desires.

———

Claims to birth control or lesbian relationships were more centered in a woman's viewpoint than free love, nonmonogamy, or interracial relationships. In the face of massive cultural power defining women as wives and mothers and of women's economic need for marriage, birth control was a step toward some control and appealed widely to women, even if a broader domestic equality in child care and housework remained elusive. Likewise, taking the lesbian path and refusing marriage, more clearly than any other practice, made visible women's potential for sexual independence from men. The voicing of these possibilities through sex radical discourses, despite the practical difficulties of living them out, subverted the monolithic power of patriarchal definitions.

Conclusion

Sex radicalism in the early twentieth-century United States belonged to no
one group and had no monolithic vision. Feminists, leftists, and bohemians,
both black and white, expressed their discontent with the inherited codes
of bourgeois marriage and sexual conduct and created oppositional visions
stemming from an emergent consciousness that these metropolitan intellectuals were best able to articulate.[130] Their visions grew out of the social and
cultural conditions of modernity in the great cities, where racial/ethnic and
intellectual interchange, radical and feminist politics, and the social and economic independence of New Women made possible new sexual subjectivities.
Attacking the rigidities and conformities of Victorian thought, sex radicals
rejected community controls over sex and claimed privacy for individuals;
they proclaimed the goodness of sex against assumptions of its sinfulness; and
they argued women's equivalent rights in these arenas.

Radically individualist claims for sexual freedom and pleasure or for
interracial sex both manifested and furthered the loosening grip of institutional marriage and expressed a potential for gender and racial equality. The
articulation of radical visions and practices destabilized prevailing definitions
and codes for women's sexuality. To protest the patriarchal restrictions of marriage and the double standard challenged women's subordination to men and
confinement to marriage. To assert the legitimacy of interracial sex delegiti-
mized coercive protection of white women and repression of black men. To
demand legality for birth control undermined women's definition as passionless wives and mothers. And to name lesbian desire raised the possibility of
women's sexual independence from men.

What these challenges and experiments in sexuality and marriage meant
in practice, however, was not the same for women and men, blacks and whites.
Sex radicals' romantic egalitarianism—"willed equality" in the words of historian Christine Stansell—was not easy to sustain.[131] It remained difficult for
women to seize these freedoms due to powerful forces of culture and psychology, material inequality, and, for African American women, racial inequality.
White men, already possessing greater social power, more readily than white
women voiced and experienced the benefits of free love and nonmonogamy.
Women continued to face pervasive social judgment for sexual activity outside
marriage, judgment that often marked their own psyches as well, and most
needed men's material support, especially when they had children. "Freeing"
nonreproductive sex promised to loosen the cultural straitjacket of motherhood

as well as ease its physical burden, yet most women continued to seek the pleasures and rewards of motherhood. Their needs as mothers and their economic
inequality formed the material basis for their greater adherence to "love,"
legal marriage, and monogamy, the way to be "good women" and earn male
loyalty. The cultural, psychological, and material power of marriage affected
lesbians as well, even as divorce and labor force participation made women
more able to survive outside marriage. Lesbians' growing visibility in the culture both broadcast the possibility of their choice and increased its stigma,
raising self-doubt and social suspicion.[132] Finally, African American women
faced racist stigmas as "bad women" by definition and so stood on shakier
ground in violating sexual codes generally, while the practice of interracial
sex seemed to free black men more than them. Some brave women did claim
radical sexual freedom publicly, but they were more likely to be outsiders, like
anarchists, artists and writers, or blues singers. Those not forced or willing to
remain outside or who sought esteem in the dominant culture needed more
circumspection.

By the late 1920s and 1930s, however, the open atmosphere of the 1910s
was fading for heterosexual radicalism, replaced by an impetus to reform marriage. Some radicals had supported marriage all along or came to do so after
youthful experiments with free love. Seen as radical in their time, these writers, especially Floyd Dell, appear with hindsight more as experimenters who
prefigured (and sometimes became) the dedicated marriage reformers of the
1920s and 1930s. They believed egalitarian relationships could be sustained
within a revised institution of marriage and sought to bring into marriage the
radicals' conception of sexual desire and activity (rather than duty and social
control) as the source of marital cohesion. While "true love" in marriage justified and purified sex in marriage for Victorians, these thinkers elevated the sex
element, while maintaining the importance of love. Clearly, when birth controllers and sex radicals invoked both love and women's sex rights as a means
to improve marriage, they were moving in a safer direction. The next chapter
documents this development in the promotion of "companionate marriage."

3

Companionate Marriage

"Y ou won by trickery," reads a note from Diana to Ann after Ann has won
her man in the silent film *Our Dancing Daughters* (1928). Joan Crawford
stars as the daring and sexually provocative but innocent flapper Diana. Anita
Page plays Ann, a traditional but scheming and manipulative woman. The
two young women have been vying for the affections of the handsome and
wealthy football player Ben Blaine. The three first come together at a dancing
and drinking party at the Yacht Club. At one point Diana leaps to a table top to
perform a jazz dance in a revealing short costume. Ben sees her and is attracted
but soon meets Ann also. Ann plays the good, old-fashioned girl; she claims not
to drink and tells him she is going home because her mother wants her. For a
few days, the two women compete for Ben. Ben, however, wants to be "sure"
of the woman he marries and is worried by Diana's wildness. Ann, on the
other hand, tells him, "I can't be modern." She asserts that she wants a home,
husband, and babies and must be "worthy of them." He proposes to Ann, and
they marry. But Ann's show of public virtue hides the fact that, encouraged by
her mercenary mother, she is marrying Ben for his money and plans to "have
a fling" after marriage. Diana, in contrast, has supportive but noninterfer-
ing parents; she may drink and stay out late, but they trust she is a good girl.
When she is hurt about Ben's rejection, they comfort her. Ben ultimately finds
Ann lying to sneak out with an old boyfriend and realizes his mistake. After a
dramatic confrontation between the women at a farewell party, Diana leaves

for Europe. Back at the club a drunken Ann dies in a fall down the stairs. Two years later Diana returns from Europe to reunite with Ben.[1]

Our Dancing Daughters brought to life an analysis of what was wrong with sexual relations in American society that social scientists, reformers, former radicals, and fiction writers were putting forward in the 1920s. In his book *The Companionate Marriage* (1927), Denver reformer Judge Ben B. Lindsey proposed a new form of marriage to make things right and save marriage.[2] He built his concept on the notion that modern young women who danced close and petted were, like Diana, fundamentally good. Women like Ann and her mother, who used the old restrictive mores to appear virtuous and trap men, were the real villains. Marriages made in this way were form without substance, not built properly on companionship, equality, and respect, in Lindsey's view. He supported woman suffrage and birth control. In the early twentieth century he fought for different legal treatment of juveniles, arguing for rehabilitation rather than harsh punishment for those under sixteen. He helped achieve the institution of a separate juvenile court in Denver, the first in the United States, in 1907, and became its judge. From his involvement with youth he came to criticize rigid moralistic approaches to sexuality that took no account of individual needs and motivations. He collaborated with journalist Wainwright Evans in magazine articles titled "The Revolt of Modern Youth" (1924) and "Companionate Marriage" (1926). They subsequently published both as books that documented the wrongs of contemporary sex morality and Lindsey's proposals for reform.[3]

Lindsey and other writers on marriage in the 1920s differed from the sex radicals. Postwar political repression had had a chilling effect on those challenging cultural norms, including marriage, and out of this climate emerged a trend toward preserving marriage by reforming it.[4] The marriage revisionists, both African American and white, drew on the heritage of both the sexual radicals and the social hygienists to redefine marriage comprehensively for a twentieth-century urban industrial society and to reconfigure perspectives on sex, privacy, and women. Their proposals represented what sex was coming to mean for a prosperous middle class, how the moral regulatory function of marriage was shifting, and how women's less domestically defined lives pressed increasingly against the confines of the traditional model of marriage.

Like the sexual radicals, these thinkers denounced the evils of unscientific, authoritarian attitudes and sexual repression, promoted the goodness and importance of sexuality, especially for women, and called for greater freedom for young couples. Yet the most popular of them were concerned not about the injustice and pain that an outdated sexual code inflicted on individuals but

Fig. 4 Ben B. Lindsey

Judge Benjamin Barr Lindsey leaving his home, 1343 Ogden Street, Denver, to walk to his office in the courthouse, 1920–25. Lindsey had a flamboyant style and enjoyed being in the public eye. Courtesy Library of Congress, Prints and Photographs Division, Reproduction No. LC-USZ62-83714.

rather about the harm it wreaked on marriage. In this sense they resembled the social hygienists, worried about social stability and supporting change to take control over sexual disorder. But the culture had changed too drastically to sustain the appeal of the social hygienists' modified Victorianism. The latter's sentimentality, prudishness, and ascetic approach to pleasure and sex were passé in the consumption-oriented 1920s. Instead, among the middle class, the economic, spiritual, and reproductive meanings of marriage were competing with a growing emphasis on the material and sexual enjoyments of life.[5] An active birth control movement continued, publicly if less dramatically, to

promote the practice of fertility control, decentering the motherhood emphasis of the social hygienists.[6] And women's achievement of the vote signaled the
irreversibility of some kind of equality for women. Thus, the marriage revisionists of the 1920s stood between the sex radicals and the social hygienists
as they melded the rhetoric of sexual freedom with the goal of transforming
but preserving marriage among the middle-class constituency that was their
audience.

The revisionists went on to detail how courtship and marriage needed to
be altered to accommodate new social realities. Their proposals were characterized by three themes: relying on the authority of science, they promoted
sexual intimacy as the glue of marriage; acknowledging the increased independence of both male and female youth in a socially diverse urban culture,
they valorized the freedom and privacy of young couples; and recognizing
the public presence and power of women, they demanded equality in marriage. Despite critiques of Victorianism, however, they ultimately reaffirmed
monogamous marriage, usually within the same race, religion, and ethnicity,
as the proper goal of youth sexual development. They supported sexuality
primarily within marriage, calling for an end to dangerous sexual behavior
among youth and to unhappy or broken marriages. What proponents of modern marriage had in common was a sense of needing to modify marriage in
response to significant social transformations.

The Context for Marriage Revisionism

In the new social and cultural world in the 1920s, sex seemed more visible and
at issue among middle-class youth. Values of personal freedom from intrusive authority became a badge of modernity, and women were empowered
with the vote and more visible as participants in paid employment. Sexualized advertising and a more consumer-oriented economy were also abrading
the stern facade of sexlessness in official culture of the Comstock era. Finally,
divorce was becoming more frequent. These dramatic phenomena combined
to consolidate changing styles of marriage. The prosperity enjoyed by the
urban middle class, though not shared by the majority of the population in
the 1920s, underlay these social and cultural changes among both whites and
African Americans.[7]

Corporate expansion and strong economic growth in the early twentieth
century fueled an expanding and prosperous middle class to whom the sexually restrictive mores of Victorian culture had become less appealing. For this

group consumption and pleasure overtook values of frugality and restraint, and these were further promulgated with the explosion of the advertising industry in the 1920s.[8] The same expansion accelerated the need for white-collar workers and thus school attendance. High schools grew dramatically, with a 650 percent increase in attendance between 1900 and 1930; university and college attendance tripled. By 1930, 60 percent of the high school–aged population and 20 percent of university-aged youth were attending these institutions, the vast majority of the latter coming from long-established white ethnic groups. A fun-oriented youth culture became especially visible among these students.[9] Many groups were excluded from the touted good life and consumer values of the 1920s because they were too poor or because they remained culturally apart.[10] But the small African American middle class did participate. Culturally, they were in some ways more part of the "national culture" than European immigrants in this period.[11] In the South from the late nineteenth century, a new black middle class of professionals and small businesspeople, often followers of Booker T. Washington's bootstraps philosophy, had built a small prosperity out of a Jim Crowed black clientele and gradually challenged the authority of an older black elite. The Great Migration brought both members of the new middle class and their clients north, while de facto segregation of the urban ghettos kept them tied to one another.[12] Between 1910 and 1930, the numbers of African American white-collar workers increased by 75 percent, and professionals in particular became more numerous. The number of black college professors multiplied nearly nine times (from 242 to 2,146). Black colleges expanded dramatically, increasing enrollments more than 600 percent between 1917 and 1927.[13]

Black and white middle-class youth in high schools and colleges were the populations among whom the dating system became firmly entrenched in the 1920s and early 1930s. Dating, inspired by working-class models, was replacing older, family-controlled forms of courtship. It took place outside the home in the world of commercial leisure and consumption; it required the man to have money to pay for entertainment; and it encouraged young women to bargain with sexual favors.[14] Among both white and African American middle-class youth, sexuality was thus more openly displayed than in the past through dress, dance, and coupling off. The sensibilities of parents and school officials were affronted by the revealing clothes of the flapper, suggestive dances, and youth demands for greater freedom. For example, on the expanding black college campuses in the 1920s, students protested the Victorian white missionary rules that limited social life and claimed the right to have fraternities and sororities and for women and men to smoke, date, and dance together as white students were doing. Young women sought the right to abandon their " 'cotton stockings and gingham dresses' " and to don "flapper skirts and stockings made of the new synthetics" like the "white girls across town," as well as the privilege of talking and dancing with boys on campus.[15] In a serialized story of black Washington society of the 1920s, narrator Davy Carr says of flappers at a dance: "[I]f the clock had been turned back ten years, [they] would have been arrested on two counts—appearing in public without sufficient clothing, and indecent dancing. However, as [flapper protagonist] Caroline says, this is 1922, and the Middle Ages are over."[16] This sexualized youth culture was undermining the cultural authority of the sexual values that had dominated among both the white and the African American middle class of the late nineteenth century.[17]

Part of what made the more sexualized youth culture possible was the greater independence of youth from family control. In practical terms the dating culture of youth was transforming courtship from an overtly family affair, in which parents, and especially mothers, took a strong role, to one managed much more by young people themselves.[18] This independence of youth was one strand in a larger cultural glorification of individual fulfillment and freedom as opposed to submission to a wider social authority and tradition. The growth of huge industrial corporations and the decline of self-employment for men may have contributed to a widespread desire for greater personal freedom and to a critique of institutions as stifling to individuality. These desires were depoliticized for many whites in the 1920s, by comparison to the radicals of the 1910s, who had made individual freedom part of a larger political critique. Instead, the strategy of achieving individual freedom through consumption began its long-lived career in this period. Middle-class African Americans, too, followed the dream of material success, but due to their experience of racial oppression, even material success carried a political meaning, proving their capacity for achievement and right to material rewards, and the yearning for freedom from control by racist whites had a clear and direct political reference point.[19] Some, notably Jewish, immigrants, also absorbed or expanded an individualist critique of traditional religious norms and controls. And sociologists like W. I. Thomas who studied immigrant lives conceptualized them as moving from the "traditional" to the "modern," from the collectivity to individualized lives.[20] The theme of personal freedom in sex, love, and marriage resonated with larger trends in the culture.

Desire for more personal freedom in sex, love, and marriage also reflected a longer-term recasting of the relationship between marriage and citizenship. An increasingly settled nation with more numerous and developed institutions needed marriage less as a means of governance or as a symbol of republican political virtue, as it had been from the colonial era into the nineteenth century. Enforcing monogamous marriage did remain an important means of state control over working-class, nonwhite, and non-Christian citizens and immigrants.[21] By the early twentieth century, white middle-class citizens, as well as immigrant radicals and African Americans, were growing restive with older expectations of marriage and traditional morality as essential to respectable citizenship status. Lindsey voiced the resentment about such controls in his books on youth and marriage, in which he relayed stories of middle-class adolescents unjustly persecuted for their sexual activities and portrayed intrusive public moral authorities as gross violators of personal freedom and privacy. Thus, as Nancy Cott has argued, "a rhetoric of household intimacy and liberty" began to prevail over assumptions of the state's right to regulate marital relations.[22]

Whether the emphasis was on the sex or on the freedom of youth that made sex more culturally visible, the most contentious issue was the changing power and place of women. Female sexuality was strictly controlled to guarantee women's value in the marriage market; and both sexual control and the channeling of women into wifehood and motherhood prevented daughters from having the same personal freedoms as sons. But woman suffrage, women's greatly expanded public roles and employment, birth control practice and activism, and feminist thinking deeply challenged Victorian gender roles and culture. These changes demonstrated that women could be active citizens in the public sphere and that wifehood and motherhood no longer fully defined their lives. For example, heterosexual professional women struggled to balance careers, marriage, and childbearing, and the rate of childlessness among women maturing in the 1920s was more than 25 percent, an extraordinary proportion, the highest in the eight decades from 1880 to 1960. Feminists were shifting away from the sole reliance on motherhood as the basis of women's power and social claims.[23] The entry of lesbianism into novels and plays popularized another sexual possibility for women.[24] Women's gains in this period were limited, but their activism and employment helped to undermine Victorian notions of female vulnerability, domesticity, and sexual innocence. Discussion of these new features of women's lives and their impact on courtship and marriage was widespread in the first three decades of the century, among African Americans as well as among whites.[25]

Both culturally and materially, employment—especially better-paid or respected professional work—most profoundly affected the conception of women's sexual and marital lives because for most women the ability to earn an independent living was probably their most significant source of power. It allowed them to decline marriage, to possess more authority within it, and to leave it when necessary. Including both married and single women, the total proportion of the female population who were in the labor force crept up from 21 percent in 1900 to 25 percent in 1930; most were single, and well over 40 percent of all single women were employed in the 1920s. This premarital experience gave women's lives more in common with men's.[26] Careers and marriage were the subject of intense debate in the 1920s due to their feminist implications for women's power and because married women were in fact employed in greater proportions than in the past. While the total proportions of all married women who held paid jobs remained small—9 percent in 1920 and 12 percent in 1930—those figures included a large proportion of black wives (33 percent of whom were employed) in both years and a 56 percent increase among white wives over the decade. Within white-collar work, rising rates of marriage were also striking: by 1930 nearly 25 percent of professional women were married, as were 32 percent of clerical workers, 33 percent of saleswomen, and 18 percent of schoolteachers.[27] Those who advocated women's right to combine career and marriage often tended strategically to underplay the challenge these new patterns posed to men's dominance in the family, but that potential was always present and surely accounted for the highly charged public debates of the decade.[28] Assumptions of, or demands for, women's equality were certainly not based solely on their paid labor force participation, but employment was deeply interwoven with the issue.

Employment was significant also because it grounded women's ability to exit marriage or to survive when men left. Since the early nineteenth century, the constraints of permanent marriage had been loosening, and with them women's restriction by coverture. Coverture, or the doctrine of marital unity, deeply constrained women in marriage; it meant that the husband's legal existence "covered" that of the wife, preventing her from acting as an individual legally or economically and generally limiting her in every arena of life. Being able to separate or divorce allowed women a way out.[29] Though separation was more readily available, divorce rates were also increasing: between 1870 and 1900, the divorce rate doubled (from 2 to 4 divorces per thousand existing marriages), and from 1900 to 1920 it nearly doubled again (from 4 to 7.7 divorces per thousand); the large majority of petitioners were women.[30] By the 1920s cumulatively, the practice and possibility of separation and divorce had frayed the cords of both marital unity and permanence and had contributed to a sense that women were not only wives but also, at least some of the time, independent persons.

The desire for individual freedom, pleasure, and privacy in a world of middle-class prosperity; female roles in the sexualized youth culture; and women's greater public presence, equality claims, and ability to leave marriage formed the context for attempts to redefine marriage in the 1920s and early 1930s. Marriage revisionists identified these social and cultural alterations as causes for concern. As Social Gospel advocate Sherwood Eddy wrote in 1929:

> No other generation in this country ever faced the insistent demand for equality between the sexes, for the economic independence of women and the abolition of a false double standard of morals. No other ever had such high-powered playthings as the auto, the radio, the moving picture, together with so much leisure and spending money. No other ever was subject to the seduction of such commercialised amusements or such a circulation of suggestive and obscene sex literature and periodicals. All such artificial stimulation is exciting human nature abnormally.[31]

Addressing this problem and proposing solutions attracted a wide variety of writers in the 1920s and 1930s.

Creators of Modern Marriage

The most famous proponents of modernizing marriage—Ben Lindsey, Floyd Dell, and Margaret Sanger—were white, but African Americans also participated in the debates. The de facto segregation of much of American cultural and intellectual life meant that discussions were often separate, with African Americans addressing issues and concerns specific to their experience, such as racist bars to intermarriage. Nevertheless, African Americans always had to attend to what whites were proposing, if only because, when translated into public policy (as in the case of social hygiene), white-initiated reforms could intrude on their lives. And certainly in some arenas, such as birth control, interracial efforts were taking place.[32] Finally, constrained as its circumstances were, the black middle class did, as noted earlier, confront some of the same issues as the white middle class in relation to the independence and sexual behavior of youth and the roles of women. For both groups popular debate was widespread and lively, although the number of African American sources here is much smaller. The discussion was conducted in print by three broad constituencies.

Former sex radicals, especially birth controllers, and other white reformers were especially vocal. Margaret Sanger, curbing her public flamboyance and radicalism in the 1920s as she sought rapprochement with physicians and greater respectability for the birth control cause, published *Happiness in Marriage* in 1926 to compete with other advice books and promote birth control as part of the new marriage.[33] Ira Wile, a New York pediatrician and analyst, worked with Sanger and served as director of the American Birth Control League in the late 1920s. Rachelle Yarros, a Russian Jewish immigrant and radical, who lived in Chicago's Hull House settlement, worked as an obstetrician-gynecologist. Straddling moderate and radical reform, she engaged in both social hygiene and birth control advocacy and, encouraged by Sanger, opened the second U.S. birth control clinic in 1923. Both produced books on sex and marriage—Wile, with writer Mary Day Winn, *Marriage in the Modern Manner* (1929), and Yarros, *Modern Woman and Sex: A Feminist Physician Speaks* (1933).[34] Floyd Dell moved from the sex radicalism of the early 1910s toward a more conventional stance as he underwent psychoanalysis with Dr. Samuel Tannenbaum in 1917, seeking what he saw as the psychic stability and freedom to leave free love behind, marry again, and have children. Settled into his marriage with suffragist B. Marie Gage, in the 1920s he published both novels and the lengthy tome, *Love in the Machine Age*, that outlined his vision of modern marriage.[35] Sherwood Eddy was a longtime YMCA missionary in India and China, a Social Gospel advocate, and ultimately a Christian socialist, pacifist, and opponent of racism. His frequent lectures at colleges in the United States and abroad led him to notice that "old conventions and standards had been shattered" and near "moral anarchy" prevailed among youth. He set out in the 1920s to study the problem of sex, reading Ellis, Sanger, and Lindsey, and interviewing single and married people, before publishing his own conclusions in *Sex and Youth* in 1929. He was liberal or radical on many social questions (and later compared Joseph McCarthy to Hitler, for example). But Eddy, like Dell and many of these writers, accepted the family as "the basic, divine unit" and the foundation of human happiness.[36]

African American activists also engaged issues of marriage in the 1920s. W. E. B. DuBois supported the birth control movement and in his voluminous writings as editor of the *Crisis* addressed marriage as part of the larger race struggle. Likewise, George Schuyler, still a socialist in the 1920s, and associated with the *Messenger* until its demise in 1928, sometimes wrote about gender and marital relations in his columns in the *Pittsburgh Courier*, a black newspaper, from 1925 to the 1960s. He continued to fight against antimiscegenation laws but gradually abandoned his former radicalism (ultimately

becoming a strong political conservative by the 1940s, although always a pro-
ponent of race equality).[37] These men supported a modern vision of marriage
that always included the right to intermarry, but their overall perspective was
not a sex radical one.

———

Writers of fiction addressed youth sexuality, courtship, and marriage, which
remained the staple of novels as they had been from the beginning of the
genre in the eighteenth century. Before the wide distribution of paperback
books (starting in 1939), the reading of fiction was concentrated in the most
prosperous and best-educated part of the public, the group that dominated
official cultural debates about sex and marriage rules. Successful novels point
to the problems that this group wanted to read about. In addition to showing
young lovers finding their way to marriage, novels in the post–World War I era
addressed relationships after marriage more than they had earlier, and women
became more numerous among the central characters. Dell wrote several novels that imagined youthful courtship as well as commenting on marriages of
the older generation. Prominent Indiana literary figure Meredith Nicholson
wrote *Broken Barriers* (1922), about the love affair of a spunky young Indianapolis working woman; it was made into a film in 1924. Nobel Prize–winning
writer Sinclair Lewis took part in the popular effort at reimagining love and
marriage in novels such as *Main Street* (1920) and *Ann Vickers* (1932); the
latter was also made into a film in 1933. Sidney Howard is best known for
his 1940 screenwriting Academy Award for *Gone with the Wind*, but his plays
had also been very successful. His 1926 Broadway production *The Silver Cord*
argued for the freedom of young people to court and marry without parental interference; it appeared as a film in 1933.[38] Novels and the films based
on them offered their readers vivid representations of the clashes between
young women's new consciousness and older ways of regulating sex and courtship. Their heroines and heroes formulated answers to conservative charges of
moral decadence and pioneered new ways to understand their sexual selves.

Among African Americans, however, where other sources are fewer, the
fiction of Jessie Fauset and the serialized story "The Letters of Davy Carr,"
published anonymously in 1925 and 1926 in the *Messenger*, provide very important evidence for middle-class perspectives on marriage. Jessie Fauset, known as
the midwife of the Harlem Renaissance, came from a poor but genteel Philadelphia family, attended Cornell University on a scholarship, and became a
teacher. She began to work with DuBois on the *Crisis* in 1912 and left teaching for full-time editorial work there in 1919. She encouraged other writers

during that fertile period in black letters, but she also wrote novels herself.[39] These works address women's work, equality, and sexual freedom, flappers, and middle-class marriage, all in the context of intraracial skin-color prejudice and passing, and were written in an incisive feminist style. Edward Christopher Williams, the first formally trained African American librarian, who worked at Howard University's library during the 1920s, also wrote fiction and plays. The child of a prominent black father and a white Irish mother, Williams was born in 1871 in Cleveland. In his Washington years he was a well-known figure among the black elite. Apparently intrigued by the modern flapper, Williams penned "The Letters of Davy Carr" as an exploration of the many types of women and romance in black Washington.[40] These writers offer a window onto the rich world of black middle-class courtship and marriage.

———

Finally, social scientific thinkers helped to shape modern marriage. The social sciences were gaining prestige and authority and expanding their academic base. By the 1920s, Chicago and Columbia had trained more than a hundred Ph.D.'s in sociology; Freudian psychoanalysis and a new psychiatry, based on understanding the "normal," were gaining adherents; the American Psychological Association, founded in 1892, tripled in size between 1900 and 1920.[41] Prominent among white social scientists were feminist psychologist Phyllis Blanchard and pioneer family sociologist Ernest R. Groves. Blanchard studied with G. Stanley Hall. From 1925 on, she worked at the Philadelphia Child Guidance Clinic and taught at the University of Pennsylvania School of Medicine. Her research on adolescent girls produced, among many writings, *New Girls for Old* (1930). With an introduction by the radical V. F. Calverton, this book shows how the marriage reformers pursued the sex radicals' desire to find an empirical basis for sexual life—"fact instead of fancy," as Calverton wrote. Blanchard addressed sex education, careers, marriage, and the problems of the modern young woman. She later coauthored a textbook on mental hygiene with Groves.[42] Groves was a prolific analyst of the development and proper form for modern marriage. He also founded the marriage education movement and taught the first university course in it at Boston University in 1922. His first degree was in divinity from Yale, and he later studied English and philosophy but then moved to sociology; his career illustrated the intellectual shift from religion to social science as the source of authority for regulating heterosexual relations. He taught sociology at the University of North Carolina from 1927 until his death in 1946 and wrote many monographs, textbooks, and popular works, including *The Marriage Crisis* and *American Marriage and Family Living* (with William F. Ogburn, both

1928) and *The American Family* (1934). Partly in response to the tremendous correspondence that developed with his readers and partly in response to the interest of university students, he began to do marriage counseling. He and his second wife, Gladys, who gradually became his partner in the practice, developed a marriage counseling service in Chapel Hill in the 1940s. They also wrote many popular magazine articles. Groves's ideas on marriage were thus promulgated through a variety of media. His attitude toward marriage was epitomized in the title of an annual conference he founded in 1934, the Conference on Conservation of Marriage and the Family; he began the conference to promote the marriage preparation courses spreading through colleges across the country, with the intent of improving and saving marriage.[43]

Sociology and social work obtained a foothold among African Americans as access to university training grew. Social worker Constance Fisher, for example, who wrote in the *Birth Control Review*'s special Negro issue of 1932, got a master's degree in social work from Western Reserve in 1929 and had a career in juvenile, maternal, and infant care programs.[44] Bettie Esther Parham, who wrote an advice column on modern families in the newspaper *New York Age* from 1935 to 1937, was director of the Home Economics Department at Dillard University in New Orleans, when home economics had hopes of claiming authority as part of the social sciences.[45]

E. Franklin Frazier was the most eminent of the black social scientists. From a working-class Baltimore family, he graduated from Howard University in 1912 and earned a master's degree in social work from Clark University. Much influenced by DuBois, Frazier supported woman suffrage, was on the political Left, and was always a passionate advocate of race equality and integration. After teaching in the Atlanta School of Social Work for some time, he returned to graduate school at the University of Chicago in 1927 for a doctorate and from that research wrote *The Negro Family in Chicago* (1932), later expanded to *The Negro Family in the United States* (1939). He fought the scientific racism still reigning in social work and sociology, but his studies of the black family have since been criticized as the source of Daniel Patrick Moynihan's infamous "matriarchy" theory in the 1960s that blamed black poverty on "too powerful" unwed mothers and "weak" black fathers. While Frazier's antiracist explanations have been ignored in this critique, there is no question that, like many white authors, he found some aspects of women's social freedoms disturbing. Frazier brought social scientific authority to the black discussion of modern marriage.[46]

Like the works by birth controllers, reformers, ex-radicals, and novelists, many white social scientific discussions of modern marriage in the 1920s

Fig. 5 Bettie Esther Parham

Bettie Parham came from a North Carolina family. Her father had prospered as he
worked his way from factory labor to business to a degree in ministry and was able
to give all his children an education. Bettie graduated from Shaw University in 1931.
For several years in the mid-1930s she wrote a column on marriage and family for
the African American newspaper the *New York Age*. She later became a successful
entrepreneur, selling beauty products for black women. Courtesy of Photographs and
Prints Division, Schomburg Center for Research in Black Culture, The New York
Public Library, Astor, Lenox and Tilden Foundations.

centered on the middle class and individual interactions within the family
rather than the family's relation to the larger society. This emphasis mirrored
the period's stresses on individual freedom and pleasure and critique of marriage and family as institutions of social order producing conformity to traditional social and sexual regulations.[47] Frazier departed from the intrafamilial
emphasis of white social scientists because of his critical perspective on the
effects of white racism on black families. Although his work is best known for
its treatment of the black working class, it also examines the middle class and
shares the concerns of white sociologists about how best to make marriage and
family serve social order.

Science, Religion, and the Myth
of Victorian Repression

Despite the divergent backgrounds of the authors considered here—some started in religion, others had long been critical of it—they shared, as Sherwood Eddy put it, the desire to find "reliable ethical standards in a universal human experience interpreted by reason, apart from traditional authority."[48] Reason meant science, both biological and social. The establishment of science as cultural authority had, of course, been under way since the eighteenth century, but scientific language about women and human sexuality had been interwoven with moral and religious language in Victorian medicine and had most often supported rather than challenged the social order prescribed by Protestant Christianity.[49] In the 1920s the cultural split between vocal and antiliberal fundamentalists and modern scientific thinkers contributed to a sharper public sense of tension between science and religion, even though liberal Jews and Protestants found intellectual accommodation with science. Science became a more dominant and pervasive source of authority, and condemnation of "superstition" became easier. In this environment marriage revisionists could more effectively mock restrictive sexual mores that no longer seemed to have much rationale among the sophisticated urban middle class. Critics stringently condemned a gap between "reality" (defined by "science" or "rationality") and the false representations and prescriptions of outmoded worldviews, often religiously defined. In Howard's *Silver Cord*, the scientist daughter-in-law announces she will use her science "to strip this house and to show it up for what it really is."[50] Frazier condemned the churches' evaluation of "all human behavior in terms of sin and righteousness" as quite unhelpful. Likewise, Lindsey called the suppression of sexual needs "unnatural" and continence an idea perpetuated by religious fanatics who saw in sex only "ugliness, original sin, and fig leaves."[51]

The term "superstition" was not thrown equally at all religions: this rhetoric came from a liberal Protestant, Jewish, or agnostic position that especially targeted Catholics, Orthodox Jews, and conservative Protestants, for whom marriage was bound up with the defense of "Western civilization and American democracy." The postwar Red Scare and public discussion of the liberalization of marriage and divorce laws in the Soviet Union led some critics to associate Lindsey's proposals with "atheistic Bolshevism." His penchant for speaking provocatively, as when he charged religious opponents with " 'bigotry and intolerance,' " heightened the controversy over his ideas. A group of liberal New York Episcopal clergy invited him to lecture to them in 1930; one asserted his own daughter was in a companionate marriage and using birth control. Lindsey spoke but soon after got into a battle with the Episcopal bishop of New York, William Manning, who was more conservative than some of his clergy. Lindsey shocked some when he sneaked into a Sunday service at which Manning denounced him from the pulpit; Lindsey interrupted the benediction to defend himself vociferously and was hauled out by police. Lindsey had been politically attacked by the fundamentalist Protestant Ku Klux Klan and ultimately lost a Klan challenge to his election in the mid-1920s. He strongly challenged such fundamentalism as "irrational," an example of "the basest instincts we have…presenting themselves under the guise of true religion and patriotism."[52]

The birth control issue, of course, made Roman Catholics a major target of sexual liberals because their demographic presence had produced political power that seriously hindered the birth control fight, as Sanger discovered. In her 1931 autobiography she denounced the Catholic hierarchy and other "hopeless dogmatists"; arrayed against them she saw "the forces of reason, of tolerance, of science—forces that embody more truly the spirit of Christ than the Church ever did." Rachelle Yarros and Ben Lindsey also cited Orthodox Jews, whom they considered excessively moralistic. All these religions were marked as not modern both by their dogmatic rather than scientific truth claims and by their authoritarian interventions into sexual behavior. As Phyllis Blanchard summarized it, the old religious prohibitions were ineffective because the "present generation is too imbued with the scientific spirit of inquiry to accept taboos simply because these are expressed by a representative of authority."[53]

The science to which marriage revisionists looked for the truth of sex was both biological and social. Research on sex hormones in the 1920s was cited by Lindsey, for example, as a way to authorize the determinism of (sexual) "love" over religious fulminations about sin: there is "a chemistry of sex, a chemistry of love" that "has its bases in the hormones secreted by the endocrine glands.…Now evidently a factor like that simply *Is*. You can't do away with it by denying it or bottling it up or laying it to original sin."[54] More prevalent than appeals to biology were appeals to psychology, including but not limited to Freudianism. Floyd Dell made the most extensive use of a Freudian model, interpreting practices like celibacy, arranged marriage, prostitution, and Victorian courtship as "neurotic" or "infantile" and defining his proposals as the path to psychological maturity and normality.[55] Finally, sociologists such as Groves and Frazier based claims about the importance of sex on a sociological (and historical) analysis of marriage as an institution. Groves presented the shift to a consumer economy, which encouraged both husband and wife to have "desires for pleasure and self-expression," as the source of marital change.[56] For all these thinkers, science demonstrated that sex was a real force in the world, the source of both problems and opportunities, that older and nonscientific worldviews could not effectively address. These writers sought to capture and guide that sexual force to strengthen marriage.[57]

The Companionate: Redefining Modern Marriage

The term "companionate marriage" was created in 1924 by Dr. Melvin M. Knight, a professor of history at Barnard College, to describe legal marriage for companionship without children. Knight asserted that the state had an interest in these marriages despite their childlessness and argued for tax changes that would encourage childbearing. Ben Lindsey popularized the term when his book was published in 1927, and it became the center of widespread public discussion. The following year he debated the merits of companionate marriage with the eccentric physical culture promoter and confession magazine publisher Bernarr Macfadden before an audience of sophisticated New Yorkers. By insisting that the new type of marriage was merely an escape for people too "lazy" to live up to the traditional moral code, Macfadden alienated his listeners, but Lindsey's liberal approach won their approval.[58] In the same year Adam Clayton Powell's Abyssinian Baptist Church in Harlem held a forum reported in the *New York Age* about "companionate marriage"; it included a paper by journalist Alice Dunbar-Nelson titled "Delinquent Colored Girls" (unwed adolescent mothers), as well as the discussion of companionate marriage by African Americans William Ferris, Yale graduate and former editor of Marcus Garvey's *Negro World*, and former Columbia University student J. Egbert Allen. Powell criticized "false modesty...on the sex question" and the failure of parents, teachers, and preachers to educate young people about sex.[59] Such discussions pointed to widespread popular interest in questions of youth behavior, sex morality, and marriage.

Advocates of reform were self-conscious liberals who opposed returning to the modified Victorianism characteristic of the social hygiene reformers. They decried excessive sexual repression for all and accepted women as sexual beings, but, unlike Emma Goldman or other sex radicals of the 1910s, they wanted to reinvent marriage to accommodate this sexualization and find new ways to guide the middle-class young safely into it. By rethinking the terms of dating, courtship, and marriage, these thinkers hoped to secure social and gender order but in a humane and distinctively modern form.

Lindsey and other marriage revisionists presented companionate marriage as a set of sexual values and conventions that could resolve the conflict between new patterns of youth behavior and what they considered an outmoded system for regulating it. Lindsey used the term "companionate marriage," which he sharply distinguished from "trial marriage," to mean a form of legal marriage that would involve access to sex education and birth control, as well as divorce by mutual consent for the childless, usually without alimony.[60] I will use the term "companionate marriage" in the broader sense of marriage that was dominated by the values Lindsey promoted: the importance of the sexual bond and education for it; the use of birth control to postpone and space children; and the acceptance of divorce as an appropriate option when the spousal relationship irretrievably broke down.

Companionate marriage modified major elements of the prevailing form of marriage: it began tentatively to challenge the prevailing social and legal standard of sole male responsibility for economic support.[61] Thus, when a man was not yet ready to be a breadwinner, this scheme facilitated early marriage through financial support for the newlyweds from their parents or from the wife's employment. The companionate vision also recognized modern women's education and paid work roles prior to or in the early period of marriage, acknowledging women's greater premarital equality and setting up a period of companionable partnership. The new model encouraged emotional and sexual intimacy rather than procreation and recognized a place for divorce in the system by easing the process for couples in this childless phase. Companionate marriage was intended to provide a legal alternative to sleeping or living together before marriage, and proponents denied that it undermined the fundamentals of marriage. Yet critics were correct to notice that companionate marriage represented both a diminution of the reproductive emphasis and an acknowledgment of the possibility of impermanence. Most important, it recognized women's new premarital roles, independence, and individuality and allowed them to work changes on the pre-childbearing phase of marriage.

Companionate marriage was also, as Lindsey never tired of pointing out, essentially what conventionally married practitioners of birth control were already doing when they postponed children. In his scheme, once the companionate phase had been successfully managed, the couple could move into "family marriage" and have children.[62] At that stage, women were expected to be primary caregivers; marriage revisionists were not displacing mother-hood as the expected goal of most women's lives. The new ideas were being propounded in a world where pressures and incentives toward motherhood remained powerful. These included religious strictures against contraception, especially from Catholicism, rural traditions of larger families, and the fact that motherhood simply continued to be the most rewarded—and often most rewarding—work that most women were allowed to do.

Additionally, motherhood was promoted by the eugenics movement, which, from the 1920s and 1930s on, pressed white middle- and upper-class people who were seen as "fit" parents to bear more children.[63] The class elit-ism and racism of the often upper-class supporters of eugenics were widely shared among whites, and some birth control proponents echoed their lan-guage. Opportunistically, Sanger and Lindsey used eugenics rhetoric in argu-ments for birth control. Lindsey claimed that the prohibition of birth control allowed "degenerates" and "social incompetents" to reproduce excessively.[64] Companionate marriage with birth control, he argued, would diminish such irresponsible childbearing.

Despite such rhetoric, the main body of companionate marriage think-ers stood in a different camp from active eugenicists, such as Paul Popenoe, who also wanted to remold marriage. Popenoe, for example, published *Mod-ern Marriage: A Handbook* in 1925, but his concerns were different. He was writing exclusively to tell men how to find, court, and marry women who could make them happy and bear healthy children. He echoed some of the themes of companionate marriage thinking by, for example, opposing exces-sive repression, and he realized that men had to accommodate modern wom-en's greater assertiveness. However, his eugenic goals made him oppose birth control, feminism, and women's careers. He believed that delaying childbear-ing confirmed couples in a selfish absorption in their own lives and "a lack of inclination for children," and that it led to sterility. He called for "a radical change in education, especially of women, which will inculcate a biological point of view in place of the uncurbed individualism and thinly disguised sex-antagonism which they now absorb, particularly in the women's separate colleges." In his view, "The whole feminist demand for the obliteration of sex distinctions and an equal share in all the world's activities is scientifi-cally unsound."[65] The central place of birth control and assertions of women's equality (however limited) in companionate marriage proposals sets them apart from Popenoe's ideas. Additionally, wary of state power, companionate marriage supporters like Sanger and Lindsey favored education and birth con-trol, not compulsory sterilization, to discourage reproduction by the "unfit."[66]

The liberal marriage revisionists treated here best exemplified the sensibilities of an emerging urban consumer culture and the powerful influence of feminism that persisted in the 1920s.

The legalization of birth control and liberalization of divorce laws necessary to make Lindsey's proposals fully viable did not take place at that time, and the creation of a legally distinct form of pre-childbearing marriage was never a practical possibility. Although conservative charges that Lindsey really meant to destroy marriage led some advocates of marriage reform to avoid the term "companionate marriage," the concept did capture a revised sense of the shape and purpose of marriage that was becoming increasingly popular in the 1920s and 1930s. Even the Roman Catholic Church, which never accepted mechanical birth control or divorce, nevertheless was widely understood to allow the rhythm method after 1931 and moved closer to accepting the notion that sexual pleasure was important to the success of marriage.[67] Lindsey's idea, then, described the direction of change in twentieth-century marriage, where duty and childbearing were less binding and divorce increasingly undermined fixity. This different conceptualization of marriage made psychological and sexual compatibility fundamental.

This modern marriage of sex, birth control, and divorce was indeed a different institution from Victorian marriage, and it both resulted from and confirmed a shift in cultural visions of sexuality, heterosexual relationships, and gender power. First, these theorists promoted sexual intimacy as the key element that created marriages and held them together. They wanted tolerance as well as guidance for youthful sex and looked to sex and an intense psychological bond as the source of the marital union. Second, they promoted the freedom and privacy of the couple relative to traditional moral and social claims and regulation. The older concept of marriage as a sacred and permanent economic and procreative institution, with political, class, and moral functions, that was grounded in larger networks of kin and community, became less salient. Finally, marriage revisionists always did obeisance to the equality of modern women. Most attributed changes in sexual mores and marriage in large part to women's new place in public political and economic arenas; they recognized the changes by criticizing patriarchal relations in marriage, though they differed on the basis of marital equality. In all these areas, marriage revisionists dimly echoed the sex radicals, although they lacked the romantic idealism and disregard for convention that marked the radicals' thought and marshaled all their arguments into support for legal marriage.

Sexual Intimacy

Advocates of companionate marriage stressed the healthiness and value of sex as part of human relations and as the glue of marriage. Some defended certain youthful premarital activities; all idealized marital sex, facilitated by birth control. Like the sex radicals, marriage revisionists represented sex as a source of energy and vitality and defined repression as unhealthy, but they did so with special relation to marriage. If you deprive men and women of the "love and companionship" of marriage, wrote Lindsey, "you either impose on them a celibacy which warps the soul and twists the inner nature, or you drive them to sexual lawlessness of the kind that is working such havoc and destruction in society today." Outside marriage, sex carried an ominous potentiality. Inside it, however, sex enriched, energized, and harmonized life. The modern world "needs more, not less, heterosexual passion to make it go round smoothly," wrote Dell in his 1930 volume *Love in the Machine Age*.[68] The new sexuality among youth represented both possibilities: forced underground, it threatened social disorder, but channeled through reformed mores and companionate marriage, it increased order by attracting young people into marriage.

Marriage reformers stressed tolerance for the youthful new morality. Lindsey portrayed himself as the rescuer of misunderstood youth, listening to their stories in his Denver juvenile court chambers, negotiating with their benighted elders, and facilitating reconciliations and marriages. He stressed young people's distance from parents, their essential innocence and sexual goodness, their adherence to their own moral code, and the hypocrisy and formalism of parental morals. One pregnant adolescent, Lindsey argues, for example, "had given herself to her lover under conditions which were 'immoral' in the sense that they violated the social code, but which were, so far as her attitude toward such an intimacy was concerned, morally impeccable." That is, she was in love, and she was not "promiscuous." Rachelle Yarros reported that engaged couples she saw in her Chicago birth control clinic often engaged in premarital sex, likewise commenting that they were not promiscuous and did not believe they were harming others. While Lindsey and Yarros preferred marriage, they recognized that not all sex outside marriage could any longer be categorized as "prostitution" or "promiscuity," as it had been by older reformers.

Jessie Fauset depicts several young flappers in her novel *The Chinaberry Tree* (1931). Set in Red Brook, New Jersey, the novel dramatizes the story of Laurentine Strange and her cousin Melissa. Laurentine is the daughter of a prominent white man, Colonel Holloway, and his black mistress, Sal Strange, a successful dressmaker. Sal and Laurentine live on the margins of the respectable black community, and Laurentine struggles with shame about her mixed-race heritage and illegitimate birth. She has been jilted by the wealthy black man Phil Hackett because of his business connections with the brother of the white Mrs. Holloway. Sal's niece Melissa comes to live with them, and her outgoing nature helps to bring her aunt and cousin out of their partially self-imposed isolation. The plot follows the two cousins' paths to marriage, Laurentine to a decent black doctor, Stephen Denleigh, and Melissa to an idealistic young reformer, Asshur Lane. Melissa and her friends, daughters of the local black middle class, are part of a modern youth culture. They party, smoke, wear makeup, flirt, and play, sing, and dance to jazz. Fauset presents them as vital, even if their sexually suggestive behavior occasionally exhibits "crudeness." While she hints at their need for guidance and restraint, she also contrasts them favorably with Laurentine, whose spirit is crippled by agonizing over outdated moralities.[69] Fauset, like Lindsey and Yarros, contrasted loving and innocent sexual activity (that would, however, still benefit by moving inside the safety of marriage) with an irrationally repressive morality that uniformly condemned all sex outside marriage. Sex could be a dangerous force, but these authors usually presented it as healthy and natural as part of youthful love leading toward marriage.

If proponents of modern marriage brightened the image of sex among unmarried youth, they apotheosized it as part of wedlock, placing both emotional and physical closeness at the heart of marriage. Anticipating marriage with Stephen Denleigh, Laurentine "felt a strange, permeating sense of well-being in being thus close to him, in being so intimate." Lindsey labeled sex with affection a "profound spiritual experience." The ideally intimate couple took a conscious and cultivated approach to sexual relations—made possible partly through sex education—as the fundamental bond of marriage, apart from its role in procreation. Calling "sex communion" the "consummation of mutual affection," Ira Wile and Mary Day Winn asserted in *Marriage in the Modern Manner* that it "makes sex pleasure not an end in itself but a means to a greater enrichment of life for both partners, a drawing together into closer spiritual relations." More lyrically, Sanger describes sexual relations as "a dance of soul as well as body, a dance in which two humans are no longer separate and distinct persons but in which their beings are co-mingled in a new and higher unity."[70] Mutually satisfying sexual relations were increasingly understood as a key component of marital happiness, and thus success.[71]

Birth control facilitated this romantic vision. DuBois pointed to the centrality of sexual intimacy when he defended birth control "so that the young people can marry, have companionship and natural health, and yet not have children until they are able to take care of them." In the same issue of the *Birth Control Review* (June 1932, its second "Negro Number"), African American social worker Constance Fisher cited "sexual maladjustment" among various sources of marriage breakdown, something she hoped birth control would help to prevent.[72] As Wile and Winn argued, "Mutual attractiveness, companionship and the sharing of life with some one else are more important for many people than the desire to create on a physical plane—that is, to have children. Indeed, too great reproductiveness frequently dissipates all these desirable features of married life." Or, as Dell's fictional heroine Janet March declaims, "[D]oing things together is quite as important as having babies."[73] In the new marriage the companionate sexual bond of the spouses took precedence.

Failure to attain a satisfying sexual relationship was often claimed to be the source of failed marriages: "Probably ignorance, selfishness, and failure in physical functioning are the rocks and reefs on which most disastrous marriages founder."[74] And when the will to union disappeared, marriage was no longer authentic. Lindsey wrote that to call an unloving marriage "holy" was to cling to "a superstition unworthy of a civilized people," and he favored allowing more legal grounds for divorce than most states then permitted.[75] Both he and other marriage reformers were technically rather conservative about recommending divorce, especially later, during the childbearing phase of marriage, but the heightened need for personal compatibility in the new marriage logically required it. As Dell summarized it, "if the relation proves unable to maintain itself by its own inner emotional strength," then it should be "formally dissolved."[76] While strongly sustaining the ideal of permanent marriage, most of these writers saw more accessible divorce as a concomitant of making sexual and emotional intimacy the source of marital cohesion.

Sexual relations were certainly important to Victorian marriage. What was new in companionate marriage proposals was the more favorable and less anxious approach to the power of sexual desire as a social force, even to some extent among unmarried youth, and the heavier dependence of the spousal bond on the formation of a strong and harmonious sexual relationship. Marriage modernizers in the 1920s and 1930s loudly proclaimed their focus on this element of married couples' lives.[77]

The Freedom and Privacy of the Couple

The obverse of the intense sexual bond of modern marriage was the greater relative distance between the couple and society—the ideal of the freedom and privacy of the heterosexual couple, which formed the second common element in companionate marriage proposals. Marriage was by definition heterosexual, but the modern version required an intensification of male-female intimacy. That intensity came not only from tightening the sexual relationship but also from loosening other ties. As the scientist heroine of *The Silver Cord* proclaimed, each partner should see the other as "apart" from all others. "That's what being in love must mean and being properly and happily married. Two people, a man and a woman, together by themselves, miles and miles from everybody, from *everybody* else." The triumphant conclusion of Dell's *Love without Money* brings male and female protagonists together in their own city apartment, "where they could be alone, and shut out the world."[78] The growing cultural emphasis on individual freedom was at work here. Feminist Suzanne LaFollette argued that the "original intention" of marriage was "as a purely personal relationship," but it had been degraded by a variety of influences such as "fear of sex,...religious superstition, and above all...the notion that the major interests of the group are essentially opposed to those of the individual and are more important than his."[79]

The central elements of Lindsey's proposal—sex education, birth control, early marriage, and divorce by mutual consent for the childless—underpinned this individualist vision that foregrounded two isolated people in love, pushing aside for the moment their links to the wider society through parents, friendship, religious and other authorities, and the economic and property functions of marriage. This kind of freedom for the individual couple marked for these thinkers not only the historical movement of progress but also the superiority of American culture. Wile and Winn contrasted modern American marriage with traditional marriage in China, where young couples lived with parents. The result was too much influence for the "older generation, a fact which certainly accounts in part for the conservatism that made China for so long a stagnant nation."[80] Although in reality marriage in the United States continued to function as an important social and legal institution, the rhetoric of modern marriage shifted to the couple's personal relationship and their right to privacy. Outside that couple relationship, these thinkers hoped, social, legal, and economic entanglements and regulations lay at considerable distance.

Several writers praised defiance of community opinion or defended even quite unconventional sexual behavior. In *The Chinaberry Tree*, Fauset voices through the physician Stephen Denleigh a powerful rejection of the shame Laurentine feels about her mother's longtime liaison with Colonel Holloway, a man she could not marry because of the color bar: " 'This was a true love match, the kind you read about—Heloise and Abelard and all that....I don't advocate their line of action and yet there is something awe-inspiring.' "

The mother, Sal Strange, is depicted as having had a happy life in which she ignored the moralistic community around her that saw being " 'mixed up with white folks' " as a sign of degradation. Lindsey himself defended an open marriage in which "Mr. and Mrs. Blank" tolerated one another's extramarital affairs; he even argued the affairs and honesty about them improved the marriage. While acknowledging it was a "dangerous experiment," he nevertheless argued that it was better to let them have freedom to experiment (and fail) than to condemn them out of hand. Because the couple was childless, Lindsey explains, "their mode of life remains their own private business" and "the effects of their experiment...individual rather than social." Reformer Sherwood Eddy announced, "In the evolution of human society, marriage has been gradually changing from an institution upheld by the State and the Church into a *private, personal relationship.*"[81] Privacy for the couple's love relationship, except for the question of children, increasingly assumed more saliency than the historical social functions of marriage.

The verbal barrage against authoritarian regulation focused on the traditional control of youth sexuality (always greater for young women). "Hands off!" these writers shouted to parents, schools, and churches hounding youth for their premarital sexual activities. Both Lindsey's *Revolt of Modern Youth* and *The Companionate Marriage* were filled with stories of "perfectly normal, healthy-minded" adolescents, especially young women, whose behavior drew the wrath of intrusive, puritanical parents and school officials. One who had gotten pregnant had been discovered by a woman teacher. The teacher, who Lindsey implies was titillated by a letter she discovered from the girl to her boyfriend, reported it to the principal, who suspended the student as a bad influence on others. Defending the young woman, who had acted out of love, Lindsey asserted, "There was nothing whatever in the situation that could justify these two savages in making an example of her."[82] Marcet Haldeman-Julius, socialist publisher and mother of Josephine, whose "companionate marriage" was featured in the national press in 1927, wrote in support of Lindsey's proposals that adults were often "jealous of youth" and had unfairly "restricted its pleasures."[83] Most of these writers (even Sanger in the new conventionality of *Happiness in Marriage*) did not overtly approve of such premarital sex and wanted to get the young people married. Yet the emphasis was very much on the right of privacy for heterosexual couples, at least the middle-class young people cited by Lindsey and Dell.

Loosening controls over middle-class youth sexuality meant a greater change for young women than for young men because class purity always depended on women's remaining virgins until marriage to class-appropriate men. Thus freedom and privacy for couples' sexual activity were not just about sex; they bespoke a female shifting away from familial control generally. As Floyd Dell wrote in his autobiography, as a youth he had been eager for young women to steal themselves "out of the safe-deposit vault of the parental home" and commit themselves to sexual love.[84] That parental control, however, had represented the stake of parents and kin in a traditional function of marriage—the formation of economic and social alliances. Marriage continued to serve some of these functions, but control was less direct.

The new marriage rhetoric denied these functions, promoted the idea of autonomy for youth, and criticized parental, most often maternal, interference. For example, a letter writer to the African American *Pittsburgh Courier*'s advice columnist explains her mother's eagerness to see her "married and settled down" before the mother's death. The columnist urges the young woman not to "risk ruining your whole life because your mother wishes to see you married."[85] In Howard's *Silver Cord*, widowed Mrs. Phelps is far more demanding: she wants to keep both sons with her in their small town, driving off one fiancée whom she dislikes and disrupting the career plans of both the other son and his scientist wife. She challenges the primacy of the husband-wife bond so central to modern marriage, complaining that "this scientific age" is making boys "forget that the bond between mother and son is the strongest bond on earth."[86] More frighteningly, one of the young women Lindsey counseled—pregnant and in love with a man of a different religion—feared her father might shoot her lover. Lindsey marries the couple and helps the woman bring her father around.[87]

Marriage revisionists also decried considerations of property or children's economic contributions that might limit the freedom of individuals to love and marry as they chose. Floyd Dell's magisterial tome *Love in the Machine Age* expounds these ideas most fully in the form of a psychological and historical theory of the transition of marriage and family from patriarchy to modernity. In early European history, he explains, the patriarchal system gave the father of a family autocratic control over serfs and slaves, wives and children. The father's ability to disinherit kept children's lives in thrall to the family and patriarchal morality. The book is a brief against this control and against patriarchy's "*property*-precepts about 'purity' or sex-fear, and its hostility to free courtship and love-choice." But, Dell argues, the effects of patriarchy persisted even when the middle class challenged the aristocracy for control, because the middle class sustained various "patriarchal customs" that subsequently "bec[a]me modern neuroses." The customs Dell condemns include binding children too closely to parents (thus not allowing them to become mature adults), sex segregation, and marriage based on property concerns and arranged by parents. In his view these customs damaged youthful freedom to form mature love relationships and marriages.[88]

Applied to the modern world, this theory allowed Dell to denounce the persistence of Victorian morality because it jealously guarded the virginity of higher-status girls in pursuit of class status and property-based marriage instead of allowing free marriage choice. It reflected Dell's own life history as a bookish working-class youth, who "was not marriageable, but very companionable"; upper-class girls felt they could be open and frank with him, but, due to his low social status, they clearly distinguished those friendly feelings "from the kind of love which is a basis for marriage," that is, with a class peer.[89] Dell sought freedom for individuals to cross such boundaries if love led them there.

In various ways a number of these writers echoed Dell's desire to deny primacy to any other family relationship except marriage and thus to detach love and marriage from economic considerations.[90] In *The Chinaberry Tree*, Fauset shows Laurentine realizing that the true importance of marriage lies in emotional closeness, not social or economic status: "It seemed to her she sensed for the first time the oneness which a successful marriage could bring, with no idea of its social benefits or security."[91] And Phyllis Blanchard criticized the pattern of daughters who sacrificed marriage to care for their parents, a common pattern in immigrant families in this period.[92] Marriage had to come first. Similarly, parents' economic need for children's labor limited early marriage among the rural African American subject of sociologist Charles S. Johnson's Alabama study *Shadow of the Plantation* (1934). Presenting his subjects as peasants isolated from the dominant culture, he noted that if couples did marry young, they often lived with parents. Their cultural difference was further marked by marriages (legal or common law) that were clear economic partnerships in which high fertility was valued. These features were quite different from the companionate marriage ideal. Despite portraying the cultural integrity and adaptiveness of the community's social codes, Johnson looked toward the introduction of values and practices "in accord with a more advanced conception of life and of social relations."[93]

That "advanced conception" involved the rhetorical ideal of intimate, individual love between a man and a woman, undisturbed by larger familial claims and unalloyed with economic considerations or roles in a larger social network. But in the long history of marriage, women's reproductive capacities as well as their labor had been objects of exchange between lineages; this exchange made marriage a more social and economic than individual venture. In the modern era, extracting the couple from familial entanglements and social regulation required greater change for women, since women experienced more family demands and more social surveillance than men did. And women relied on marriage economically: marriage could never be solely about "love" for them. Altering the status of women was thus essential to the project of reforming marriage.

Equality for Women

The third element that characterized the companionate marriage discourse was obeisance to the notion that women were—and ought to be—emerging from traditional subordination into something (more) like equality with men. These writers exuded a sense that the modernity of which their ideas were a part required a new egalitarian comradeship in marriage. Lindsey put it most baldly: "The contention I am making for these changes in our marriage code is in reality nothing but…another step forward" in the fight for women's "right to control their destiny as individuals who are no longer in slavery." Ideas of "masculine supremacy or of female frailty and weakness" are "illusions," noted Wile and Winn. Eddy argued that modern marriage must be based on "*liberty, equality, cooperation, and growth,*" and that "there must be equality in the democratic home."[94] Focusing narrowly on the home and the couple's relationship, many marriage reformers failed to attend to women's weaker position in the broader social, economic, and legal organization of gender, which undermined equality within marriage. Still, they addressed certain aspects of wives' subordinate place.

Careers and employment were prominently linked to the notion of women's equality in companionate marriage. Single women's paid employment made earlier marriages possible, as Dell insistently argued. "It is through having careers—or starting out to have them" that young women "find their best opportunities" to meet men and to marry. And their wages then allowed couples to marry even if the man could not support them both.[95] Hence, critics of female wage earning were out of date: "The recognition of women's work outside the home…as *being a part of the marriage system*, and not something alien and hostile to it, would modernize our socioeconomic system at this point."[96] Besides facilitating heterosocial encounters and early marriage, employment was understood to make women more financially savvy and able to hold their own with husbands once they did marry. It benefited marriage by giving the wife "a greater understanding of the value of money" and "an increased sense of power and security."[97] Longer-term employment for wives had an obvious logic that feminists in the 1920s promoted, but it was much more controversial. The expectation of premarital and sometimes pre-child-bearing female employment, however, was incorporated into Lindsey's model of the companionate.

On a more personal front, the democracy of modern marriage meant that the subservience of wife to husband was to be replaced by a relationship of greater emotional and intellectual equality. As Eddy asks, "Does the husband really want a mere permanent housekeeper, a faithful drudge, an unpaid servant, or does he desire a real life companion and a friend…?" This was a different companionship from the Victorian variety, however, because women were now presumed to be more than domestic angels; their participation in the public world made them fuller persons with the ability to do more than serve others. *New York Age* columnist Parham pointed out that excessive sacrifice on the part of one or the other spouse can lead to "disappointing and undesirable results." Her gender neutrality masks the usual pattern, which Yarros makes clear: "Marriage has often destroyed the individuality of women."[98] Instead, mutual respect and a more rounded comradeship were to characterize the modern marriage.[99] Negative images of domineering husbands or lovers and dependent and passive wives implicitly promoted gender equality in the literature of marriage revision. Nineteenth-century Americans had modified male dominance through critiques of male adultery, intemperance, and cruelty.[100] Marriage revisionists of the 1920s critiqued smaller actions such as the tradition of wives' personal service to husbands. In his novel *Ann Vickers*, for example, Sinclair Lewis exposes the inadequacy of Ann's first husband, Russell Spaulding, in part through showing his insensitive expectation of such service. Russell and a male guest, for example, sit and discuss real estate while their wives wash dishes: "[I]t never occurred to either of them that these working wives should not order their husbands' meals, hire and—especially—fire servants, see that their husbands' socks were darned," and perform myriad other caretaking tasks that were not reciprocated by the men. Similarly, in *The Chinaberry Tree*, Fauset reveals the poor potential of one flapper's first suitor, Malory Forten, when he presumes the right to dictate her public behavior. He "believed in…a rather definite place for women" and once told her, " 'I didn't like your dancing that vulgar dance. That sort of thing isn't…the kind of thing I like from a girl whom I'm expecting to be my wife.' "[101] This type of authority violated the democratic code of modern marriage.

Passive or submissive women were similarly criticized for their failure to live up to the modern ideal. Using highly pejorative language, Groves celebrated the passing of the "slave type of woman, whose existence centered in her husband's comfort, and the child-like wife." And in *The Chinaberry Tree*, Laurentine begins in a state of passivity and dependence on male approval, praying for "a home life like other women, a name, protection."[102] Fauset presents this neediness as a problem, whose solution is Laurentine's claiming of the capacity for self-sufficiency and independence. These images, along with birth control rhetoric of women's biological freedom, were fundamental to the definition of modern marriage as a relationship of male and female equality.

The rhetoric of sexual intimacy, the freedom and privacy of the couple, and women's equality appears throughout the writings on companionate marriage in the 1920s. Sexual intimacy was to provide a more mystical unity for the modern couple, reinforcing and ultimately supplanting the cohesion of Victorian wedlock built on the partnership of reproduction and household economy. The couple, through courtship and especially in marriage itself, was to be granted a much larger degree of freedom and privacy to cultivate that sexual bond and to create a relationship of psychological closeness. The closeness was to be founded on relations as individual persons rather than primarily as beings with roles in wider social and economic networks. Finally, to make this marriage viable, women's equality was necessary. The suppression of women's sexual natures and their restriction from the freedom and privacy available to men had come to be seen as harming marriage. For modern marriage to be possible, these writers proclaimed, women had to become, and be treated as, men's equals.

Companionate Marriage and the Superiority of Modern American Culture

Companionate marriage seems in most ways to have been a domestic American concern, a set of guidelines to direct youth away from what reformers felt was the potential anarchy of social freedom and back toward a safer institution for sexual and emotional energies. Yet for many proponents this conception of marriage also represented what was uniquely modern and superior about American culture.

Companionate marriage discourse, especially the emphasis on equality for women, recapitulated but revised conceptions of American society as the acme of an evolutionary hierarchy spanning "savagery" to "civilization." Most nonwhite and colonized peoples were seen as closer to the former than the latter. Nineteenth-century anthropologists had characterized American (and European) civilization as superior to the savage or barbaric, among other things, by its patriarchal culture and extreme gender differentiation—dominant, controlled, public men and protected, chaste, domestic women. They portrayed simpler societies around the world as degrading and overworking women, while presenting American women as possessing respect and high status. The social changes of the early twentieth century, particularly women's visibility in the public worlds of employment, politics, and leisure, as well as men's turn toward a more aggressive style of masculinity, were altering those roles and thus their place in the claim of superiority.[103] Twentieth-century anthropologists revised the earlier schema. Margaret Mead, for example, rejected evolutionary and racist theories and criticized male dominance. She even compared "primitive" societies favorably to the United States in regard to teaching the young about sex. She left behind the authority of nineteenth-century Protestant moralism, relying instead on the legitimizing force of science. However, despite her positive portrayals of some aspects of these other societies, she judged them lacking in individual freedom. She also, in historian Louise Newman's words, continued the tradition of "assess[ing] the United States' purported cultural superiority to other nations in terms of its supposedly superior gender relations (western women are free and have the most choices)."[104]

Companionate marriage literature illustrates this modern framing of the U.S. sense of national superiority. Companionate marriage writers understood their proposals for a marriage bargain between more equal partners as part of American cultural modernity, and as the Victorian domestic image lost its ascendancy, equality for women in voting and in marriage became the new sign of American cultural superiority. These writers associated domineering men and submissive women with the past or with cultural or class "others." Dell, for example, described patriarchy as an outmoded stage of civilization. He then blamed its persistence on non-Americans, claiming that modern changes "are…profoundly resisted…by the special patriarchal traditions of particular 'racial' groups" (though he names none). He condemned what he saw as authoritarian immigrant parents who tried to maintain traditional cultural authority over their children. Sanger also strongly identified immigrants as excessively male-dominant, citing the "traditional and unfortunate attitude of many foreign born men toward their wives. Women were not made merely to serve the physical and sexual needs of husbands, with no obligation on the part of the latter except to provide a house and to pay the bills." Frazier echoed the distinction between American- and foreign-born when he explained the divorce of an American black woman from her Jamaican-born husband: quoting the American woman, he said that West Indian black immigrants brought with them the attitude that " 'the men were lords and the women worked as slaves,' " surely a very loaded terminology.[105]

Sanger and Yarros also linked female submissiveness with the past and/ or with the foreign. As Sanger wrote in *Woman and the New Race*, women of the past had submitted passively to degradation, but modern women were demanding "complete freedom." She described with horror the prostitutes – "women of all races huddled together in Oriental degradation"—that she saw on her Asian travels, while Yarros pointed to the Italian and east European Jewish immigrant women who felt shamed and controlled by authoritarian husbands.[106] The tone of these descriptions was somewhat sympathetic, but the images more strongly conveyed the sense that such women were somehow inadequate, that they had failed actively to take on the roles of modern women, while their husbands lacked the democratic decency of native-born American men. The marriage revisionists, then, even the African American Frazier, reproduced in modified form the perspective of American cultural superiority that had characterized late nineteenth-century social theorists.

Conclusion

The marriage revisionists who described and promoted companionate marriage in the 1920s sought to sustain an ideal of love-based legal marriage in a modern urban world. Material and cultural transformations in the lives of the white-collar classes, especially in the political and social roles of women, had loosened the framework of Victorian marriage. Secular and scientific authority were diminishing the power of Anglo-Protestant culture. Consumption was more salient in the middle class and its youth culture; immigration was increasing ethnic diversity; the birthrate was declining and the divorce rate accelerating; and women were pursuing education, employment, and politics. In this context the sexual moderation, moral regulatory functions, and polarized gender roles of Victorian marriage were giving way. In applying a new label to marriage, the assorted social reformers and ex-radicals supporting companionate marriage were making explicit in public discourse that the place and functions of marriage were changing. In reality, continuities abounded: marriage remained the end point of most long-term heterosexual relationships, the locus of most childbearing, a substantial means of social regulation, and the main work of most women's lives. Nevertheless, the rhetoric of sexual intimacy, freedom and privacy, and equality for women both signaled and encouraged new understandings and expectations. The promotion of companionate marriage was a significant historical turning point.

Despite wide agreement among marriage revisionists on sex, privacy, and equality, however, important differences existed over exactly what the new marriage meant in practice, especially in terms of women's power and authority. The largest and most popular group of white writers, including Ben Lindsey and Floyd Dell, supported birth control and flapper styles but equivocated on more substantive forms of equality. African American writers as a group were more accepting of a pragmatic equality based on black wives' frequent employment. Black feminists went further and, with white feminist writers, produced prescient images of a more fully egalitarian marriage than more conventional figures could imagine.

4

Modern Marriage:
Three Visions

The wives had a common bond in having desired something more than
the conventional lot of womankind. College had been, to each of them,
part of a youthful program of rebellion, emancipation, self-realization.
And they had this in common, too, that they had given up their plans for
careers and economic independence, and become happily married. But if
they had given up without much regret their defiant early hopes, it had
not been an abject renunciation of their principles; their surrender was to
love and not to convention, for the men they married had been men who
sympathized with their rebellion, perhaps loved them for it.

—Floyd Dell, *Janet March*

Despite agreement on the broad themes characterizing visions of modern marriage—sexual intimacy, freedom and privacy, and equality for
women—marriage revisionists had significant differences. They varied over
the exact nature and importance of sex, its gendered meanings, the extent
of couples' individual freedom from the larger community or liberty to cross
racial boundaries in marriage, and housework and wives' employment. The
differences reveal three broad and overlapping visions of modern marriage.
These visions do not represent the ideas of three mutually exclusive groups
of thinkers, because some writers had a foot in more than one camp, but
they do convey the range of possibilities conceivable for those who wanted
change but remained committed to legal marriage. The "flapper marriage"
was the most widespread form. It can best be understood as modernizing
male dominance through unions in which vital, modern, yet pliant flapper sweethearts formed relationships with sensitive yet still masterful men.
A second type, most common among African American writers, was the
"partnership marriage," in which competent and often employed modern
women created marriages with responsible men that contributed to a stable
community. Finally, a third, minority type was the "feminist marriage,"
in which both sex and work (paid and unpaid) involved greater equality
between women and men.[1] These differences among marriage thinkers illu-
minate aspirations to sexual satisfaction, individual freedom, and women's

and black equality, as well as a number of anxieties—about the uncontrol-lability of sex, social instability, and the dangers of women's power and independence.

The differences among these types emerge most clearly in memorable images of character types and behavior that appeared both in marriage tracts and in popular fiction. While most writers agreed on the general principles of modern marriage, the dramatization of the people they imagined capable of enacting it (or not) reveals what they actually meant by more sex, free-dom, and equality. Popular fiction intervened in the prevailing discourse of marriage and provided readers with new narratives and values and revised models of how people could or should think and feel, ones that competed with the versions inherited from the nineteenth century. Readers respond to fiction in diverse and unpredictable ways. The representation of a style of personality or way of resolving sexual or marital problems does not guar-antee that readers will imitate it, but it does expand the range of possibili-ties. The fact that fiction can compete so compellingly with existing values explains why novel reading has been a moral battleground since the eigh-teenth century, with conservatives decrying the sexualizing effects of reading novels (on girls especially). The novels of the 1920s often created a world in which some characters moved from (what was represented as) the Victorian to the modern and in which others failed to do so. These characters served to legitimize or delegitimize for readers certain kinds of subjectivities and forms of heterosexual relations that facilitated or obstructed the achievement of modern marriage.[2] They helped to normalize certain character types and demonize others, who, most often among proponents of flapper marriage, were women with power.

Flapper Marriage

Flapper marriage involved the defining presence of the modern young woman who entered into it. Wearing anti-Victorian short and boyish clothing that de-emphasized the hips and breasts of the maternal body, often smok-ing and drinking to show she rejected traditional femininity and claimed male privileges, the flapper represented the quintessentially modern woman of the middle class in the 1920s.[3] In this male-centered vision the woman was active and modern but also a sweet, generous, and essentially innocent figure who put her man first, while the man was usually older, confident, and in charge.

Janet March

Floyd Dell's novels illustrate this model perfectly. In his novel *Janet March* (1923), protagonist Janet and her family live in the Midwest; she is the tomboy daughter of a college-educated mother and a liberal father who wants to escape the influence of his Victorian businessman father and to be his own man. Refusing authoritarianism, the Marches "wished to remain young; and so, inevitably, their children had more freedom." Mrs. March "wasn't suspicious of unfamiliar ideas, wasn't dogmatic in rejecting them." As Janet moves through adolescence, she grows tired of younger men who had never "entertained a thought that could not be quelled by the touch of a gentle hand"; she wants "masculine certitude, an authority," and a man "she didn't feel superior

Fig. 6 Floyd Dell

Floyd Dell, 1921 portrait by Marjorie Jones. Married since 1919, Dell would have been thirty-three or thirty-four years old in this photo. Despite his turn in this period toward more conventional views of marriage, his clothing continues to suggest a hint of the bohemian. Photo Courtesy of Floyd Dell Papers, The Newberry Library, Chicago.

to." She moves to Chicago and sleeps with an older artist she has fallen in love with. The relationship does not last. She then quits college, moves to New York, and gets involved with a family acquaintance, Roger, a bookstore owner sixteen years her senior.[4]

Roger represents the modern man, sensitive, thoughtful, eager for something more intense and beautiful than "the dull responsibilities of workaday life." An important part of what he wants is the "pagan right" to pleasure unspoiled by outdated religious rules. He especially wants freer sexual relationships with women, but he is not interested in the cheap pickups his male friends go out with; he wants a woman he can talk to (thus both sex and equality for women). Roger has had his own share of pain caused by a puritanical girlfriend who could not abandon the virginal ideal and later ended up committing suicide after becoming pregnant by another man. He needs Janet to provide the beauty and intensity he longs for.[5]

Janet is open, willing to try sex, and not intimidated by the old morality. Bolder than some writers on the premarital sex issue, Dell presents Janet's early liaison as valuable: "She had known that he had the secret of the freedom she desired," and she is grateful for this knowledge about sex, which brings her maturity and freedom. Janet is contrasted with Roger's earlier girlfriend, Sally, whom he characterized as "'afraid of [her] body, afraid of life!'"[6]

Janet is a capable and modern young woman of the world. She does not, however, pursue a career. She says she may be a feminist but is neither "interested in the vote" nor in secretarial work or economic independence, thus distinguishing herself from the passé suffragists as well as from modern career feminists.[7] Having worked as a filing clerk during her summer vacation, she has learned that work is not an adventure. Instead, she wants "to be in on something exciting" but thinks the only way to do it is through a man: "'The trouble is that a girl can be of so little use to a man who is doing things. I realize that. He is giving her a look-in on his adventure but what is she giving him? I really feel very humble when I think of that side of the problem.'" Janet and Roger marry. She works in his bookshop while he writes. After getting pregnant, she ultimately concludes: "'One has to risk something—create something! All my life I've wanted to *do* something with myself. Something exciting. And this is one thing I *can* do. I can—' she hesitated—'I can help create a breed of fierce and athletic girls, new artists, musicians, and singers—'."[8] Thus, all of Janet's modernity ends up returning her to women's maternal destiny.

Janet March briefly illustrates how flapper marriage both presented itself as modern and sustained male dominance. As feminist Florence Seabury wrote in a critique of the novel, Janet is "ultimately orthodox"; having "claimed her right to all experience and experiment," she "finally raises her banner on the platform of fireside and nursery."[9] Critiquing women's claims to citizenship and paid work, this vision denigrated the struggles of feminists for public equality; yet even in the private arena it undermined female desire and channeled women's energies back to motherhood and the emotional nurturance of men. In this depiction of modern marriage several character types demonstrated desirable and undesirable social and emotional traits and showed that women with power were unattractive and often reprehensible. The types were the new sexual man and woman, puritanical and controlling matriarchs, lesbians, and employed wives.

The New Sexual Man and Woman

Companionate marriage writers invoked science to stress the importance of sexuality and the fact that women, too, had sexual natures, which men were urged to respect and support. They also revalued men's sexuality, which was tainted with negative Victorian images of excess. But along with changes, comfortable maternal images persisted, reflecting the discomfort many writers felt in contemplating female sexual desire.

To support women's sexuality, reformers called for new, more sensitive behavior among men. Men were advised to restrain jealousy and set aside male possessiveness and obsessions with purity in women, as well as to accept and enjoy sexual activity without guilt. Lindsey approvingly cited the case of a rational and modern man who married a young woman with a child born out of wedlock. This man rejected "the old traditional masculine attitude that he must marry a 'Pure Woman.'" Within marriage, men were called to be tender and protective and, to some extent, to take responsibility for women's sexual response.[10] The beginning of women's sexual empowerment thus required adjustments among men.

But men were also reassured of the basic goodness of their natures. In *Revolt of Modern Youth*, Lindsey asserted that "'morality' doesn't play much part in the reactions of the normal lad—not if he is the healthy young animal he should be." Even at a young age, however, most girls were intolerant, bigoted, and judgmental. And adolescent boys, seeking girls' approval, might sadly turn in the same direction.[11] Appropriately modern men, however, embodied the natural goodness of sex, avoiding the crippling dogmas of the past. This characterization of male and female sexuality valorized male sexual desires and labeled female sexual fears and resistance irrational and outdated.[12]

On the other hand, despite the acceptance of premarital sex by Dell and a few others, it generally remained difficult for male (and even some female) writers to escape the sense of women as the recipients of men's sexual agency. Lindsey, for example, asked one young flapper about "close dancing": "[D]on't you feel that [the boys] are taking liberties with your person? Don't you resent it?" She did not. But though she did not support his suggestion of victimization, she did deny active sexual interest; he reports her as claiming she got no "thrill" from the dancing as the boys did (who were "fools," in her view). Confirming an underlying innocence, then, Lindsey clearly enjoyed reporting to shocked moralists "how much more restrained and well poised she is than they have any notion of." Similarly, the scientist daughter-in-law in *The Silver Cord* (though not a flapper like Janet March) displaces female desire onto the male when she speaks of offering her husband "[t]he enjoyment of my body" but says nothing of her own desire.[13] The ideal woman was thus neither moralistic and sexually withholding nor mature and sexually assertive; rather, she was inexperienced and/or accepting of male initiative. In other words, she was not a full sexual subject as men were.[14]

Anxiety about the destabilizing effects of young women's involvement in sex was assuaged by images of young women who wanted to be mothers. Lindsey, for example, envisioned the "apparently oversexed and apparently reckless and pleasure-loving little flapper....There is a delicacy, and fineness, a spirituality, an unearthly sweetness about these young girls" despite the makeup and wildness. And, he proclaimed, "They are not fresh bodies offered for the pleasure of men but bodies offered to the agony and bloody sweat of motherhood. That is what it really means with most of them, whether they and we are conscious of it or not." In *Ann Vickers*, Sinclair Lewis's bold story of a young feminist, Ann, like Dell's heroines, matures by opening up to heterosexual love. But she, too, is shown as attracted to a powerful older man, extremely eager to have a child, and feeling at her best during pregnancy.[15] In these imaginings the dangers of uncontrolled female sexuality were displaced onto the safe maternal urge.

Thus, despite the new emphasis on women's sexual response, many marriage revisionists also continued to stress women's biological role in reproduction. Some asserted that the desire to bear children was, as Ernest Groves put it, women's "most fundamental urge." Dell even assimilated male sexuality to this model by citing "modern psychological science" to confirm that men also have parental instincts.[16] Thus, the stress on women's sexual nature did not lead to a vision of female sexual subjectivity and power apart from maternity.

Puritanical and Controlling Matriarchs

The mocking of sexual repression (something that continues today as a powerful weapon of ridicule and judgment against critics of sexualized culture)
blossomed during the 1920s in popular culture. The critics used these images
of repression to indicate the absence of a scientific outlook and thus a lack of
modernity in their targets. Janet March's mother, Penelope, exemplified the
modern, liberal, and accepting parent who gave her child freedom to explore
and find her own way. But delineators of flapper marriage created many more
female characters who dramatized excessive female power as stereotypically
puritanical and controlling older women. These character types, from the
laughable to the threatening, undermined the legitimacy of sexual control
and the Victorian style of respectable womanhood. Images of women were
most common, although men were sometimes depicted as antisexual.

Lindsey offered portraits of some old-fashioned men, often ministers,
who were rigid, eager to see the devil in the new youth freedom, and yet also
hypocritical, covering up sexual scandals in their own churches and lives. A
cruel Ku Klux Klan minister father who opposed his daughter's marriage, for
example, was caught by his daughter sleeping with a young girl he was trying to save. Yet, ultimately, this man appears more as a pathetic victim than
as a sinister force. As the daughter tells Lindsey, "[Father] had been awfully
strict with himself, I suppose; and he must have had it boiling around inside
of him, and the temptation was too much." The daughter's modern, youthful
wisdom provides forgiveness for the father and release from his destructive
moral authoritarianism.[17]

Puritanical women characters, however, were much more common than
men and frequently more ominous. In *Ann Vickers*, for example, Sinclair
Lewis imagines a female character who embodies the evils of repression.
Ann's assistant superintendent at the industrial home she heads is Mrs. Keast,
who "had, possibly as a result of fifty-five years complete abstinence from
tobacco, alcohol, laughter, sexual excitement, and novels, a dark bagginess
under her eyes, and twitching fingers." At first a humorous figure, Keast later
threatens Ann with blackmail. Even more reprehensible were Victorian-style
wives whose hatred of sex deprived their husbands and harmed their children.
For example, Mrs. Hill, the puritanical mother of a flapper named Millie, tells
Lindsey, " 'Sex is repulsive but necessary, and it's a sin to take pleasure in such
a thing.' " Lindsey gives her a scientific lecture explaining how her sexual
ignorance and that of her husband led to their conflicts over sex and thus
to divorce. By contrast, the enlightened modern daughter pities her mother,

exclaiming to Lindsey, " 'Poor Mother,...So damn' good—and so dumb!' " But she also blames her, saying, " 'Mother's the immoral one in our family.' "[18]

The figure of the controlling matriarch often included but went beyond the evils of sexual puritanism. This stereotype was used to attack women's power over marriage. The matriarch infantilized sons and protected daughters from premarital sex, thereby violating the freedom and privacy of young couples. In *Love without Money*, Floyd Dell labels a controlling mother figure, Mrs. Cedarbloom, "a natural-born policewoman." She tries to dominate her daughter Gretchen as they battle over Gretchen's plan to quit finishing school, and she so fears the topic of sex that when marriage is mentioned, she acts "as if there were a bad smell in the room." And in Howard's *The Silver Cord*, Mrs. Phelps's daughter-in-law calls her "a type that's very common in this country...a type of self-centered, self-pitying, son-devouring tigress, with unmentionable proclivities suppressed on the side"—implying incestuous feelings toward the son.[19] The extreme caricatures convey a powerful tone of misogyny.

These stereotypes of repressive women illustrated the declining moral authority of Victorian womanhood in the 1920s in general and the particular discomfort of several of the white male marriage revisionists with women's familial and sexual authority. The writers attacked the ways these mothers, operating within the older model of marriage as the anchor of essential social and economic alliances, used their authority to influence children's marriage choices. The mothers recognized that marriage remained vital to women's social status and survival, a reality masked by the companionate vision of marriage as a free-floating bond between two autonomous individuals. In this sense attacks on mothers who openly pursued social and economic interests through marriage were a significant ideological move that disempowered women.[20]

The Lesbian

Negative depictions of the lesbian also served as an attack on women's power among advocates of flapper marriage. The "bonds of womanhood" among women in the nineteenth century had provided emotional support and political potential for many women and helped make possible the partnerships among women known as Boston marriages. But by the 1920s such relationships increasingly connoted the potential for homosexuality, which was emerging more fully into popular cultural consciousness with the spread of Freudian thought and the growing visibility of urban homosexual subcultures.[21] In this atmosphere some marriage revisionists articulated homophobic ideas, though they did not go unopposed.

A psychoanalytic framework depicting homosexuality as a " 'fixation' of arrested development" became common and was mentioned in some of the companionate marriage writings.[22] Floyd Dell, however, was truly and negatively obsessed with homosexuality and integrated it into his theory of the difficulties facing modern marriage. Dell's relationship with poet Edna St. Vincent Millay and his attempt to "cure" her of her attraction to women were surely part of the background to his theories.[23] His ideas describe lesbianism as a threatening force that could interrupt the formation of the heterosexual couple.

Dell did not consider heterosexuality a spontaneous capacity but understood it as something to be achieved by correct development. Patriarchy, he claimed, produces a "welter of neuroticism" that keeps the young from appropriate goals—"emotional independence of their parents" and "full capacities of heterosexual love." Wrong development occurred where patriarchal practices kept males and females apart. Among the well-to-do, for example, "the unwholesome fashionable practice of sex-segregated schools brings young people into a homosexual atmosphere, which delays when it does not drastically set back their psychic growth. These homosexual 'crushes' are conventionally ignored, particularly in girls' schools," because, he contended, homosexuality had been considered less threatening to the social order than heterosexual experiment among girls. He disagreed. He suggested that the supposed sexlessness, even "spirituality," of female institutions masked the deviant nature of some women's relationships. His protagonist Gretchen in *Love without Money* is almost seduced by a teacher at the finishing school she is eager to leave; she sleeps with her boyfriend in part to prove to herself that she is not a lesbian. Dell feared the blocking of "mature" heterosexuality, replacing Havelock Ellis's more tolerant vision of sex "as a variety of responses . . . to a variety of stimuli" with a Freudian definition of sex "as a series of reactions along a path of development."[24]

Dell mentioned both men and women but revealed greater concern about women. Graduates of men's colleges, he argued, learned to exploit "socially inferior girls," but women's college graduates might fail to marry. Dell's greater anxiety about women emerged in his account of the danger of "unconscious homosexuality," which he says may appear as " 'prudishness,' " " 'unapproachable purity,' " or " 'ambition and application to work which leaves no room for interest in the other sex.' " Lindsey sketched a similar picture of questionable female types, scoffing at the "nerves" and "'peculiarities'" and possible "perversions and disorders" caused by "bottled-up sex" in celibate women who believe they have sublimated their sexual energy in "feminist careers." The extreme threat posed by such women is represented in Lewis's *Ann Vickers* when a decadent lesbian character pushes one young woman to suicide.[25] These descriptions denigrated unmarried career women, sometimes partnered with women, who were coming under scrutiny as old-fashioned, repressed, and/or possibly lesbian in the 1920s.[26]

For Dell and, less intensely, for a few others, homosexuality represented women's independence from men and as such a threat to the new marriage. But this implication did not go unchallenged. A number of feminist writers lacked these fears and valued close ties among women. Several women authors promoted the virtues of close female friendship. Bettie Esther Parham, who wrote the *New York Age*'s advice column, "The Modern Family," saw danger in women's overabsorption in the marriage relationship and abandonment of old friends. Jessie Fauset and Edward C. Williams depicted female friendships very positively in their stories.[27] Psychologist Phyllis Blanchard called for tolerance for homosexuality, whether "sublimated" or expressed, and noted hopefully that women's modern freedom allowed such women to support themselves without marriage. But it was Sanger who most pointedly appeared to be answering Dell when she challenged the new homophobia in her 1931 autobiography. She openly admitted to falling in love with other girls, as well as boys, in her school days and wrote, "I often laugh as I read the advice given by some authors on sex psychology and hygiene, especially when it refers to sex intimacies between girls in adolescence." Though she cautiously explained that the relationships were seldom sexual, she also strongly asserted that "[g]irls need each other's affection and love during adolescence as much as they need sunshine and air."[28] For all Sanger's intensity about heterosexual love, she, like several other writers, retained a feminist sense of women's need for close relationships with other women.

The figure of the lesbian, then, was one of contention among marriage revisionists. For Dell she represented a wrong turn on the path of psychosexual development and a woman far too strong and independent for his tastes. For several feminists, the lesbian required acknowledgment as something out of the ordinary but evoked neutrality or sympathy. Like the caricatures of antisexual and controlling Victorian mothers, the lesbian image made vivid the desire among some of the most prominent marriage revisionists to control women's power.

The Employed Wife

Growing female labor force participation was key to the general sense of women's equality in the 1920s, and premarital/pre-childbearing employment supported marital equality. Wives' employment carried a strong feminist charge but clashed with the prevailing male breadwinner ideology and with most women's practical entanglement in powerful social and emotional demands within the family.[29] In the social world within which marriage revisionists were writing, on the one hand, wives' employment was in fact rising. The proportion of all married women officially in the paid labor force doubled from 6 to 12 percent between 1900 and 1930, although this statistic masks the much higher proportion of employed African American wives than of white wives (33 percent of black vs. 10 percent of white wives by 1930).[30] However, for most women marriage to a breadwinner male continued to be the major if not sole source of livelihood.

A number of writers noted that the old-fashioned pattern—women's economic dependence in the household and the separate spheres that dependence underlay—posed hazards for marital equality and unity. If the man has the "privilege" and "stimulus" of his public labors, Eddy worried, but "the woman has all the handicaps, all the drudgery, all the housework, all the monotony,…then the two may unconsciously and unwittingly begin to grow apart." Childbearing brought special vulnerability. Women dread motherhood, Lindsey asserted, because under present social arrangements, "the bearing and rearing of children places the woman at the husband's mercy."[31] Cultural and social expectations of women's domestic responsibilities, combined with employment discrimination and lack of alternative child care and housekeeping for all but the well-to-do, strained the equality values of modern marriage.

Yet marriage revisionists who were most anxious about women's power and independence denied or refused to address the problem. Dell was most conservative on this issue, strongly opposing careers for women. He accepted only premarital jobs that helped women find husbands and labeled careers "infantile"; "any theoretical idealization of woman as a wage worker…is at the same time a depreciation of the importance to her of mating and maternity," and "she is being robbed of her sexual rights." Lindsey recognized the benefits of employment to wives' independence but concluded it was not "practicable or possible under our present social order." Yet he also opposed what might have been some alternative to wives' dependence—state assistance to families with children. In the end, along with Eddy and Groves, he relied on "a trained ethical sense" (and occasional judicial support orders) to keep the husband from taking advantage when the wife had no income.[32] For these writers the only support for women's equality in marriage lay in private arrangements and a male sense of obligation—truly a foundation of sand. And without children, a wife had no claim on her husband in the companionate scheme; Lindsey opposed alimony in case of divorce for childless women. This denied the reality of women's economic inequality, even without children.[33] In an American context where strong hostility to state provision for families dominated the political landscape, there was little solid basis for women's equality in marriage, and most marriage revisionists did not argue for serious change.[34] Women's dependency in marriage was still central to their vision.

Flapper marriage was supposed to serve as a model for modern relationships in which sex was a valued rather than a fearful quantity, in which dating and married couples enjoyed a secure and respected privacy and independence from families of origin, and in which the qualities of male domination and female submissiveness were gone. Yet this most popular and visible version of modern marriage was articulated in ways that reasserted the male dominance no longer acceptable in its Victorian form. Men were urged to soften their control, to be respectful and democratic, to be rational and modern, yet they still exercised more power than women. Women's sexuality was promoted but then reimagined as maternal. Women who exercised some authority—by being "puritanical" or "controlling matriarchs" who managed their children's marital choices—were attacked as vicious and unmodern. Women who chose other women sexually were targeted as deviant. And no solutions were envisioned for the economic inequality of wives. But perhaps the most striking symbol of the ongoing inequity of this version of modern marriage was the flapper herself.

In *Black Oxen*, her best-selling novel of 1923, Gertrude Atherton presents the seasoned father of a flapper explaining modern girls to a friend:

> The emancipated flapper is just plain female under her paint and outside her cocktails. More so for she's more stimulated. Where girls used to be merely romantic, she's romantic...plus sex instinct rampant.... There's no virginity of mind left, mauled as they must be and half-stewed all the time, and they're wild to get rid of the other. But they're too young yet to be promiscuous, at least those of Janet's sort, and they want to fall in love and get him quick. See the point?

The bold, brave modernity of the flapper lay precisely in her youthful exuberance, basic innocence, and continued orientation to men and marriage. It also lay in her willingness to cast aside the caution about sex and pregnancy women were trained to have in the world of the double standard. Her equality lay in being a good sport about sex, not in making the same claims for a public work life as men. Above all, the flapper was generous toward men. As Millie tells Lindsey, "[B]elieve me, when I fall in love I'm not going to be stingy."[55]

Lindsey also imagined the flapper's open and giving nature producing an undemanding wife. Perhaps the ultimate in generosity was voiced by a mature and modern wife Lindsey counsels when her husband has had an affair. She has learned that " 'love is never delivered on demand; . . . the true way to get it is to claim nothing and demand nothing, and simply to welcome it as a gift.' "[56] This particular vision of modern marriage, then, required women to reject the fact that marriage remained for most their means of livelihood and source of social status—and to step into a kind of abstract sexual equality with men without making substantial demands of those men and also without claiming the right to the kind of employment that could support independence. In flapper marriage the element of modern society that was disturbing to many—the unprecedented autonomy of young women—was drained of its frightening qualities with images of women as innocent, maternal, and still dependent on men. But, pervasive as this vision was, it did not wholly monopolize the discussion of what modern marriage should be.

African American Partnership Marriage

African American women participated in the development of companionate marriage with African American men. Here I address the shared vision that a number of black men and women articulated in relation to the new marriage norms. African Americans emphasized the general themes of sexual intimacy, greater freedom and privacy for the couple, and women's equality, yet their conceptions were modified by the needs and context of African American life. Due to the racist sexualization they faced, the need for group cohesion, the claims for equal citizenship rights, and economic marginality, this version of modern marriage put less emphasis on sex and privacy and incorporated wives' paid work. Many of these features are indicated in Edward Christopher Williams's story "The Letters of Davy Carr."

"The Letters of Davy Carr"

"The Letters of Davy Carr" was published anonymously as a serialized romance between January 1925 and June 1926 in the *Messenger*, which had shifted from socialist and race politics to a middle-class cultural focus by the mid-1920s. The story, set in Washington, D.C., centers on the youngest daughter of the middle-class Rhodes family. Caroline Rhodes, a grade-school teacher and a dark and lively beauty with "all the best and worst points of the modern flapper," alternately fascinates and horrifies the priggish narrator, Davy Carr.[37] Davy is a well-educated single man, native of a "little provincial Southern city," sojourning in Washington, D.C., in 1922 to do research for a book on the slave trade. While boarding with the Rhodes family, Davy writes letters to his war buddy back in New York describing "colored society" in the nation's capital.[38] With the charming Caroline always as a comparison, he catalogues African American female types. He describes the "dicty" upper-class women he meets in the prosperous Anacostia neighborhood, including a "vamp" and women who flirt with one another's husbands. Then he inventories a variety of young middle-class women, from the stylish to the frumpy to the "hard and sophisticated."[39]

The plot picks up when, off on a date in Baltimore, Caroline is abducted by her sleazy gambler escort and has to be rescued by Davy from possible rape. Davy becomes irritable with Caroline's flirtatious independence and procession of boyfriends but remains deluded about the reasons for his mood until the end, when, about to leave Washington, he realizes he is in love with her. They have it out, make up, and kiss. Marriage is clearly in the offing. Thus the story both asserts the basic goodness and marriageability of the flapper, lightly mocking provincial moralism, and at the same time confirms traditional dicta of feminine decorum and the need for masculine protection.

The ideal black husband in these sources was a man of professional achievement and culture who was respectful of women, proud, honest, and courageous in facing the burdens of race prejudice, and dedicated to the race. He was not characterized by strong sexual desire as in the Dell novels. The race man Davy Carr, researcher of the slave trade and supporter of the Dyer Anti-Lynching Bill in Congress, though perhaps somewhat old-fashioned in his manners, represents this kind of man and is, therefore, the proper partner for Caroline. A more modern example is the sensitive Dr. Denleigh in Fauset's novel *The Chinaberry Tree*. A supporter of birth control who practices among poor immigrants, he also represents the voice of science and reason as he gently entices Laurentine Strange from the morass of Victorian sexual shame over her illegitimacy and white father and helps her to blossom in the new relationship with him. Upright and honorable men like this are contrasted with the figure of the male "sport," who aggressively exploits women and does not do real work. One such character is Morris H. Jeffreys in the "Davy Carr" story, the handsome gambler, too well dressed for proper masculinity, who abducts Caroline.[40] The exemplary men have a masculine authority and heterosexual credentials, but their manliness stems from moral integrity more than from sexual force, exhibiting a restraint highly practical in the context of white racist stereotypes of black men.

Protagonist Caroline Rhodes resembles the Lindsey flappers. She is "no conventional doll-baby" but energetic, vibrant, and modern; she will make her own courtship decisions, despite the concerns of her parents.[41] Like Lindsey's Millie, Caroline is free in her manners. Fussed at by her "Victorian" mother and elder sister, Caroline smokes and constantly visits Carr's room to chat. He describes how she sat in his room, "swinging her silk-clad legs with the abandon of a small boy, and regaled [him] in terms piquant and interesting, if a trifle startling at times, with her very modern views of the woman question, fellows, and marriage.... [I]t was decidedly refreshing, but I am not sure that it was not more shocking than anything else."[42] Yet both danger and modesty ultimately restrain her. Caroline "has a mind of her own, originality, and courage," as well as true inner beauty that far outshines the artificial "product of the beauty culturist's art," but she learns from the near-rape episode the lesson that young women cannot be too free. Her own instincts also pull her back: when she realizes she has fallen in love, she reins in her modern feminine assertiveness and modestly stops visiting Carr's room. She reprimands him for a kiss he imposes on her because she does "not want to seem to be seeking" him and does not want to be seen as "that kind of a girl."[43] Men and women remain different and subject to different rules, and Carr notes—with some irony—that "in spite of the suffragettes" he is unsure about female equality because women are so different from men.[44] Carr's self-mocking tone does not undermine the message of moral and social caution that pervades the story: safety and propriety require preserving female modesty and male initiative.

In these ways Caroline is similar to the white flapper image. She differs in that she uncontroversially pursues a career. At the story's opening, she is an elementary teacher, taking night courses at Howard University to obtain certification as a secondary school teacher and thus a higher salary. She tells Davy that one cannot marry without a fat paycheck. With some old-fashioned male regret, he wonders, "Has it come to that?"[45] Yet Caroline's teaching and further education are part of a culture of middle-class black achievement—her more serious older sister is a Wellesley graduate. It is also a contribution to the wider community as well as to her future marriage. Education and paid work for these women are not a distraction from marriage but an important contribution to it.

The "Davy Carr" story points toward some of the distinctive features of African American companionate marriage. Black marriage revisionists promoted the importance of a good sexual relationship in marriage but did so in a more understated way than several prominent white writers. They advocated independence and privacy for the married couple yet continued to envision marriage as part of a wider African American community and its struggle for race advancement. In addition, their strong opposition to the role of marriage law in shaping segregation produced greater support for the freedom of interracial couples to marry than white marriage revisionists showed. Finally, their support for spousal equality rested on a firmer foundation than that of many whites due to economic realities requiring a higher level of employment for black wives.

African American Conservatism about Sex

Claims for sex, supported by science and rejection of a "puritanical" past, were promoted in some form by both African American and white marriage revisionists, but there were some broad racial differences as well. African Americans took a relatively more conservative position on sexual expression. The background of this tendency lay in the postemancipation history that made sexual respectability so central to black status due to the sexualized racism directed against both black men and women. Middle-class African Americans were keenly aware of this situation and often felt anxious if sex were treated too casually.[46] In "Davy Carr" a friend of Davy's strongly voices the older sensibility:

> The "flappers" of this age seem to know far more than their mothers do, and they read books which their grandmothers would have burned, and go to plays which—thirty years ago—would have been debarred from any stage. But in this case if the truth has made them free, it has not made them clean. There is only this difference noticeable to me—they are far coarser than the generations which have gone before. Personally, I cannot see that this is a gain.

While Williams presents an ironic view of the foibles of the old-fashioned, his preference seems finally to fall on the side of sexual restraint.[47]

White sex liberals in the 1920s sometimes attempted to invert traditional racist scorn for supposed black immorality by arguing that such freedom from "Puritanical" rules "might contribute a welcome leaven to the conventionality of current sex *mores*."[48] Frazier definitively rejected such thinking: slavery's brutal heritage of "250 years of promiscuous sex relations" made restraint and order a priority. "While we appreciate the position of those who feel that because the Negro is not overburdened with an outworn tradition he might contribute to a more rational attitude towards sex relations," Frazier wrote, "at the present time the normal functioning of the family is necessary in order to save us from many of our problems." Frazier was an atheist who could be caustic about churches, and, of course, he used modern social scientific language, but his sense of caution about sexual comportment was not very different from that of more conventional black leaders like Mary Church Terrell, the club woman who had worked to establish recreation centers for black troops as part of the social hygiene efforts during World War I.[49] Likewise, DuBois wrote of the need "to steer between the Scylla of prudery and the Charybdis of unbounded license," to keep the freedom of Harlem from leading to "crime, gambling, sexual depravity, waste, luxury."[50] He also reacted against the exoticization of black life in some Harlem Renaissance fiction, as in McKay's *Home to Harlem*.[51] Thus, while black marriage revisionists deployed the myth of Victorian repression, their thinking also continued to echo the politics of respectability through which African Americans managed racism.[52]

Some white writers on marriage made expressive sexuality much more fundamental to their critique and their vision. Lindsey's accounts of youthful difficulties, for example, often made sexual repression seem like the cause of every difficulty. Likewise, though she had publicly abandoned support for free love by the 1920s, Sanger continued to stress the importance of sexuality in extremely romantic rhetoric.[53] Compared with these two, African American writers seem moderate.

Nevertheless, it is important not to exaggerate the differences. Though Lindsey and Sanger had greater public visibility, not all white proponents of companionate marriage made such overblown claims about honest and freer sex as the key to human happiness. Ernest R. Groves, like Frazier, was deeply concerned about sex as a disruptive force. He favored birth control when used to help a couple financially, for example, but worried about the separation of sex and love: "[W]ith the coming of the idea of contraception an impetus is given to those who seek sex as an experience by itself."[54] African American writers were similarly cautious, avoiding the dramatic language of Lindsey and Sanger but having much in common with other white writers.

Puritanical and Controlling Women

A few African American images can be found comparable to those of anti-sexual and controlling women in the flapper marriage sources, but they carry a different charge. Jessie Fauset portrayed old-maidish types, but they were more comic than threatening. In *Plum Bun*, for example, Miss Hettie Daniels, an elderly housekeeper, is mocked for her "great fetish" of "sexual morality,"

Fig. 7 Jessie Fauset

Portrait of Jessie Fauset, n.d. Known as the midwife of the Harlem Renaissance, Fauset assisted other writers through her position as literary editor of the NAACP's *Crisis* from 1919 to 1926, in addition to producing her own novels. A 1905 graduate of Cornell University, she shows pride in her educational accomplishments by wearing her Phi Beta Kappa key. Courtesy of Photographs and Prints Division, Schomburg Center for Research in Black Culture, The New York Public Library, Astor, Lenox and Tilden Foundations.

for having "held out" against men and "kept [her] pearl of great price untarnished." Women like this have let the all-important experience of love and marriage pass them by.[55]

Jessie Fauset does create one controlling and evil matriarch figure, but her emphasis is on race betrayal more than female power in her depiction of the interfering mother Olivia Cary in *Comedy: American Style*. Olivia resembles the mothers in Lindsey's, Howard's, and Dell's writings; she is cold and antisexual and married her husband only because of his light color. Her husband's mother had told him that a good woman was always cold, and Olivia "was cold enough, freezing, in fact! She did not run after him. She gave him no inkling of any liking." Yet she married him because he could father children who would be able to pass for white. Olivia is also extremely manipulative, and Fauset condemns Olivia's management of her daughter Teresa, which ends a promising romance with a visibly black man and produces a very unhappy marriage to a penny-pinching, racist Frenchman.[56]

But more important than Olivia's exercise of maternal control are the traitorous values that guide her—the desire to be white and to abandon the race. She seizes Teresa from her dark-skinned fiancé, Henry Bates, proclaiming she would " 'rather see her dead' " than married to a visibly colored man and thus exposed to the "insult" and "sense of inferiority" that African Americans had to face. Henry's honesty, courage, and loyalty to the race represent the racial virtue that Olivia conspicuously lacks. Most damning of all, Olivia sees her dark younger son, Oliver, as the " 'mill-stone around our necks' " that has kept the whole family from passing for white. Her elder son, Christopher, denies her the name of mother when he discovers that she has been inducing Oliver to act as a butler when she entertains white club women. Later, when Oliver discovers the full truth of his mother's dislike, he commits suicide.[57]

Certainly, the deployment of Olivia's character as a figure of evil who lacks real motherly love matches those in *The Silver Cord*, *Companionate Marriage*, and Dell's novels, but the emphasis is on race betrayal more than on female management of an archaic marriage system that crushes individual freedom. Olivia does crush the freedom of Teresa and Henry, but their freedom signifies less about their rights as independent persons than about their loyalty to the black community—and her lack of it. Fauset's use of the controlling matriarch figure thus highlights the more communal orientation of African American marriage thought.

African American Marriage and Community

Although African Americans bowed to the reality of greater youth freedom from parental direction, on the whole they voiced a less radically individualist notion of the couple and in many ways sustained the older conception of marriage as a broad social and economic partnership. Several factors encouraged this. In general, the deprivation of public status and roles in the larger society and political system made even the private households of African American communities assume more "public" functions than was true for most white families in this period. For example, the denial of public accommodations, as in hotels and restaurants, meant that a network of elite black families, often related by blood and marriage, served a vital community function by hosting leaders and members of black organizations when they traveled across the nation.[58] In addition, those who aspired to be part of the new middle class of this period sometimes accomplished it by marrying into the old black elite, further sustaining the social structural functions of marriage for these groups. And economic need led to cooperation as well: Fauset's *Comedy* favorably depicts two generations of the Blanchard family moving in together to cope with the economic disaster of the Great Depression.[59]

Several writers asserted the broad social and political importance of marriage. DuBois wrote that when men and women compromise and make sacrifices, marriage can be "the center of real resurrection and remaking of the world." In the *Crisis*, he described his own daughter Yolande's marriage in 1928 as redolent of wider social significance, not just the joining of two individuals but "the symbolic march of young and black America," conveying a "sense of new power...a new race; a new thought; a new thing rejoicing in a ceremony as old as the world."[60] His new son-in-law, the brilliant and popular young poet Countee Cullen, was homosexual, something widely suspected in fashionable Harlem circles and very likely known to DuBois. But marriage for DuBois was something as much socially as personally meaningful; he was immensely proud that his daughter was marrying one of the rising stars of Harlem's cultural renaissance. As the marriage quickly soured and he tried to save it, DuBois privately fell back on an older view: sex was not "'the main thing about marriage,'" he wrote to Cullen.[61] DuBois's public account of the wedding echoed the traditional emphasis on the importance of regularized marriage as part of race advancement, even as he celebrated the rising power of African Americans in the 1920s.[62] Fauset, too, linked marriage and social involvement, describing the most admirable marriages as those centered not on selfish consumerism or an exclusive domesticity but on work and service beyond the married couple. For example, in *The Chinaberry Tree*, Asshur Lane's idealism and Tuskegee training mark him, rather than the materialistic Malory Forten, as the appropriate partner for Melissa. In *Comedy: American Style*, Christopher Cary, son of Olivia, the cruel mother obsessed with whiteness, asks dressmaker Phebe Grant to marry him. His proposal includes asking her help with his "life's work" of restoring his father, who has been devastated by the suicide of his other son. Phebe agrees: "I'll marry you. I'll help you." She thus enters the marriage in a partnership intended to support the extended family. Fauset understood marriage neither as "adventure in romance [n]or as a means to an end."[63] It was not to be focused exclusively inward, on the heterosexual bond, but rather to serve as the central relationship in which partners could share work that was linked to race advancement or the larger community.

This difference between whites and blacks, however, should also not be exaggerated. Eddy also warned against too great isolation of the couple—an "introverted absorption in each other." And Groves, more conservatively than Lindsey or Dell, wanted more community oversight of courting couples. He also continued to see marriage and family as the basis of social order—the inspiration for men "to achieve great things in the world of business" and the locus of child rearing, which he understood as a social duty.[64] But overall, the whites' conceptualizations were more privatized and personal in focus, with less attention to the connectedness of marriage with a wider social world. And, viewed in the aggregate, black thinkers were more likely to de-emphasize individualist claims and rationales for reform. Thus, as in their cautious approaches to sexuality, African Americans emphasized social meanings, connections, and responsibilities more than private relationships or pleasure.

Interracial and Interethnic Marriage

However, in one area—the question of marriage across racial lines—African Americans supported the freedom of the individual couple from social and legal regulation much more strongly than did white marriage revisionists. The very social freedom of youth that companionate marriage advocates accepted and praised did, of course, make possible greater social mixing in the 1920s, though black-white mingling on a level of equality and potential marriage remained extremely rare, due both to social harassment and to law. Thirty of forty-eight states prohibited black-white marriage in 1919 (and a number also banned Asians, Native Americans, and/or Mexicans from marrying whites).[65] Although not positively advocating intermarriage (as black sex radicals did),

African American marriage revisionists always reserved the right of individuals to make such choices. While some white marriage revisionists accepted interethnic (European) and interreligious marriages, on the race issue their nascent liberalism faded.

Among whites, Ben Lindsey and Rachelle Yarros were the most liberal on racial, ethnic, and religious difference. Yarros, who was Jewish, voiced a powerful criticism of eugenics, which opposed interracial or interethnic marriages, for its racial bias. Quoting an academic authority, she associated eugenics with "'ancestor worship, anti-Semitism, color prejudice, anti-feminism, snobbery.'"[66] Lindsey does mention a black-white marriage on the periphery of one of his stories and does so without comment. More directly, he defends a Protestant-Jewish marriage of two young people opposed by the interfering Protestant (and Klan) father. He asserts that several years later the marriage has turned out well.[67]

Others were more cautious. Sherwood Eddy and Ernest Groves both warned explicitly against allying with people of different backgrounds on the grounds of potential instability. Groves opposed "trial marriage" precisely because the lack of "serious commitment" could lead young people to ignore "differences of race, class, religion, or taste." Eddy addressed intermarriage directly, arguing that marriage was less "likely to be happy, and therefore successful," when Catholic and Protestant, believer and nonbeliever, or "a member of the white and a member of the coloured race" were joined. His concern for making marriages work led him to hesitate before such challenges. He mentioned without naming "one of the most radical Negro leaders in America" (probably DuBois) as denying interest in intermarriage out of concern about harassment by white society. Eddy continues, "Many inter-racial marriages, that personally might have proved happy, have been rendered bitter and unhappy by the treatment the two parties or their children have received. It is to be hoped that some day we may rise above our racial prejudice in these matters, but at present this is an unpleasant and hard reality that must be faced."[68]

The "unpleasant and hard reality" of racism was everywhere on the rise in the early part of the century, and conservatives actively invoked it on the issue of interracial relationships. In a backlash against potential mixing, white racists especially targeted both the social freedom of young white women and the associated possibility of those women pursuing sexual relationships with black men, as when Virginia enacted a "racial integrity" law in 1924 that targeted white women who bore mixed-race children.[69] In the northern states where intermarriage was legal, informal harassment against such relationships sharpened, and legislators made many (though unsuccessful) attempts to pass laws against it in this period. Such an attempt was made in New York State in the aftermath of a case of marriage between a white man and a mixed-race woman. In 1924 the young scion of a wealthy New York family, Leonard Rhinelander, unbeknownst to his family, married a mixed-race, working-class woman, Alice Jones. Horrified at the news, his father enticed him away and then compelled him to initiate an annulment suit. The suit failed, but in 1926 a bill to ban black-white marriages was brought before the legislature (and failed). The reaction of Rhinelander's family and of many whites, however, showed the continued unthinkability of legal intermarriage for most whites (as well as of unmarried black male–white female relations).[70]

Far more common than marriage, which was so widely illegal as well as socially condemned, was the long tradition of powerful white men pursuing sexual liaisons with women of color. White conservatives never addressed this issue, but African Americans did. The white Llewellyn Nash in Fauset's *Comedy: American Style* was the fictional representative of a figure long condemned by African Americans. Attentive and interested in marriage until Phebe reveals she is "colored," Nash then seeks her as a mistress. The upright and self-sufficient Phebe refuses.[71]

African Americans criticized this kind of racism intensely, though many were pragmatic about the difficulties of interracial marriage or uninterested in it altogether. One letter to the editor of the *Chicago Defender*, a black weekly, objected to so much front-page coverage of the Rhinelander case. "Amalgamation does not help the Race, for we don't want to join the other race, but surpass them and hold our own. . . . So place these unloyal incidents on the back page."[72] DuBois, in an article from 1920 that Eddy may have been referring to, labeled intermarriage inexpedient because it involved "too great a strain" and because most blacks wish "to build a great black race tradition." However, he maintained "the moral and legal right of individuals" to marry across the line if they wish.[73] Frazier was also deeply concerned about producing stable marriages but as early as 1925 took a strong stand for the right of intermarriage. Intermarriage was the most provocative aspect of "social equality," as it was known, which meant mingling in arenas of personal association such as eating, socializing, or marrying. He argued that "class restrictions [i.e., applied to a legally defined class such as a racial group] upon marriage are a denial of the democratic principle." He also opposed building an "isolated and self-sufficient Negro culture," arguing that social mingling would have a more democratizing and assimilating effect.[74] Most powerfully, Frazier used science in the form of Freudianism to compare southern white racist thinking, with its fanaticism about intermarriage, to the thought patterns of the insane. He posited a "Negro-complex" as the source of dissociated and overly emotional thinking, whereby a white woman's respectful address of a black man would lead other whites to ask her "whether she would want a Negro to marry her sister" (a seeming displacement of the more obvious implication that the woman herself might be willing to marry a black man).[75] Most simply, following the logic of companionate marriage ideology, Fauset voices through *Plum Bun*'s heroine Angela the critique that " '[l]ove ... is supposed to be the greatest thing in the world but look how we smother and confine it. Jews mustn't marry Catholics; white people mustn't marry coloured—'." Rudolph Fisher addresses the same theme in a 1925 short story where racism also keeps a very light-skinned black woman and a darker man apart because she is constantly mistaken for white.[76]

And among African Americans support for intermarriage was not just the province of a few intellectuals or leaders. It was discussed in major black newspapers such as the *Pittsburgh Courier* and the *New York Age*. Besides following the introduction of antimiscegenation legislation in Congress and the states, the papers published many stories of individuals who had married across the color line (or tried to). They tended, like Fauset's character, to advance love as the legitimizing factor. The *New York Age* featured prominently a series in 1924 that condemned a Jewish man for abandoning his black common-law wife of twenty years, who was suing him for $500 per month alimony and to defend her good name. A headline proclaimed that she had had a "Good, Moral Life, Esteem and Good Will of Neighbors." "Mamma Lizzie Found Life's Romance When She Met 'Papa Fat,'" read another headline.[77] Similarly, the *Courier* ran a story in 1929 called "Taking the 'Color Question' Out of Marriage!" that quoted whites saying, " 'I love him' " and " 'I have a right to marry whom I please' " as they married African Americans, Chinese, and Asian Indians. The subtitle ran, "The Hue and Cry of Nordics over Recent Interracial Marriages Have Proved That Skins May Differ 'But Affections Dwell in Black and White the Same.' "[78] While it was certainly true that intermarriage in practice was not a burning issue for most, the question of possessing the right to it touched a resonant chord with the black public.

Marriage across social boundaries challenged the social and legal functions of marriage in reproducing class, racial, and ethnic groups and hierarchies.[79] The hesitation of most white companionate marriage thinkers to encourage such crossing reveals the limits of their individualism about marriage choice and their implicit acceptance of the regulatory role of marriage in the prevailing racial order. Lindsey's positive account of a Protestant-Jewish marriage may illustrate historian Matthew Frye Jacobson's argument about the increasing amalgamation in this period of the nineteenth-century hierarchy of European immigrant groups into a single "Caucasian race" and the simultaneous heightening of the black-white polarity in U.S. racial thinking after 1920.[80] White marriage revisionists were unwilling to contest the black-white boundary. But opposition to racism and the clear recognition that antimiscegenation laws stigmatized African Americans led the latter to support the freedom of individuals to marry as they chose.

———

Promoting freedom and privacy for the couple valorized autonomy both for individual lovers and then for the couple vis-à-vis the larger social order. In some ways this vision reflected shifting social realities, as the expansion of a capitalist industrial economy in the nineteenth century had weakened the grip of patriarchal family relations through geographic mobility and individual wage labor for women as well as men. In the more cosmopolitan urban America of the 1920s, greater youth freedom in courtship meant a broadening of marriage choice in terms of European ethnicities and class, moving beyond a rigid Anglo-American middle-class endogamy. But whites' rhetoric of freedom and rejection of marriage as social regulation revealed its limits in their caution about crossing racial boundaries. African American marriage revisionists, in contrast, always thoroughly rejected the racist interference of antimiscegenation law.

Women's Equality and the Employed African American Wife

Compared with proponents of flapper marriage, African American marriage revisionists, women and men, seemed somewhat less anxious about women's place. As "Davy Carr" shows, a traditional emphasis on male primacy in gender relations persisted. However, women's equality had a stronger basis in African American marriage due to the economic struggles that frequently made wives' employment crucial, even in the middle class. This reality leavened the impact of the dominant culture's idealization of the domestic wife and underlay more consistent support for wives' employment among African Americans, though rationalized by economic need more than by gender equality per se. It also led to greater domestic sharing, according to the memories of black professional women of this era.[81]

The case of E. Franklin Frazier demonstrates the double position of African American thinkers, as participants in both the dominant white and the

African American cultures. As is well known, in his major work, *The Negro Family in the United States* (1939), Frazier expressed considerable concern about black single mothers in the urban working class, and he preferred, among two-parent families, those where the wife held little or no employment. He was eager to support male breadwinners in the working class, where he argued that race progress was greatest when black men got manufacturing jobs, for then "the authority of the father in the family has been strengthened," and the wife has lost some of hers. In this way, black working-class "ideals and patterns of family life [could] approximate those of the great body of industrial workers." Additionally, Frazier's biographer reports that it was extremely important to Frazier that his own wife need never take a job.[82]

Yet, aside from his own wife, Frazier offered more mixed views about middle-class women. Concerned not only with the stability of black marriages but also with the economic fragility of the middle class, he worried about dependent wives who nagged their husbands for money. Some middle-class wives, he claimed, followed standards of consumption set by whites and pushed their husbands into illicit gambling as a source of cash. Perhaps for this reason he seemed more comfortable with the employed middle-class wife than with the wage-earning wives among the poor urban migrants. He criticized both "matriarchal" and "patriarchal" family forms as unmodern and implicitly suggested that, for the "Brown Middle Class" at least, the "democracy" of the dual-career couple was a better model. Perhaps because the working class, as a large proportion of the total black population, concerned whites more and was especially vulnerable as the target of racist social policy, Frazier felt a greater need to encourage conformity to the dominant ideal of marriage among them. Frazier's perspective on the working class seems not unlike that of the white female social welfare reformers of the early twentieth century. Although those reformers were often employed, unmarried, childless, and/or partnered with women, they applied the standard of the male breadwinner–dependent wife family to the poor women whom they intended to assist, just as Frazier did to the black working class.[83] But regardless of Frazier's wishes, the economic need for many working-class and middle-class black wives to hold jobs created a different context for the discussion among African Americans.

In general, employed wives appear more often and more uncontroversially in African American marriage sources. DuBois, acknowledging black women's rates of employment, urged acceptance of their "economic freedom." "We cannot imprison women again in a home or require them all . . . to be nurses and housekeepers." And in Fauset's works, the female protagonists

do devote themselves to husbands—to nurture and restore black men struggling in a racist world—but their earning capacities are part of how they
accomplish that task. Thus, in *Comedy*, when Christopher Cary discovers his
depressed father has lost most of the family money, fiancée Phebe Grant
invites him and his family to move into her home with her and her mother,
where her home ownership as well as her earnings at a dress shop could help
sustain them.[84]

Positive portrayals of the employed wife appeared not only in sophisticated fiction and sociology but also in more popularly oriented newspaper
features. Some noted how the employed wife benefited the black family.
New York Age columnist Parham, for example, urged professional women to
marry and keep their work, envisioning these "accomplished Negro women"
as providing their race with "the things it needs for a stabilized future—
cultured refined homes and families that only superior training can guarantee."[85] George Schuyler's well-known column, which ran in the *Pittsburgh
Courier* from 1924 to 1966, occasionally included material on marriage and
supported wives' employment. On 30 November 1929, he included several
arguments—that patriarchy was outmoded, that a wife needed to help out
economically, and that her work also made a better marriage because "she is
more of a real partner than ever before, which is perfectly proper." No doubt
affected by the deepening Depression, the *Courier* editorialized in 1930 that
the working wife should be accepted. Instead of being "helpless, perfumed,
and patronized," the modern working wife, the editor wrote, was an "intelligent, informed, energetic partner in the task of supporting the home." White
male marriage revisionists were seldom this positive. In this sense, as Frazier
himself pointed out in 1960, black women's independence " 'has provided
generally a pattern of equalitarian relationships between men and women
for Americans.' "[86]

African Americans, then, were full participants in the creation of
modern marriage, stressing sexual intimacy, freedom and privacy for the
couple, and women's equality. They stood apart from proponents of flapper
marriage, however, in a less flamboyant approach to sex, a greater concern
for race loyalty and community connection for the married couple, and a
greater acceptance of wives' employment. Most important, they sharply
attacked a major form of social interference with marital freedom—antimiscegenation laws—and they were not obsessed with reshaping and
reclaiming a domestic and maternal role for wives as were proponents of
flapper marriage. African Americans pioneered a pragmatic egalitarianism—partnership marriage.

Feminist Marriage

In addition to different emphases by white supporters of flapper marriage and African American thinkers, a few writers more markedly challenged existing conceptions of male-female sexual difference and pushed equality demands further. Strong feminist claims for women's right to sexual fulfillment differed from briefs for accepting young women's premarital experimentation. Feminist demands for wives' employment separated those committed to securing materially based equality for women from those who primarily sought to eradicate inegalitarian attitudes or who accepted wives' wage earning for family survival. Rachelle Yarros, Jessie Fauset, Bettie Parham, and, more ambivalently, Sidney Howard, Sinclair Lewis, Ira Wile and Mary Winn, and Ernest Groves delineated men and women who could populate feminist marriage—where equality in both sex and work was imagined. These were minority images that could not be widely heard or aspired to at the time, but they show how a feminist perspective found a small niche within companionate marriage discourse. Jessie Fauset's *Plum Bun* (1928) provides a fictional model of the feminist middle-class romance.

Plum Bun

Fauset's 1928 novel is a bildungsroman that takes a light-skinned protagonist, Angela Murray, through tests of character until she accepts her race and her talents and abandons the unworthy search for wealth and ease through passing for white. Artistically talented, Angela comes from a modest but respectable black family in Philadelphia but longs for more and hates the "curse" of her race that always weighs on her.[87] After her parents die, she moves to New York and passes for white, pleased with "this sense of owning the world" that came from being "free, white and twenty-one."[88] She begins to plan to marry a white man, as the route to social freedom and power. She attends an art class, where she meets bohemian whites and a man named Anthony Cross, who is attracted to her and later reveals himself to be black. At a Greenwich Village party she meets a wealthy white man, Roger Fielding, who pursues her and later persuades her to have an affair, though she had been expecting a marriage proposal. Gradually she becomes disillusioned with her situation, realizing she is not really in love. Unable to improve the relationship or move it toward marriage, she leaves and throws herself into her art work and starts to see Anthony again. After some slightly contrived difficulties and misunderstandings—Anthony thought she was white and had begun a relationship with Angela's estranged, nonpassing sister, Virginia—Angela wins a fellowship to study painting in Paris and ultimately is reunited with Anthony there.

Roger and Anthony represent opposed models of manhood as well as race. The white Roger is wealthy and knows how to flatter Angela and manipulate free love ideas to entice her to sleep with him. Pressing her to become his mistress in a "love-nest," he argues that " 'the happiest couples in the world are those who love without visible bonds.' "[89] Most important, he is not independent and will not marry without his wealthy father's approval—he is " 'not entirely [his] own master.' "[90] Roger is thus sexually exploitative and also dependent. By contrast, Anthony Cross exemplifies the ideal man. A talented artist, he is serious, poor, and not materialistic: "[He] would seek for the expression of truth and of himself even at the cost of the trimmings of life."[91] He falls in love with Angela but, believing she is white, breaks off their relationship after admitting his race to her. She delays her own similar admission. He explains that he has passively allowed others to believe he is white but that ultimately he has always been honest: " 'I have never denied my colour; I have always taken up with coloured causes.' " Bitter and wild earlier in his life, out of grief over his father's lynching, he had later concluded " 'that for my father's sake I would try to make something of myself.' " This integrity and loyalty to the race lead him to sacrifice (as he supposes) his love for her. Angela thinks, "Here was honour, here was a man!" Anthony's manhood is independent and honorable, even if he is poor; it is not based on money or on exploiting women as Roger's is.[92]

Angela develops into a modern woman in terms of both sex and work. She begins with the plan to use her sexuality to capture a rich white man and marry him, but she learns the perils of this as well as turning against it ethically. A white woman friend voices a powerful critique of the double standard and women's difficult balancing act when trying to use sex in this way: it is " 'the hardest game in the world for a woman.... If we don't give enough we lose them. If we give too much we lose ourselves. Oh, Angéle, God doesn't like women.' "[93] Angela does indeed step over the line by sleeping with Roger. Here Fauset shows her in a more traditional style, as overcome by her almost maternal feelings. Wet from a rainstorm, "[he] looked so like a little boy.... All her strength left her; she could not even struggle, could not speak. He swept her up in his arms."[94] But Angela moves beyond this denial of her own rational choice. After leaving Roger, she recognizes the "perfectly pagan" (i.e., actively sexual) desire that led her into the affair. She has extricated herself competently and is not morally ruined by the action; she has just made a mistake. When he returns, offering marriage, she brusquely says, " 'Go away, Roger. I don't want to be bothered with you!' "[95]

Angela becomes mature also through entering fully into her work life as an artist. She moves from seeing her artistic gift as an "adjunct" to a life of "pleasure" and "freedom" to taking her painting seriously and working hard enough to win a fellowship to study in Paris; "her talent...had now become the greatest, most real force in her life."[96] Her integrity is complete when she comes out as black to support a visibly black fellowship winner who, after winning, has been then denied affordable passage to Paris due to race prejudice.[97] Having abandoned her morally questionable early trajectory, she is rewarded—after achieving this independence and self-respect—by being reconnected to her almost-lost lover, Anthony.

Plum Bun exemplifies a feminist variant of the modern romantic journey toward marriage. Angela begins as a traditional woman who seeks to make her way in the world only through a man, using her wiles and even slighting the need for love. She realizes her mistake, learning to abandon material desires for the sake of love and honesty, even if it requires sacrifice. She accepts her sexual desires and takes responsibility for them. And she accepts and develops her own talent and finds a life work. This is a vision of feminist marriage.

Feminist Sexual Subjects

In contrast to the lively yet still demure young women of flapper marriage, feminist figures claimed more sexually. The widespread acknowledgment of women's sexual desire in this period did not mean that women were actually understood to "possess" their own sexuality, and certainly there were limits to what was imagined by these feminists who believed in marriage.[98] They were not sex radicals. They wanted sex still to be based on love and opposed passion that threatened marriage. In *Plum Bun*, Angela regrets the "hot-headed wilfulness of youth" that had led her "to throw aside the fundamental laws of civilization for passion" with Roger. And Yarros argued that monogamy and the restraint of some passions were good things, not just "the arbitrary dictates of priest or politician."[99] Yet within these limits feminist writers did imagine women with a sexual self-possession that differed from the mere vivacity of flappers. Feminist writers also wrote about male figures who respected women; they strenuously critiqued the double standard and imagined women with active desire taking sexual initiative; and they showed female characters making rational sexual choices that considered their own interests.

To match strong modern feminists, these writers depicted egalitarian men who were sensitive to women's needs and respectful of their autonomy. Yarros, for example, described with approval the many "intelligent young men" who had come to see her to learn about how to give their brides sexual pleasure. Such men were rightfully avoiding the Victorian brutality that feminist and free love reformers had documented in the late nineteenth century.[100] Fauset creates a laudable husband in Christopher Cary. More like a traditional female figure, he stresses his loyalty to his wife, Phebe, above all. While she is in New York, being tempted to escape her burdens in an affair with an old flame, he, unaware of her situation, worries about her absence but remembers "how sweet and true and utterly decent" she is.[101] His faithfulness seems to ensure hers. These ideal men's sexual drive is less prominent than their consideration of women, by comparison to the men imagined by the creators of flapper marriage.

In creating female characters, feminist writers enunciated powerful critiques of the double standard and the assumption that only men have, or should have, sexual agency. In *The Chinaberry Tree*, the inhibited Laurentine feels her desire for a kiss but is too afraid to express it; she calls herself a "fraidy-cat," but the authorial voice blames men: Laurentine embodied "all those virtues and restraints which colored men so arrogantly demand in the women they make their wives." Yarros asserts the anger of the "modern sophisticated young girl or woman" at the assumptions of some sex advice manuals that the woman "is an instrument to be tuned and played upon by the artist man."[102]

Much more clearly than supporters of flapper marriage, feminist writers imagined that women's sexual agency constituted more than responding to men and more than being mothers. Sanger's radical romanticism persisted even in the neutralized prescriptions of *Happiness in Marriage*. She echoed the tone of her radical years when she proclaimed the joys of sex and that both "[m]en and women have been endowed with this dynamic energy which we name passion." Yarros likewise scorned repressive views such as those of a rabbi who saw women as "instruments of men's pleasure" and who believed it sinful for women to show desire. The modern women, she said, "is not ashamed of passion, and is not averse from taking the initiative in sex matters" and claims a "normal," "legitimate and even noble joy in sex relations."[103] Fauset also depicts female characters attracted to male bodies and describes such feeling in one woman as "a raging fire" within her.[104] These writers definitely wished to claim a specifically sexual, not only reproductive, nature for women.

An extension of women's active desire and initiative was their pursuit of desire in a rational and self-interested way. They are not overcome with shame or desire or overwhelmed by male power when faced with the possibility of sexual interaction. In *Ann Vickers*, for example, Ann rejects a seduction attempt by one of her college professors. He charges her with not wanting to be a "real woman," with "timidity," and with being "[s]hocked." But she replies, "I'm not shocked at all!...I'd have a lover, if I wanted him enough."[105] Not only are women capable of making rational sexual choices, but they also recognize the complexity of the sexual arena and are justified in acting self-interestedly. Fauset, for example, recognized that antipuritanism could be a ploy, not a straightforward value, when Roger mocks Angela for resisting a kiss—he just wants to gain sexual access.[106] She shows the female "good sport," who dropped such hesitance and was sexually open and generous to men, as unwise due to the unevenness of the sexual playing field. Women like this open themselves up to exploitation. Angela explains her decision to sleep with Roger: "[H]er surrender was made out of the lavish fullness and generosity of her heart; there was no calculation."[107] But the novel clearly shows that this choice was a mistake. Without denying the primacy of sexual love, these portrayals return us to the sense of marriage as, after all, a matter for some "calculation," just as it had always been for women with property. Calculating feminists, however, allowed space for women like Angela to choose to be sexually active and not to be "ruined" by it. Yarros noted that modern young people, women as well as men, feel that "they have a right to occasional indulgences. They do not see why society should object to this degree of freedom, provided there are no children."[108] Women may have faced an unequal world, but, much more powerfully than the flappers, these female characters claimed sexual subjectivity.

Feminists opened up the field of sexuality to women in a way that more conventional thinkers did not, yet that opening also closed off options that many women were attached to. The Victorian notion of women's sexual and moral superiority, for example, received a decided critique from feminist thinkers as well as others. Sanger wanted women to accept their sexual selves and condemned female prudishness or "simpering innocence" as ruinous for marriage. Yarros reported seeing in her medical practice a generational shift from the pre–World War I era wives, who disliked sex and yet submitted to it to keep their husbands happy, to postwar young wives, who wanted sexual satisfaction for themselves. While sympathetic to the older group, she expected them to seek professional help to deal with the "habit of repression." Among groups she lectured to and in her own circles, she also encountered more old-fashioned women. She described these often "intelligent and refined" women as chiding her when she defended men's desires and argued for women's; they did not want to abandon their sense that women were superior to men because women had fewer sexual desires.[109] Yarros, like Sanger, condescended to such women and saw them as threats to their own and their children's marital happiness. The feminist marriage thinkers consigned them to the category of the unmodern.

The Housewife

Besides sexuality, feminist marriage thinkers differed from others on questions of work—both domestic and public. The housewife and her labor were fraught with challenges to equality, and feminist thinkers were sharper critics of dependency than other marriage writers. Wile and Winn cited the example of "the successful husband who grows faster, socially and intellectually, than the hardworking wife who has helped him to win his place, and thereafter, becoming tired or ashamed of her, turns to pastures new." They also wrote sympathetically of homemakers' "disadvantageous position, psychologically." These wives are humiliated by having to ask husbands for money because husbands as earners "feel martyred" by having to "turn over the check to the wife." Significantly, Yarros also uses the term "humiliation" to describe the feelings of a formerly wage-earning woman turned dependent wife.[110]

These feminists looked for a more collaborative arrangement, not unlike Crystal Eastman and some of the women radicals. Sanger argued that men often let marriage "drift into a sort of master-slave relation"; in her view, the "mutual acceptance of household duties by the husband as well as the wife does more than any other single thing toward the creation of that splendid comradeship and companionship which are the solidest foundations of permanent homes and happy marriages."[111] *New York Age* columnist Parham likewise called modern husbands and wives "co-partners in both the family set-up itself and the household activities." She linked housework sharing to women's employment, accepting that employed wives still had to take responsibility to "maintain the morale of the home," but arguing that wives' sympathetic listening should be reciprocated with husbands' sharing "more of the household responsibilities."[112] Ira Wile and Mary Winn likewise asserted that when men were not sole breadwinners, they should help with housework; they noted, however, that men were often backsliders on this front. Wile and Winn even challenged the sexual division of labor itself, arguing there was no "inviolable line" between women's and men's work, including child rearing.

"The fact that a woman has borne children does not necessarily mean that she is the best person to bring them up." Yarros echoed Charlotte Perkins Gilman in calling for cooperative arrangements to address both housekeeping and child care.[113]

These feminist views are in contrast to those of the few male authors to discuss housework. Sherwood Eddy's proposal for sharing stemmed from his concern that a woman's submersion in domesticity would dull her and harm marriage. Even when the wife was not employed, he wrote, the husband ought to help with the dishes; but he also advised the wife to postpone some kitchen work if necessary so as to spend time with her husband "to share in their reading and cultural tastes." If she does all the housework, he asks, "how much would she have to share when she does come into the living room?" Eddy was certainly influenced by feminist arguments; he cites a passage from Sanger on shared housework. More conservatively, Floyd Dell argued that a widowed father doing housework constituted failure to provide a "standard of adult masculinity" for a son.[114] Not surprisingly, female marriage revisionists, who had careers, felt more keenly than the men the inequity of female responsibility for household labor. But in this sensibility they were up against prevailing legal and popular assumptions that husbands owned wives' domestic labor.[115]

The Employed Wife

More extensively discussed than housework was wives' employment. Feminist marriage thinkers incorporated greater acceptance of women's paid work. The account of flapper marriage has demonstrated how in the 1920s, as Nancy Cott has argued, "the ballast anchoring harmony between the sexes to sexual parity in the public world as well as the bedroom" was lost.[116] Equality between the sexes had devolved to mean equity in sexual and psychological relations more than in political and economic ones. Feminist marriage thinkers objected to this majority perspective, supporting wives' employment more consistently. On this issue, their views overlapped with those of African American proponents of partnership marriage.

But feminist visions like Fauset's went beyond economic partnership to include not just jobs for wives but careers, which not only assisted the economic well-being of black families but also promoted gender equality and underpinned the modern woman's individuality. In *The Chinaberry Tree*, Laurentine is desperate to be respectably married. Her journey in the novel is toward a more independent sense of self. She learns from a new friend, a trained nurse named Millie Ismay, "that there was something in life besides marriage." She takes pride in her abilities as a skilled seamstress and dress designer, which gave her a "small independence." All this leads to a growing equality with her new lover, Dr. Denleigh, whereby she was "emerging from his aegis, to wear one of her own which enabled her to walk side by side with him."[117] Fauset grew progressively more committed to this view: in her final novel, *Comedy: American Style*, which addresses married life most fully, Fauset supports employment for wives more completely than in any other work, for both its psychological benefits and its financial contribution.[118] Marriage was absolutely important to Fauset. She saw it as a base of "safety" and "assurance," a "foundation" from which "an ambitious woman might reach forth and acquit herself well."[119] But her fiction offered very positive portrayals of women's competencies of both talent and earning as the basis of a more egalitarian partnership within marriage.[120] These views were echoed by Parham, though she stressed the benefits to marriage. Employment, she argued, fostered wives' "intellectual growth" and created mutual sympathy between husband and wife, enabling each to better appreciate the other's problems.[121]

Among whites, Yarros also made paid work central to wives' equality. As the means to equity she listed paid employment first (coming later to birth control, child care provisions, and laborsaving devices). She advocated every woman's being trained for an "independent economic career," called for elimination of "unfair discrimination" in employment, and noted that bearing fewer children made it more possible for married women to do other work.[122] The feminist portrayals still included, like most accounts of marriage, the understanding that women would take responsibility for young children, probably leaving paid employment for a time.[123] But economic and psychological equality was more deeply structured into marriage in this vision than in flapper marriage.

Sometimes white male writers, like the black men cited earlier in this discussion, supported wives' careers (more frequently than they supported shared housework or imagined women as equal sexual subjects). Playwright Sidney Howard, novelist Sinclair Lewis, physician Ira Wile (with coauthor Mary Winn), and sociologist Ernest Groves in particular allowed or advocated two-career marriage. Thus, the heroic scientist daughter-in-law in Howard's *Silver Cord* plans to continue her career, declining to be identified solely as wife and mother. Lewis's *Ann Vickers* likewise presents a feminist heroine who is triumphant at finding a lover and having a child at forty but who is also a successful professional woman. She proclaims to her lover, "I'll always have jobs—you may as well get used to it—it makes me only the more stubborn a feminist, to be in love!" Ira Wile and Mary Winn propounded the uses of a wife's career for relieving the husband "from the nervous pressure of too great financial responsibility," giving the wife greater financial acuity, and providing the marriage "greater emotional stability" due to the wife's "increased sense of power and security."[124]

Ernest Groves described in fascinating detail the problem of the two-career marriage, one guesses probably drawing on his own. His account reveals both the embeddedness of the gender division of labor and the power of economic inequality. Included in his book *American Marriage and Family Relationships* (1928), the passage could almost have been written in the 1960s. Setting aside husbands who wanted to keep women in their traditional place, he catalogued the troubles of even sympathetic men. He could not pry apart the association of women with domestic labor, for example, arguing that, unless they live in an apartment with "practically no housekeeping or household responsibilities," the husband "cannot prevent her having greater obligations for the maintenance of family life than he himself has." Here he demonstrates the power of ongoing cultural expectations of women's domestic labor owed to the husband. Groves recognized the rising standards of living that impelled some middle-class wives to earn income, and he approved. Yet he could not envision the family making its "indispensable contribution to the state" without women's domestic labor. Hence, he argued, a wife should take employment only if she could do so "without detriment to her particular family circle."[125]

It was also very difficult for Groves to conceive of a woman equally talented as her husband in nondomestic labor. He could imagine a husband sacrificing "his own interests and inclinations in order to help his wife find outlet for her desires," for example, by moving somewhere that was less good for the husband. Yet such a choice might not work out due either to the woman's lack of "detachment" from family (required by paid work) or perhaps to her lack of "any adequate ability or talent which can possibly furnish the success she expects." And if she did have the "detachment," family life might then become "deficient in its yield of satisfaction" (for whom, one wonders). In the end, "extraordinarily gifted" wives might do all right, but others would not, since usually the man's sacrifice was less good for the family because of his greater earning power.[126] That earning power represented the economic grounding of gender inequality. Although Groves's delineation of the issues reveals a male-centered perspective, it accurately represents the pragmatic difficulties that more thoroughly feminist thinkers also faced.

Enormous obstacles confronted women attempting to combine paid work with marriage. Legal interpretation and public policy opposed equality by sustaining the male breadwinner ideology and husbands' ownership of wives' labor.[127] In a context where wives' domesticity remained the ideal for most and the reality for the majority, both black and white, and where pervasive and deeply rooted prejudice limited women's employment opportunities, only the tiny group of professional women could find the cultural and economic conditions enabling them to combine career and marriage. About 3 percent of all (employed and nonemployed) adult women pursued professional or managerial careers in 1920, rising to 4 percent in 1930. Only one-fifth of this tiny 1920 professional cohort (or .6 percent of all adult women) were married, rising to one-quarter of the 1930 group (or 1 percent of all adult women).[128] Even those who managed the combination faced extremely powerful pressure to continue assuming responsibility for housework, children, and emotional nurturance generally, forms of work that were as substantial as they were undervalued, even sometimes by feminists. Psychologist Lorine Pruette, author of a study entitled *Women and Leisure* (1924), argued that the industrial revolution had made women's household tasks fewer and easier. She noted women's "longing for something more. Their faces are marked by the strain of too much leisure; the faces of their men are marked by the strain of too much labor." Dismissing the value of unpaid household labor, Pruette praised the new woman for having given up what the traditional wife clung to—her "right to a living without working."[129] The feminist champions of careers thus could not at this historical moment provide answers to the equality issue for the large majority of women, but they limned the features of the problem that second-wave feminists took up again once many more wives were wage earners in the post–World War II period and especially the 1970s.

Like African American partnership marriage, the feminist variant of companionate marriage confronted culturally and socially loaded features of the conventional marriage system. The African American marriage revisionists had exposed the racism of the antimiscegenation laws and the moral inadequacy of the liberalism of Eddy, Lindsey, and Groves. The small number of feminist writers challenged the way marriage reproduced male sexual and economic power in the hobbled imagining of women's sexuality and the shackling together of women and domestic labor. They dared to imagine women as sexual subjects apart from maternity, and they pressed the importance of shared housework and, especially, paid work as the foundation of women's equality.

Conclusion

These three versions of modern marriage reflect the range of visions artic- ulated by companionate marriage thinkers. Flapper marriage was unques- tionably the most widely disseminated form, depicted in popular novels and films as well as in Lindsey's serialized books. It built on the alterations to the Victorian middle-class world; the modern sense of individualism; the urban freedoms of youth, especially the increased education, employment, and citi- zenship of women; the expansion of consumer culture; and the open acknowl- edgment of and public demand for birth control. But flapper marriage was also an effort to sustain male primacy, if not stark domination, in marriage. It was meant to contain some of the unnerving possibilities of the modern world, particularly the separation of women's sexuality from maternity, more casual sexual relations outside marriage, and women's burgeoning presence in the paid workforce. And because the goal was to sustain marriage and the social and sexual order it stood for, flapper marriage also meant homogamy. "Like marrying like" was said to give better odds of permanence, but it also made interethnic, and especially interracial, mating seem dangerous. These white thinkers were racial liberals, not full-fledged eugenicists, but imagining a mixed-race society was beyond their capability.

African American partnership marriage was invisible to most whites but actively debated and lived by middle-class black people. Rhetorically similar to flapper marriage in its self-conscious modernity in relation to birth control, sex, youth independence, and women's equality, this version of modern mar- riage accommodated to the racist world African Americans faced. Scientific views of sex and birth control were less flamboyantly asserted. The need of the wider black community for commitment and involvement from married couples dampened the individualist impulse to couple withdrawal and privacy in flapper marriage. The urgency of black wives' employment gave the eco- nomic partnership model readier acceptance. And fervent antiracist principle led to absolute condemnation of antimiscegenation law.

Feminist marriage was the province of a few articulate feminist intel- lectuals, black and white, sensitive to women's autonomy and equality across all aspects of marriage. In feminist marriage women claimed sexual desire and took initiative, and their bodies were not entirely "offered to the agony and bloody sweat of motherhood," as Lindsey claimed.[130] The authors of this vision did not express hostility toward women who considered their own inter- ests in marriage, and they were alert to the benefits of wives' employment not only for economic assistance but also for upholding women's equality as individuals. Not free lovers but supporters of marriage, these thinkers sought to overcome the traditional conflict between women's equality as sexual and public persons and a male-centered conception of marriage.

Feminist marriage, like African American partnership marriage, was a minority perspective in part because the cultural and material conditions that could have grounded efforts to live out the vision did not yet exist for many women. Margaret Sanger's treatment of the questions of work and sex in *Happiness in Marriage* illustrates how the realities of most women's situation limited articulation of a feminist position. Sanger apparently wrote the book in part to compete with Marie Stopes's *Married Love*.[131] In supporting the institution of marriage in the first place, Sanger's book departed from her own now discreet but continuing practice of free love. But in its fairly conventional approaches to both work and sex, it showed her attempt to appear more respectable and to reach a mainstream audience, not primarily professional women but average (presumably white) women.

Sanger's strongest statements on women's work were her claims for shared housework. She also demanded a guaranteed budget for the at-home wife so as to give her more financial control.[132] Ultimately such an arrangement, like her proposal for housework sharing, depended on the husband's willing cooperation, which, as critics of dependency had noted, was often not forthcoming. On the question of careers, *Happiness in Marriage* was more conservative than the subsequent reflections on her own life in her autobiography. In the latter she admitted her own pleasure both in the work of nursing itself and in her ability to share financial responsibility with her first husband.[133] But in *Happiness in Marriage*, Sanger mentioned wives' employment only in relation to the early companionate phase of marriage and did not dwell on the question of careers as Fauset and Yarros did, or even as much as Wile and Winn or Groves.[134] Instead, her equality claims were carried by her intense romanticism about women's sexual force.

The greater emphasis on sexuality accorded with Sanger's personal philosophy and with her life's work on birth control. But even on sex she pulled her punches in this book, falling back on traditional gender dynamics. In her account of courtship she presented men as the natural pursuers in sex, leaving women to "cultivate" and "direct" men's desire.[135] While Sanger claimed women's right to sexual satisfaction, nowhere did she present women's full claims to desire and initiative in the way that Fauset and Yarros did.

In the arenas of both work and sex, then, Sanger was softening her perceived radicalism in this book and reaching for a more conventional audience.

The book did not sell well in any case, perhaps because she was not as explicit about sex as her audience was ready for.[156] Still, her decisions on the approach surely point to her and her publisher's sense of what the reading public would accept. She was likely right to guess that a majority of American wives would have had difficulty making the claims that Fauset or Yarros made for sex or careers. As Sanger asserted, "There is reason to expect that most normal women will continue to seek self-development and self-expression in the fields of marriage as well as motherhood."[157] She was speaking to the practical realities of most domestic white wives, supporting greater equality for them within the confines of traditional sexual and work roles rather than through sharp challenges to those roles.

5

Sexual Advice for Modern Marriage

In 1940 Columbia University psychologist Carney Landis published a study of 295 women, divided in half between psychiatric patients and "normal" women, closely matched for age and social background. He found that "the sex adjustment of the average marriage is far from ideal." Mrs. K., aged thirty-one and married for six years, provided one example:

> During this time she had never experienced orgasm. She said that she found their first sex relations after marriage satisfactory and free from emotional upset, but she did not respond adequately. Although her husband had made every attempt to help work out a satisfactory adjustment, her response was always the same and she continued to play a completely passive role. She said that she would probably never desire sexual relations with her husband except for the fact that she knew that this was a normal part of married life. She remarked, "I like the idea of my husband wanting me and I always hope it will cement our relationship." When asked, "How do you usually feel when intercourse is over?" she said, "I can't say that I'm satisfied. I have a feeling of affection though I may not know what it's all about. Also, I have thought that I expected too much of sex. More than actually exists. I am not too disappointed." She said that the most satisfactory part of her love life with her husband consisted in

his displays of affection.... [S]he said that she feared that she was not normal physically.[1]

Mrs. K. exemplified the difficulties some women faced in enjoying sexual intimacy and equality within marriage. While she clearly had a conception of what was by that period considered sexually normal, she seemed fatalistic about her inability to experience it. Yet she knew it was important to her marriage. This standard of normality could well have come from the many manuals of advice on marital sex available by the early Depression years, when she married.

To define the sexual side of companionate marriage was the task of the physicians, psychologists, and sociologists who published numerous marriage manuals that appeared on bedside tables in the 1920s through the 1940s. The marriage revisionists of the 1920s had outlined the moral, historical, and scientific rationales for companionate marriage. The advice writers increasingly assumed companionate marriage as normative and went on to offer detailed prescriptions for sexual relations in marriage. They informed readers not only about birth control but also about the all-important process of "sexual adjustment" in marriage.[2] The books discussed sexual difficulties and outlined physical positions and techniques to help, always urging appropriate consultations with physicians when needed.

Sexual advice authors pursued two of the fundamental themes of companionate marriage: they attempted to meld equality for women with sexual intimacy as the essential cement of modern marriage. Women's firmer place in the public world as citizens and wage earners lay behind this sexual advice just as it had undergirded the creation of companionate marriage as a whole. These works delineated a particular new sexual ideal in marriage—the "cult of mutual orgasm."[3] This advice was based on the argument that women had suffered in the past but were now ready to claim marital equality—in sex now as well as in general respect and decision making. The books opened up often confining Victorian prescriptions for female sexuality, although they also established new standards of sexual performance for both women and men. This part of the impetus for advice on marital sex lay in the continuation of marriage revision from the 1920s, with its emphasis on new rights for women.

In addition, particular historical circumstances of the Depression and World War II influenced this advice literature. First, economic hardship increased the demand for birth control as married couples became desperate to limit their families. A market for commercial contraceptives, over-the-counter remedies covertly marketed as contraception (condoms as well

Fig. 8 Ernest R. Groves and Gladys Hoagland Groves

Ernest and Gladys Groves in their Chapel Hill, North Carolina, home, probably in the 1940s. He taught family sociology and marriage education courses at the University of North Carolina from 1927 until his death in 1946. Gladys, a younger second wife trained as a teacher and social worker, wrote, lectured, and taught part-time at local colleges while their children were young. The two wrote books of marriage advice and started a marriage counseling service together. Courtesy of North Carolina Collection, University of North Carolina Library at Chapel Hill.

as so-called feminine hygiene products), flourished. The birthrate declined, dipping below replacement rate in 1933. The birth control movement began to achieve some judicial if not legislative success, due to the public demand for contraception as well as to the power of political arguments for helping people on relief to reduce their childbearing. A U.S. Court of Appeals decision in 1936

(*United States v. One Package of Japanese Pessaries*) on the importation of a package of Japanese pessaries (which Margaret Sanger had had mailed to Dr. Hannah Stone) reinterpreted the Comstock law of 1873 to allow an exemption for contraceptives prescribed by physicians. And in 1937 the American Medical Association endorsed birth control. While far from freely available, contraception had achieved a strong presence in U.S. society by the end of the Depression years.[4] The wider use of birth control focused more attention on sex within marriage and could well have expanded the interest of many people in sexual advice literature, even though the books often, in the earlier years, were not able to give explicit birth control instruction.

Countering the influence of feminist-influenced companionate marriage and birth control, the Depression raised social anxieties about the stability of marriage and about male authority. Conservatives were distressed when birthrates fell and also when the marriage rate plummeted by 25 percent between 1929 and 1932, fearing that these portended the decline of the traditional family. Paul Popenoe established his Institute of Family Relations in Los Angeles in 1930, where he promoted positive eugenics—more reproduction by those he deemed genetically desirable—through marriage counseling. Divorce rates had spiked after World War I and then remained much higher than in the prewar years, with those marrying during the 1920s divorcing at twice the rate of those married prior to the war.[5] Male unemployment rose, and because female-dominated occupations were not as hard hit by the Depression, more married women entered the workforce. Among married women, the employment rate grew from 12 percent in 1930 to 17 percent in 1940. Married women also became a larger proportion of the total female labor force: in 1930 married women formed 29 percent of all wage-earning women (while single women formed 54 percent, and divorced or widowed 17 percent). By 1940, however, married women formed 36 percent of the total (vs. single women's 49 percent, and divorced or widowed women's 15 percent).[6] These changes threatened a major foundation of masculinity—the male breadwinner role. Sociological studies of the time and subsequent oral histories suggested that unemployed men could suffer from shame, depression, and loss of familial authority, and that some women lost sexual interest in their husbands as a result.[7]

Feminism's struggle for individual rights for women faced greater challenges in this atmosphere, though rhetorical nods to women's rights continued along with commitment to the male breadwinner marriage. Anxiety about the latter was reflected in the intense public and legislative hostility to married women's employment. (Governments at all levels proposed and passed bills legitimating employment discrimination against married women during these years.) New Deal social welfare legislation acknowledged women primarily as wives and mothers, not as individuals or wage earners like men, and New Deal–supported art and theater likewise presented the wife primarily as the "faithful comrade" in the family's struggle rather than as an individual. At the same time, the increasingly influential experts of social science (including family sociology) aimed "to revitalize and reassert the primary importance of the family" and women's place in the home.[8] As part of this effort, in 1934 Ernest Groves initiated the annual Conference on the Conservation of Marriage and the Family at the University of North Carolina, at which scholars, clergy, physicians, and social service workers from around the nation gathered to promote effective marriage preparation. World War II sustained this concern for strengthening families, though Groves hoped they would be "families of modern spirit" that recognized women's individuality. In 1941, as president of the National Conference on Family Relations, he argued both that "the status of women should go forward with an increasing momentum" and also that "wholesome marriage and family life" were essential to repairing the world after the war was over.[9] Advice works on marital sex formed an important part of this larger effort to protect marriage and traditional gender roles within it from these potentially destructive forces.

Finally, the wider presence of gay men and lesbians in the large cities and in cultural representations made an alternative to heterosexual identities more visible. Over the first three decades of the century, both in social practice and in medical analysis, heterosexual and homosexual were becoming starker and more exclusive categories.[10] This was particularly true for middle-class men, for whom masculinity had seemed under siege from the corporate organization of work and from feminist activity long before the Depression had threatened their economic power. And feminist activity, by promoting women's independence, itself was often associated with lesbianism. During the Prohibition years, lesbians and gay men achieved considerable cultural visibility in New York theater districts and publications and in speakeasies and nightclubs; the popular media reported on drag balls. Even in the 1920s, the New York state legislature had revised obscenity laws to prohibit representations of homosexuals on Broadway (as in the 1926 play *The Captive*), but after the end of Prohibition in 1933, the state extended its surveillance of popular entertainment through liquor licensing laws, defining the mere presence of homosexuals in a bar as "disorderly." These actions forced direct discussion of homosexuality and people with overtly homosexual styles out of the public sphere, but they also suggest the defensive posture of conventional moralists in this period.[11] Psychologist Lewis Terman's creation in 1936 of the Masculinity-Femininity (MF) scale for personality testing reflected this concern with sustaining prevailing gender differences; homosexuality, seen to violate those differences, was an important concern for him. The impact of this hostile discourse was reflected in Landis's 1940 study, which reported that it was "more difficult to obtain information on this particular subject [homoerotic feelings or activities] than on any other phase of the personal life."[12] In this context, improving marriage was in part a way to sustain the male-dominant heterosexual gender order.

Sexual advice works often reflected these anxieties, attempting to shore up male authority within marriage through sexual activity, even as they sought to promote sexual satisfaction for women.[13] They also broadcast their revisions in the context of an ongoing culture of feminine modesty and the double standard, as well as the material reality of most married women's financial dependency, which made it difficult for them to assert themselves in relation to their husbands. Further sustaining husbands' primacy was judicial interpretation of domestic relations. Courts understood the marital bargain to mean that women owed "consortium"—sex, household labor, and companionship—in return for men's obligation of financial support. Despite women's legal independence in some areas, then, what persisted was "the very core of marital unity, the husband's private control of his wife's body."[14]

As a result of these conflicting influences, marital sexual advice works often contained contradictory messages. On the one hand, they sought to support men and reassure them of their power in marriage. On the other, they sustained a feminist impulse to improve the sex lives of women. At a historical moment in which women were no longer so completely identified with reproduction, these works revealed a cultural struggle over a new concept of female sexuality—whether it would continue to be understood primarily as reproductive and serving men, or understood at least partly as belonging to women themselves. Whatever their contradictions, however, the books found an eager audience.

The Emergence of Sexually Explicit Marriage Manuals

People were asking physicians and other authorities about sex in marriage long before published manuals began to proliferate in the 1930s, and their needs motivated several of the early physician authors to put their advice into print. Physician H. W. Long published his book in 1919 because he claimed that married people had come to him, as to many doctors, "for counsel and advice regarding...their sex life." Writing the book saved his patients from the embarrassment of speaking about their problems and saved him time as well. Joseph Collins published *The Doctor Looks at Love and Life* in 1926 with similar assertions. The Dutch physician-writers Johannes Rutgers and Theodoor Van de Velde likewise claimed to be moved by the sexual suffering of their patients.[15]

Long's book, which is quite sexually explicit, had a limited audience due to censorship under the Comstock law. His book could "be sold, thanks to our prudish public, only to the [medical] profession," who he hoped would lend it to patients.[16] After 1930 this situation changed. Birth control crusader Mary Ware Dennett won a 1930 case in New York's Second Circuit Court of Appeals against the post office banning of the sex education pamphlet she had written for her sons. An English translation of Van de Velde's very explicit *Ideal Marriage* was allowed in the United States in the same year. Then in 1931, under revised obscenity rules in the tariff law, British birth controller Marie Stopes's 1918 book *Married Love* was finally allowed into the United States. The British Dr. Helena Wright's book *The Sex Factor in Marriage* was also admitted in 1931.[17] Congress and the courts had accepted the argument that scientific discussions of sex with a serious purpose deserved protection that prurient writings did not. Prior to 1930, Long's text was the most detailed and direct in its physical descriptions of U.S.-published sources examined here. But, freed from Comstock censorship by court decisions in 1930 and 1931, much more sexually explicit manuals intended for a lay audience flooded onto the market in the Depression years.[18]

Besides the sympathetic motives of various physicians (and the chance to earn money from these popular publications), the impetus for many advice manuals on marital sex came from the birth control movement and the marriage education movement. The public visibility of Stopes, Sanger, and many other birth control advocates elicited desperate appeals for help from individuals all over North America and Britain. In addition, from the beginning, birth control clinics found clients had more complicated problems than the need for contraception alone. Thus, Sanger's New York Birth Control Clinical Research Bureau began a "Marriage Relationship Clinic" in fall 1931 "to promote mutual understanding of the physical and psychological aspects of the sex relationships."[19] Hannah Stone, the medical director of Sanger's clinic on Sixteenth Street, and her husband, urologist Abraham Stone, managed this marriage counseling project, working first out of marriage consultation centers at the Labor Temple and the Community Church in New York City and then in the Clinical Research Bureau itself.[20] Based on their experience, the Stones published *A Marriage Manual*, in question-and-answer format, in 1937. Other works emerging in the context of the birth control movement include those of Sanger, Stopes, Rachelle Yarros, William J. Robinson, Wright, and Millard S. Everett.[21]

The second source of sexual advice texts was the marriage education movement. Debates about companionate marriage and the social changes in women's lives in the 1920s prompted courses on marriage in schools and other institutions. The Young Women's Christian Association in Chicago, for example, offered a ten-week course on marriage in 1929 that was attended by the young secretarial workers who were a major clientele. Course topics included budgets, children, careers, and "The Physiological Side of Marriage," among others.[22] These marriage courses were especially common at colleges and universities. The Central Young Men's Christian Association College in Chicago offered a course addressing marriage, out of which grew one of the most popular books, *The Hygiene of Marriage* by Millard S. Everett. He also credited birth control leaders for inspiration, showing the overlap between birth control and marriage education groups.[23] The careers of Ernest R. Groves and Gladys H. Groves exemplify the development of this social scientific approach and its shift from marriage education courses to the work of marriage counseling. Student interest and letters of inquiry responding to the Groveses' earlier books and articles prompted them to start publishing specific advice works in the 1930s, including *Sex in Marriage* in 1931 and an extensive revision and expansion of it, coauthored with their daughter Catherine Groves (Peele), entitled *Sex Fulfillment in Marriage*, in 1942; the latter was based on the three authors' marriage counseling case records. Gladys also published a general marriage advice work for women, *The Married Woman*, coauthored with physician Robert Ross in 1936. Dr. Max Exner's publication of *The Sexual Side of Marriage* (1932) represents a similar trajectory, but he moved from the sex education work of social hygiene into sex education for marriage.[24] Physicians and social scientists like these were publishing prescriptive versions of a growing professional consensus about the vital role of sexual intimacy in creating cohesive and happy marriages.

Unlike the social hygiene or sex radical movements or companionate marriage thinkers, the group propagating marital sex advice manuals includes no identifiable African Americans. African Americans may well have been interested in such advice. The possibility of a " 'Marriage Advice Bureau' " at the Harlem branch of Sanger's Birth Control Clinical Research Bureau was raised in 1932 but was apparently not pursued; the branch struggled to attract enough clients for its regular birth control work and was closed in 1937.[25] African Americans were, however, involved in marriage education work. The black National Association of College Women, for example, was "sponsoring a series of lectures on 'Building Healthy Sex Attitudes' and 'Modern Marriage' for local college women students" in Greensboro, North Carolina, in 1937.[26] And in 1942 Gladys Groves, who was teaching marriage education courses in several black colleges close to Chapel Hill, instituted at North Carolina College for Negroes (Durham) a one-day version of Ernest's annual Conference on the Conservation of Marriage and the Family. There, from 1942 to 1951, black professionals in medicine, social work, and education gathered to hear from white (and a few black) experts on problems of sex and marriage education.[27] However, none of these black professionals focused solely on the sexual aspects of marriage or apparently produced any marriage advice works. The small number of black professionals tended to be quite stretched in their responsibilities, and they may also have hesitated to specialize in sexual problems due to the ongoing stigmatization of black sexuality. Black people visited white clinics, and black readers probably read advice works by whites, but I have found no published works of marital sexual advice by black authors.[28]

The authority claimed by marriage advice authors was predominantly scientific, but some relied on other forms of legitimation. Despite the widespread criticism of "superstition," religion retained substantial social and cultural power, and several authors cited religious figures as supporters of their sexual advice projects. Some books included endorsements by clergy. Some even cited Catholics, unusual because the genre often discussed birth control. Van de Velde drew on a Roman Catholic pastoral advice work from 1870 arguing the importance of female orgasm, though that position was based on the old belief that orgasm was linked with conception.[29] In the preface to her American edition, Stopes cited an approving letter from a Jesuit who praised her for treating in "'beautiful'" and "'delicate language'" the problems of "'those who, through ignorance or want of thought, make shipwreck of their married happiness.'" Stopes sought clerical support by writing to the participants at the Anglican bishops' Lambeth Conference in 1920, claiming she had a prophecy from God that sex was not for procreation only. They were unreceptive, but in 1930, moved by the arguments of the more diplomatic Helena Wright, they did give "limited approval" to birth control.[30] This was only, however, for those who felt a "moral obligation to limit or avoid parenthood." They condemned birth control used "from motives of selfishness, luxury, or mere convenience."[31]

No writers cited personal experience to legitimate their claims to sexual knowledge, but Marie Stopes, Isabel Hutton, Helena Wright, and probably others did draw on their own experiences, as well as those of people they treated or counseled. The first version of Stopes's famous chart of the periodicity of women's sexual desire was based on her own experience, supplemented with that of women she knew from suffrage circles. Hutton explained in her 1960 autobiography that she wrote her marriage manual based on her "own past ignorance and difficulties" as well as patients' questions, but in the manual itself she refers only to patients. Wright freely admitted to her biographer in the 1980s the connection of her book to her own life.[32] Van de Velde alludes to the "rare opportunities" for observation of the actions of the uterus after orgasm, observations "impossible" in regular coitus so only possible after "*intensive stimulation...without actual coitus.*"[33] How could he have made such observations? On patients? Or on his wife?[34] Likewise, Helena Wright offers a lyrical description that seems unlikely to have come from a patient: "As the act proceeds, the intensity of pleasure rises, thought is abandoned, a curious freeing of the spirit, very difficult to describe, takes place."[35] But at this historical moment professional status and science were the preeminent factors that could remove sex from the realm of the obscene and give the power to speak. As the physician introducing the American edition of Van de Velde's book asserted, *Ideal Marriage* was written "scientifically, completely, without a scintilla of eroticism."[36]

Medicine overwhelmingly dominated as the source of legitimacy for speaking about sex, but women authors may have also implicitly drawn on the legitimacy provided by their status as wives. The twenty-six works examined here had twenty-eight authors, nineteen of them men and nine women. More than two-thirds were physicians—fourteen men and five women. The female doctors were all married, and two were writing as coauthors with physician husbands. The nonphysician women, Sanger, Gladys Groves and her daughter (marriage educators/counselors), and Stopes, a biologist turned birth control advocate and marital adviser, were all married as well. Gladys Groves chose her status as wife rather than as a professional to identify herself in the preface to the book she coauthored with a male physician colleague; advertising the book as "[c]ombining science and practicality," perhaps she sought to play on readers' potential sense of connection with an ordinary, nonprofessional married woman.[37]

Finally, Stopes, Sanger, and Yarros made a feminist position central to the authority of their voices, explicitly linking the quest for better sexual experience for women to rejection of patriarchal ideology, not just to scientific enlightenment. As Sanger put it, new desires for "a more abundant" love life resulted as women attempted "to change their position from that of docile, passive child bearers to comrades and partners."[38] As the Depression years advanced, overt claims for feminism became muted. Arguments for equity for women in marital sex persisted, but they were mixed into a brew of contradictory advice that included not only critiques of male technique and pity for women's sexual distress but also woman-blaming and male claims for sympathy. The effects on women readers likely varied both by author and by the contexts in which women sought to act on the advice.

Marital Sex Advice Manuals

Making companionate marriage work was not easy. As sophisticated middle-class people increasingly absorbed the perspective of psychology, they learned that it could be difficult, especially for women, to overcome their sexual socialization. People required guidance. From the 1920s through the 1940s, a variety of experts seized this opportunity to produce sex advice manuals for married couples.[39] They sought both to reform sexual behavior and to encourage "modern" ways for married people to think about sexual relations.

Many of the manuals addressed here were extremely popular and remained in print into the 1960s. Five were not fully explicit in the treatment of sex. Physicians wrote three of these—Collins and birth control advocates Robinson (1922) and Yarros (1933). Sanger's *Happiness in Marriage* (1926) and reformer Sherwood Eddy's *Sex and Youth* (1929) offered some but minimal details.[40] These books treated marriage broadly, including some advice on sex relations per se, though in far more romantic and general style than most post-1930 works. Original publications of foreign works were often earlier, but they did not appear in the United States until 1930 and after. The remaining twenty-one works were quite direct in describing sexual anatomy, physiological processes, and positions for intercourse. People's hunger for sexual knowledge kept a number of these explicit texts in print for many years. As of 1948, one reviewer suggested that sales of marriage manuals over the previous twenty years had totaled 2 million, with a large secondhand market in addition to that number. Van de Velde's *Ideal Marriage*, conservative about gender roles, densely technical, but very detailed about sexual relations, was one of the most popular; in 1962 it was being reprinted for the forty-second time since 1941. It remained a top seller until the late 1960s brought David Reuben's *Everything You Always Wanted to Know about Sex (But Were Afraid to Ask)*.[41] Ernest and

Gladys Groves's first sex advice effort, *Sex in Marriage* (1931), went through two more editions (1940 and 1943); their next work, *Sex Fulfillment in Marriage* (1942), an extensive revision and expansion of the first, was republished in 1947, 1951, 1957, 1960, and 1965. Hannah and Abraham Stone's popular book *A Marriage Manual* (1935) was expanded in 1937, reprinted in 1939, completely revised in 1952, and revised and published for a final time in 1968. One of the longest-lived might have been Dr. H. W. Long's *Sane Sex Life and Sane Sex Living* (1919), some version of which was being advertised in a flyer collected by the Kinsey Institute in 1977.[42] These writers created a framework for talking about marital sex that remained dominant until the challenges of second-wave feminism.

The advice manuals continued the reshaping of the cultural meanings of sex begun by marriage revisionists of the 1920s in several ways. First, they set up a new sexual ideal that linked sex closely to the fulfillment of the companionate model. This meant making sexual intimacy a stronger element in the bond of marriage and affirming the modern vision of sexuality as a source of health and vigor, less thoroughly connected with reproduction than marital sex in the past. Additionally, demanding equality for women, these writers urged women's active participation and orgasmic pleasure. These emphases were distinct from those in the majority of Victorian writings, which expressed concern about "excess," more often focused on sex for reproduction, and did not stress women's sexual desires or rights.[43]

Next, the books diagnosed sexual failure—what kept couples from achieving the ideal. Though they involved both men and women, sexual difficulties were understood as more complex and frequent among women than among men. The fundamental problem was the lack of women's full sexual participation and orgasmic pleasure. Male impotence and anxiety were also addressed but much less than women's problems. When women were unhappy with sex, they resisted it, and marriages then suffered from a lack of sufficient, fulfilling, and mutual sex to seal the companionate bond. Both sexual intimacy and women's equality in it thus failed to be achieved.

The books also indicated the predominant causes of sexual failure. They attributed sexual strains to ignorance of anatomy and basic sexual functioning but, more important, to bad, but distinct, attitudes among women and men as well as to inadequate technique. Women were characteristically described as fearful and sexually resistant due both to fear of pregnancy and to prudery. Yet domineering male sexual attitudes and selfishness were also criticized as a source of conflict. Marriage writers drew on their own observations (of patients or clients) and on some of the early studies of sex to substantiate their assertions.

Because they were able to be much more sexually explicit after 1930, these books offered direct advice on how to achieve mutual sexual satisfaction, spelling out a new vision of sex, separated from reproduction, more frequent and extensive, standardized into appropriate stages and physical positions, and incorporating women's orgasm. The new norms exhibited a complex gender politics of sexual relations. They sustained men's dominance in many ways yet also opened some space for women's sexual claims.[44]

These marriage manuals often demonstrated greater support for women than the works of psychoanalysts, who during the 1940s wrote about women in an increasingly misogynist way. Many psychoanalysts attacked women as mothers and for emasculating both husbands and sons with their domestic tyranny. They also refocused women's sexuality on reproduction and affirmed that female passivity and male sexual control and aggression were natural. By contrast, most of the authors examined here, while also enmeshed in assumptions of male dominance, attempted to be more evenhanded.[45]

Ideal Sex

The crusade for better sex was a crusade to improve marriage by making sex more satisfactory, especially for women. Since companionate marriage relied on sexual intimacy as the primary marriage bond, bad sex, according to these books, led to unhappy marriages and divorce. The U.S. edition of Helena Wright's book claimed that "[s]tudies of American divorce records point specifically to ignorance about mutually satisfying practices in sex intercourse as a major cause for divorce."[46] To address this problem the books defined a new ideal that they contrasted with the Victorian alternative—bad sex, which was fundamentally about pleasure and privilege for men and suffering and reproduction for women. Bad sex was based in fear and ignorance. Marriage advisers sought both to change that reality where it existed and to root out people's belief that that was how things naturally were. They drew on new social scientific work to critique the nineteenth-century concept of a hierarchy of races and civilizations; they evoked a Boasian cultural relativism to condemn Victorian repression of women's sexuality.

In promoting a more leisured and heightened sexual experience, marital sex advisers referred to historically and culturally varied literatures from outside Europe and North America. They sustained the Orientalist notion that these other cultures were more sexual than Europeans/North Americans, but they reversed the Victorian valence of that idea.[47] In their view, modern, egalitarian marriage showed American (or European) superiority over other cultures in which they believed women were oppressed. However, they decided the other cultures had a better approach to sex. They undermined readers' assumptions by showing that other cultures had different customs, such as exposing rather than covering various body parts; this created a useful distance on prudish American mores.[48] Eleven of these works specifically cited either "Oriental" or "primitive" cultures or both as exemplary for their more positive valuation of sexuality generally and cultivation of women's sexual pleasure in particular. The "achievement of a successful sex-life" is the "universal experience of primitive peoples, and of Eastern civilizations," wrote Helena Wright (who had served as a medical missionary in China), due to their recognition of the importance of sex and of teaching it to their youth. She credited both "Indians" and "Arabs" for such knowledge.[49] Van de Velde likewise cited both "Oriental civilizations" and "the primitive 'barbarian's' appreciation of the woman's desire and pleasure; even though in other departments of life, he despises his partner, overworks her like a beast of burden, and disposes of her as a piece of property, he is, on this point, much superior to the average man of Western civilization."[50] No one strongly promoted this literature—the Stones noted that Oriental erotic literature recommended dozens of positions for sex that were "altogether fantastic." But citation of works like the *Kama Sutra*, the Chinese "Bridal Books," the *Ars Amatoria* by Ovid, and *El Ktab* by the "famous Muslim Sage, Omar Haleby," made readers aware of alternative cultural traditions with more pleasure-centered sexual views.[51] While these writers authorized themselves with science above all, the exoticism of these references added spice to the new sexual ideal.

Acknowledging cultural differences also undermined the notion that sexual behavior was a natural or "instinctive" response. Instead, sex was described as a conscious performance that employed good techniques to attain physical satisfaction. The Groveses wrote that "sex instruction is ignored because of a false confidence in the instinctive nature of sex. It is assumed that sex can take care of itself." Like hunger, this basic human appetite "needs understanding and guidance."[52] This perspective justified sex education, the giving of marital advice, and the publication of these books.

———

Sexual advice writers set their definitions of ideal sex apart from those of the dominant Victorian writers first by urging more frequent sexual activity and arguing its healthfulness and value, rather than its danger. (Even radical Victorians like free lovers generally supported moderation and feared "excess" of passion.) Putting this ideal into practice necessitated separating sexuality from reproduction through birth control, so couples could have more intercourse without increasing pregnancies. The books echoed the public demand for birth control that surged due to economic straits during the Depression; its legal status improved after the 1936 court decision *United States v. One Package*. The manuals treated birth control as a very desirable part of marriage that would protect women's health, limit family size, and improve sexual relations, achieving the intense sexual intimacy fundamental to companionate marriage.

A few of these works continued to deplore "excess" and worry about draining energies as the Victorians did. In their first book, for example, the Groveses claimed the early years of marriage are the time when "temptation of excess is greatest."[53] But most of these writers conveyed the idea that sex would invigorate, not debilitate, people. Support for frequent, nonreproductive sex distinguished their views from the predominant Victorian prescriptions. Birth control pioneers like Sanger believed that this had an obvious liberatory effect on women because birth control could release women from the fear of pregnancy and allow their sexual desires to be expressed more freely. Theoretically, women could then act sexually more as men were able to, without bodily consequences beyond the sex act itself. They could become sexual "individuals." (How much women wanted to separate sex from its reproductive consequences is another question.)

Ideal sex also included women's orgasmic pleasure and active participation. Van de Velde captured the model echoed by almost all subsequent advice givers. He advocated prolonged sexual activity that was intended as an antidote to the stereotypically brief, male-centered sexual act. In Sanger's words, such a brief encounter was like "a hurried meal over a lunch counter" and usually unsatisfying to women. Mutuality was essential, for "[c]ommunion-mating...implies *equal rights and equal joys in sexual union*," Van de Velde argued.[54] The stress on mutual pleasure in itself actually meant a focus on women's pleasure, since men's satisfaction was generally assumed as easy and, indeed, necessary to the act itself. In ideal sex, men were to be equally concerned with women's pleasure and not just their own.

But a woman's needs were not solely her husband's responsibility. Rather, as Sanger noted, a woman should be an "active, equal partner." These manuals strongly rejected female inactivity. Stopes wrote that a "wife should not be content (as too many wives are) to be a meek and passive instrument...; she has an active part to play." Groves and Ross noted that a woman's activity produced an orgasm more quickly for her. In more old-fashioned terms, Dr. Charles Clinton argued female passivity made the "exchange of sex magnetism" impossible, thus harming the quality of the sexual experience.

Women's activity in the sex act was also understood to contribute to men's emotional as well as physical pleasure. A woman's resistance to being "awakened," argued the clergyman who introduced Helena Wright's book, will cause the husband to be "deeply disappointed" and "hurt in his very spirit by [her] coldness."[55] This perspective may also indicate men's desire to escape the Victorian assumption of women's purity and their own lesser moral status. Everett argued women should "be equally frank in the admission of a desire for sexual pleasure, so that the burden of 'immorality' will not have to be shouldered entirely by the husband."[56] The demand for women's pleasure and activity reflected not only a claiming by women of sexual equality in companionate marriage but also a wish by men, in their own interest, for women to affirm men's sexuality by their own equal response.

The picture of ideal marital sex in these books expressed two themes of companionate marriage—sexual intimacy and women's equality. "Excess" was less of a concern; more sex was good, and birth control was essential. Women's sexual pleasure and active participation were valorized. Men were to appreciate and support women's sexuality because women's response was necessary to complete men's. Here was a new womanhood and new manhood for the twentieth century: the modern woman took active pleasure in sex and was less exclusively domestic and maternal. The modern man showed sexual vigor but was sensitive to a woman's desire. In companionate marriage this modern woman and man united sexually.

Sexual Failure

In the real world of clinic patients and advice seekers, however, the ideal often seemed far away. Many couples were failing to achieve satisfying non-reproductive sex, and wives especially were becoming alienated. Men's sexual troubles, primarily impotence, were mentioned, but they took far less space in the manuals than women's. Universally, male, female, and joint authors stressed women's fears, lesser (or more buried) desire, failure or slowness in being aroused, eagerness for but lack of sexual satisfaction, resentment, and resistance as enormous obstacles to happy marriage. Dr. Hutton, for example, noted women were often "apprehensive and fearful" when first seeing the husband naked with an erect penis.[57] They also thought women, whether due to natural differences or to moral fears, had a "less imperious" sexual instinct and so "move[d] much more slowly" toward readiness for intercourse.[58] And intercourse less often produced sexual satisfaction: Stopes proclaimed that 70 to 80 percent of middle-class married women were "deprived of the full orgasm through the excessive speed of the husband's reactions" or other "maladjust-ment." Yarros in her Chicago clinic practice found among women patients of all types that most were "eager to learn how they can have a more satisfactory sex life in marriage."[59] Many women found unpleasant experiences merely added to their frequently negative socialization about sex to produce disinter-est or resistance. The Groveses noted that a woman who "forces herself to go through the motions" when uninterested may develop a "permanent aver-sion to sex activity" or, if unsatisfied, may "protect [herself] from another such experience by a mask of indifference."[60] Such experiences could lead to unhappiness or divorce.

Marriage manual writers referred not only to experience with their own patients or clients but also to the early studies of sex to substantiate the diffi-culties they sought to alleviate. The sex studies of the 1920s and 1930s, as well as Kinsey's later and better-known one, supported the idea that women's lack of sexual response was a major problem for marriage. The studies did not use random sampling or other twentieth-century methodological improvements and clearly reflected the biases of the researchers, who often found what they expected to find. However, both the research process and its findings offer important evidence of experts' concerns in the period and in general ways substantiate that many women had serious complaints about sex.[61]

Although temperamental differences or incompatibility were the most common complaints among married people who were unhappy, Katharine B. Davis did find that sex was the second most common complaint among women. Dr. Gilbert V. Hamilton found the same for both men and women.[62] Davis was an early woman Ph.D. in social science who had headed the New York State Reformatory for Women before starting her research while working for Rockefeller's Bureau of Social Hygiene. She carried out her study in 1920 on college and club women. Hamilton was a physician who recruited 100 middle-class New York married men and the same number of women for his study in the 1920s. Davis reported that many women found their own "sexual intensity" less than their husbands': in 62 percent of cases, the women rated their hus-bands' sex impulse greater than their own, while only 30 percent rated it equal to their own.[63] Gynecologist Robert Latou Dickinson based his conclusions on patient information from a nearly fifty-year practice (1880s to 1930). Hamilton and Dickinson both found that men wanted more sex and/or tended to set the rhythm of sexual frequency, while women were passive and less desiring. Ham-ilton discovered that women wanted more talk and affection while men wished their wives were more passionate.[64] Dickinson bluntly described typical inter-course among a select group of 100 cases for whom he had more information:

The characteristic coitus of these couples is brief and physiologically male, the female remaining passive and isolated. Once or twice a week there takes place, without preliminaries, an intromission lasting up to five minutes at the end of which the husband has an orgasm and the wife does not. Both man and woman know that the woman has no animating desire. She submits without welcome to the embrace.... There is no other topic upon which a woman will talk with so much grief and bitterness.[65]

Women's reporting of lesser sexual interest accorded with prevailing expectations that women should be more modest about sex; still, the unanimity of the results is striking and suggests the power of this discourse as an expression of some female experiences. Dickinson's knowledge of his long-term women patients gives credence to his assertion that women were often angry about this pattern.

Historian Elaine May's study of late nineteenth-century and early twentieth-century divorce cases confirms this gender dynamic. Overwhelmingly, "men complained that women declined 'reasonable marital intercourse'" while women often used the term "sexual abuse," by which they meant distaste for husbands' sexual advances, too great frequency, or oral sex. And women in 1920 made these complaints as much as those in 1880. Psychologist Landis found in his 1940 study that such feelings of disgust "occurred almost exclusively in those women who rarely, if ever, achieved orgasm." Such gendered patterns contributed to serious marital tensions in which lack of female orgasm was a central issue.[66]

Most of the early sex studies confirmed the lack of orgasm as statistically widespread. Hamilton found 46 of his 100 women subjects either had never had an orgasm or were doubtful about it. Dickinson found in a group of 442 cases for which he had data that 26 percent of women reported never experiencing an orgasm with their husbands, while another 25 percent reported they experienced it only sometimes or rarely. Psychologist Lewis Terman, in his 1930s study of marital happiness, found that one-third of the wives were "inadequate" in orgasm (defined as having them never or only sometimes), and that those who did not have orgasms were more likely to refuse sex. Finally, Kinsey's much larger study of 8,000 women, begun in the late 1930s, again found that about one-third of women rarely responded to orgasm, another third did so about half the time, and the last did so "a major portion of the time."[67] These studies were in many ways oriented to discovering this "fact," which was constructed as a problem by the new ideology of companionate marriage.[68] However, not all the data fit. Terman reported that some nonorgasmic women were still happy in marriage, and his research did not support the idea that this problem was "the one major cause of unhappiness in marriage." But this qualification was not as widely repeated as the view that orgasm was essential. Kinsey's female study reiterated the wisdom: "[O]ur data confirm what many clinicians have regularly seen, that the persistent failure of the female to reach orgasm in her marital coitus, or even to respond with fair frequency, may do considerable damage to a marriage."[69]

Male impotence, whether total or through premature ejaculation, was less often cited as a difficulty, though a number of advice works mentioned it. Its obvious disruption of the sex act certainly made it a barrier to the ideal sexual relationship and indeed to marriage itself. The Stones tell of an impotent man whose puritanical wife did not realize anything was wrong for two years but after medical consultation was able to get the marriage annulled. Some books gave the topic only a page or two, while the massive Van de Velde text ignored it altogether. Only urologist Dr. Edwin W. Hirsch focused on male impotence as a central sexual problem, and even he emphasized women's role in alleviating it. The early sex studies that included men also downplayed the problem. Kinsey's study discussed it only in relation to old age, noting its minimal occurrence among younger men (less than 1 percent of men below age thirty-five).[70] Clearly, in the view of both advice writers and researchers it was women rather than men who had the greater role in sexual maladjustment.

Causes of Sexual Failure

Marriage manuals indicated directly and indirectly several factors that underlay this epidemic of sexual failure, including lack of knowledge, male domination, female prudery, and homosexuality. Ignorance about anatomy, sexual relations, and birth control stemming from inadequate sex education was an obvious cause. More important, however, were gendered attitudes: male domination and neglect of women's needs and female (and occasionally male) puritanism about sex.[71] (Men's puritanism sometimes meant thinking women should not like sex and sometimes meant applying ascetic views to both themselves and their wives.) Homosexuality was also seen as a disruptive force, although marriage manuals' readership of engaged or already married couples made the topic less salient than in the companionate marriage literature, with its emphasis on strengthening a heterosexual youth culture. The books described these threats to heterosexual success as products of censorship of sexual information, as well as patriarchal marriage, female passionlessness, and sex segregation. Although they sometimes cited "organic" or "constitutional" causes for sexual deficiency, they focused on knowledge and attitudes as primary.

Lack of basic sex education and the suppression of contraceptive knowledge and devices were universally cited as problems. The physician author of the foreword to Everett's book asserted "the crying need for making information *fully available* to all classes."[72] Certainly formal sex education was rare, and many people learned about sex not from parents or teachers but from slightly older peers. Researchers cited striking instances of lack of knowledge: Dickinson reported thirteen patients who remained virgins after marriage and were completely ignorant that penetration was supposed to occur.[73] And in the early 1930s, even though harassment of birth control clinics and speakers declined, the Comstock law (and many state-level versions) remained in force and continued to limit the spread of scientific birth control information.

But more important than mere ignorance as an obstacle to achieving ideal sexual relations were men's and women's attitudes about sex. Male domineering and female prudery were posited as major barriers to mutual sexual satisfaction that marriage writers urged readers to overcome; they implicitly criticized male dominance and sympathized with women. Books from the 1920s through the 1940s treated both issues, but over this period the books discussed here shifted the balance of responsibility for the problems from men to women.

Writers in the 1920s and early 1930s repeatedly cited domineering male attitudes as the source of women's dislike of sex and lack of pleasure. Though tales of horrific wedding nights that alienated wives forever were presented with greater critical distance by 1940 and often described as "exaggerated," they remained common in these texts.[74] Legally, wives had an obligation to provide sexual service, but these writers questioned the wisdom of men's claiming their "marital rights" on the wedding night without regard for women's feelings. Stopes, Robinson, and Long said such force was essentially rape, often producing, in Long's words, *"a shock to the bride from which she may not recover during all the subsequent years of married life!"*[75] Men's beliefs in their rights stemmed from the notion that marriage involved conquering and owning women, which modern women resisted. As Joseph Collins wrote, "Woman's resentment against being looked upon and treated as property is frequently displayed in frigidity." Frigidity and this imperial attitude were bound up together, according to Dr. LeMon Clark, as the frigid woman provided a challenge to the young man seeking victory in the sexual struggle. The answer was to alter the notion of conquest and substitute mutuality. "When we bring young men up to view love and its fruits as a mutually satisfying experience and remove from it the element of conquest, the frigid type of woman will find herself almost completely neglected."[76]

Men's harsh domination over women and their aggressive assumption of sexual property rights were understood to damage marriage by crippling women's pleasure in sex and the intimate bond it was supposed to create. The modern ideal husband was instead supposed to help his wife to achieve sexual pleasure. He needed, according to Dr. Wright, "to put himself imaginatively into his wife's personality" and learn how she can feel more sexual intensity. Sanger criticized the man obsessed with conquering many women: "The man who is notoriously promiscuous is most often he who is unable to awaken the deeper love of any one woman"; such a man instead offers only "disappointment." Rather, the man who knows "the inner secret of sexual harmony and happiness—this is the man who is the master of love, and the real leader of humanity toward the future."[77] This feminist voice pointed to the sexual harm wrought by traditional roles as well as their unfairness and demanded that men change.

But despite these writers' considerable sympathy for women, they did not exempt them from blame for their own sexual suffering. They criticized some women's notion that sex was only for reproduction, that other sex was bad, and that women were morally superior due to their passionlessness. The Groveses noted that women often saw sex as a "necessary evil."[78] Reproduction, of course, was fundamental to most women's sexual lives. Their actual vulnerability to pregnancy was one difficulty, but even more important was the belief that "sexual union should serve primarily the purpose of race propagation."[79] The birth control campaign was built on the vision that not all sex had to mean reproduction for women, and when advocates felt able to move beyond the culturally safer arguments based on the health of mothers and children, they asserted that fear of pregnancy disrupted the quality of marital sex. Manual writers acknowledged reproduction as primary, but most stressed the development of other meanings for sex. As Van de Velde put it, humanity had evolved to make the sex urge and the reproductive urge "increasingly separate, distinct, and independent," and among "civilized races" the reproductive drive was no longer the leading one.[80] Women like Lindsey's Victorian matriarchs, who clung to motherhood, were hurting themselves and their marriages.[81]

But even apart from women's focus on reproduction, advice writers blamed "ascetic, puritan principles" for the "unnatural condition" of frigidity.[82] Men might impose these views and thereby damage women's responsiveness. Stopes told the story of a "prudish" husband who responded ignorantly and insensitively to a wife's request to kiss her breast and thus "inhibited her natural desire."[83] And Dr. Clark asserted, "Some men feel that there is something just a little 'unladylike'...in a woman who gives herself up to the complete enjoyment of intimate sexual contact. This feeling rarely fails to communicate itself to the woman, and is another potent cause of apparent sexual apathy."[84]

But more often it was not men but women with "unworthy ideas about sex" who could be their "own worst enemy," claimed Dr. Wright. Marriage advice writers identified and criticized a culture of female victimization and moral superiority that they believed was counterproductive to modern, egalitarian marital sex. Dr. Hutton strongly denigrated the attitudes of some women "that a wife leads an almost martyr-like existence, subjecting herself to the will and desires of her husband." Eddy proffered a wedding night horror story to counter tales of brutal men: "[T]he young wife said in substance: 'If I have to satisfy your lust I will do it, but I say in advance that I loathe and despise it, and you for wanting it.'" The next day she found her husband weeping and "[f]rom that day to this that home has been sheer hell to that man."[85] Most recognized women's dilemma of combining modesty and restraint before marriage with the expectation of accepting and enjoying sex afterward, but they condemned those who persisted too long with restraint.[86] Antisexual ideas allowed wives to feel justified in resisting and criticizing their husbands for sexual advances rather than encouraging them to recognize their own dislike of sex as a problem. As the Groveses wrote, the woman must "cease to take pride" in her "outgrown maidenly reserve" and see herself humbly learning from her husband rather than flattering herself on her "superiority of delicacy."[87] Recognizing that the double standard had allowed women a certain leverage based on this attitude of sexual reserve, Groves and Ross argued things were different in modern marriage: "The woman who takes the more normal attitude of wanting to give up to the man as completely as possible...is happier, and in the long run more powerful."[88] This theme of antiprudery sustained the attack on older styles of female power that was also evident in the condemnation of the controlling Victorian matriarch in the companionate marriage literature.

Finally, echoing the broader acknowledgment of homosexuality as a social and psychological entity by the 1930s, a few advice manuals discussed it in relation to marital sex. It was not a large theme, but a number of authors briefly mentioned it, echoing Dell and others who saw same-sex attraction as an adolescent phase.[89] Most identified it as a mild threat on the margins of normal development, something caused by prudery and sex segregation that could be overcome with proper mixed-sex socializing, sex education, and the cultivation of "normal" heterosexual impulses.[90] A smaller number of works posited homo-sexuality either as an effect or as a cause of heterosexual failure in marriage. Dr. Rutgers pointed to male insensitivity when he characterized lesbianism as a possible effect of "Coarse Love-Making of Uninformed Man," while Groves and Ross noted that men who do not get enough intercourse "often become rather effeminate."[91] Conversely, Drs. Stone, Clinton, and Edward Podolsky identified homosexual feeling as a source of frigidity.[92] The homosexual alternative was clearly a "spectral presence" in these works and was associated with hetero-sexual failure, especially the crippling of female heterosexual response.[93]

In condemning domineering male approaches, female prudery, and homo-sexuality, the marriage manual writers were criticizing the Victorian gender order. They were promulgating modern manhood and womanhood: men with cooperative and egalitarian attitudes toward women, women with a nonmor-alistic acceptance of sex, who together could create marriages with heterosex-ual intimacy and pleasure. Although they tried evenhandedly to demonstrate both male and female responsibility for women's difficulties in marital sex, by the 1940s, when feminism had less of a public presence, they tended to blame women more. This shift is visible, for example, in the changes made by Ernest and Gladys Groves in their substantially revised 1942 manual.[94] Where their 1931 book had emphasized the man's need to cater to the woman's different or more complex sexual sensibility, the later one focused on her need to follow him. Both books contain chapters on the husband's and the wife's part in sex and assert that both spouses must strive to make sex a success. But while in the earlier book, the chapter on the husband's part is longer than the chapter on the wife, the reverse is true in the 1942 book. The later book adds a good deal to the discussion of the woman's responsibility, including three additional paragraphs that elaborate: "[T]he woman is generally more inhibited about sex than the man.... If, however, the man, because his attitude toward sex is likely to be less warped, has to assume more or less the rôle of teacher, the woman should pride herself on her aptness as a pupil."[95] In general, the tone of the texts published after the mid-1930s became harsher toward women, calling for greater effort on women's part and urging them to abandon their inhibitions and respond more fully to their husbands in sex.[96]

The Gender Politics of Sexual Advice

The final task of these marital sex manuals was to offer pragmatic advice on how to overcome the sexual problems so vividly recounted, advice that reveals the struggle between claiming a new equality for women and supporting a more sexualized masculinity. The manuals combated ignorance by providing basic sexual information on anatomy and intercourse, but more important, they set standards to guide readers in four areas—the separation of sex from reproduction; initiative and the timing of sex; normative intercourse; and female orgasm. It is in the details of these standards that contradictory messages appear. Many prescriptions potentially supported women's greater equality in sex, including contraceptive use, attention to women's periodic rhythms of desire, foreplay, and clitoral stimulation for female orgasm. Yet in its account of normal sex and the timing and control of it, especially male initiative, this advice sustained a male dominance that undermined the goals of women's active participation and pleasure. Still, for women with greater power to negotiate sexually, this literature could have offered substantial support for improving their sexual lives in marriage.

Overcoming sexual ignorance was a basic and pervasive goal in these texts. Evidence from Landis's 1940 study confirmed the need, as he found "an attitude of disgust toward sex in general . . . was more common in those who had none or only inadequate information in childhood."[97] To that end, many of the books offered substantial sections of explicit anatomical and physiological lessons. Sanger, publishing in 1926, was brief, spending 10 pages out of 230 on the topic "The Organs of Sex and Their Functions," while Van de Velde, in his extremely technical tome, filled close to half of its 320 pages with detailed information on human sexual parts and functioning. The Stones took about one-third of their book to describe male and female organs as well as reproductive processes.[98] Many books also described intercourse. Dr. Hutton, for example, devoted 16 of 151 pages to a section titled "The First Sex-Act," the organs, and fertilization, including detailed diagrams of women's pubic area, the penis, and side views of both male and female pelvises, showing all the internal organs. Eleven books display anatomical diagrams, and ten of those include the clitoris, several copying Robert Latou Dickinson's careful drawings. (Some advice books were more complete than many medical anatomy texts. Dickinson was an exception among anatomy text illustrators in the mid–twentieth century in that he included the clitoris in illustrations and discussed it, while most such texts did not.)[99] For readers with little sex education, the books provided substantial information, but marriage manuals that followed Dickinson were supporting more woman-oriented knowledge.

Beyond basic information, however, the detailed advice offered illuminates the gender politics of marriage manuals. The announced purpose of most texts throughout the period continued to be tightening the marriage bond by improving marital sex, with a strong focus on helping women. However, the

PLATE IV

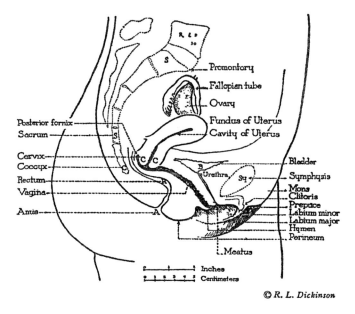

© *R. L. Dickinson*

FEMALE ORGANS, SIDE VIEW

A vertical section through the middle of the body. The generative
organs are shown in heavy outline; the urinary organs and other
parts of the body in lighter outline.

Fig. 9 Female Reproductive Anatomy

This diagram, by gynecologist Robert Latou Dickinson, appeared in the 1943 edition
of *Sex in Marriage* by Gladys and Ernest Groves. It reflects Dickinson's attentiveness
to female anatomy, including the clitoris, which other medical illustrators often omit-
ted. It was originally published in Dickinson's *Human Sex Anatomy* (1933).

details reveal the more buried theme of sustaining male dominance through
a more sexualized masculinity that resembled the male style of the Victorian
male sporting culture more than that of the Christian gentleman.[100] Throughout the advice the interests of women and of men were intertwined, producing ambivalent and conflicting messages.

Ongoing pronatalist cultural traditions and the work of eugenicists had
some impact on these works, which conveyed the idea that marriage nor-
mally led to childbearing. However, separating sex from reproduction was
fundamental to the advice about sexual relations. Birth control was essential,
but more was involved than restricting fertility per se. In the broader goal

of making sex harmonious, frequent, and lifelong, underpinning the spousal intimacy that cemented companionate marriage, birth control was one important element. Most authors, still fearful of prosecution, continued not to give entirely explicit contraceptive instruction, but their support for it was usually clear. (Van de Velde's *Ideal Marriage* differed in that he did not openly discuss birth control, since he was still a Catholic when he wrote that book.) In his *Hygiene of Marriage* (1932), Everett devoted four out of thirteen chapters to it, making a case for its legitimacy as well as describing laws, listing clinics, and distinguishing hearsay knowledge from knowledge based on the scientific method. He refers to the diaphragm as a "device" without a description or diagram, though he does describe intrauterine devices, spermicides, condoms, withdrawal, and rhythm (safe periods) clearly. Just a few years later, after the *United States v. One Package* decision in 1937, the Stones gave more detailed accounts and assessments of most available methods.[101]

The books did not merely promote birth control; they gave sharp advice on appropriate forms. Contraceptive methods that were ineffective or interfered with a smooth sexual experience were criticized as sources of sexual dissatisfaction. On these grounds, marriage authors condemned the rhythm method, abstinence, withdrawal, and the belief that female orgasm was required for conception.

Rhythm, whose scientific basis had been discovered in 1929, was widely taken as an acceptable method for Catholics after the papal encyclical *Casti Conubii* (1930) offered a more positive view of marital sex apart from procreation. Although the encyclical still strongly condemned birth control, its new view of marital sex meant that sexual intercourse gained a higher moral status than it had once had, even at times when conception could not occur—in the safe period and in menopause. Some American Catholics interpreted this as legitimizing the rhythm method, which Catholic doctor Leo J. Latz promoted in his book *The Rhythm of Sterility and Fertility in Women* (1932).[102] The marital advice works addressed here, however, often criticized rhythm both as ineffective contraception and as harmful for sex relations. Dr. Maurice Chideckel stated bluntly, "As to safe periods, there are none."[103] While others noted the method was useful for Catholics (presumably as opposed to nothing at all), they also pointed to its negative impact on the relationship: "It would certainly disrupt the emotional life to have it necessary to limit intercourse to certain days, relatively few in number, in the monthly cycle, placing both partners under an undue and unnecessary strain."[104]

Withdrawal and abstinence were believed to have similar drawbacks. Coitus interruptus (or withdrawal), wrote William Fielding, "is known to be a prolific cause of nervous disorders, hysteria, and numerous other disturbances.

It has been found in these cases that health is regained when complete coitus is performed under conditions which remove the fear of pregnancy."[105] And abstinence, self-evidently, contradicted the pro-sex perspective of these works. Everett considered it "[m]ost injurious and most irrational" and "a crime against the nervous system which can be justified only by a medieval mind" (i.e., the Catholic Church).[106]

Additionally, some writers found it necessary to counter the myth that conception could not occur without a female orgasm (suggesting the popular persistence of this ancient belief). The seventeenth-century sex manual *Aristotle's Masterpiece*, which promulgated this view, remained in print and in use well into the nineteenth century.[107] "[M]any a young husband has impregnated his wife when he least expected to do so, thinking that because he alone experienced the orgasm, that therefore conception was impossible," noted Dr. Long in 1919.[108] This method also obviously violated the imperative for female pleasure. Educating readers about this myth undermined the identification of women's sexual feeling with reproduction alone.

The practical advice on contraception generally, whether specifics were given or not, favored the diaphragm as a method, because "sensation is not affected, and the normal sequence of the sexual act is not disturbed."[109] This support for a female-controlled method of contraception had the potential to be empowering to women (at least those who could afford private doctors from whom they could obtain diaphragms and who had the private bathrooms in which to deal with them), in contrast to methods that relied on men's control, especially withdrawal. Overall, separating sex from reproduction through birth control was supposed both to support women's equality in sex and to promote easier sexual relations, benefiting both men and women.

But it was not just birth control that was called for. The manuals also more subtly altered the relationship of sex and reproduction by countering popular myths and cultural taboos against sexual activity during menstruation and pregnancy, after childbirth, and during and after menopause. They most consistently argued that sex was permissible in pregnancy with moderation and that women's desire and thus active sexual life continued past menopause. This was distinctly different from most Victorian marriage manuals, which defined menstruation, pregnancy, and postmenopause as inappropriate times for sex. There had been a long history of cultural prohibition on sex during menstruation, from the Bible to *Aristotle's Master-Piece*, to modern texts.[110] Everett and others asserted that it was safe to have sexual intercourse until the last two months of pregnancy, "provided consideration and care are exercised." Most books upheld a customary six-week postpartum ban on intercourse as necessary to women's health, although Van de Velde reduced that to two weeks.[111] The vast majority of advice writers also agreed that the erotic impulse continued after menopause. Dr. Clinton asserted that women "need not cease to be wives after they can no longer be mothers.... in any really successful marriage the menopause does not mean the end of sexual life."[112] Somewhat less often, these writers argued that sex was acceptable during menstruation. Wright noted that some women feel their strongest desire during menstruation. "Nature is a better guide than any rule of ours, and if the spontaneous wish for intercourse appears very markedly, it is wise to allow it free expression." Clark more cautiously suggested that the woman might not wish to offend "the esthetic feelings of her husband," but that if her desire were strong and both found it acceptable, "there is no physiological objection to it."[113]

The general tendency of these works was to expand the times when sexual activity was permissible and to detach that activity from the female reproductive rhythms. As Fielding noted, defending sex after menopause, "It appears, therefore, that sexual desire is not necessarily dependent upon ovulation." This was a significant change in the conceptualization of female sexual desire, disconnecting it from biological reproduction more than ever before.[114] The obvious result was to promote greater regularity of (nonprocreative) intercourse and to outline a female sexual subjectivity less shaped by the reproductive role, a benefit to "modern" women who wanted to develop their sexual lives in a new way and to men whose sense of themselves may have been built more on their sexuality than in the past.

Finally, the separation of sex from reproduction facilitated more frequent sexual activity than Victorians had supported. While most of the twentieth-century writers explained that individual capacity and desire should govern frequency, in the end they tended to refer to findings of actual averages—two to three times per week (often cited from Robert Latou Dickinson's studies)—which then might be labeled "normal," or they cited historic authorities, most notably Martin Luther, who is reported to have recommended sex twice a week.[115] By contrast, nineteenth-century advice was most commonly to have intercourse once a week.[116]

———

Who took initiative and controlled the timing of these more frequent sexual relations formed a second, and contested, theme of the advice, in which assumptions of men's control predominated but arguments for women's influence were also voiced. Here there was a partial shift away from the Victorian emphasis on sexual restraint in marriage, in which supposedly more passionless wives helped husbands to hold their passions in check by setting limits and claiming deference (a practice promoted by the evangelical reformers who created Victorian mores but one always in tension with the legal and social power of actual husbands).[117] Instead, as the critique of prudery indicates, such women were urged to reject antisexual ideas and respond to male sexual approaches. But this "correction" of a supposedly female-biased Victorian prescription appears more like public reclaiming of male sexual prerogatives that had always been part of patriarchal gender order, though shoved into the shadowy underside of official Victorian culture.[118] Discussion of initiative and timing revealed the tension between this conventional male initiative and the new requirement that women both enjoy and actively participate in sex.

Persisting beliefs in a different, and more aggressive, male nature, reinforced by custom, underpinned male initiative. In many ways the proponents of companionate marriage and the sexual advice writers were recuperating the concept of male sexual necessity (the enduring popular notion that men had to have sexual intercourse to preserve their health). The social hygienists had worked hard but unsuccessfully to undermine this idea in their sex education programs of the 1910s. The promotion of sex as good, healthy, and natural in the new marriage literature, of course, included women, but it also carried an edge of denying Victorian critiques of male excess. Lindsey, for example, told stories of outside attractions among married people in which he interprets the fact of attraction as a sign of vigor and normality. He argued that monogamy did not come naturally to all and should not be forced but should grow organically from good relationships. Jealousy, not infidelity, he claimed, was the greatest "crime against marriage."[119] Lindsey acknowledged that women might feel such attractions, but all his examples except one were men. Women, he said, tended to be more inhibited because they "have such a horror of unchastity." A theoretically gender-neutral point, then, had the practical effect of legitimizing the extramarital freedom that men had long exercised. In a context where the possibility of divorce made marriage more fragile, married women might have experienced men's freedom as psychologically and economically threatening. But Lindsey reframed that freedom as an expression of a man's need of and right to sex rather than a sign of betrayal.

The trope of male hunter and female hunted was pervasive. Even Sanger asserted that "[n]ature and tradition have decreed that Man shall be the wooer, the pursuer, the huntsman." The Stones saw men as "sexually the more aggressive and active," and many authors littered their texts with variants of these stereotypes.[120] Gladys Groves and coauthor Robert Ross made an awkward attempt to combine male dominance and female participation when they claimed that "he is by nature and education fitted to be the leader and she the active partner in matters of sex."[121] Such assumptions, combined with the emphasis on correcting female prudery, led to a general expectation of male sexual initiative and female deference and response. Several writers did propose that the woman also could take some initiative after the period of marital adjustment, or when the man was fatigued, or to create variety. Wright and Hutton both suggested that "later in marriage" the woman could be quite forward or even "play the dominant part."[122] But they clearly understood such initiative as exceptional.

Some writers told women they should not deny men sex, advice that accorded with the judicial interpretations that wives owed household and sexual service in return for support.[123] Norman Himes said a pregnant woman might wish to give up sex, but he warned her to "realize the strain she places upon a man.... Stubbornness in these matters does not make for marital harmony." Again, even Sanger argued that some men could not control their desires and might commit adultery if denied sex.[124] A couple of authors edged toward the coercive, as when the Stones suggested that "a woman frequently prefers to be forced to do the thing that she may very much desire herself" (though they urge women not to be passive in this way).[125] In the background, of course, was the reality of most women's vulnerability and dependence within marriage, creating the need to please men. As physician Maurice Chideckel explained, men were "naturally polygamous," and women had to make them monogamous by keeping them sexually happy in marriage. A male perspective appeared in the framing of women's hesitations as irrational or selfish and as an obstacle to the sexual intimacy. Van de Velde stated it most baldly: "The demand that the woman's wishes shall be paramount and alone decide [when and whether to have intercourse], is... both unjust and, what is practically more important, incorrect. It offends against the *fundamental principle of sexual altruism*, just as much as does the traditional view of male 'rights' and female 'duties,' which Mrs. Stopes condemns."[126] Van de Velde allowed that patriarchal Victorian marriage was unfair, but in calling for "altruism" he obscured the imbalance of power and disputed the claim Stopes made for women's control.

In this claim Stopes, and a number of other writers, countered men's power of initiative with the argument that women should influence the timing of sex, appearing to echo nineteenth-century demands for deference to women. Sanger wrote, for example, that in the beginning of marriage the husband should take the initiative but later the woman should "dominate the relation."[127] But the rationale for this deference was no longer the value of holding sex in check but rather the goal of female sexual satisfaction, based on the theory of female periodicity.

Periodicity was the idea that women experienced cycles of greater and lesser sexual desire or receptivity, related to their menses. Havelock Ellis had asserted this idea, and Sanger, Stopes, and Fielding all cited him. Stopes additionally did her own research ("on a number of individual records," which her biographer notes were actually suffragist friends whose husbands were away in the war) that showed a typical pattern of two "wave-crests" of desire in a menstrual month, usually right before menstruation and eight or nine days after, or about two weeks apart. Van de Velde agreed with the observation of a common (though not universal) premenstrual desire but argued that other crests were individually variable and *"not typical of the race."*[128] He resisted the idea that women should assert control over the timing of sex on such a basis.

But the concept of female periodicity of desire was very widespread. Half of these works asserted its existence and used it to qualify the general assumption of male sexual initiative.[129] Because it was important for women to get pleasure in sex, it was useful for them and their male partners to be aware of women's periodic potential for greater desire and to let it "regulate in some degree the time and the frequency of the sexual relations."[130] The cycles were, in Stopes's words, "the foundations on which the edifice of the physical expression of love may be built."[131] Adapting to these biorhythms helped fulfill several aspects of good sex: following the rhythm would make marriage "more interesting, more stimulating, more poetic and infinitely more mysterious"; a woman might find it easier to "take an active part" during the "time of her greatest desire"; and she was "more apt to obtain an orgasm at that time."[132]

The advice on periodicity qualified but did not trump the assumption of male initiative. Women were often urged not to tell men their desires directly but rather to resort to indirect signals such as *"little flirtations,"* which sustained female modesty.[133] However, as part of the guidance for achieving more satisfactory sexual relations, with women's participation and pleasure, this advice did urge both women and men to listen and attend to women's bodies and provided women with a scientific rationale for doing so.[134]

In addition to standards for contraception, initiative, and the timing of sex, these works laid out for readers a normative vision of sexual relations, which included attention to the woman's sexual needs though also obeisance to symbols of male dominance. Pleasure was ideally to be attained within "normal intercourse," which involved a proper sequence of stages and bodily positions. For Van de Velde normal sex aimed at "consummation of sexual satisfaction"; it included love-play (foreplay) to arouse the woman adequately, and it concluded with ejaculation of semen into the vagina with simultaneous orgasm. He, Stopes, and Sanger described a series of stages that were meant to prolong the act and thus to arouse the woman. Van de Velde's account is most elaborate, with four stages—the prelude, love-play, sexual communion, and afterglow. The prelude involved flirtatious conversation to rouse interest in sexual activity. Love-play meant physical stimulation, such as kissing of all sorts, prior to coitus.[135] As Van de Velde notes, "There are numberless delicate differentiations and modifications of sexual pleasure... which can banish the mechanical monotony."[136] This stage was centered on bringing women's desire to an active state. Stopes urged husbands, for example, to "[r]emember that each act of union must be tenderly wooed for and won, and that no union should ever take place unless the woman also desires it and is made physically ready."[137] And the emphasis was not merely physical but also psychological. Men were urged to be attentive and loving, to speak, not just to arouse the woman physically: "Words play the first part; the husband tries to show his wife how much he loves and desires her, and so evokes in her mind the feeling of being desired."[138] Next, "sexual communion" with orgasm of both spouses was considered the supreme sexual experience. And finally, afterglow included lying together, staying awake, and maintaining the romantic feeling through the husband's "caresses and sweet words," which were meant to show love and concern for the wife, demonstrating that sex was not just selfish desire on his part.[139] Almost all the manuals of the 1930s and 1940s prescribed these different stages of sex, especially foreplay.

In institutionalizing the preliminary pleasuring of women as a standard feature, sexual advisers were rejecting the idea that these noncoital approaches were immoral or disgusting. Van de Velde promoted the "genital kiss" (cunnilingus), for example. Groves and Ross argued that in the honeymoon period sexual "relief" without full intercourse (apparently, mutual masturbation) could be part of the woman's "educational process," though clearly regular intercourse was expected later. Alternatives to male intromission were thus acceptable as foreplay.[140]

Alternatives were not, however, acceptable in the "consummation." Van de Velde admitted that more "minor stimuli" could bring about ejaculation, "[b]ut the glorious consciousness of having tasted the supreme pleasure, and the soothing, complete relaxation are lacking, and with them the psychic effect, at once tender and triumphant, of an ideally successful *coitus*." And the Stones warned, "Erotic sex play can be termed perverse when it serves as the sole means of sexual gratification and comes to be preferred to normal sexual union."[141] Van de Velde strongly associated this "normal sex" with male dominance, but other writers did so less or not at all. Dr. Long, for example, though he also assumed regular coitus as standard, was much more tolerant of alternative ways of coming, all in the interest of making sure both partners experienced orgasm.[142] Regardless of their position on equality, these writers understood normal sex to begin with foreplay and conclude with male intromission and ejaculation.

This perspective also necessitated the rejection of the nineteenth-century contraceptive technique known as karezza. Karezza had been popularized by Dr. Alice Stockham in the late nineteenth century, and the Oneida Community had practiced it earlier. It meant sexual intercourse without orgasm, achieved through strong mental control and minimizing of movement during intromission. It served as contraception but also accorded well with the Victorian sense that sex involving the loss of semen was energy-draining.[143] The early works considered here praised karezza. H. W. Long's *Sane Sex Life and Sane Sex Living* (1919) said it lifted sex "into the realm of *mental* and *spiritual* delight"; he considered it a contraceptive method. Stopes (writing originally in 1918) also represented a transitional perspective, suggesting that karezza could be useful for an "undersexed" man, "conserving the man's vital energy" while offering the woman the "physical nerve-soothing she requires."[144] However, marriage manuals of the 1920s to 1940s (when they mentioned it) more often opposed this practice due to their stress on the importance of orgasm. Van de Velde, for example, called Stopes's view a "*contradiction in terms*" because lack of orgasm would not be soothing but rather "must lead to a perpetual and increasing dissatisfaction and unrest, an accumulating genital congestion and profound emotional irritation and exasperation." Besides producing physical problems, Clinton asserted, avoiding orgasm "is manifestly contrary to the intention of Nature."[145] Although these writers considered lack of orgasm bad for both women and men, they considered it much more difficult for men. The expansive but attenuated and restrained pleasure that some late Victorians found in karezza now appeared both inadequate and harmful. Normative intercourse had to include the final satisfaction.

The normative vision of intercourse also included various coital positions that spouses could try, in the interest of variety and improving sexual satisfaction for the woman. Several writers did not rank the positions in terms of preferability and seem genuinely to have promoted alternatives to what many still noted as "most common"—the male superior or missionary position. Helena Wright asserted that the "desire for something new" could be a cause of marriage breakdown, and so variety was useful to sustain marriage. Many married couples use only one position, which they believe is "right," but this is "a pity." "Theoretically speaking there can be no such thing as a 'right' or a 'wrong' position." She suggested four alternatives to the missionary position—woman prone on top, woman "astride," woman sitting on man's lap, and side to side.[146] Despite this openness, however, several works either implicitly or explicitly sustained the normativity of the male-superior position as a symbol of what some—but not all—considered an appropriate male dominance. Van de Velde, for example, said quite explicitly of the woman-astride position that its disadvantage was the "complete passivity of the man and the exclusive activity of his partner. This is directly contrary to the natural relationship of the sexes, and must bring unfavorable consequences if it becomes habitual. Therefore, on these (profoundly psychological) grounds alone, we cannot recommend the choice of this attitude."[147] Others indicated woman-superior positions were appropriate only when the man was somehow less powerful than the norm— when his penis was "disproportionately small," when he was "temporarily or permanently less vigorous sexually than the wife," or when he was fatigued, marking these possibilities as exceptions.[148] The advice works opened up possibilities, then, but also revealed fears that shifting physical positions might destabilize men's normal dominance in the sex act. The best-selling Van de Velde stood out in this regard. In this sense, although these authors insisted on female pleasure as essential to good marital sex, their normative vision of sex often adhered to symbols like the male-superior position and marginalized alternative sexual practices that did not center on orgasm through penetration.

Finally, the question of female orgasm was central to all these works, but disagreement over its proper nature divided the authors as they confronted the increasing salience of the theory of the vaginal orgasm. Freud had famously created this theory in his *Three Essays on the Theory of Sexuality* (1905) in order to explain heterosexual women's transfer of libido from the original female object, the mother, to a male object, suggesting that during a period of latency in adolescence, the vagina became eroticized. A fully mature, that is, heterosexual, woman experienced sexual pleasure in her vagina, not her clitoris.[149] Subsequent psychoanalytic thinkers (including some women) maintained this idea, increasingly grounding female heterosexuality in women's bodily difference from men and implicitly sustaining the link of sex with reproduction, since vaginal intercourse was necessary for pregnancy. They also set up what Kinsey and Masters and Johnson later argued was an impossible goal—orgasm in the vagina.[150]

The marriage advice writers examined here, however, some of whom were physicians though not psychoanalysts, were divided in their view of the vaginal orgasm. Only half of the authors of the twenty-one more explicit texts appear to have accepted the concept of vaginal orgasm in some form, and only half of those seriously promoted it. Van de Velde, for example, claimed that sensations of the vagina and the clitoris were "distinctive and dissimilar" and that in "ideal communion" the focus would be on the vagina. Everett called clitoral/vulval orgasm "less complete." Ernest and Gladys Groves did not allude to the vaginal orgasm in their original 1931 book (*Sex in Marriage*). In the revised text of 1943 (*Sex Fulfillment in Marriage*), they inserted one sentence suggesting that vaginal sensation could develop "after repeated pleasurable intercourse."[151] This and other mentions were perfunctory, and eleven authors did not discuss the vaginal orgasm at all.

The majority instead emphasized the clitoris, even those that also mentioned the vaginal orgasm. Among the five earlier and less explicit books, only Sanger's even presented any anatomical detail on female orgasm, and she named the clitoris as the "special seat of sex sensitiveness in woman." The larger cluster of more explicit texts from the 1930s also predominantly focused on the clitoris. Both the earlier and the later Groves books, like many others, discussed the biological correspondence of the clitoris and the penis, the sensitivity of the clitoris, and the presence of erectile tissue in the clitoris. Even Clark, while favoring the "maturity" of the vaginal orgasm, described the clitoris as "the point which ignites the powder train of nerve sensation leading to the deeper organs." Wright posited the vaginal orgasm as a theoretical more than an actual phenomenon, since "[n]early all women find vaginal sensation through...the gateway of clitoris sensation." And in a work focused on male impotence and the need for women to be more sexually responsive to alleviate it, Dr. Hirsch also discussed only the clitoris and its need to be "genuinely stimulated." Even the works of the 1940s, when the Freudian perspective was a strong presence in the culture, all made clitoral stimulation fundamental to the sex act and a prime skill that husbands needed to learn.[152]

Collectively, these texts give the impression that some authors knew about the emphasis of psychoanalysts on the vaginal orgasm and felt compelled to nod to their authority. Yet even those who acknowledged the vaginal orgasm as the ideal did not necessarily denigrate the clitoral form. As Van de Velde put it, the differences between them were like the differences between "two fine kinds of wine."[153] Regardless of division on the nature of female orgasm, these advice works clearly promoted sexual relations that were as intense and pleasurable for women as for men. Despite the containment of this pleasure within marriage and often in sexual positions that seemed to symbolize male dominance, the practical emphasis of these works on women's pleasure and their frequent sidestepping of the vaginal orgasm represented a significant divergence from the more misogynist psychoanalysts of the same period.[154]

Making female orgasm a standard expectation, of course, represented both benefits and pressures for women. It created demands for men to be tender and thoughtful in sex and to encourage wives' pleasure. It also legitimized for women readers of the texts their right to sexual pleasure. Groves and Ross phrased the issue to express subtly the underlying exchange: "If one is to put time and trouble into having intercourse, one should get something out of it, and one must insist on the husband's sharing that view."[155] On the other hand, the pressure for orgasm also intensified the critique of prudery and produced some harsh judgments of women. The Stones argued that such a woman who was sexually unresponsive "must make every effort to obtain an insight into the nature of her disability, to recognize her deficiency, and to appreciate the importance of correcting it." Most extremely, they seemed to suggest faking orgasm: "[E]ven if her sexual desire is not very strong, a wife need not constantly emphasize the fact of her indifference to her husband, or always inform him of her lack of response. At times it may even be well for her to simulate an interest in the sex act and to indicate a greater reaction to sexual stimulation. This in itself might help to create a greater marital harmony, and aid in gradually correcting her sexual indifference."[156] Performance anxiety in the context of women's dependence within marriage could not well promote real equality of sexual entitlement.

Wives whose social or economic power could partially counterbalance marital inequality would have been in the best position to benefit from these advice works. Sex studies of the period show this was the case. Experience, age, education, or class could offer women some leverage. Landis found that women were more likely to achieve orgasm, the more premarital experience they had with men and the less the age difference between themselves and older husbands. Kinsey likewise found that women with more education or a higher social class background attained orgasm more readily than women with less.[157] Greater relative equality helped women claim sexual pleasure for themselves.

———

Considered as a whole, this marriage advice literature worked to revise the cultural formulation of female sexuality in two major ways, compared with the Victorian era: separating (respectable) women's sexuality from its near-total identification with reproduction, and replacing passionlessness with the cultivation of female response as essential to good marital sex. Yet both changes were undermined not only by contradictory tendencies within the texts themselves but also, more important, by the material contexts within which readers were receiving them.

Married women's sexuality was separated from reproduction in these writings not only by contraception but also by the prescription for increased frequency of sex and the undermining of old taboos against sex during pregnancy, postpartum, and during menopause, even during menstruation. These ideas potentially opened to women a pattern of sexual activity more similar to men's, less specifically conditioned by reproductive rhythms and responsibilities.[158] Yet, however much actual women desperately sought to take control of their fertility, the link between their sexual desire and activity and their reproductive capacity was deeply rooted and not always unwelcome. Motherhood remained a major source of most women's dignity and culturally acknowledged value in society, and many women had grown up feeling that motherhood was the legitimation of sex (as advice works' struggle against such ideas shows).[159] Reflecting the power of this identity, Hannah and Abraham Stone gave a different twist to the popular notion that conception could not occur without female orgasm: they reassured readers that failure to reach orgasm would not affect a woman's fertility at all. This could have been comforting to women who had trouble with sex but valued their ability to be mothers.[160] For these reasons the promotion of nonreproductive sex very likely had ambivalent meanings for many women.

Attacking old taboos surrounding women's reproductive cycles while maintaining the male right of sexual initiative also opened women to male demands for more continual sexual activity on the still overwhelmingly unequal ground of marriage. This pressure is seen when advice authors charged women with selfishness or prudery if they did not wish to respond to men's desires. Women had lost a right of resistance based in passionlessness or purity. What remained was grounded in women's bodily difference, whereby women could use the concept of their sexual periodicity to mitigate male sexual demands or channel them to times of women's own desire. Because these authors often drew on their own experience (if female) or observations of patients or clients, this phenomenon suggests that many women subjectively experienced their reproductive cycles, their biological difference from men, as tightly linked to their sexual feelings. The advice books in turn reinforced this link in their prescriptions. Although they promoted birth control, the advice by no means fully disrupted the link between women's sexuality and reproduction.

Cultivating women's sexual responsiveness was the other major shift from Victorian prescriptions, but, however touted in this literature, this effort was hamstrung by the advice works' acceptance of male initiative and male control of the normative sexual act and, more important, by most women's social and financial dependency within marriage and the ongoing double standard in the culture. The promotion of clitoral stimulation for orgasm was indeed a very significant and helpful effort, as was demonstrated by the marriage counseling programs of Abraham Stone and colleague Dr. Lena Levine in New York City in the 1940s. The message that women's orgasms were most effectively induced by clitoral stimulation assisted couples to improve their sexual techniques and women to achieve orgasm. But these women were also "uneasy with the feeling that their bodily rhythms should determine the dynamic of the love-making and felt unable to make the men 'wait.' "[161] Earlier studies reported similar findings. Dickinson found in his gynecological practice many women who knew how they could come but did not tell their husbands. One said, " 'I was a good actress, I hid it. I thought something was terribly wrong with me.' " The Groveses noted on the basis of their marriage counseling work that "numbers of women, in practice, believe themselves immodest if they indicate to their husbands their need or desire for sex union." Landis's 1940 study suggests that in the face of so many other pressures, advice works could often be ineffective. As one woman said, " 'All these positions the books tell about seem absurd. I am discouraged with all our sex relations....[M]y husband...is very unhappy because I don't respond, so I pretend I do. It's of no consequence to me.' " The investigator concluded unsurprisingly that "women may adjust to very inadequate sex relations rather than disrupt the total marriage situation. The extreme emphasis that is placed on the importance of good sex adjustment seems hardly justified because so many marriages survive with this handicap."[162] Women hesitated before men's power over them in marriage; they needed to please husbands; and they faced persistent cultural messages that "good women" did not really want or certainly would not ask for sexual stimulation. These realities countered many women's assertion of desire or encouraged them to fake responses.

These texts contain elements in strong tension with one another. The contending discourses emanating from feminist, revisionist, and more conservative cultural voices created contradictory meanings even within individual works. On the one hand, they supported female-controlled contraception and clitoral stimulation, which increased possibilities for women's sexual comfort and satisfaction. In addition, the belief in periodicity of female desire did create a basis for women to claim some control over the timing of sexual activity on the basis of their own desire. On the other hand, they sustained male dominance in a new, more sexualized form by assuming a more aggressive male nature, sexual need, and initiative, as well as by representing the male-superior position and orgasm through male intromission as standard and sometimes as symbolic of proper gender order.

Due to the serious limitations of this advice literature from a feminist perspective, some scholars have argued that this revision of sexuality and marriage "was a revolution on men's terms," that was oriented to men's sexual well-being, that could "legitimate men's sexual claims on women," and that constituted "an acknowledgment of women's sexual desire" but not their "sexual sovereignty."[163] In many ways these assessments are right. What the sexual advice could mean to individual women depended on the context of their lives, which included a still highly male-dominant culture and the economic subordination of women, both grounded in the deeply unequal partnership of marriage. And marriage was what the manuals promoted; they did not contemplate women's discovery of bliss in celibacy, free love, or lesbianism. Sexual advice manuals made a significant and fascinating contribution to the discourse of modern women's sexuality, but they existed in a landscape still shadowed by the power of marriage to define women's lives. Given that reality, some of the changes seemed more readily to benefit men than women.

It is likely that claims for women's sexual rights in this period could only have achieved wide distribution embedded within a revised but still male-dominant model of marriage. Yet this framework did not completely overwhelm the elements that spoke to women's sexual needs, and it remains historically significant that such elements appeared in the texts. Their presence was a testament to the earlier arguments and struggles of feminists and sex radicals, which also helped provide a new language with which to talk about sex.[164] And certainly some readers of advice works testified to the sense of empowerment that the books could give.[165] These sexual discourses, entrenched within marriage, could not provide equality or autonomy for women, but, as Nancy Cott has asked, "[W]hat transformation in sexual ideology alone could have done so?"[166]

The extraordinarily independent-minded British physician Helena Wright, whose 1930 advice manual built in part on her own early experiences of sexual dissatisfaction, told her biographer fifty years later that she and her husband had both been virgins at marriage, and pleasure had been elusive for her. Unlike many women, however, she talked about it: " 'Peter,' I said, 'I find this a bore.' " She used her medical research skills to learn more and then told him they were going to experiment, and they did. Wright became a stalwart contributor to the British birth control movement, working as chief medical officer at a London birth control clinic for thirty years. There she began to do psychosexual counseling and then wrote several sexual advice and sex education books. She told her patients, including Catholics, that they had the right of "personal judgment" about birth control. She was above all committed to the sexual education of women and tried to teach them "freedom from fear—fear of sex, fear of taboos, fear of public opinion." Though Wright was more confident and socially powerful than most women through education and wealth as well as occupation, she not only fought for sexual freedom and satisfaction for herself but also used her position to empower other women.[167]

Conclusion

In Tess Slesinger's short story "On Being Told That Her Second Husband Has Taken His First Lover" (1935), the husband confesses an affair to his wife and asks her if she can " 'love [him] in spite of anything.' " She asks the same, and he says, " 'Anything, *but no gents.*' " The double standard is palpable as she thinks to herself, "[O]ne thing is clear: one gent, and you will have lost the large part of your power over him." As he leaves the house for work and, she is sure, to see his lover, she does not "sweep the cups and saucers off the table" nor "scream" nor "turn on the gas" nor "fall in a heap sobbing on an empty bed," but rather, thinking of both the second and the first husband, stands "at the kitchen sink letting the water run to grow hotter, and [says] to the cold walls reproachfully, 'Oh Dill, Dill...oh Jimsie, Jimsie...' "[1] Women still needed to do the emotional and sexual work of keeping their husbands happy, while men could more readily take advantage of the new liberal mores.[2] For all the hyperbole about women's status and the new morality, much remained the same.

Some women accepted the challenge of sexual independence and rejected what they saw as women's dependent and sentimental ways of clinging to marriage. They wanted women to be as game as men in facing the vicissitudes of sexual relationships. As anthropologist Ruth Benedict said to her friend Margaret Mead, in regard to a mutual friend: "[N]o one can sink lower than to hold onto a husband who wants to end a marriage."[3] But, as sophisticated professional women living in New York City and participating in an avant-garde intellectual world, these women were exceptional. Probably more common was the stance of New York journalist Marjorie Hillis in her book *Live Alone and Like It* (1936), in which she advised single and divorced women not to pity themselves. If you sing "poor me," Hillis asserts, "Not only will you soon actually be all alone; you will also be an outstanding example of the super-bore." Instead, women should learn to enjoy living alone. Hillis subverts the cheerleading, however, as she lets slip the ulterior motive: to remain glamorous and interesting enough to attract a man. Pamper yourself with little luxuries, she says, to make a good impression, and learn to be "a better companion, which involves being a good listener."[4] In either case women were being told to rein in their expectations of men.

Slesinger's portrayal of women's emotional pain or Hillis's sense of the second-best quality of the single life countered the bold romantic optimism of Goldman, Sanger, or Jessie Fauset about women's sexual lives. Slesinger, Hillis, and other astute and pessimistic women writers took ironic, if not cynical, perspectives on love and marriage that resembled the mixed feelings of wives cited by marriage revisionists—dissatisfaction, yet resignation in the face of men's advantage. These writers acknowledged that marriage had changed; its rigidity and expected permanence were dissolving. What remained the same was the fact that women needed marriage more than men did. Freedom's gains were attended by losses. Because women could get paid employment, the nature of the marriage exchange had altered. They were losing their claim on deference and loyalty from men, losing the protections (limited as they may have been) that law and public opinion allowed in recognition of women's weaker position. In Ursula Parrott's novel *Ex-Wife* (1929), one fictional character argues, "The principal thing that relieving women from the dullness of domesticity did, was to relieve men from any necessity of offering stability in return for love, fidelity and so on." She suggests women should "dynamite the statue of Susan B. Anthony, and start a crusade for the revival of chivalry."[5] Because economically most women still were hard-pressed to earn enough to support themselves, and because emotionally and culturally marriage remained the predominant measure of women's success and normalcy in life, marriage, with all its limitations, continued generally to be the most attractive choice for women. As writer and editor Edith M. Stern wrote in *Men Are Clumsy Lovers* (1934), "Unfortunately, men are still as essential to women's happiness as they were in the benighted days before there were Careers."[6]

A few decades later neither stoicism nor nostalgia for chivalry engaged the young women of second-wave feminism who began to challenge male dominance in all arenas of life, including sexuality and marriage. Looking back, they saw only compromises, not equality, in the forms of modern marriage that they had inherited and instead demanded a comprehensive transformation of the deeply rooted patriarchal patterns that oppressed women and warped the relations between the sexes.[7] Yet the thinkers addressed in this study lived in different times and could not envision the same goals that late twentieth-century feminists could.

Reformers and radicals of the early twentieth century confronted a historic and entrenched institution. Only a radical few could imagine alternatives to marriage in the way that is possible in the twenty-first century. Many were deeply attached to marriage as a cultural sign of full adulthood and the locus of childbearing and child rearing. Most of the thinkers addressed here did not wish to destroy it, believing that it was essential to social order and a civilized nation. Furthermore, marriage continued powerfully to structure social and cultural life. Many men perceived rightly that marriage sustained their privileges as men. Many women found it difficult to abandon the social honor that marriage bestowed (and protection from the harassment sexually active single women faced); most needed the access it provided to men's greater economic resources. In a society whose political leaders generally opposed public provision for child care, this was especially important. In addition, conservatives were able to mobilize inflammatory charges of communism, irreligion, and moral decadence not only against radicals but even against reformers like Lindsey who were committed to marriage. It is no wonder that companionate marriage did not revolutionize heterosexual relations.

Certainly modern marriage still gave the greater advantage to men. It promoted a more sexualized masculinity that sanitized the male "animal" that Victorian conventions had repressed. The vital boyfriend and husband of the new marriage desired a flapper wife who would respond to and support his sexuality. Indeed, *Esquire* magazine, begun in 1933, began to depict women as valuable not for domesticity and childbearing but primarily as sexual objects.[8] Perhaps, as women made gains in the world beyond the family, the more male-oriented strains of the new marital thinking were functioning, especially among whites, to reclaim more direct male control of women within it.[9] The critique of women's attachment to their birth families and of powerful mothers-in-law articulated such a desire for control. And the anxiety about lesbianism and the punitive pathologizing of women's relations with one another that were so evident, especially in Floyd Dell's writings, expressed resentment over the possibility of women's sexual independence from men. Thus, second-wave feminists were right to see the continuity of male dominance in the concept of modern marriage that emerged in the 1910s and 1920s and had become the predominant framework by the 1940s.

Reaction against women's claims and independence clouded the cultural scene in the 1940s and 1950s. Women's increasing presence in the paid workforce sparked much of the response. Men's recruitment for war and a growing war economy drew more and more women into waged work. Between 1940 and 1950, the proportion of all women in the labor force grew from 27 to 30 percent; even more dramatically, the proportion of married women in paid work increased from 17 to 25 percent.[10] During the war, single women became the focus of moral anxiety in cities with large industries, and some locales instituted curfews and other moral surveillance. Married women's employment also raised concerns about both unattended children and extramarital sex.[11] The upheavals of war did have an impact. Postwar divorce rates spiked, for example, with more men than women initiating legal actions, divorcing wives who had had affairs while the men were in the armed services.[12] Particular wartime conditions, then, combined with the traditional patriarchal suspicion of women's deviousness to raise alarms about women's sexuality.

Both mothers and employed women received an undue amount of vitriol. Two best-selling antifeminist diatribes appeared in the 1940s. Philip Wylie's *Generation of Vipers* (1942) attacked mothers for suffocating and emasculating their sons, while Ferdinand Lundberg and Marynia Farnham's *Modern Woman: The Lost Sex* (1947) excoriated career women for acting like men and denying their desires for conventional marriage and motherhood. Both used psychoanalytic concepts to ground their charges.[13]

The war and postwar years witnessed the great popularity of the psychoanalytic perspective. The controversies over female sexuality within the Freudian tradition since its arrival in the United States had settled by the 1940s into an understanding of the vaginal orgasm as "a standard through which women's sexual impulses were deemed healthy or pathological."[14] In the broad range of nonpsychoanalytic marital advice works, the influence of psychoanalysis in the 1950s also produced an increasing insistence on the vaginal orgasm. (Alfred Kinsey questioned the concept in *Sexual Behavior in the Human Female* [1953], but his view had little impact until the 1960s.) Some writers criticized earlier works for putting too much responsibility on men and instead blamed women for their sexual failures. This outlook coincided with larger cold war anxieties about moral decline and the weakening of American families.[15]

The cold war and the baby boom in the 1950s in some ways reinforced men's dominance in marriage as defensive nationalism again linked marriage and conventional gender roles tightly to social and political order. Social commentators trumpeted a "marriage crisis," as in the 1920s. Fears persisted of the loss of male-female difference, of weak men, and of women who were too powerful or sexual. Anxious social critics urged the better containment of sex and of women in marriage to maintain the strength of the family and the nation.[16] Middle-class and more educated families were encouraged to have more children, and many did so, understanding it as an expression of good citizenship. The birthrate reversed its 150-year decline, and popular culture generated ubiquitous images of happy wives and mothers.[17] Middle-class married women in suburbia certainly faced significant conservative pressures in the 1950s. This was the situation about which Betty Friedan complained in *The Feminine Mystique* (1963).

Yet at the same time the postwar culture included much more acknowledgment of married women's nondomestic employment and political participation than Friedan recognized. And their labor force participation continued to climb, rising from 25 to 32 percent of all wives between 1950 and 1960. Figures still included a higher proportion of black than of white wives, but the white rate of growth was greater. Married women took paid jobs to support a higher standard of living for their families and to pay for higher education for their children, as well as for personal satisfaction. Better-educated white middle-class wives were also drawn by the labor market needs of an expanding economy—for clerical workers, nurses, and teachers. Black wives continued in waged labor to help their more economically strained families. But, as Friedan's National Organization for Women stressed in the 1960s, all married women wage earners faced gender discrimination and the burden of the double day, and black women faced racial discrimination in addition.[18]

These developments accompanied the establishment of companionate marriage not only as the predominant prescriptive ideal but also as popular understanding and practice. Age of marriage dropped in the 1950s, as though Ben Lindsey's exhortations to let young people marry early and have a legitimate sex life were finally being heard. Social scientists reported that Americans espoused companionate marriage's norms of emotional intimacy and greater psychological equality of men and women. African American periodicals propagated the ideal of sexual intimacy and women's sexual equality and suggested black married couples were facing the same issues as whites. Working-class as well as middle-class couples expressed the sense that women's sexual enjoyment should be part of marriage. And by the 1960s the Roman Catholic Marriage Encounter movement was promoting intense emotional relationships between spouses for a more middle-class, suburban Catholic population.

Although open support for birth control was impossible due to ongoing church opposition, in other ways the movement's vision of marriage resembled earlier reformers' emphasis on the couple pair-bond.[19] By the 1960s, then, American marriages had shifted substantially from nineteenth-century patterns, although new pressures had arisen in relation to sexuality, childbearing, and employment for married women.

Outside marriage, other developments set the stage for the massive protests of women's and gay and lesbian liberation. In the 1960s, single women college students began to engage in sexual relations at rates more similar to those of men. "Permissiveness with affection" began to characterize the day-to-day mores of many youth, although this change was hampered by the difficulty single women had in obtaining birth control and by the even greater difficulty in getting abortions. Other single people, attracted to their own sex, took part in the lively gay and lesbian subculture, often centered around bars, that had emerged in the postwar period. But they had to face police harassment and criminal sanctions against their sexual relationships.[20] Despite much liberalization in sexual practices by the 1960s, official sexual values continued to center on marriage, heterosexuality, and reproduction.

Then radical feminism and the new gay and lesbian liberation movement came on the scene in the late 1960s and 1970s and addressed the many buried tensions involved in these social and sexual changes. They critiqued marriage and heterosexuality as a whole and proclaimed sexual liberation as central to their demands. Women's liberation groups called for greater access to contraception and abortion, and black feminists additionally denounced racist sterilization practices as well as black nationalist demands that women focus on motherhood to build up the black population.[21] At the same time the Supreme Court was loosening restrictions embodied in the 1873 Comstock law that earlier sex radicals like Margaret Sanger had fought. In *Griswold v. Connecticut* (1965), the Court struck down legal prohibitions on contraception, and it extended those rights to single people in 1972 in *Eisenstadt v. Baird*. After New York made abortion legal in 1970, the Supreme Court invalidated other state laws against abortion in its *Roe v. Wade* decision of 1973. These decisions implied that the sexual relationship apart from procreation was fundamental to marriage and that the state's right to intervene in it had limits. And, though the Court framed the cases in terms of privacy rights, the justices also implicitly confirmed the claims of feminists that women were not defined only by their reproductive role.

But beyond reproductive rights, feminists of the early 1970s denounced the entire framework of heterosexuality, from gender role socialization to dating and marriage, as grounded fundamentally in an inequality that was not natural but socially created. They pointed to the basis of that inequality in employment and pay discrimination, in cultural concepts of women as "naturally" suited to child care and domesticity, and in men's violence in rape and woman battering. They proclaimed women's rights as individuals and called for sexual liberation. Anne Koedt's article "The Myth of the Vaginal Orgasm" attacked the response that many marriage manuals were promoting by the 1950s and reclaimed the clitoris. Women's faking of orgasms was understood as a reaction both to self-centered male lovemaking and to the social and financial dependency that produced their need to please men. Heterosexual feminists claimed sexual freedom and sought to transcend the drive for security in marriage. Sexual self-determination and the capacity for independence from men—so much more possible for women of this era who were accustomed to employment—lay at the heart of women's liberation.[22]

Feminist rebellion also laid open the possibility of lesbian sexuality. Many lesbians participated in the new women's movement, but previously heterosexual women also followed their revolutionary thinking toward a lesbian choice, especially in the early 1970s. The gay liberation movement made same-sex relationships more public and demanded acceptance. Lesbianism became a symbol of self-determination and independence from men. Lesbian feminists pioneered a broader and more fluid understanding of women's sexuality and sexual relations that separated sexual desire from gender roles and shifted the focus off penetration and the missionary position that was so prevalent in marriage advice manuals. Lesbians celebrated the clitoris as the source of women's pleasure, and heterosexual feminists did, too.[23]

Feminists divided among themselves over sexual issues in complicated and painful ways from the 1970s to the 1990s, but they had irrevocably recast the terms of women's sexuality. Assertions of fixed differences between men and women are now always contested, and, indeed, the relationships among sex, gender, and sexuality have loosened altogether. Women's sexual desires are assumed, and single women can openly pursue sexually active lives. Even conservative Christian evangelicals, who strongly opposed women's and gay liberation, began in the 1970s to advise clitoral stimulation to enhance marital sex.[24]

Marriage, formerly the only officially acceptable situation in which women could be sexually active, now exists as one of many choices. There are more social settings where gay men and lesbians need not hide their relationships. Cohabitation competes with marriage, although less so in the United States than in other parts of the world. To be sure, vocal conservative

American religious and political groups continue to condemn these alternatives, but they are not able to stop them. Yet marriage also remains popular. Almost everywhere in the United States it still confers legal and financial benefits that some lesbians and gay men also seek to gain. It retains a powerful cultural hold.[25]

The companionate marriage of the 1920s emerged in a very different world, and yet it prepared the ground in important ways for today's developments. It was designed for an image of modern women, who would hold a larger place in the public world than their mothers and claim some kind of equality. This marital arrangement was intended to reconfigure the inherited cultural patterns of gender relations that discomfited many urban women and men of the early twentieth century. Most prominently, incorporating birth control and romantic sexual love, it left behind the Victorian emphasis on sexual restraint and moderation, epitomized by the respectable lady. It redefined women as less maternal and more sexual and redefined marriage as a union of privacy, sexual companionship, and greater interpersonal equality. The most prevalent version of companionate marriage did not drastically alter gender roles, but it did provide a functional modern form for the middle-class family, with its emphasis on home as an arena of consumption and leisure. Built on bonds of romantic love, the modern marriage was supposed to be less tied down by traditional networks of kin and community. This made it more fragile but also more flexible.[26] The intense and private heterosexual relationships this pattern allowed may have loosened ties to mothers and older women that some young wives wanted to escape in order to define modern marital roles for themselves. But heterosexual intensity could also isolate women from potential support. Modern marriage resembled Victorian marriage in that it remained the most culturally valued situation in which to rear children, and women remained their principal caretakers. From one perspective, then, companionate marriage appears as a historic adaptation to broad social and economic changes of the twentieth century that did not dramatically change women's place.

But this was not an impersonal structural change. Men and women, both white and African American, were agents of this development. The women insisted they had specifically sexual and not only maternal desires; they sought greater freedom from familial authority; and they hoped for relationships of equality and sexual satisfaction. In their writings they portrayed some women trying to live out these new possibilities. By putting such images into public discussion, no matter how overshadowed by cute flappers in popular fiction and film, feminist women writers did counter male-centered perspectives and opened to their readers possibilities beyond the kind of subordination that had characterized Victorian marriage. But as long as women's material, social, and cultural inequality continued to be embedded in law and everyday life, it remained much more difficult for even those women who were thinking in new ways actually to live out their visions. A feminist ideal for egalitarian relations remained very much a minority hope in the early to mid-twentieth-century United States.

Although invisible to most whites, African Americans were participants in these contentions and changes, but the historical legacy of racism produced some distinctive emphases. Whatever their actual experiences or private views, this cultural reality continued to make it a delicate balancing act for black women to venture open support for modern women's sexual claims. Popular entertainers like Billie Holliday did so but beyond the margins of respectability. Yet at the same time, African American public discussion of marriage normalized more egalitarian arrangements on the basis of black wives' much greater labor force participation as well as traditions of community participation. This situation existed due to racism and economic exigency—hardly desirable conditions. But it did foreshadow what became the majority pattern later in the century. African American sociologist E. Franklin Frazier's words of 1960, when he said that black women's "spirit of independence and self-assertion...has provided generally a pattern of equalitarian relationships between men and women for Americans," now sound particularly prophetic.[27] Gender parity requires comprehensive cultural change to reenvision the relations of men and women, but also essential is less disparity of material circumstances, which African American couples were somewhat more likely to experience.

Altering the deeply embedded cultural conventions governing sexuality and marriage was a massive project that both feminists and more conservative reformers could attempt but neither control nor accomplish as they wished. When Rachelle Yarros, Jessie Fauset, Helena Wright, and Gladys Groves bent over their desks, writing to document, imagine, and promote marriages of economic partnership and sexual camaraderie for the women of their day, they surely reached and heartened some of our grandmothers and mothers and thus helped to shape our world, in which feminists continue to strive for the freedom, equality, and sexual and reproductive self-determination of all women.

Selection of Marriage Manuals

Chapter 5 is based on an analysis of twenty-six books on sex and marriage. Five—four from the 1920s and one from 1933—form a separate category of early works with significantly less focus on sexual intercourse per se. Most of these transitional works were still building the case for companionate marriage and treated sex rather briefly, or in Sanger's case very romantically, as part of that. However, they differ from the lengthy and heavily medical—physiologically and anatomically detailed—advice works on marital sex that poured out later. The remaining twenty-one books are of this type. One of these, a physician-authored text that could only be sold to physicians, was published in 1919; another appeared in 1927, the remainder in the 1930s and 1940s (in the United States, sometimes earlier in Britain or Europe).

This latter sample of works was chosen through a combination of their accessibility and varied references to their popularity or usefulness by other contemporary marriage writers or later historians. Accessibility (in libraries but especially used-book stores) was itself a sign of popularity in that some works had multiple printings. Theodoor H. Van de Velde's *Ideal Marriage*, for example, was first published in German in 1926 and English in 1928 (Britain) and 1930 (United States). Repetition of themes in later works showed not only the influence of earlier ones but also the elaboration and reinforcement of a basic framework for understanding marital sex problems that then remained in place until second-wave feminism.

The books are listed in chronological order of appearance in English in the United States.

I. Earlier, Less Explicit Texts

William J. Robinson, *Married Life and Happiness, or Love and Comfort in Marriage*, 4th ed. (1922; repr., New York: Eugenics, 1929)

Joseph Collins, M.D., *The Doctor Looks at Love and Life* (New York: Doubleday, Doran, 1926)

Margaret Sanger, *Happiness in Marriage* (New York: Blue Ribbon, 1926)

Sherwood Eddy, *Sex and Youth* (New York: Doubleday, Doran, 1929)

Rachelle Yarros, *Modern Woman and Sex: The Feminist Physician Speaks* (New York: Vanguard, 1929)

II. More Explicit Texts

H. W. Long, *Sane Sex Life and Sane Sex Living* (New York: Eugenics, 1919)

William J. Fielding, *Sex and the Love-Life* (New York: Blue Ribbon, 1927)

Th. H. Van de Velde, M.D., *Ideal Marriage: Its Physiology and Technique* (1926 [Germany]; New York: Random House, 1930)

Marie Stopes, *Married Love: A New Contribution to the Solution of Sex Difficulties* (1918; repr., New York: Putnam, 1931)

Helena Wright, M.D., *The Sex Factor in Marriage* (New York: Vanguard, 1931)

Ernest R. Groves and Gladys H. Groves, *Sex in Marriage* (1931; 3rd ed., New York: Emerson, 1943)

Millard S. Everett, *The Hygiene of Marriage* (New York: Vanguard, 1932)

M. J. Exner, M.D., *The Sexual Side of Marriage* (1932; New York: Eugenics, 1937)

Isabel Emslie Hutton, M.D., *The Sex Technique in Marriage* (1923 [Britain]; 1932 [U.S.]; New York: Emerson, 1949)

Charles A. Clinton, M.D., *Married Sweethearts: The Role of Sex Behavior in Marriage* (New York: Macfadden, 1933)

Charles A. Clinton, M.D., *Sex Behavior in Marriage* (New York: Pioneer, 1935)

Edwin Hirsch, M.D., *The Power to Love: A Psychic and Physiologic Study of Regeneration* (New York: Knopf, 1935)

Gladys Groves and Robert A. Ross, M.D., *The Married Woman: A Practical Guide to Happy Marriage* (Cleveland, Ohio: World, 1936)

Maurice Chideckel, M.D., *The Single, the Engaged, and the Married* (New York: Eugenics, 1936)

Hannah Stone, M.D., and Abraham Stone, M.D., *A Marriage Manual: A Practical Guide-Book to Sex and Marriage* (New York: Simon and Schuster, 1937)

Dr. J. Rutgers, *How to Attain and Practice the Ideal Sex Life* (1922 [Germany]; New York: Falstaff Press, 1937)

LeMon Clark, M.S., M.D., *Emotional Adjustment in Marriage* (St. Louis: Mosby, 1937)

Norman Himes, *Your Marriage: A Guide to Happiness* (New York: Farrar and Rinehart, 1940)

Ernest Groves, Gladys Groves, and Catherine Groves, *Sex Fulfillment in Marriage* (New York: Emerson, 1942)

Edward Podolsky, M.D., *The Modern Sex Manual* (New York: Cadillac, 1942)

William S. Sadler, M.D., and Lena K. Sadler, M.D., *Living a Sane Sex Life* (New York: Wilcox and Follett, 1944)

Notes

Introduction

1. Marge Piercy, *Small Changes* (Garden City, N.Y.: Doubleday, 1973), 5, 4, 8, 12, 16–17.
2. Ibid., 18, 20–21, 22–25, 30, 35–38, 493–94. Piercy could almost have been using as an outline Beverly Jones's "The Dynamics of Marriage and Motherhood," in *Sisterhood Is Powerful: An Anthology of Writings from the Women's Liberation Movement*, ed. Robin Morgan (New York: Vintage, 1970), 46–61. See also Jane Gerhard, *Desiring Revolution: Second-Wave Feminism and the Rewriting of American Sexual Thought, 1920 to 1982* (New York: Columbia University Press, 2001), 81–116.
3. Judith Schwarz, Kathy Peiss, and Christina Simmons, "'We Were a Little Band of Willful Women': The Heterodoxy Club of Greenwich Village," in *Passion and Power: Sexuality in History*, ed. Kathy Peiss and Christina Simmons, with Robert A. Padgug (Philadelphia: Temple University Press, 1989), 118–37; Crystal Eastman, "Bed-Makers and Bosses" (1923), in *Crystal Eastman on Women and Revolution*, ed. Blanche Wiesen Cook (New York: Oxford University Press, 1978), 83–85; Helen Hull, *Labyrinth* (New York, 1923).
4. Margaret Sanger, *Happiness in Marriage* (New York: Blue Ribbon, 1926), 38, 125–33; Rachelle Yarros, *Modern Woman and Sex: The Feminist Physician Speaks* (New York: Vanguard, 1929), 61–67; Ernest R. Groves and Gladys Hoagland Groves, *Sex in Marriage* (New York: Emerson Books, 1943).
5. Although "whiteness" was expanding to incorporate a wider array of people of European descent by the 1920s, whites still seldom acknowledged or discussed people of other races. Matthew Frye Jacobson, *Whiteness of a Different Color: European Immigrants and the Alchemy of Race* (Cambridge, Mass.: Harvard University Press, 1998), 91–135.

6. Vicki L. Ruiz, *From Out of the Shadows: Mexican Women in Twentieth-Century America* (New York: Oxford University Press, 1988), 51–71; Judith E. Smith, *Family Connections: A History of Italian and Jewish Immigrant Lives in Providence, Rhode Island, 1900–1940* (Albany: State University of New York Press, 1985), 114–17; Susan Porter Benson, *Household Accounts: Working-Class Family Economies in the Interwar United States* (Ithaca, N.Y.: Cornell University Press, 2007), 17; Charles E. Johnson, *Shadow of the Plantation* (Chicago: University of Chicago Press, 1934), 47–58. Among secular Jewish immigrants of the early twentieth century, however, there is evidence of considerable interest in books on sex and marriage, as well as a Yiddish translation of Margaret Sanger's *What Every Girl Should Know*. See Eli Lederhendler, *Jewish Responses to Modernity: New Voices in America and Eastern Europe* (New York: New York University Press, 1994), 140–58. Some second-generation immigrants also did adopt some of the youth-controlled courtship practices of the new marriage model by the 1920s and 1930s. See Randy D. McBee, *Dance Hall Days: Intimacy and Leisure among Working-Class Immigrants in the United States* (New York: New York University Press, 2000), 29–36, 198–238. On theorizing the relationship of dominant and other cultural views, see Raymond Williams, *Schooling and Capitalism: A Sociological Reader*, ed. Roger Dale, Geoff Esland, and Madeleine MacDonald (London: Routledge and Kegan Paul, 1976), 202–10.

7. Judith Stein, "Defining the Race, 1890–1930," in *The Invention of Ethnicity*, ed. Werner Sollors (New York: Oxford University Press, 1989), 266n82; Evelyn Brooks Higginbotham, *Righteous Discontent: The Women's Movement in the Black Baptist Church, 1880–1920* (Cambridge, Mass.: Harvard University Press, 1993), 187; Michele Mitchell, *Righteous Propagation: African Americans and the Politics of Racial Destiny after Reconstruction* (Chapel Hill: University of North Carolina Press, 2004), 76–81.

8. Stephanie Coontz, *Marriage, a History: How Love Conquered Marriage* (New York: Penguin, 2005), 53–56, 88–89, 154–55.

9. Amy Dru Stanley, "Marriage, Property, and Class," in *A Companion to American Women's History*, ed. Nancy Hewitt (Malden, Mass.: Blackwell, 2002), 193–205; Nancy Cott, *Public Vows: A History of Marriage and the Nation* (Cambridge, Mass.: Harvard University Press, 2000), 3, 11–13, 26–27, 57, 66, 80–96.

10. Coontz, *Marriage*, 145–46.

11. Hendrik Hartog, *Man and Wife in America: A History* (Cambridge, Mass.: Harvard University Press, 2000).

12. Mary P. Ryan, *Cradle of the Middle Class: The Family in Oneida County, New York, 1790–1865* (New York: Cambridge University Press, 1981); Paul Johnson, *Shopkeeper's Millennium: Society and Revivals in Rochester, New York, 1815–1836* (New York: Hill and Wang, 1978); Allan Greer, " 'The Queen Is a Whore!': Gender, Language, and Politics in the Lower Canadian Rebellion of 1837–1838," in *Rethinking Canada: The Promise of Women's History*, ed. Veronica Strong-Boag, Mona Gleason, and Adele Perry (Toronto: Oxford University Press, 2002), 59–74.

13. Michel Foucault, *Discipline and Punish: The Birth of the Prison*, trans. Alan Sheridan (New York: Vintage, 1979), and *The History of Sexuality*, vol. 1, trans. Robert Hurley (New York: Vintage, 1980), 68–70, 103–22; Lynn Hunt, "Foucault's Subject in *The History of Sexuality*," in *Discourses of Sexuality: From Aristotle to AIDS*, ed. Domna C. Stanton (Ann Arbor: University of Michigan Press, 1992), 86–87; Thomas Laqueur, *Solitary Sex: A Cultural History of Masturbation* (New York: Zone Books, 2003), 270; Ryan, *Cradle of the Middle Class*, 126, 160–61.

14. Helen Horowitz, *Rereading Sex: Battles over Sexual Knowledge and Suppression in Nineteenth-Century America* (New York: Vintage, 2003), 358–436; Timothy J. Gilfoyle, *City of Eros: New York City, Prostitution, and the Commercialization of Sex, 1790–1920* (New York: Norton, 1992), 106, 113–15, 181–96; Christine Stansell, *City of Women: Sex and Class in New York, 1780–1860* (Chicago: University of Illinois Press, 1982), 171–92. Charles Rosenberg refers to the code of traditional male sexual freedom as the traditional masculine ethos, which he argues existed in tension with the ideal of the Christian gentleman. See Charles Rosenberg, "Sexuality, Class and Role in 19th-Century America," *American Quarterly* 25 (1973): 140.

15. John D'Emilio and Estelle Freedman, *Intimate Matters: A History of Sexuality in America* (New York: Harper and Row, 1988), 113; Horowitz, *Rereading Sex*, 50–55, 265–70.

16. Laqueur, *Solitary Sex*, 209–21, 267–302; Rosenberg, "Sexuality, Class and Role," 135–40, 152; Cott, *Public Vows*, 17–23; Barbara Welter, "The Cult of True Womanhood," *American Quarterly* 18 (1966): 151–74; Greer, " 'The Queen Is a Whore!' " 63–65.

17. Nancy Cott, "Passionlessness: An Interpretation of Victorian Sexual Ideology, 1790–1850," in *A Heritage of Her Own*, ed. Nancy F. Cott and Elizabeth H. Pleck (New York: Simon and Schuster, 1979), 162–81. The long-standing ascetic Christian ideal had coexisted with the earlier understanding of sexuality as a powerful force within every individual which needed to be controlled. Ryan, *Cradle of the Middle Class*, 79.

18. Horowitz, *Rereading Sex*, 45–122, 269–70; D'Emilio and Freedman, *Intimate Matters*, 161–65; Coontz, *Marriage*, 177–78; Karen Lystra, *Searching the Heart: Women, Men, and Romantic Love in Nineteenth-Century America* (New York: Oxford University Press, 1989), 6–7. Lystra argues that "passionlessness was not a dominant ideal within middle- to upper-middle-class American marriages," pointing to the prominence of sexual matters in the love letters and noting that "purity" did not contradict "legitimate sexual expression," that is, within a loving marriage. She does acknowledge, however, that many thinkers believed women's sexual endowment was milder than men's and that most proponents of romantic marital love advocated "moderate sexual indulgence." This marital romanticism coexisted with, and, she argues, may have been intensified by, public reticence about sexuality; see Lystra, *Searching the Heart*, 58, 60, 75–76, 79, 101–2, 88–91.

19. Smith-Rosenberg, "Beauty, the Beast, and the Militant Woman"; Charles Walter Clarke, *Taboo: The Story of the Pioneers of Social Hygiene* (Washington, D.C.: Public Affairs Press, 1961), 75; David J. Pivar, *Purity Crusade: Sexual Morality and Social Control, 1868–1900* (Westport, Conn.: Greenwood, 1973), 32, 51–65, 78–121; Mary Odem, *Delinquent Daughters: Protecting and Policing Adolescent Female Sexuality in the United States, 1885–1920* (Chapel Hill: University of North Carolina Press, 1995), 8–37.

20. Gilfoyle, *City of Eros*, 187.

21. Horowitz, *Rereading Sex*, 14, 299–318, 357–436.

22. D'Emilio and Freedman, *Intimate Matters*, 159–63.

23. Ibid., 56–61, 73–85, 272–84; Janet Farrell Brodie, *Contraception and Abortion in 19th-Century America* (Ithaca, N.Y.: Cornell University Press, 1994), 180–224; James Mohr, *Abortion in America: The Origins and Evolution of National Policy, 1800–1900* (New York: Oxford University Press, 1978); Linda Gordon, *Woman's Body, Woman's Right: Birth Control in America*, rev. ed. (New York: Penguin, 1990), 95–101, 153–54; Stanley L. Engerman, "Changes in Black Fertility, 1880–1940," in *Family and Population in Nineteenth-Century America*, ed. Tamara K. Hareven and Maris Vinovskis (Princeton, N.J.: Princeton University Press, 1978), 126–53.

24. D'Emilio and Freedman, *Intimate Matters*, 58–59; Gordon, *Woman's Body, Woman's Right*, 19–22.

25. Andrea Tone, "Black Market Birth Control: Contraceptive Entrepreneurship and Criminality in the Gilded Age," *Journal of American History* 87 (2000): 435–59.

26. Gordon, *Woman's Body, Woman's Right*, 219.

27. Floyd Dell, *Love in the Machine Age: A Psychological Study of the Transition from Patriarchal Society* (New York: Farrar and Rinehart, 1930), 6. Examples of this perspective include Sidney Ditzion, *Marriage, Morals, and Sex in America: A History of Ideas* (New York: Bookman, 1953), and Edward M. Brecher, *The Sex Researcher*, with foreword by William H. Masters and Virginia E. Johnson (Boston: Little, Brown, 1969).

28. Cott, *Public Vows*, 157.

29. Daniel Horowitz, *The Morality of Spending: Attitudes toward the Consumer Society in America, 1875–1940* (Chicago: Ivan Dee, 1985), xxvi–xxvii.

30. Lewis A. Erenberg, *Steppin' Out: New York Nightlife and the Transformation of American Culture, 1890–1930* (Westport, Conn.: Greenwood, 1981).

31. Sharon R. Ullman, *Sex Seen: The Emergence of Modern Sexuality in America* (Berkeley: University of California Press, 1997), 23, 103–9; Lary May, *Screening Out the Past: The Birth of Mass Culture and the Motion Picture Industry* (New York: Oxford University Press, 1980), 96, 97, 102.

32. Barbara Miller Solomon, *In the Company of Educated Women: A History of Women and Higher Education in America* (New Haven, Conn.: Yale University Press, 1985), 43–61; Eleanor Flexner, *Century of Struggle: The Woman's Rights Movement in the United States* (1959; repr., New York: Atheneum, 1970); Lynn Y. Weiner, *From Working Girl to Working Mother: The Female Labor Force in the United States, 1820–1980* (Chapel Hill: University of North Carolina Press,

1985), 18–30; Joanne Meyerowitz, *Women Adrift: Independent Wage Earners in Chicago, 1880–1930* (Chicago: University of Chicago Press, 1988); Sarah Deutsch, *Women and the City: Gender, Space and Power in Boston, 1870–1940* (New York: Oxford University Press, 2000), 78–114; Christine Stansell, *American Moderns: Bohemian New York and the Creation of a New Century* (New York: Holt, 2000), 28–30.

33. Ullman, *Sex Seen*, 75; Roderick Phillips, *Untying the Knot: A Short History of Divorce* (New York: Cambridge University, 1991), 210; Jesse F. Battan, "The 'Rights' of Husbands and the 'Duties' of Wives: Power and Desire in the American Bedroom, 1850–1910," *Journal of Family History* 24 (1999): 165–86. In terms of the now commonly used statistics on probability of divorce, the probability of divorce in existing U.S. marriages in 1910 was about 15 percent versus 45 percent in 2000. Robert Schoen and Vladimir Canudas-Romo, "Timing Effects on Divorce: 20th Century Experience in the United States," *Journal of Marriage and Family* 68 (2006): 755.

34. E. Anthony Rotundo, *American Manhood: Transformation in Masculinity from the Revolution to the Modern Era* (New York: Basic Books, 1993), 227–32.

35. Carroll Smith-Rosenberg, "The Female World of Love and Ritual: Relations between Women in Nineteenth-Century America," and "The New Woman as Androgyne: Social Disorder and Gender Crisis, 1870–1936," in Smith-Rosenberg, *Disorderly Conduct: Visions of Gender in Victorian America* (New York: Knopf, 1985), 53–76, 245–96; Lisa Duggan, "The Trials of Alice Mitchell: Sensationalism, Sexology, and the Lesbian Subject in Turn-of-the-Century America," *Signs* 18 (1993): 791–814; Leila J. Rupp, *A Desired Past: A Short History of Same-Sex Love in America* (Chicago: University of Chicago Press, 1999), 45.

36. Daniel T. Rodgers, "In Search of Progressivism," in *The Promise of American History: Progress and Prospects*, ed. Stanley I. Kutler and Stanley N. Katz (Baltimore: Johns Hopkins University Press, 1982), 126–27; John Burnham, "The Progressive Era Revolution in American Attitudes toward Sex," *Journal of American History* 59 (1973): 885–908.

37. Sheila Rowbotham and Jeffrey Weeks, *Socialism and the New Life: The Personal and Sexual Politics of Edward Carpenter and Havelock Ellis* (London: Pluto Press, 1977); Warren Susman, "'Personality' and the Making of Twentieth-Century Culture," in Susman, *Culture as History: The Transformation of American Society in the Twentieth Century* (New York: Pantheon, 1984), 271–85; John Higham, "The Reorientation of American Culture in the 1890s," in Higham, *Writing American History* (Bloomington: Indiana University Press, 1970), 79, 84.

38. Joseph Singal, "Towards a Definition of American Modernism," *American Quarterly* 39 (1987): 7–26; Stansell, *American Moderns*, 75–80, 225.

39. Gordon, *Woman's Body, Woman's Right*, 153–54, 186–245; Ellen Chesler, *Woman of Valor: Margaret Sanger and the Birth Control Movement in America* (New York: Simon and Schuster, 1992), 34, 65–73, 81–88.

40. Like Susan Porter Benson in *Household Accounts*, I use "partnership" to indicate a sense of "shared responsibility and joint enterprise" in marriage, more than

that which characterized the prescriptive (and implicitly middle-class) marriages
of more divided gender roles.

Chapter 1: Education for Social Hygiene

1. The text of the pamphlet was published as "Friend or Enemy?" in *Social Hygiene*
   2 (1916): 481–99. The cover is pictured and distribution discussed in another
   article by Exner, "Social Hygiene and the War," *Social Hygiene* 5 (1919): 280,
   285. *Social Hygiene*, which became the *Journal of Social Hygiene* with volume 8
   (1922), will be referred to hereafter as *SH* or *JSH*.
2. Exner "Friend or Enemy?" 490, and "Social Hygiene and the War," 289. Peter
   Stearns explains that the Victorian emotional style encouraged such intense
   responses to mothers in *American Cool: Constructing a Twentieth-Century Emotional Style* (New York: New York University Press, 1994), 36.
3. Exner, "Social Hygiene and the War," 281–83, 286, 289. The army's response
   showed the clash of the moral and scientific: though the military encouraged the
   lectures and pamphlets, its campaign to control venereal disease in France was
   made effective also by the requirement that every soldier undergo preventive
   medical treatment within three hours of having sexual contact. The U.S. Army
   did indeed have lower rates of venereal disease than other Allied forces, but it was
   not all due to sexual restraint. Allan M. Brandt, *No Magic Bullet: A Social History
   of Venereal Disease in the United States since 1880* (New York: Oxford University
   Press, 1985), 102–15.
4. Brandt, *No Magic Bullet*, 9–13, 16–18, 22; Jeffrey P. Moran, *Teaching Sex: The
   Shaping of Adolescence in the Twentieth Century* (Cambridge, Mass.: Harvard
   University Press, 2000), 1–20; Paul Boyer, *Urban Masses and Moral Order in
   America, 1820–1920* (Cambridge, Mass.: Harvard University Press, 1978), 200.
   The term "social hygiene" was coined in 1907, according to William F. Snow,
   "Progress, 1900–1915," *SH* 2 (1916): 37.

   The most important existing treatments of this movement are Brandt,
   No Magic Bullet; Moran, *Teaching Sex*; and Julian B. Carter, "Birds, Bees, and
   Venereal Disease: Toward an Intellectual History of Sex Education," *Journal of
   the History of Sexuality* 10 (2001): 213–49. My treatment differs from theirs in
   its greater emphasis on women and on the role of African Americans. A useful
   earlier study is Bryan Strong, "Ideas of the Early Sex Education Movement in
   America, 1890–1920," *History of Education Quarterly* 12 (1972): 129–61.
5. Snow, "Progress," 39.
6. American Social Hygiene Association, "The Association's Tenth Year, 1914–24,"
   JSH 11 (1925): 283–90; Moran, *Teaching Sex*, 68–75.
7. Brandt, *No Magic Bullet*, 9–13.
8. John C. Burnham, "The Cultural Interpretation of the Progressive Movement,"
   in *Paths into American Culture* (Philadelphia: Temple University Press, 1988),
   208–28; Daniel T. Rodgers, "In Search of Progressivism," *Reviews in American
   History* 10 (December 1982): 113–32. On the racism of elites, see Judith Stein,

"Defining the Race 1890–1930," in *The Invention of Ethnicity*, ed. Werner Sollors (New York: Oxford University Press, 1989), 79–80, and T. J. Jackson Lears, *No Place of Grace: Antimodernism and the Transformation of American Culture, 1880–1920* (New York: Pantheon, 1981), 107–9. On Progressives' racism, see David W. Southern, *The Malignant Heritage: Yankee Progressives and the Negro Question, 1901–1914* (Chicago: Loyola University Press, 1968).

9. Boyer, *Urban Masses*, 207–10; Gilman M. Ostrander, *American Civilization in the First Machine Age, 1890–1940* (New York: Harper and Row, 1970), 27; Jane Addams, *The Spirit of Youth and the City Streets* (1909; repr., New York: Macmillan, 1957), 108; Henry S. Curtis, "The Relation of Public Recreation to Problems of Sex," *JSH* 10 (1924): 204–5.

10. Quotation from Josephine L. Baldwin, "Theaters, Nickelodeons, and Amusements," in *The Sunday School and the Teens*, ed. John L. Alexander (New York: Association Press, 1913), 282; and Harriet McT. Daniels and Gertrude K. Griffith, "Home Conditions and the Adolescent Girl," in the same volume, 188. Addams, *The Spirit of Youth*, 6, 13, 18–19; Robert A. Woods and Albert J. Kennedy, eds., *Young Working Girls: A Summary of Evidence from Two Thousand Social Workers* (Boston: Houghton Mifflin, 1913), 6. See also Kathy Peiss, *Cheap Amusements: Working Women and Leisure in Turn-of-the-Century New York* (Philadelphia: Temple University Press, 1986).

11. Charles W. Eliot, "Public Opinion and Sex Hygiene," in *Report of the Sex Education Sessions of the Fourth International Congress on School Hygiene and of the Annual Meeting of the Federation* (New York: American Federation for Sex Hygiene, 1913), 15–16.

12. Linda Gordon, *Woman's Body, Woman's Right: A Social History of Birth Control* (New York: Grossman, 1976), 277–78; John S. Haller, *Eugenics: Hereditarian Attitudes in American Thought* (New Brunswick, N.J.: Rutgers University Press, 1963), 79, 6–7. Americans not of British stock first outnumbered Anglo-Americans in 1914. Ostrander, *American Civilization*, 27, 277.

13. Winfield Scott Hall, "The Relation of Education in Sex to Race Betterment," *Social Hygiene* 1 (1914): 69; Exner, "Social Hygiene and the War," 289.

14. Gordon, *Woman's Body, Woman's Right*, 136. For a full statement of the eugenic position of some social hygienists, see Roswell H. Johnson, "Adequate Reproduction," *SH* 5 (1919): 223–26. G. J. Barker-Benfield also notes the connections between white middle-class men's class and racial fears and their desire to control white women in *Horrors of the Half-Known Life: Male Attitudes toward Women and Sexuality in Nineteenth-Century America* (New York: Harper and Row, 1976), 122.

15. Maurice A. Bigelow, *Sex-Education: A Series of Lectures Concerning Knowledge of Sex in Its Relation to Human Life* (New York: Macmillan, 1916), 60.

16. Arthur B. Spingarn, "The War and Venereal Diseases among Negroes," *SH* 4 (1918): 339; Bettina Aptheker, "Woman Suffrage and the Crusade against Lynching, 1890–1920," in *Woman's Legacy: Essays on Race, Sex, and Class in American History* (Amherst: University of Massachusetts Press, 1982), 56–61; Eric Foner, *Nothing But Freedom: Emancipation and Its Legacy* (Baton Rouge: Louisiana State University Press, 1983), 59–61.

17. In September 1893, for example, a black man who argued about prices with a white woman selling produce at the market in Roanoke, Virginia, was subsequently lynched. News reports had claimed he assaulted her. Ida B. Wells-Barnett, "A Red Record," in *The Land of Contrasts, 1880–1901*, ed. Neil Harris (New York: George Braziller, 1970), 155–58; "In the Jim Crow Car," *Crisis* 4 (May 1912): 39–40. Mary White Ovington, in "Segregation," *Crisis* 9 (January 1915): 142–45, points out how segregation makes black women "appear as all of one kind [bad]," not divided between good girls and bad girls. Alfreda Duster, transcript of interview, 8, 9 March 1978, 24, Black Women Oral History Project, Schlesinger Library, Radcliffe College, Cambridge, Massachusetts. Deborah Gray White notes, "From emancipation through more than two-thirds of the twentieth century, no Southern white male was convicted of raping or attempting to rape a black woman." White, *Ar'n't I a Woman? Female Slaves in the Plantation South* (New York: Norton, 1985), 164. Raymond Wolters, *The New Negro on Campus: Black Colleges and Rebellions in the 1920s* (Princeton, N.J.: Princeton University Press, 1975), 322–23.

18. Mary Church Terrell, *A Colored Woman in a White World* (1940; repr., New York: Arno, 1980), 165, 181, 207, 216; Langston Hughes, *The Big Sea* (New York: Hill and Wang, 1940), 301; Nannie Helen Burroughs, "12 Things the Negro Must Do for Himself / 12 Things White People Must Stop Doing to the Negro," pamphlet, n.d., 24–25, Box 46, Nannie Helen Burroughs Collection, Library of Congress, Washington, D.C.

19. Gerda Lerner, ed., *Black Women in White America* (New York: Random House, 1972), 436; Mary Church Terrell, "The Duty of the National Association of Colored Women to the Race," *African Methodist Episcopal Church Review* 16 (January 1900): 352; Stephanie Shaw, "Black Club Women and the Creation of the National Association of Colored Women," *Journal of Women's History* 3 (1991): 10–11; Evelyn Brooks Higginbotham, *Righteous Discontent: The Women's Movement in the Black Baptist Church, 1880–1920* (Cambridge, Mass.: Harvard University Press, 1993), 193–94.

20. "Purity Congresses," in Subject Files, Mary Church Terrell Collection, Library of Congress, Washington, D.C., Microfilm, Reel 16; Terrell, *Colored Woman*, 183–84, 296–98, 417; "Editorial," *Crisis* 17 (November 1918): 9.

21. W. E. B. DuBois, ed., *Morals and Manners among Negro Americans*, Atlanta University Publications, No. 18 (Atlanta: Atlanta University, 1914); Stein, "Defining the Race 1890–1930," 266n82.

22. DuBois, *Morals and Manners*, 35, 16, 93–94, 90–91.

23. James R. Grossman, *Land of Hope: Chicago, Black Southerners, and the Great Migration* (Chicago: University of Chicago Press, 1989), 145–57; Evelyn Brooks Higginbotham, "African-American Women's History and the Metalanguage of Race," *Signs* 17 (1992): 258–62.

24. Brandt, *No Magic Bullet*, 8; Charles Walter Clarke, M.D., *Taboo: The Story of the Pioneers of Social Hygiene* (Washington, D.C.: Public Affairs Press, 1961), 56–63; William Freeman Snow, "Pioneer Experiences," *SH* 5 (1919): 579–82.

25. Clarke, *Taboo*, 57–62; John Burnham, "The Progressive Era Revolution in American Attitudes toward Sex," *Journal of American History* 59 (1973): 890–91, 894, 98; Brandt, *No Magic Bullet*, 9–10, 40.

26. Ruth Rosen, *The Lost Sisterhood: Prostitution in America, 1900–1918* (Baltimore: Johns Hopkins University Press, 1982), 14–15; Philadelphia Association for the Protection of Colored Women, *Report* (Philadelphia, 1912), Terrell Collection, Subject Files; Peter Collier and David Horowitz, *The Rockefellers: An American Dynasty* (New York: Holt, Rinehart and Winston, 1976), 63, 105–7.

27. Clarke, *Taboo*, 61; Burnham, "Progressive Era Revolution," 897; O. Edward Janney "Pioneer Experiences," *SH* 5 (1919): 578–79; James Bronson Reynolds, "Pioneer Experiences," *SH* 5 (1919): 582–84; "Grace Hoadley Dodge," in *Notable American Women*, ed. Edward T. James, Janet Wilson James, and Paul S. Boyer (Cambridge, Mass.: Harvard University Press, 1971), 1:489–92; Lavinia L. Dock, *Hygiene and Morality: A Manual for Nurses and Others* (New York, 1910), 110–11.

28. Reynolds, "Pioneer Experiences," 582–83; Clarke, *Taboo*, 65; Moran, *Teaching Sex*, 28.

29. Philadelphia Association for the Protection of Colored Women, *Report*, 1, 3, 4; Charles H. Wesley, *A History of the National Association of Colored Women's Clubs, Inc.: A Legacy of Service* (Washington, D.C.: NACWC, 1984), 19.

30. Charles W. Eliot, "Introduction," and Bertha Stuart, "Teaching Phases: For Girls," in *The Social Emergency: Studies in Sex Hygiene and Morals*, ed. William Trufant Foster (Boston: Houghton Mifflin, 1914), 3, 164.

31. Clarke, *Taboo*, 61–63, 73–74, 83; Brandt, *No Magic Bullet*, 38.

32. Exner, "Social Hygiene and the War"; Brandt, *No Magic Bullet*, 53–60, 71–79; Moran, *Teaching Sex*, 68–76, 98–100; Michael Imber, "The First World War, Sex Education, and the American Social Hygiene Association's Campaign against Venereal Disease," *Educational Administration and History* 16 (1984): 47–56; Carter, "Birds, Bees, and Venereal Disease," 218. Government support for even this more narrowly VD-focused education, however, began to decline in the late 1920s, as the sense of wartime urgency faded. General public ambivalence about the broader type of sex education and the vulnerability of teachers to parental disapproval meant that throughout the 1920s and 1930s occasional, usually disease-focused, programs were the primary form of sex instruction where it existed at all in the public education system. For more, see Moran, *Teaching Sex*, 109–17.

33. William T. Foster, "Statewide Education in Social Hygiene," *SH* 2 (1916): 309–29.

34. Ibid., 310–18.

35. Ibid., 318–23, 328–29.

36. Charles Rosenberg notes that Victorian sex reformers also argued from the authority of science. "Sexuality, Class and Role in 19th-Century America," *American Quarterly* 25 (1973): 141–42. See also Cynthia Eagle Russett, *Sexual Science: The Victorian Construction of Womanhood* (Cambridge, Mass.: Harvard University Press, 1989), 13.

37. William Trufant Foster, "The Social Emergency," in *The Social Emergency: Studies in Sex Hygiene and Morals*, ed. William Trufant Foster (Boston: Houghton Mifflin, 1914), 11; Dock, *Hygiene and Morality*, 131; Brandt, *No Magic Bullet*, 46, 114.

38. Maurice A. Bigelow, "Pioneer Experiences" *SH* 5 (1919): 575. See also "Pioneer Experiences," *SH* 1 (1915): 567–89, and biographical information on authors, *SH* 1 (1915): 453–55.

39. American Federation for Sex Hygiene, *Report of the Annual Meeting of the Federation* (New York, 1913), 151. In 1910, 30 percent of the membership of the Society for Sanitary and Moral Prophylaxis was female, according to Brandt, *No Magic Bullet*, 24–25. Jeffrey P. Moran notes that social hygiene had fewer women than purity groups but more than more "masculine" reform groups. "'Modernism Gone Mad': Sex Education Comes to Chicago, 1913," *Journal of American History* 83 (1996): 486.

40. Brandt, *No Magic Bullet*, 50–51; Boyer, *Urban Masses*, 200; Paul S. Achilles, *The Effectiveness of Certain Social Hygiene Literature* (New York: American Social Hygiene Association, 1923), 24, 27, 36; Robert Dickinson and Lura Beam, *A Thousand Marriages: A Medical Study of Sex Adjustment* (Baltimore: Williams and Wilkins, 1931), 228. Dickinson unfortunately did not date his cases, but internal evidence suggests this subject was speaking between 1915 and 1920. Bigelow, "Pioneer Experiences," 575.

41. American Federation for Sex Hygiene, *Report of the Special Committee on the Matter and Methods of Sex Education* (New York, 1912), 2–3; Bigelow, *Sex-Education*, 34, 99–100; M[ax] J. Exner, *Problems and Principles of Sex Education: A Study of 948 College Men* (New York: Association Press, 1915), 21; George J. Fisher, "Sex Education in the Young Men's Christian Association," *SH* 1 (1915): 228–30; Laura B. Garrett, "Sex Hygiene for Children before the Age of Fifteen," *SH* 1 (1915): 260. Moran also discusses the theme of integration of sex education into other instruction; *Teaching Sex*, 58.

42. Carter, "Birds, Bees, and Venereal Disease," 240.

43. Garrett, "Sex Hygiene for Children," 258.

44. Charles G. Gaffney, "A Father's Plan for Sex Instruction," *SH* 1 (1915): 270.

45. Richard H. Tierney, S.J., "The Catholic Church and the Sex Problem," in *Report of the Sex Education Sessions*, 65–71. Institutional Catholicism centered in the immigrant communities was in the 1910s marginal to Protestant-dominated Progressive reform, of which social hygiene formed a part. The only Catholic figure I found who was at all connected with the early social hygiene movement was James Cardinal Gibbons of Baltimore, whose obituary in the *Journal of Social Hygiene* identified him as an honorary vice president of the American Social Hygiene Association from 1913 on. He was described as a "man of broad and liberal human interests, profoundly American in all his thinking and endeavor," probably to distinguish him from what Protestant reformers saw as the alien masses of Roman Catholics. *JSH* 7 (1921): 158. Not until after 1920 did Catholicism begin to be assimilated into what was considered "mainstream" American culture. Debra Campbell, "'Flannery O'Connor Is Not John Updike,'" *American*

Quarterly 43 (1991): 333–34. By 1928 another priest addressed a gathering of social hygienists less critically. He employed the movement's by then standard rhetoric about sex education while vigorously rejecting any link between social hygiene and birth control; Alphonse M. Schwitalla, S.J., Ph.D., "The Aims and Achievements of Social Hygiene," *JSH* 15 (1929): 1–7. Moran, "'Modernism Gone Mad,'" 502–5, and *Teaching Sex*, 66.

46. Charles W. Eliot, in "Pioneer Experiences," *SH* 5 (1919): 569–71; Florence M. Fitch, "What Are Our Social Standards?" *SH* 1 (1915): 558; Exner, *Problems and Principles*, 31; Walter M. Gallichan, "Prudery and the Child," *SH* 5 (1919): 349–53; Miriam C. Gould, "The Psychological Influence upon the Adolescent Girl of the Knowledge of Prostitution and Venereal Disease," *SH* 2 (1916): 204–5.

47. David Macleod argues that YMCA and Boy Scout workers were similarly focused on middle-class youth in *Building Character in the American Boy: The Boy Scouts, YMCA, and Their Forerunners, 1870–1920* (Madison: University of Wisconsin Press, 1983), 35.

48. *Report of the Sex Education Sessions* of the Fourth International Congress on School Hygiene and Annual Meeting of the American Federation for Sex Hygiene (New York, 1913), 102; Wilbur F. Crafts, "Safeguarding Adolescents against Community Moral Perils," in *The Sunday School and the Teens*, ed. John L. Alexander (New York: Association Press, 1913), 306–12; Fitch, "What Are Our Social Standards?" 558; Lewis A. Erenberg, "Everybody's Doin' It: The Pre-World War I Dance Craze, the Castles, and the Modern American Girl," *Feminist Studies* 3 (1975): 157; Bigelow, *Sex-Education*, 174. Quotation from *Beauty for Ashes* by Albion F. Bacon, reviewed in *SH* 1 (1915): 300.

49. Several early studies by social hygienists asked boys about sources of sexual information. Results showed that from half to nine-tenths of subject groups (predominantly high school or college boys) had gained their first knowledge from boy or girl companions, usually boys, and only a tiny fraction had learned from parents, doctors, or other "reliable" sources. See Exner, *Problems and Principles*, 5–6; Achilles, *Social Hygiene Literature*, 37; M. W. Peck and F. L. Wells, "On the Psycho-Sexuality of College Graduate Men," *Mental Hygiene* 7 (1923): 697–714; and Walter L. Hughes, "Sex Experiences of Boyhood," *JSH* 12 (1926): 265. Peck and Wells asked boys where they received "adequate" rather than first instruction about sex, so their figures are weighted much more toward parents. Exner's sample was of college men, and he found 8 percent claiming to have first heard about sex from either parents or other "good" sources, such as a doctor or the YMCA (but excluding books), while 90 percent had learned from boy or girl companions. Achilles' sample included some working-class adolescents and men but mostly high school or college students; again, 8 percent reported learning from parents, while 52 percent learned from companions. Hughes's sample included boys who worked in mills as well as high school boys, rural and small town. Four percent of his subjects reported learning from parents, and 88 percent from companions.

50. Achilles, *Social Hygiene Literature*, 70, 34, 47; Fisher, "Sex Education in the Young Men's Christian Association," 227; Hughes, "Sex Experiences of Boyhood," 267.

51. Bigelow, *Sex-Education*, 168.
52. Ibid.; Robert S. Lynd and Helen Merrell Lynd, *Middletown: A Study in Modern American Culture* (New York: Harcourt, Brace, and World, 1929), 117, 118, 137–39, 140; Beth L. Bailey, *From Front Porch to Back Seat: Courtship in Twentieth-Century America* (Baltimore: Johns Hopkins University Press, 1988), 13–19; Alfred C. Kinsey et al., *Sexual Behavior in the Human Female* (1953; repr., New York: Pocket Books, 1965), 242–43, 298–300, 339 (table 83); Daniel S. Smith, "The Dating of the American Sexual Revolution: Evidence and Interpretation," in *The American Family in Social-Historical Perspective*, 2nd ed., ed. Michael Gordon (New York: St. Martin's, 1978), 432.
53. Ben Lindsey claimed and Kinsey's study of men confirmed some shift in the partners of middle-class single men from prostitutes to companions of their own groups. Ben B. Lindsey, "The Promise and Peril of the New Freedom," in *Woman's Coming of Age*, ed. Samuel D. Schmalhausen and V. F. Calverton (New York: Liveright, 1931), 454–55; Alfred C. Kinsey, Wardell B. Pomeroy, and Clyde E. Martin, *Sexual Behavior in the Human Male* (Philadelphia: Saunders, 1948), 413.
54. Johnson, "Adequate Reproduction," 225; Bigelow, *Sex-Education*, 186, 198, 83. The final quotation is Bigelow's citation from C. Gasquoine Hartley, *Truth about Woman* (1913).
55. Bigelow, *Sex-Education*, 82 (quoting Hartley, *Truth about Woman*). Bigelow subsequently warns very explicitly against feminist "proselyting" of younger women on the subject of sex and urges that young women be protected by education, 85. Dock, *Hygiene and Morality*, 61, 136.
56. Katharine B. Davis, *Factors in the Sex Life of Twenty-Two Hundred Women* (New York: Harper, 1929), 367; Dickinson and Beam, *A Thousand Marriages*, 357.
57. Anna L. Brown, "Sex Education in the Young Women's Christian Association," *SH* 1 (1915): 584; Gould, "Psychological Influence," 195, 198, 201, 205.
58. Bigelow, *Sex-Education*, 58, 167, 191; Fitch, "Social Standards," 554; Achilles, *Social Hygiene Literature*, 75; Rachelle Yarros, "Experiences of a Lecturer," *SH* 5 (1919): 215.
59. Bigelow, *Sex-Education*, 193, 117, 188. On nineteenth-century gynecological surgery, see Ronald G. Walters, *Primers for Prudery: Sexual Advice to Victorian America* (Englewood Cliffs, N.J.: Prentice-Hall, 1974), 73–74, and Barbara Ehrenreich and Deirdre English, *For Her Own Good: 150 Years of the Experts' Advice to Women* (New York: Doubleday, 1979), 123–25.
60. For example, see Wanda Gag, "A Hotbed of Feminists," in *These Modern Women: Autobiographical Essays from the Twenties*, ed. Elaine Showalter (Old Westbury, N.Y.: Feminist Press, 1978), 132. Sex studies include Robert L. Dickinson and Lura Beam, *The Single Woman: A Medical Study in Sex Education* (Baltimore: Williams and Wilkins, 1934), 135; Gilbert V. Hamilton and Kenneth MacGowan, *What Is Wrong with Marriage* (New York: Boni, 1929), 245; Lewis Terman, *Psychological Factors in Marital Happiness* (New York: McGraw-Hill, 1938), 321; Kinsey et al., *Human Female*, 242–44, 268, 298–301, 331.

61. Achilles, *Social Hygiene Literature*, 36.

62. Bigelow, *Sex-Education*, 184–85, 197–98; Achilles, *Social Hygiene Literature*, 18 (citing a sex education pamphlet for girls called "The Girl's Part" by Mabel Ulrich).

63. Thomas Walton Galloway, "The Responsibilities of Religious Leaders in Sex Education," *SH* 7 (1921): 142. Quotations from Bigelow, *Sex-Education*, 74, and Curtis, "Relation of Public Recreation to Problems of Sex," 203. See also Clarke, *Taboo*, 73; Clark W. Hetherington, "Play Leadership in Sex Education," *SH* 1 (1914): 38; and Moran, *Teaching Sex*, 47.

64. Bigelow, *Sex-Education*, 191, 178, 180, 136. The difference was evident, for instance, in cautions against masturbation, which was still considered vaguely harmful though not a cause of insanity. Although all writings about boys mention masturbation as a problem, the corresponding literature about girls does not. These writers thought that more boys than girls masturbated or else that it was not as serious a problem for girls. See Achilles, *Social Hygiene Literature*, 11–20. For another example with similar assumptions, by a feminist physician, see Yarros, "Experiences of a Lecturer," 215.

65. Hall, "Race Betterment," 70; American Federation for Sex Hygiene, *Report of the Special Committee on the Matter and Methods of Sex Education*, 8; Achilles, *Social Hygiene Literature*, 11, 16, 34, 35, 82; Bigelow, *Sex-Education*, 59–60; Edward Keyes Jr., "Can the Law Protect Matrimony from Disease?" *SH* 1 (1914): 9; Exner, "Social Hygiene and the War," 284–91; *Report of the Sex Education Sessions*, 140.

66. Achilles, *Social Hygiene Literature*, 14.

67. Bigelow, *Sex-Education*, 40; E. S. Shepherd, "Vice Crusades," *Medical Critic and Guide and Dietetic and Hygienic Gazette* 18 (June 1915): 229; F. I. Davenport, in *Report of the Sex Education Sessions*, 120.

68. John Higham, "The Reorientation of American Culture in the 1890s," in *Writing American History* (Bloomington: Indiana University Press, 1970), 73–102; Macleod, *Building Character*, 47; Peter Filene, *Him/Her/Self*, 2nd ed.(Baltimore: Johns Hopkins University Press, 1986), 70–72; E. Anthony Rotundo, *American Manhood: Transformations in Masculinity from the Revolution to the Modern Era* (New York: Basic Books, 1993), 222–46.

69. Bigelow, *Sex-Education*, 185, 112; Edward O. Sisson, "Educational Phases," in *The Social Emergency: Studies in Sex Hygiene and Morals*, ed. William Trufant Foster (Boston: Houghton Mifflin, 1914), 96. See also Filene, *Him/Her/Self*, 91–92.

70. Peck and Wells, "Psycho-Sexuality of College Graduate Men," 16; Achilles, *Social Hygiene Literature*, 71–72, 84; Exner, "Social Hygiene and the War," 284–91.

71. Bigelow, *Sex-Education*, 185, 148–49, 6; Garrett, "Sex Hygiene for Children," 261–62.

72. Johnson, "Adequate Reproduction," 225; Laura B. Garrett, in *Report of the Sex Education Sessions*, 103; Bigelow, *Sex-Education*, 197.

73. Gould, "Psychological Influence," 204; Fitch, "Social Standards," 550.

74. Yarros, "Experiences of a Lecturer," 212, 216; Sisson, "Educational Phases," 97; Bigelow, *Sex-Education*, 191, 187–88, 116–17.

75. Karl S. Lashley and John B. Watson, "A Psychological Study of Motion Pictures in Relation to Venereal Disease Campaigns," *SH* 7 (1921): 200, 204–5.

76. Carter, "Birds, Bees, and Venereal Disease," 241–46.

77. Davenport, in *Report of the Sex Education Sessions*, 116–21, 124; Charlotte Perkins Gilman, *Women and Economics*, ed. Carl Degler (1898; repr., New York: Harper and Row, 1966).

    The only other social hygiene thinker who approximates Davenport's assertion of equivalent female sexual force is Exner, who argues that, while women *generally* control themselves better than men and express their sex instinct through affection rather than "passionate desire," "there is a considerable proportion of women in whom sex impulses are just as imperious as in most highly sexed men." "Friend or Enemy?" 488.

78. Davenport, in *Report of the Sex Education Sessions*, 123–24.

79. The dissertation was published under F. I. Davenport, Ph.D., as *Adolescent Interests: A Study of the Sexual Interests and Knowledge of Young Women*, Archives of Psychology, No. 66 (New York, 1923). She thanks her Columbia advisers, R. S. Woodsworth and A. T. Poffenberger, but also Leta Hollingworth of Columbia Teachers College, one of the pioneer women psychologists combating Victorian orthodoxies on sex differences. See Rosalind Rosenberg, *Beyond Separate Spheres: Intellectual Roots of Modern Feminism* (New Haven, Conn.: Yale University Press, 1982), 84–86, 95–113.

    In 1924 Davenport published a much-expanded version of the dissertation under the name Isabel Davenport, Ph.D., *Salvaging of American Girlhood: A Substitution of Normal Psychology for Superstition and Mysticism in the Education of Girls* (New York: Dutton, 1924). For account of the origins of the study, see pages 17–20, 22–28; the quotation is from page 7.

    Backgrounds of the students are described in Davenport, *Adolescent Interests*, 8.

    The desire for sex information was widespread. Moran notes that "even groups of junior high school girls in the 1920s were reportedly banding together to request 'talks on menstruation—their reproductive organs and explanation of many questions that were puzzling them'"; *Teaching Sex*, 101.

80. Davenport, *Adolescent Interests*, 12, 21, 32–24, 58; Davenport, *Salvaging of American Girlhood*, 109, 142. The long-lived belief that conception could not occur without orgasm ("passion") emerged in one question; *Salvaging of American Girlhood*, 185.

81. Davenport, *Adolescent Interests*, 12, 34–36, 42.

82. Davenport, *Salvaging of American Girlhood*, 20–21, 128; Davenport, *Adolescent Interests*, 30. The other psychologist is quoted in Achilles, *Social Hygiene Literature*, 100.

83. Davenport, *Salvaging of American Girlhood*, 5, 209, 212, 227–29, 244, 240–41.

84. Bigelow, *Sex-Education*, 168; Fitch, "Social Standards," 560.

85. Galloway, "Responsibilities of Religious Leaders," 149; Ostrander, *American Civilization*, 123, 256. One summary of social hygiene work noted that the ASHA tried primarily to reach professional and business groups most likely to be "influencing public thought and action." "The Association's Tenth Year, 1914–1914,"

289; Burnham, "Progressive Era Revolution," 899; Exner, "Social Hygiene and the War," 288; Lashley and Watson, "Motion Pictures," 181; Eric Schaefer, *"Bold! Darling! Shocking! True!": A History of Exploitation Films,* 1919–1959 (Durham, N.C.: Duke University Press, 1999), 21–29.

86. Jane Addams's *Spirit of Youth,* as well as *A New Conscience and an Ancient Evil* (New York: Macmillan, 1912), which deals with prostitution, Woods and Kennedy's *Young Working Girls,* and Alexander's *The Sunday School and the Teens* exemplify the overlap of the settlement house movement and social hygiene. Addams participated in the antiprostitution work that directly preceded social hygiene. But sexual behavior is central to the "problems" defined by all these authors, who support sex instruction as one of the solutions. See especially George Fisher, "The Physical Life of the Adolescent," in *The Sunday School and the Teens,* ed. John L. Alexander (New York: Association Press, 1913), 232; Woods and Kennedy, *Young Working Girls,* 94.

87. *Report of the Special Committee on the Matter and Methods of Sex Education,* 19; Dr. C. F. Hodge, *Report of the Sex Education Sessions,* 141; Addams, *Spirit of Youth,* 13, 15, 27–28, 37; Mary E. Odem, *Delinquent Daughters: Protecting and Policing Adolescent Female Sexuality in the United States, 1885–1920* (Chapel Hill: University of North Carolina Press, 1995), 45.

88. Hodge, in *Report of the Sex Education Sessions,* 141; Addams, *Spirit of Youth,* 13, 15–16; Lebert Weir, "The Recreational Phases," in *The Social Emergency: Studies in Sex Hygiene and Morals,* ed. William Trufant Foster (Boston: Houghton Mifflin, 1914), 77–78; Woods and Kennedy, *Young Working Girls,* 111, 42, 54; John Garber, "Dance Halls," in *The Sunday School and the Teens,* ed. John L. Alexander (New York: Association Press, 1913), 272–73; Daniels and Griffith, "Home Conditions," 186–87; Louise de Koven Bowen, *The Public Dance Halls of Chicago* (Chicago: Juvenile Protective Association of Chicago, 1917), 6.

89. Daniels and Griffith, "Home Conditions," 187–88; Woods and Kennedy, *Young Working Girls,* 60–67; Odem, *Delinquent Daughters,* 49–52.

90. Achilles, *Social Hygiene Literature,* 34, 47; Harry H. Moore, "Teaching Phases: For Boys," and Arthur Evans Wood, "Economic Phases," in *The Social Emergency: Studies in Sex Hygiene and Morals,* ed. William Trufant Foster (Boston: Houghton Mifflin, 1914), 130–52, 62; Woods and Kennedy, *Young Working Girls,* 123; Harry A. Wembridge, "A New Emphasis in Social Hygiene Education," *SH* 7 (1921): 160.

91. Foster, "Statewide Education," 322, 329; Exner, "Social Hygiene and the War," 279–80; Brandt, *No Magic Bullet,* 79, 95.

92. Exner, "Friend or Enemy?" 485–89; Foster, "Statewide Education," 328; Woods and Kennedy, *Young Working Girls,* 123; Achilles, *Social Hygiene Literature,* 16–17, 13–14.

93. Odem, *Delinquent Daughters,* 3–4.

94. Mary Bularzik, "Sexual Harassment at the Workplace: Historical Notes," *Radical America* 12 (July–August 1978), 25–43; Peiss, *Cheap Amusements,* 51. Abraham Bisno, an early organizer of the garment workers' union, gives an unusually frank account of his own sexual approaches to women who were his employees when

his family ran a clothing contracting shop in Chicago in the 1890s. See his memoir, *Abraham Bisno, Union Pioneer*, foreword by Joel Seidman (Madison: University of Wisconsin Press, 1967), 64–65. Also Peiss, *Cheap Amusements*, 51.

95. Woods and Kennedy, *Young Working Girls*, 17, 26–28, 108, 101, 104; Garber, "Dance Halls," 270–73; W. I. Thomas, *The Unadjusted Girl*, ed. Benjamin Nelson (1923; repr., New York: Harper and Row, 1967), 117, 119; Margaret Dreier Robbins, "One Aspect of the Menace of Low Wages," *SH* 1 (1915): 358–62; Joanne Meyerowitz, "Sexual Geography and Gender Economy: The Furnished Room Districts of Chicago, 1890–1930," *Gender and History* 2 (1990): 280.

96. Woods and Kennedy, *Young Working Girls*, 34, 37, 52, 105, 107, 108; Peiss, *Cheap Amusements*, 178–84.

97. Thomas, *Unadjusted Girl*, 70–97; Judith E. Smith, *Family Connections: A History of Italian and Jewish Immigrant Lives in Providence, Rhode Island, 1900–1940* (Albany: State University of New York Press, 1985), 75–76; John D'Emilio and Estelle Freedman, *Intimate Matters: A History of Sexuality in America* (New York: Harper and Row, 1988), 198–200. In his vivid account of women workers in the garment industry, Abraham Bisno asserts strongly how grateful immigrant peasant women were to have work that, unlike farm work, was confined to definite hours and that also earned wages. See Bisno, *Abraham Bisno*, 178, 212. See also Meyerowitz, *Women Adrift*, 12–20, 92–116; Peiss, *Cheap Amusements*, 69–70; Odem, *Delinquent Daughters*, 48; Randy D. McBee, *Dance Hall Days: Intimacy and Leisure among Working-Class Immigrants in the United States* (New York: New York University Press, 2000), 210–18.

98. Garrett, "Sex Hygiene for Children," 258–59; Margaret Eggleston, *Womanhood in the Making* (New York: George H. Doran, 1923), 174, 179, 181; Brown, "Sex Education at the YWCA," 584; Bigelow, *Sex-Education*, 176; Woods and Kennedy, *Young Working Girls*, 23, 156; Yarros, "Experiences of a Lecturer," 216, 220.

99. Woods and Kennedy, *Young Working Girls*, 99, 156; Hall, "Race Betterment," 74; Addams, *Spirit of Youth*, 43; Eleanor Rowland Wembridge, "Social Backgrounds in Sex Education," *JSH* 9 (1923): 65–67, 76.

100. Garrett, "Sex Hygiene for Children," 264; Achilles, *Social Hygiene Literature*, 7, 22–23, 34, 66–67. Lashley and Watson noted that one-third of the men they interviewed in their preliminary work did not understand the term "sexual intercourse," but they argued that in films at least the meaning was clear from the context, and they advised the use of scientific rather than popular terms. "Motion Pictures," 209–10.

101. Wembridge, "A New Emphasis," 161; Woods and Kennedy, *Young Working Girls*, 124, 85–88, 100; 162–63; Ella Reeve Bloor, in *Report of the Sex Education Sessions*, 90–91. Mother Bloor, later a Communist, supported sex education and referred to teaching children about the "sacredness" of motherhood. Certainly, some working-class people thought in the same terms as the social hygienists. See also Leslie Woodcock Tentler, *Wage-Earning Women: Industrial Work and Family Life in the United States, 1900–1930* (New York: Oxford University Press, 1979), 109; Dorothy Richardson, "The Long Day: The Story of a New York Working Girl" (1905), in *Women at*

Work, ed. William L. O'Neill (Chicago: Quadrangle, 1972), 73–74; Thomas, *Unadjusted Girl*, 119–20; Wembridge, "Social Backgrounds," 69; Peiss, *Cheap Amusements*, 110. In addition, many European peasant societies from which immigrants came allowed some sexual intimacy—either petting or intercourse—as a sign of having a serious relationship expected to end in marriage. Thomas, *Unadjusted Girl*, 141; Louise Tilly and Joan Scott, *Women, Work, and Family* (New York: Holt, Rinehart and Winston, 1978), 38–39.

102. Spingarn, "War and Venereal Diseases among Negroes," 335–36; "A Campaign among Negroes," *SH* 5 (1919): 630; Charles V. Roman, "The American Negro and Social Hygiene," *JSH* 7 (1921): 43–44; Brandt, *No Magic Bullet*, 116–17.

103. Spingarn, "War and Venereal Diseases among Negroes," 339; "Campaign among Negroes," 630–31; Arthur B. Spingarn, "The Health and Morals of Colored Troops," *Crisis* 16 (August 1918): 166, 168.

104. Reports and Documents, War Camp Community Service, Terrell Collection, Library of Congress.

105. Spingarn, "Campaign among Negroes"; "Charles V. Roman," in *Dictionary of American Negro Biography*, ed. Rayford W. Logan and Michael R. Winston (New York: Norton, 1982), 532–33; William F. Snow to Arthur B. Spingarn, 12 December 1921, in Arthur B. Spingarn Papers, Library of Congress, Washington, D.C.; Kenneth M. Gould, "Progress, 1920–21," *SH* 7 (1921): 321.

106. Franklin O. Nichols, Memorandum to Dr. William Snow, 11 November 1921, in Spingarn Papers; Franklin O. Nichols, "Some Public Health Problems of the Negro," *JSH* 8 (1922): 283, 285; "News and Notes," *JSH* 9 (1923): 243–44; "Association Notes," *JSH* 14 (1928): 247–48; "Health of the Negro," *JSH* 15 (1929): 99; "Social Hygiene Institutes for Physicians," *JSH* 19 (1933): 460; "News and Abstracts," *JSH* 20 (1934): 455–57; Jean B. Pinney, "1932 in Review," *JSH* 19 (1933): 28, 32; William Montague Cobb, "Medical History," *Journal of the National Medical Association* 45 (1953): 301–4; obituary of F. O. Nichols, *New York Times*, 4 February 1955.

107. Mary S. Edwards, "Popular Health Education in Simplest Terms," *JSH* 20 (1934): 177–89.

108. Minutes of NACW Conventions, 1920, 1930, 1939, in Terrell Collection, Library of Congress; Sallie Stewart to Mary Church Terrell, 14 December 1925, in Terrell Collection, Moorland-Spingarn Research Center, Howard University, Washington, D.C.

109. Franklin O. Nichols, "A New Opportunity for Schools," *Opportunity* 4 (September 1926): 287–89; Nichols, "The Attitudes of Patients towards Syphilis, Based on Interviews with 300 Male Negro Patients at Harlem Hospital, New York City," *JSH* 19 (1933): 153, 155.

110. Spingarn, "War and Venereal Diseases among Negroes," 335, 340; Nichols, "Public Health Problems of the Negro," 281–83, 285; Roman, "The American Negro," 44–45; Ruth Reed, "Illegitimacy among Negroes," *JSH* 11 (1925): 86–88; Nichols, "Social Hygiene and the Negro," *JSH* 15 (1929): 409. Although Spingarn was white, and Reed probably was, I have relied only on arguments that paralleled those made by black writers.

Some of these "problems" (such as illegitimacy), of course, had little to do with the spread of venereal disease, but concern about them all was characteristic of the moral views of the black reformers as of the white. Any behavior seen as morally "disordered" was generally considered to contribute to venereal disease.

111. Spingarn, "The War and Venereal Diseases among Negroes," 335–39; Nichols, "Some Public Health Problems of the Negro," 282; Nichols, "The Attitudes of Patients towards Syphilis," 151–59.

112. See above, note 4. Franklin O. Nichols, "Social Hygiene in Racial Problems—the Negro," *JSH* 18 (1932): 451; Nichols, "Social Hygiene and the Negro," 410. Of all the commentators cited, only Ruth Reed approached a culturally relativist framework in her discussion of lower-class difference from middle-class norms of legal marriage and sexual respectability.

113. Spingarn, "War and Venereal Diseases among Negroes," 341; "Social Welfare Program for Negroes in North Carolina," *JSH* 13 (1927): 176–77; Nichols, "Social Hygiene and the Negro"; "Social Hygiene Institutes for Physicians," *JSH* 19 (1933): 460; "News and Abstracts," *JSH* 20 (1934): 456; "An All-Community Problem," *JSH* 10 (1924): 426.

114. Linda Gordon, "Black and White Visions of Welfare: Women's Welfare Activism, 1890–1945," *Journal of American History* 78 (1991): 578, 586.

115. Roman argued for leaving women "the freedom and responsibility of a decision" on matters of childbearing, in "American Negro," 45–46. DuBois also supported birth control. See "A Word from Dr. DuBois," *Birth Control Review* 3 (September 1919): 15. Mary Church Terrell, "Talk to the Young Men of Howard University Academic Department," March 1925, Terrell Collection, Moorland-Spingarn Research Center. One respondent in DuBois's 1914 study made a comment similar to Terrell's: "I regret to say, as a whole, Negro men have not and do not accord our women that respect and attention so much in evidence in Southern white men" [presumably toward white women]. *Morals and Manners*, 32. On celibacy, see Nichols, "A New Opportunity for Schools," 287. Only DuBois criticized female celibacy. See "The Damnation of Women," in DuBois, *Darkwater: Voices from Within the Veil* (1920; repr., New York: Schocken, 1969), 184–85.

116. I have found no responses to sex education by blacks. The Achilles study did include two groups of blacks but often did not cite them in aggregate statistics. They seemed to be middle-class young people who resembled middle-class white groups in their responses and differed similarly from the "continuation school" (working-class) group. Achilles, *Social Hygiene Literature*, 10, 22.

117. Jean B. Pinney, "The Twentieth Year: A Summary of Activities of the American Social Hygiene Association during the Year 1933," *JSH* 20 (1934): 14–45.

118. Benjamin C. Gruenberg, "Sex Education in Secondary Schools: 1938," *JSH* 24 (1938): 533–34; Vivian Hadley Harris, "The Status of Sex Education in Public Educational Institutions," *SH* 7 (1921): 167–80; U.S. Public Health Service, *Sex Education: A Symposium for Educators* (Washington, D.C.: U.S. Public Health Service, 1927); John Newton Baker, *Sex Education in High Schools* (New York: Emerson, 1942), 39–40, 19, 42–46, 28. Baker noted that religious opposition was present in about 5 percent of the situations he surveyed and that it was not always

successful. Catholics sometimes could accept sex education if assured that birth control would not be mentioned. Moran's article on the Chicago experiment details Catholic opposition in " 'Modernism Gone Mad.' " He notes a widespread culture of opposition to adolescent sex that made many parents accept the more moralistic disease-prevention focus of the occasional programs in preference to sustained course instruction on sexual development, in *Teaching Sex*, 99.

119. "Conference on Education for Marriage and Family Social Relations, 1934, Final Report," *JSH* 22 (1936): 13, 28; Walter H. Brown, M.D., "Social Hygiene in the College Curricula," *JSH* 17 (1931): 261–70; M. J. Exner, "The Status of Sex Education in the Colleges," *JSH* 17 (1931): 441–58; Edward L. Keyes, "Social Hygiene and the National Association," *JSH* 11 (1925): 515–19; Pinney, "Twentieth Year," 32–34.

120. Nichols, "Racial Problems," 449–51; Pinney, "1932 in Review," 32; "News and Abstracts," *JSH* 20 (1934): 455–56; "News and Abstracts," *JSH* 24 (1938): 572.

121. Newell W. Edson, "Love in the Making: An Article Directed to Boys," *JSH* 11 (1925): 272–82; Max J. Exner, *The Question of Petting* (New York: Association Press, 1926); Paul Popenoe, "A College Education for Marriage," *JSH* 25 (1939): 168–70.

122. Exner, *Petting*, 9–11, 1920; Maurice A. Bigelow, *Sex-Education*, rev. ed. (New York: American Social Hygiene Association, 1936), 253–54; Baker, *Sex Education in High Schools*, 17; Gruenberg, "Secondary Schools," 536; "Conference on Education for Marriage and Family Social Relations, 1934: Final Report," *JSH* 22 (1936): 9, 16; Brandt, *No Magic Bullet*, 157.

123. Carter, "Birds, Bees, and Venereal Disease," 218, 248.

Chapter 2: Sex Radical Challenges to Marriage

1. Gertrude Marvin, "Anthony and the Devil," *Masses* 5 (February 1914): 16.

2. Mari Jo Buhle, *Women and American Socialism, 1870–1920* (Chicago: University of Illinois Press, 1981), 274, 280–81; Daniel Aaron, *Writers on the Left* (New York: Avon, 1961), 184–85; Carole R. McCann, *Birth Control Politics in the United States, 1916–1945* (Ithaca, N.Y.: Cornell University Press, 1994), 19, 40–41; Maurice A. Bigelow, *Sex-Education: A Series of Lectures Concerning Knowledge of Sex in Its Relation to Human Life* (New York: Macmillan, 1916), 84, 192.

3. See Nancy Cott, "Giving Character to Our Whole Civil Polity: Marriage and the Public Order in the Late Nineteenth Century," in *U.S. History as Women's History*, ed. Linda K. Kerber, Alice Kessler-Harris, and Kathryn Kish Sklar (Chapel Hill: University of North Carolina Press, 1995), 107–21.

4. George Chauncey, *Gay New York: Gender, Urban Culture, and the Making of the Gay Male World, 1890–1940* (New York: Basic Books, 1994), 171.

5. Ibid., 67. This chapter draws on the published writings of a wide range of sex radicals in the 1910s through 1930s, as well as previous scholarship on the sex radicals. An outstanding discussion of the pre-1920 period is Christine Stansell's *American Moderns: Bohemian New York and the Creation of a New Century* (New

York: Holt, 2000). Other works include Alice Wexler, *Emma Goldman in America* (Boston: Beacon, 1984); Candace Falk, *Love, Anarchy, and Emma Goldman*, rev. ed. (New Brunswick, N.J.: Rutgers University Press, 1990); Linda Gordon, *Woman's Body, Woman's Right: A Social History of Birth Control in America*, rev. ed. (New York: Penguin, 1990); Ellen Chesler, *Woman of Valor: Margaret Sanger and the Birth Control Movement in America* (New York: Simon and Schuster, 1992); Nancy Cott, *The Grounding of Modern Feminism* (New Haven, Conn.: Yale University Press, 1987); Ellen Kay Trimberger, "Feminism, Men, and Modern Love: Greenwich Village, 1900–1925," in *Powers of Desire: The Politics of Sexuality*, ed. Ann Snitow, Christine Stansell, and Sharon Thompson (New York: Monthly Review Press, 1983), 131–52; Trimberger, ed., *Intimate Warriors: Portraits of a Modern Marriage, 1899–1944* (New York: Feminist Press, 1991); Lillian Faderman, *Odd Girls and Twilight Lovers: A History of Lesbian Life in Twentieth-Century America* (New York: Penguin, 1992); Leila Rupp, "Feminism and the Sexual Revolution in the Early Twentieth Century: The Case of Doris Stevens," *Feminist Studies* 15 (1989): 289–309; Judith Schwarz, *Radical Feminists of Heterodoxy*, rev. ed.(Norwich, Vt.: New Victoria Publishers, 1986); Thadious Davis, *Nella Larsen: Novelist of the Harlem Renaissance* (Baton Rouge: Louisiana State University Press, 1994); Lois Palken Rudnick, *Mabel Dodge Luhan: New Woman, New Worlds* (Albuquerque: University of New Mexico Press, 1984); Leslie Fishbein, *Rebels in Bohemia: The Radicals of the Masses, 1911–1917* (Chapel Hill: University of North Carolina Press, 1982); Margaret C. Jones, *Heretics and Hellraisers: Women Contributors to the Masses, 1911–1917* (Austin: University of Texas Press, 1993); Kevin White, *The First Sexual Revolution: The Emergence of Male Heterosexuality in Modern America* (New York: New York University Press, 1993); Kevin J. Mumford, *Interzones: Black/White Sex Districts in Chicago and New York in the Early Twentieth Century* (New York: Columbia University Press, 1997).

The sexual thought of the African American radicals connected with the New York periodical the *Messenger* (1917–28) seems to have drawn little interest. See Theodore Kornweibel Jr., *No Crystal Stair: Black Life and the Messenger, 1917–1923* (Westport, Conn.: Greenwood, 1975); and Jervis Anderson, *A. Philip Randolph* (New York: Harcourt Brace Jovanovich, 1972).

6. Henry F. May, *The End of American Innocence: A Study of the First Years of Our Own Time, 1912–1917* (Chicago: Quadrangle, 1964); Ann Douglas, *Terrible Honesty: Mongrel Manhattan in the 1920s* (New York: Farrar, Straus and Giroux, 1995); Stansell, *American Moderns*, 4–8, 40–67; David Levering Lewis, *When Harlem Was in Vogue* (New York: Knopf, 1981); John D'Emilio and Estelle Freedman, *Intimate Matters: A History of Sexuality in America* (New York: Harper and Row, 1988), 227; Joanne Meyerowitz, "Sexual Geography and Gender Economy: The Furnished Room Districts of Chicago, 1890–1930," *Gender and History* 2 (1990): 274–96; Chauncey, *Gay New York*, 34; Daphne Duval Harrison, *Blues Queens of the 1920s* (New Brunswick, N.J.: Rutgers University Press, 1988); Hazel Carby, " 'It Just Be's Dat Way Some Time': The Sexual Politics of Women's Blues," in *Unequal Sisters: A Multicultural Reader in U.S. Women's History*, 2nd ed., ed. Vicki L. Ruiz

and Ellen Carol DuBois (New York: Routledge, 1994), 330–41; Carby, "Policing the Black Woman's Body in an Urban Context," *Critical Inquiry* 18 (1992): 738–55; Ann duCille, "Blues Notes on Black Sexuality: Sex and the Texts of Jessie Fauset and Nella Larsen," *Journal of the History of Sexuality* 3 (1993): 418–44; duCille, *The Coupling Convention: Sex, Text, and Tradition in Black Fiction* (New York: Oxford University Press, 1993); Angela Davis, "Ma Rainey and Bessie Smith," in *Sexy Bodies: The Strange Carnalities of Feminism*, ed. Elizabeth Grosz and Elspeth Probyn (London: Routledge, 1995), 231–65.

7. Davis, *Nella Larsen*; Langston Hughes, *The Big Sea* (New York: Hill and Wang, 1940); Wayne F. Cooper, *Claude McKay: Rebel Sojourner in the Harlem Renaissance* (Baton Rouge: Louisiana State University Press, 1987), ix, 71; Kenneth Lynn, "The Rebels of Greenwich Village," *Perspectives in American History* 8 (1974): 335–77; Hutchins Hapgood, *A Victorian in the Modern World* (New York: Harcourt Brace, 1939); Blanche Cook, ed., *Crystal Eastman on Women and Revolution* (New York: Oxford University Press, 1978); Emma Goldman, *Living My Life*, ed. Richard Drinnon and Anna Maria Drinnon (New York: New American Library, 1977), 650, 660, 662–63; Margaret Anderson, *My Thirty Years' War: The Autobiography, Beginnings, and Battles to 1930* (New York: Horizon, 1969); Floyd Dell, *Homecoming* (New York: Farrar and Rinehart, 1933); Leonard Wilcox, *V. F. Calverton: Radical in the American Grain* (Philadelphia: Temple University Press, 1992); Stansell, *American Moderns*, 67–68, 79, 81; Douglas, *Terrible Honesty*, 412.

8. George Lipsitz, *Time Passages: Collective Memory and American Popular Culture* (Minneapolis: University of Minnesota Press, 1990), 8; Lewis Erenberg, *Steppin' Out: New York Night Life and the Transformation of American Culture, 1890–1930* (Westport, Conn.: Greenwood, 1981); Kathy Peiss, *Cheap Amusements: Working Women and Leisure in Turn-of-the-Century New York* (Philadelphia: Temple University Press, 1986); Meyerowitz, "Sexual Geography"; John D'Emilio, "Capitalism and Gay Identity," in *Powers of Desire: The Politics of Sexuality*, ed. Ann Snitow, Christine Stansell, and Sharon Thompson (New York: Monthly Review Press, 1983), 100–113; Joseph Singal, "Towards a Definition of American Modernism," *American Quarterly* 39 (1987): 19–20; Mumford, *Interzones*; White, *First Sexual Revolution*, 80–105; Stansell, *American Moderns*, 3, 61.

9. A growing literature documents how European immigrant groups struggled to achieve the socially constructed status of whiteness. Matthew Frye Jacobson, *Whiteness of a Different Color: European Immigrants and the Alchemy of Race* (Cambridge, Mass.: Harvard University Press, 1998), 75–82, 92–97; Stansell, *American Moderns*, 25–26, 67–68.

10. Max Eastman, *Love and Revolution* (New York: Random House, 1964), 81–82; William J. Robinson, *What I Believe* (New York: Eugenics, 1927), 201; Mumford, *Interzones*, 134, 143. Many sources illustrate awkward or patronizing white relations with blacks. See Goldman, *Living My Life*, 650, 660, 662–63; Anderson, *Thirty Years' War*, 82; Tess Slesinger, *The Unpossessed* (1934; repr., Old Westbury, N.Y.: Feminist Press, 1984), 241–335. Also Jones, *Heretics and Hellraisers*, 110–32; Douglas, *Terrible Honesty*, 81–82; Haim Gnizi, "V. F. Calverton, a Radical Magazinist for Black Intellectuals, 1920–1940," *Journal of Negro History* 57 (1972): 241–44, 248–51.

11. Faderman, *Odd Girls*, 99; Kathleen A. Brown and Elizabeth Faue, "Revolutionary Desire: Redefining the Politics of Sexuality among American Radicals, 1919–1945," in *Sexual Borderlands: Constructing an American Sexual Past*, ed. Kathleen Kennedy and Sharon Ullman (Columbus: Ohio State University Press, 2003), 274.

12. Freedman and D'Emilio, *Intimate Matters*, 230–31; Mumford, *Interzones*, 157–71.

13. Wexler, *Emma Goldman*, 118, 122; Anderson, *Thirty Years' War*, 54–55; Margaret Marsh, *Anarchist Women, 1870–1920* (Philadelphia: Temple University Press, 1981), 10, 45–46, 69–75; Angus McLaren, "Sex Radicalism in the Canadian Pacific Northwest," *Journal of the History of Sexuality* 2 (1992): 527–46; John C. Spurlock, *Free Love: Marriage and Middle-Class Radicalism in America, 1825–1860* (New York: New York University Press, 1988), 107.

14. Chesler, *Woman of Valor*, 57; Dell, *Homecoming*, 55; Buhle, *Women and American Socialism*, 271; Gordon, *Woman's Body, Woman's Right*, 236.

15. Jervis Anderson, *This Was Harlem, 1900–1950* (New York: Farrar, Straus and Giroux, 1981), 106, 120; Anderson, *A. Philip Randolph*, 87. A number of *Messenger* writers were West Indian immigrants. "Ku Klux Klan Leaders Well Fitted to Correct Morals of Communities," *Messenger* 3 (October 1921): 261–62. Also Nina Miller, *Making Love Modern: The Intimate Public Worlds of New York's Literary Women* (New York: Oxford University Press, 1999), 158–59.

16. Paula Giddings, *When and Where I Enter: The Impact of Black Women on Race and Sex in America* (Toronto: Bantam, 1984), chaps. 8–11; Evelyn Brooks Higginbotham, *Righteous Discontent* (Cambridge, Mass.: Harvard University Press, 1993), 185–229; Davis, *Nella Larsen*, 142; Jessie Rodrique, "The Black Community and the Birth Control Movement," in *Passion and Power: Sexuality in History*, ed. Kathy Peiss and Christina Simmons, with Robert Padgug (Philadelphia: Temple University Press, 1989), 145; *Birth Control Review* 3 (September 1919); Schwarz, *Heterodoxy*, 58, 79; Gloria T. Hull, *Give Us Each Day: The Diary of Alice Dunbar-Nelson* (New York: Norton, 1984).

17. Marsh, *Anarchist Women*, 153; Buhle, *Women and American Socialism*, 250–51; Cott, *Grounding of Modern Feminism*, 39–43.

18. The situation did not improve until a federal appeals court ruled in 1930 in favor of publishing birth control advocate Mary Ware Dennett's sex education books. Chesler, *Woman of Valor*, 97–103, 126–31, 266–67; Falk, *Love, Anarchy, and Emma Goldman*, 140–46.

19. Rodrique, "The Black Community and the Birth Control Movement," 145; *Birth Control Review* 3 (September 1919).

20. Goldman, *Living My Life*, 587.

21. Chesler, *Woman of Valor*, 161, 168; Gordon, *Woman's Body, Woman's Right*, 243–45.

22. Disputants included Upton Sinclair, *Modern Quarterly* manager John Collier, and Communist H. M. Wicks in 1927. Aaron, *Writers on the Left*, 184–85; Upton Sinclair and V. F. Calverton, "Will the Family Pass? A Debate Entitled, Is Monogamy Desirable?" *Modern Quarterly* 4 (1927): 34–41; John Darmstadt [John Collier], "The Sexual Revolution," *Modern Quarterly* 4 (1927): 137–48;

H. M. Wicks, "An Apology for Sex Anarchism Disguised as Marxism," *Daily Worker*, 9 June 1927.

23. Leonard Wilcox, "Sex Boys in a Balloon: V. F. Calverton and the Abortive Sexual Revolution," *Journal of American Studies* 23 (1989): 18.

24. Kathleen A. Brown and Elizabeth Faue, "Social Bonds, Sexual Politics, and Political Community on the U.S. Left, 1920s–1940s," *Left History* 7 (Spring 2000): 9–45; Brown and Faue, "Revolutionary Desire."

25. Anderson, *Thirty Years' War*, 7–10, 212–25; Trimberger, *Intimate Warriors*, 1–32; Lynn, "Rebels of Greenwich Village"; Janet Sharistanian, "Afterword," in Slesinger, *Unpossessed*, 359–86; Stansell, *American Moderns*, 347.

26. Kornweibel, *No Crystal Stair*; Lewis, *Harlem*; DuCille, "Blues Notes"; Miller, *Making Love Modern*, 144, 149.

27. Carby, " 'It Just Be's Dat Way' "; Davis, "Ma Rainey and Bessie Smith"; Douglas, *Terrible Honesty*, 412.

28. Deborah E. McDowell, introduction, and Nella Larsen, "Quicksand," in Larsen, *Quicksand and Passing*, ed. Deborah E. McDowell (New Brunswick, N.J.: Rutgers University Press, 1986), xiii–xiv, 6; Raymond Williams, *Marxism and Literature* (Oxford: Oxford University Press, 1977), 128–35; Chris Weedon, *Feminist Practice and Poststructuralist Theory* (New York: Blackwell, 1987), 170–72.

29. William L. O'Neill, *The Last Romantic: A Life of Max Eastman* (New York: Oxford University Press, 1978), 54; Nathan Hale, *Freud and the Americans: The Beginnings of Psychoanalysis in the United States, 1876–1917* (New York: Oxford University Press, 1971), 271, 309–10; Douglas Clayton, *Floyd Dell: The Life and Times of an American Rebel* (Chicago: Dee, 1994), 140.

30. Rudnick, *Mabel Dodge Luhan*, 85–86; Schwarz, *Heterodoxy*, 37–38, 85; Faderman, *Odd Girls*, 64, 67–72, 76, 83, 93; Chauncey, *Gay New York*, 228, 234, 243, 248; Stansell, *American Moderns*, 153, 206.

31. Michel Foucault, *The History of Sexuality*, vol. 1, trans. Robert Hurley (New York: Vintage, 1980), 6–8.

32. May, *End of American Innocence*, 6–7, 333–47; Douglas, *Terrible Honesty*, 31–34; Claude McKay, *A Long Way from Home* (1937; repr., New York: Harcourt, Brace, and World, 1970), 229; Larsen, "Quicksand," 39.

33. Samuel Schmalhausen, "The Freudian Emphasis on Sex," in *The Sex Problem in Modern Society*, ed. John Francis McDermott (New York: Modern Library, 1931), 61–62.

34. Max Eastman, *Enjoyment of Living* (New York: Harper, 1948), 88, xiv–xv; Jacques Fischer, "The Sex Impulse in Man," in *The Sex Problem in Modern Society*, ed. John Francis McDermott (New York: Modern Library, 1931), 48; Hapgood, *Victorian in the Modern World*, 364.

35. Warren Susman, *Culture as History* (New York: Pantheon, 1984), 272–80; Lipsitz, *Time Passages*, 8–12; Lawrence Birken, *Consuming Desire* (Ithaca, N.Y.: Cornell University Press, 1988); Edith Summers Kelley, *Weeds* (1923; repr., New York: Popular Library, 1972), 65–66, 81; A. A. Roback, "Sex in Dynamic Psychology," in *Sex in Civilization*, ed. V. F. Calverton and S. D. Schmalhausen (New York: Macaulay, 1929), 165–66; Roland Marchand, *Advertising the American Dream: Making Way for*

Modernity, 1920–1940 (Berkeley: University of California Press, 1985), 120–60; Elaine May, *Great Expectations: Marriage and Divorce in Post-Victorian America* (Chicago: University of Chicago Press, 1980), 75–91, 137–55; Schmalhausen, "Freudian Emphasis on Sex," 59; Freedman and D'Emilio, *Intimate Matters*, 234.

36. William J. Robinson, "Sexual Continence and Its Influence on the Physical and Mental Health of Men and Women," in *Continence*, ed. William J. Robinson (New York: Eugenics, 1930), 4–5; Roback, "Sex in Dynamic Psychology," 144–46.

37. Dell, *Homecoming*, 164.

38. Sigmund Freud, "Civilized Sexual Morality and Modern Nervousness" (1908), in Freud, *Sexuality and the Psychology of Love*, ed. Philip Rieff (New York: Collier, 1963), 20–40; Cott, "Giving Character to Our Whole Civil Polity," 121, 110–11, 118–19.

39. Tessie Liu, "Teaching the Differences among Women from a Historical Perspective," in *Unequal Sisters: A Multicultural Reader in U.S. Women's History*, 2nd ed., ed. Vicki L. Ruiz and Ellen Carol DuBois (New York: Routledge, 1994), 576, 579, 581. Liu brilliantly elucidates how women's reproductive role is crucial to the maintenance of "race," because the notion of race is built on the belief in (different) common biological descents or families. She notes that "class" in Europe was originally based on a similar belief that certain families (aristocrats) were fit to rule over others; "class" became "race" with colonialism and the extension of the rule of Europeans over others of a different skin color elsewhere in the world. See also Ann Laura Stoler, "Carnal Knowledge and Imperial Power: Gender, Race, and Morality in Colonial Asia," in *Gender at the Crossroads of Knowledge: Feminist Anthropology in the Post-modern Era*, ed. Micaela di Leonardo (Berkeley: University of California Press, 1991), 51–101.

40. Ann Laura Stoler, *Race and the Education of Desire* (Durham, N.C.: Duke University Press, 1995), 183; Peter T. Cominos, "Late-Victorian Sexual Respectability and the Social System," *International Review of Social History* 8 (1963): 18–48, 216–50; Charles Rosenberg, "Sexuality, Class and Role in Nineteenth-Century America," *American Quarterly* 25 (1973): 131–53; Helen Lefkowitz Horowitz, *Rereading Sex: Battles over Sexual Knowledge and Suppression in Nineteenth-Century America* (New York: Vintage, 2003), 125–43.

41. Giddings, *When and Where I Enter*, 85–94.

42. This chapter slights class differences among whites, as a number of the white sex radicals came from middle-class or even upper-class backgrounds. See Lynn, "Rebels of Greenwich Village," and Wexler, *Emma Goldman*, 39.

43. Goldman, "Jealousy," in *Red Emma Speaks: An Emma Goldman Reader*, ed. Alix Kates Shulman (New York: Schocken, 1983), 221; Goldman, "Love and Marriage," in *The Traffic in Women and Other Essays on Feminism* (1917; repr., New York: Times Change Press, 1970), 39; see also Elizabeth Stuyvesant's story of her eleven-year free relationship, "Staying Free," in *These Modern Women: Autobiographical Essays from the Twenties*, ed. Elaine Showalter (Old Westbury, N.Y.: Feminist Press, 1978), 96–97.

44. Jonathan Katz, *The Invention of Heterosexuality* (New York: Penguin, 1995); Steven Seidman, *Romantic Longings: Love in America, 1830–1980* (New York:

Routledge, 1991), 60–61. Elsie Clews Parsons, like many feminists, saw women and men as more alike than different; *The Old-Fashioned Woman: Primitive Fancies about the Sex* (1913; repr., New York: Arno, 1972), v–vi.

45. Neith Boyce, "The Bond," in Trimberger, *Intimate Warriors*, 75–77, 95; for more on the separation of male and female culture, see Kelley, *Weeds*, 103, 181–83.

46. Elsie Clews Parsons, "Changes in Sex Relations," in *Our Changing Morality: A Symposium*, ed. Freda Kirchwey (1924; repr., New York: Albert and Charles Boni, 1930), 46; see also Edwin Muir, "Women—Free for What?" in ibid., 80.

47. "Zora Neale Hurston," in *Notable American Women: The Modern Period*, ed. Barbara Sicherman and Carol Hurd Green (Cambridge, Mass.: Harvard University Press, 1980), 361–63; Zora Neale Hurston, *Their Eyes Were Watching God* (1937; repr., Urbana: University of Illinois Press, 1978), 30, 37, 40–41, 49, 52, 85–87, 198–99, 206, 210, 236.

48. Hutchins Hapgood, "The Story of a Lover," in Trimberger, *Intimate Warriors*, 144; "Confessions of a Feminist Man," *Masses* 5 (March 1914): 8.

49. Dell, *Homecoming*, 164.

50. On the new manhood, see John Higham, "The Reorientation of American Culture in the 1890s," in *Writing American History*, ed. John Higham (Bloomington: Indiana University Press, 1970), 60–103; White, *First Sexual Revolution*; Anthony Rotundo, *American Manhood: Transformations in Masculinity from the Revolution to the Modern Era* (New York: Basic Books, 1993), 227; Gail Bederman, *Manliness and Civilization: A Cultural History of Gender and Race in the United States, 1880–1917* (Chicago: University of Chicago Press, 1995), 218–32; Eastman, *Enjoyment of Living*, 362; Hapgood, *Victorian in the Modern World*, 86–100; Martin Summers, *Manliness and Its Discontents: The Black Middle Class and the Transformation of Masculinity, 1900–1930* (Chapel Hill: University of North Carolina Press, 2004), 8–9, 149–57; "Spurious Social Equality," *Messenger* 4 (September 1922): 490; J. A. Rogers, "Who Is the New Negro, and Why?" *Messenger* 9 (March 1927): 68; Langston Hughes, *Not without Laughter* (1930; repr., New York: Knopf, 1968); Suzanne LaFollette, *Concerning Women* (New York: Albert and Charles Boni, 1926), 100.

51. Emma Goldman, "The Hypocrisy of Puritanism," in *Anarchism and Other Essays* (1917; repr., New York: Dover, 1969), 167; W. J. Robinson, *Sex, Love, and Morality* (New York: Eugenics, 1928), 31; Robinson, *Birth Control* (New York, 1916), 37–38; Robinson, *Continence*, 11; Margaret Sanger, *Woman and the New Race* (New York: Brentano's, 1920), 116; Chandler Owen, "Love—Once More!" *Messenger* 5 (February 1923): 602.

52. Dell, *Homecoming*, 199.

53. Rotundo, *American Manhood*, 231–32; Isabel Leavenworth, "Virtue for Women," in *Our Changing Morality*, ed. Freda Kirchwey (1924; repr., New York: Albert and Charles Boni, 1930), 98, 103; Dell, *Homecoming*, 160; also Dell, "Can Men and Women Be Friends?" in *Our Changing Morality*, ed. Freda Kirchwey (1924; rept., New York: Albert and Charles Boni, 1930), 184–93.

54. Hapgood, *Victorian in the Modern World*, 160; Sanger, "Why the Woman Rebel?" *Woman Rebel* 1 (March 1914): 8; Goldman, "Love and Marriage," 40.

55. Martha Hodes, "The Sexualization of Reconstruction Politics: White Women and Black Men in the South after the Civil War," *Journal of the History of Sexuality* 3 (1993): 402–17; D'Emilio and Freedman, *Intimate Matters*, 218–19; Mumford, *Interzones*, 100.

56. Hazel Carby, *Reconstructing Womanhood: The Emergence of the Afro-American Woman Novelist* (New York: Oxford University Press, 1987), 174; Darlene Clark Hine, "Rape and the Inner Lives of Black Women in the Middle West: Preliminary Thoughts on the Culture of Dissemblance," in *Unequal Sisters: A Multicultural Reader in U.S. Women's History*, 2nd ed., ed. Vicki L. Ruiz and Ellen Carol DuBois (New York: Routledge, 1994), 342–47; Mumford, *Interzones*, 48.

57. Davis, *Nella Larsen*, 1–10, 56, 66–67, 75, 87–90, 119–22, 128–52; Larsen, "Quicksand," 109; Carby, "'It Just Be's Dat Way,'" 332–33; Wilson Moses, "Sexual Anxieties of the Black Bourgeoisie in Victorian America: The Cultural Context of W. E. B. DuBois's First Novel," *Western Journal of Black Studies* 6 (1982): 202–11; duCille, "Blues Notes on Black Sexuality," 418–44; Pamela Barnett, "'My Picture of You Is, after All, the True Helga Crane': Portraiture and Identity in Nella Larsen's *Quicksand*," *Signs* 20 (1995): 575–600; Judith Butler, *Bodies That Matter: On the Discursive Limits of "Sex"* (New York: Routledge, 1993), 178–79.

58. Hurston, *Their Eyes*, 31–32, 24–28, 43, 54; Hazel Carby, "Fiction, Anthropology, and the Folk: Zora Neale Hurston," in *New Essays on Their Eyes Were Watching God*, ed. Michael Awkward (New York: Cambridge University Press, 1990), 71–93; Victoria W. Wolcott, *Remaking Respectability: African American Women in Interwar Detroit* (Chapel Hill: University of North Carolina Press, 2001), 153.

59. Carby, "'It Just Be's Dat Way,'" 337–40.

60. To the extent that blues women sang about or enacted a sexuality that seemed more free of class control, they were challenging the existing gender order just as white working-class women were. See Peiss, *Cheap Amusements*, 88–114; Tera Hunter, *To 'Joy My Freedom: Southern Black Women's Lives and Labors after the Civil War* (Cambridge, Mass.: Harvard University Press, 1997), 172–74.

61. Lawrence Levine, *Black Culture, Black Consciousness* (New York: Oxford University Press, 1977), 226, 270–79, 284; Erenberg, *Steppin' Out*, 166; duCille, "Blues Notes," 428.

62. Schmalhausen, "Sexual Revolution," 406.

63. Hurston, *Their Eyes*, 54–55, 66, 74, 139.

64. Goldman, "Love and Marriage," 44; Goldman, "The Traffic in Women," in *The Traffic in Women and Other Essays on Feminism* (1917; repr., New York: Times Change Press, 1970), 20.

65. *Woman Rebel* 1 (March 1914): 6, 8; 1 (April 1914): 16; 1 (June 1914): 31; Eastman, *Enjoyment of Living*, 362; Stuyvesant, "Staying Free," 97. Radical and feminist Agnes Smedley also articulated a powerful antimarriage position, but she was not able to come to terms with sexuality, voicing extreme vulnerability in that regard, both inside and outside marriage, in *Daughter of Earth* (1929; repr., New York: Feminist Press, 1987), 188–207.

66. Some black writers used leftist terms to discuss marriage without necessarily opposing the institution. Chandler Owen argued that women's fear of being old maids was "capitalistic" and had "its roots in the desire to be 'respectable' and to have legitimate children who can inherit property," "Women and Children of the South," *Birth Control Review* 3 (September 1919), 9. Lee Selman, "Is Marriage a Failure?" *Messenger* 9 (February 1927): 34.

67. Sinclair and Calverton, "Will the Family Pass?" 38; Darmstadt [Collier], "The Sexual Revolution"; V. F. Calverton, *The Bankruptcy of Marriage* (New York: Macaulay, 1928), 60–62, 165–66, 205, 244–47, 216, 301.

68. C. E. Ayres, "Domesticity," in *The New Generation: The Intimate Problems of Modern Parents and Children*, ed. V. F. Calverton and Samuel D. Schmalhausen (New York: Macaulay, 1930), 387. See Wicks's attack on Darmstadt [Collier], "An Apology for Sex Anarchism." Collier wrote to Dell that he approved any conduct and "any natural and healthy social and sexual relations" that "prove subversive of fundamental institutions, customs and ideas upholding the existing social order (or disorder), and lead to the overthrow of the property class and its domination." John Darmstadt [John Armistead Collier] to Floyd Dell, 30 January 1927, Box 2, John and Phyllis Collier Collection, Walter Reuther Library, Wayne State University, Detroit, Michigan.

69. V. F. Calverton, "Red Love in Soviet Russia," *Modern Quarterly* 4 (1928): 185.

70. Deborah Gray White, *Too Heavy a Load: Black Women in Defense of Themselves, 1894–1994* (New York: Norton, 1999), 70–72; W. E. B. DuBois, "So the Girl Marries," *Crisis* 35 (June 1928): 207–9. On different black legal marriage rates, see Samuel H. Preston, Suet Lim, and S. Philip Morgan, "African-American Marriage in 1910: Beneath the Surface of Census Data," *Demography* 29 (1992): 1–3, 12–13.

71. Selman, "Is Marriage a Failure?" 34; Hurston, *Their Eyes*, 170–71. For another critique, see the poem by Ann Lawrence, "The Fallen Woman," in which "marriage ties" are excoriated as "sacred lies" that leave victims of male seduction as outcasts; *Messenger* 7 (August 1925): 301.

72. Goldman, *Traffic in Women*, 38–43; Elizabeth Gurley Flynn, "Men and Women" (1915), in Rosalyn Fraad Baxandall, ed., *Words on Fire: The Life and Writing of Elizabeth Gurley Flynn* (New Brunswick, N.J.: Rutgers University Press, 1987), 102.

73. Calverton, *Bankruptcy*, 60–61; Wilcox, *V. F. Calverton*, 20.

74. Dell, *Homecoming*, 279–80, 291; Hapgood, *Victorian in the Modern World*, 159.

75. Dell, *Homecoming*, 350; Wexler, *Emma Goldman*, 95.

76. Elsie Clews Parsons, *The Family* (New York, 1906), 347–49. See Jones, *Heretics and Hellraisers*, 36, on the public outcry caused by the book, which sold only 3,904 copies.

77. Sanger, *New Race*; Chesler, *Woman of Valor*, 247, 244; Phyllis Blanchard, "The Long Journey," in *These Modern Women: Autobiographical Essays from the Twenties*, ed. Elaine Showalter (Old Westbury, N.Y.: Feminist Press, 1978), 108–9.

78. Sinclair and Calverton, "Will the Family Pass?" 38–39; Darmstadt [Collier], "Sexual Revolution," 139; Thomas Kirksey, "Sex Expression in Literature," *Messenger* 9 (October 1927): 314.

79. Chandler Owen, "The Passing of Novelty," *Messenger* 1 (November 1917): 22; Owen, "Marriage and Divorce," *Messenger* 5 (March 1923): 629–31; McKay, *Long Way from Home*, xi, 307, 229; Cooper, *Claude McKay*, ix; Claude McKay, *Home to Harlem* (1928; repr., New York: Pocket Books, 1965), 5, 13; Sinclair and Calverton, "Will the Family Pass?" 41; Slesinger, *Unpossessed*, 308; Hapgood, "Story of a Lover," 143.

80. Hapgood, *Victorian in the Modern World*, 156, 413; Stansell, *American Moderns*, 278; Wilcox, *V. F. Calverton*, 55.

81. Zora Neale Hurston, "Sweat," in *I Love Myself When I Am Laughing and Then Again When I Am Looking Mean and Impressive: A Zora Neale Hurston Reader* (Old Westbury, N.Y.: Feminist Press, 1979), 197–207 (quotations on page 207); see also Hurston, "Pants and Cal'line," in *I Love Myself*, 186–87, and *Their Eyes*, 180, 218–19; Larsen, "Quicksand," 104–9. In "Passing," Larsen links the woman's jealousy directly to her fears about security in marriage; *Quicksand and Passing*, ed. Deborah E. McDowell (New Brunswick, N.J.: Rutgers University Press, 1986), 221.

82. Goldman, "Jealousy," 219–21; Falk, *Love, Anarchy, and Emma Goldman*, 58–59; Baxandall, *Words on Fire*, 21–22; Chesler, *Woman of Valor*, 173–74, 250–51. See also Rupp, "Feminism and the Sexual Revolution"; Stansell, *American Moderns*, 297–300. Elizabeth Stuyvesant in the *Nation* perhaps hinted at nonmonogamy when she foresaw "room in my life for other close relationships"; "Staying Free," 97. Anthropologists Margaret Mead and Ruth Benedict practiced free love without publicly proclaiming it. Like Sanger, both relied on marriage to present a conventional public self and as a kind of anchor to their lives. Lois W. Banner, *Intertwined Lives: Margaret Mead, Ruth Benedict, and Their Circle* (New York: Vintage, 2003), 9, 217–19.

83. Falk, *Love, Anarchy, and Emma Goldman*, chap. 4; Trimberger, "Introduction," Boyce, "The Bond," Hapgood, "Story of a Lover," and Hapgood-Boyce letters, all in *Intimate Warriors*, 19–25, 107–14, 144–45, 204–31.

84. Dell, "Can Men and Women Be Friends?" 193; LaFollette, *Concerning Women*, 152–53. Dr. Robinson also countenanced extramarital relations on the grounds of sexual need or even preference; Robinson, *Sex, Love, and Morality*, 31–32, 42, 49; Robinson, *What I Believe*, 110–11. See also Judith Walkowitz, *City of Dreadful Delight: Narratives of Sexual Danger in Late-Victorian London* (Chicago: University of Chicago Press, 1992), 158, on differing male and female views of the seriousness of sex in the Men and Women's Club of the 1880s.

85. Slesinger, *Unpossessed*, 66, 146, 294–95, 307, 276, 315.

86. Wexler, *Emma Goldman*, 279–80; see also Goldman, *Living My Life*, 202; Sanger, *New Race*, 181–82; Larsen, "Quicksand," 62, 104, 107–17.

87. Calverton, *Bankruptcy*, 301; Calverton, "Are Women Monogamous?" in *Woman's Coming of Age*, ed. Samuel D. Schmalhausen and V. F. Calverton (New York: Horace Liveright, 1931), 478–79; Schmalhausen, "The Sexual Revolution," 360; Owen, "Love—Once More!" 602; Robinson, *Sex, Love, and Morality*, 83. Owen and Robinson see it more as a natural difference. See also Walkowitz, *City of Dreadful Delight*, 159–60.

88. Hapgood, in *Intimate Warriors*, 152; Eastman, *Enjoyment of Living*, 378, 511–12; Sinclair and Calverton, "Will the Family Pass?" 41; Wilcox, *V. F. Calverton*, 55–57; White, *First Sexual Revolution*, 116–26; see also the interview with Miriam Allen DeFord in *From Parlor to Prison*, ed. Sherna Gluck (New York: Vintage, 1976), 159.

89. Slesinger, *Unpossessed*, 306; Leavenworth, "Virtue for Women," 103; Charles Rosenberg, "Sexuality, Class and Role in 19th-Century America," *American Quarterly* 25 (1973): 139. A cartoon by George W. W. Little called "Nauseating Nordics" points to white women's repressed sexuality to explain lynching accusations: A white woman is depicted as "The sex-starved female who is always being 'attacked by a brutal Negro'" in *Messenger* 10 (February 1928): 32.

90. Post–Civil War repeals were part of a general movement against discriminatory law, based partly in black voting strength. See David H. Fowler, *Northern Attitudes towards Interracial Marriage: Legislation and Public Opinion in the Middle Atlantic and the States of the Old Northwest, 1780–1930* (New York: Garland, 1987), 221–22, 273; Mumford, *Interzones*, 164–68; Peggy Pascoe, "Race, Gender, and Intercultural Relations," *Frontiers* 12, no. 1 (1991): 6; Gilbert Stephenson, *Race Distinctions in American Law* (1910; repr., New York: Negro Universities Press, 1969), 78–79; Michael Grossberg, *Governing the Hearth: Law and the Family in Nineteenth-Century America* (Chapel Hill: University of North Carolina Press, 1985), 127, 139. Fowler finds efforts to pass anti-intermarriage laws from 1890 to 1930, while Mumford highlights the period 1920 to 1940. Absolute numbers of intermarriages remained tiny: At the turn of the century about 10 percent of (the small number of) northern urban blacks married whites; by the 1920s and 1930s, after the Great Migration, proportions fell to .5 to 1 percent. Paul R. Spickard, *Mixed Blood: Intermarriage and Ethnic Identity in Twentieth-Century America* (Madison: University of Wisconsin Press, 1989), 272.

91. The efforts of the NAACP certainly contributed to preventing passage of these laws. Editorial, "Civil Rights," *Messenger* (March 1919 supplement): 9. Mumford, in *Interzones*, 163–64, 166–67, notes that nationalist leader Marcus Garvey was an exception in supporting legal prohibition of intermarriage. In actual practice the freedom to form interracial relationships seems not to have been a priority concern for most African Americans. Black popular singers, for example, like most race leaders, rarely commented on interracial relationships; when they did so, they warned listeners against them. See Levine, *Black Culture and Black Consciousness*, 289.

92. Other whites more mildly pointed to the biological artificiality of prohibiting black-white sex. See Ayres, "Domesticity," 366–67, 387; anonymous white letter writer to the *Crisis* 36 (July 1929): 242. Dr. Robinson wrote in 1928 that miscegenation was not in itself immoral but was so if children resulted, due to the harm done to them. *Sex, Love, and Morality*, 149–50. Eugene O'Neill, *All God's Chillun Got Wings and Other Plays* (London: Jonathan Cape, 1925); V. F. Calverton, "Introduction," in *Anthology of American Negro Literature*, ed. V. F. Calverton (New York: Modern Library, 1929), 8; McKay, *Long Way from Home*, 336–37; Mumford, *Interzones*, chap. 7, quotations from 122, 179.

I did not find evidence of white radical debate about national/ethnic intermarriage either, though some of them practiced it (white Protestant Max Eastman with Jewish Ida Rauh, for example). See Eastman, *Enjoyment of Living*, 496.

93. Wilbert Holloway, "Senator Lynch of Mississippi," *Messenger* 9 (May 1927): 152; "Civil Rights," 9; "Who's Who," *Messenger* 4 (July 1922): 445–46; Lisa Lindquist Dorr, "Arm in Arm: Gender, Eugenics, and Virginia's Racial Integrity Acts of the 1920s," *Journal of Women's History* 11 (1999): 143–66. Peggy Pascoe traces the legal challenges to these laws in "Miscegenation Law, Court Cases, and Ideologies of 'Race' in Twentieth-Century America," *Journal of American History* 83 (1996): 44–69.

94. "Civil Rights," 9; George Schuyler, "Emancipated Women and the Negro," and "When Black Weds White," *Modern Quarterly* 5 (1928–30): 361–63, and 8 (1934–35): 11–17.

95. Chandler Owen, "The Cabaret—A Useful Social Institution," *Messenger* 4 (August 1922): 461; Owen, "The Black and Tan Cabaret—America's Most Democratic Institution," *Messenger* 7 (February 1925): 97, 99; "Month's Best Editorial," *Messenger* 4 (September 1922): 490–91; Mumford, *Interzones*, 153–55. Whites' fear of black men's sexuality may account for the fact that black women, rather than men, singers of blues's sexual lyrics were taken up as commercial commodities in the 1920s. duCille, *Coupling Convention*, 165n17.

96. See *Messenger* short stories by Lovett Fort-Whiteman, "Wild Flowers," *Messenger* 5 (February 1923): 603–7; S. Miller Johnson, "The Golden Penknife," *Messenger* 7 (August 1925): 280–83, 298–301; George W. Little Jr., "So It Goes," *Messenger* 9 (December 1927): 345–47, 361, and Little, "An Aframerican Fable," *Messenger* 10 (January 1928): 7; Jean Toomer, "Becky" and "Bona and Paul," in *Cane* (1923; repr. Harper and Row, 1969), 8–13 and 134–53; Anderson, *A. Philip Randolph*, 79.

97. [Josephine Cogdell], "Temptation," *Messenger* 9 (October 1927): 303. Her identity is revealed in McKay, *Long Way from Home*, 346–47. See also "Raggedybag, by a Young Nordic Southerner," *Messenger* 9 (November 1927): 324.

98. Reba Cain, "Dark Lover," *Crisis* 36 (April 1929): 123, 137–38; Mumford, *Interzones*, 179, 100, 169.

99. Spickard, *Mixed Blood*, 302; Larsen, "Passing," 216–22. The jealousy portrayed in *Passing* may have been fueled by Larsen's real-life awareness of her husband's affair with a white woman; see Davis, *Nella Larsen*, 324.

100. Toomer, *Cane*, 59, 61, 52, 65–67; Kirksey, "Sex Expression in Literature," 314. See also McKay, *Long Way from Home*, 278–81.

101. Larsen, "Quicksand," 61, 103; Larsen, "Passing," 165–76.

102. More black men and white women than white men and black women have married, and intermarriage was legally possible only outside the South until the 1967 *Loving v. Virginia* Supreme Court decision declaring antimiscegenation laws unconstitutional. In the South, unmarried relationships of white men and black women would have been the dominant form. Spickard, *Mixed Blood*, 262–63, 269–78.

103. Couples also used douching and withdrawal. Gordon, *Woman's Body, Woman's Right*, 62–64, 95–115; Ruth Rosen, *The Lost Sisterhood: Prostitution in America, 1900–1918* (Baltimore: Johns Hopkins University Press, 1983), 99.

104. McCann, *Birth Control Politics*, 3; Sanger, *Woman and the New Race*, 28, 53, 94, 180, 229–30.

105. Gordon, *Woman's Body, Woman's Right*, 62.

106. Ibid., 231.

107. Gail Bederman, *Manliness and Civilization: A Cultural History of Gender and Race in the United States, 1880–1917* (Chicago: University of Chicago Press, 1995), 200; Gordon, *Woman's Body, Woman's Right*, 135–58.

108. Augustus Hand, *U.S. vs. One Package*, 86 F2d 737 (1936), 5–6, quoted in Chesler, *Woman of Valor*, 373.

109. Robinson, *Birth Control*, 119. See also Joseph D. Cannon, "Large Families and the Steel Strike," *Birth Control Review* 4, no. 1 (1920): 11–12; and Robert Blatchford, untitled, *Birth Control Review* 12, no. 1 (1928): 21.

110. Goldman chose a middle ground of portraying herself as having a medical condition preventing conception, yet also as choosing to decline medical treatment for it; *Living My Life*, 58. Several of the "modern" women who wrote autobiographical essays in the *Nation* in 1926–27 had decided against motherhood. See Showalter, *These Modern Women*, 7; Crystal Eastman, "Birth Control in the Feminist Program," in *Crystal Eastman on Women and Revolution*, ed Blanche Wiesen Cook (New York: Oxford University Press, 1978), 47; Slesinger, *Unpossessed*, 61, 345, 348.

111. Owen, "Marriage and Divorce," 630; Owen, "Women and Children of the South," 9, 20; Mary Burrill, "They That Sit in Darkness," *Birth Control Review* 3 (September 1919): 5–8. I have found only one example of a black "race suicide" argument, by Alice Dunbar-Nelson (in "Woman's Most Serious Problem," *Messenger* 9 [March 1927]: 73, 86), where she expresses concern that educated and employed black married women are having few or no children and that mothers' employment is harmful to the well-being of black children.

112. Owen, "Women and Children of the South," 9; Isaac Fisher, "A Voice from the South," *Birth Control Review* 3 (September 1919): 14; J. A. Rogers, "The Critic," *Messenger* 7 (April 1925): 165. Linda Gordon argues that black women social welfare reformers in the early twentieth century were more critical of male sexual abuse of women than comparable white women reformers were, in "Black and White Women's Visions of Welfare: Women's Welfare Activism, 1890–1945," *Journal of American History* 78 (1991): 579, 587.

113. Rodrique, "Birth Control and the Black Community"; Constance Fisher, "The Negro Social Worker Evaluates Birth Control," *Birth Control Review* 16 (June 1932): 174–75; and other articles in this issue and in the September 1919 and May 1938 issues. Also, W. G. Alexander, "Birth Control for the Negro…A Fad or a Necessity," *Journal of the National Medical Association* 24 (August 1932): 34–39; Jamie Hart, "Who Should Have the Children? Discussions of Birth Control among African-American Intellectuals, 1920–1939," *Journal of Negro History* 79 (1994): 80.

114. Larsen presents characters speaking of decisions not to have children but does not mention birth control directly in "Quicksand," 103, and "Passing," 168.

115. Helen Hull, *Labyrinth* (New York, 1923), 15–17, 24–26, 30, 68, 72, 92, 148–49, 185–86, 189, 339.

116. See, for example, Crystal Eastman, "Now We Can Begin" and "Marriage under Two Roofs," in *Crystal Eastman on Women and Revolution*, ed Blanche Wiesen Cook (New York: Oxford University Press, 1978), 56, 78. Some women may not have wished to give up power over an arena they could still claim authority in; see Trimberger, *Intimate Warriors*, 28. Dell, "Adventures in Anti-Land," and Max Eastman, "Confession of a Suffrage Orator," *Masses* 7 (October–November 1915): 199–210, 201–5; Dell, *Intellectual Vagabondage: An Apology for the Intelligentsia* (New York: George H. Doran, 1926), 170–72, 174. Hutchins Hapgood took on more of an active parental role in practice than many men but may have feared his own feminization as a result. See *Intimate Warriors*, 30. Darmstadt [Collier], "Sexual Revolution," 147; Calverton, *Bankruptcy of Marriage*, 263; McLaren, "Sex Radicalism," 536.

117. William J. Robinson, *Dr. Robinson and St. Peter* (New York: Eugenics, 1931), 38; Diana Frederics [pseud.], *Diana: A Strange Autobiography* (1939; repr., New York: Arno, 1975), 226. On women who married but also had same-sex relationships, see Banner, *Intertwined Lives*, and Milford, *Savage Beauty*.

118. Carroll Smith-Rosenberg, "The Female World of Love and Ritual" and "New Woman as Androgyne," in Smith-Rosenberg, *Disorderly Conduct: Visions of Gender in Victorian America* (New York: Knopf, 1985), 53–76, 245–96; Faderman, *Odd Girls*, 48–54. Historians have qualified Smith-Rosenberg's assertion that women's relationships were fully accepted prior to the late nineteenth century by pointing to sanctions against relationships seen as too great a violation of conventions or male authority. Lisa L. Moore, " 'Something More Tender Still Than Friendship': Romantic Friendship in Early-Nineteenth-Century England," *Feminist Studies* 18 (1992): 499–520; Marylynne Diggs' " 'Romantic Friends' or a 'Different Race of Creatures'? The Representation of Lesbian Pathology in Nineteenth-Century America," *Feminist Studies* 21 (1995): 317–40.

119. Eric Garber, "A Spectacle in Color: The Lesbian and Gay Subculture of Jazz Age Harlem," in *Hidden from History: Reclaiming the Gay and Lesbian Past*, ed. Martin Duberman, Martha Vicinus, and George Chauncey Jr. (New York: Penguin, 1989), 318–31; Faderman, *Odd Girls*, 62–92; Chauncey, *Gay New York*, 227–67, esp. 230–31, 311–13; Mumford, *Interzones*, 73–92; Freedman and D'Emilio, *Intimate Matters*, 288.

120. Chauncey, *Gay New York*, 230–31, 311–13; Paul S. Boyer, *Purity in Print: The Vice Society Movement and Book Censorship in America* (New York: Scribner's, 1968), 224–26; Frederics, *Diana*, 112.

121. Calverton, *Bankruptcy of Marriage*, 117, 162; Roback, "Sex in Dynamic Psychology," 152–53; G. V. Hamilton, "The Emotional Life of Modern Woman," in *Woman's Coming of Age: A Symposium*, ed. Samuel D. Schmalhausen and V. F. Calverton (New York: Horace Liveright, 1931), 227–28; Ayres, "Domesticity," 366, 384; Schmalhausen, "Freudian Emphasis on Sex," 64.

122. Chauncey, *Gay New York*, 253–54. Estelle Freedman notes that in women's prisons before 1940, African American inmates were represented as sexual aggressors with white women, one more stigma black women writers might have wished to avoid; see "The Prison Lesbian: Race, Class, and the Construction of the Aggressive Female Homosexual, 1915–1965," *Feminist Studies* 22 (1996): 399. Deborah McDowell argues that Larsen's *Passing* expresses lesbian desire, but it is not explicit in the text; McDowell, introduction, in *Quicksand and Passing*, xxiii. On blues women, see Sandra Lieb, *Mother of the Blues: A Study of Ma Rainey* (Amherst: University of Massachusetts Press, 1981), 124; Harrison, *Black Pearls*, 103–4; Joan Nestle, "Excerpts from the Oral History of Mabel Hampton," *Signs* 18 (1993): 925–35. Angela Davis notes that some male blues singers also acknowledged lesbian relationships and that Rainey mentioned male homosexuality; see "'I Used to Be Your Sweet Mama,'" 259–61.

123. Goldman, *Living My Life*, 555–56, 173, 269; Falk, *Love, Anarchy, and Emma Goldman*, 105–9, 140. Goldman's comrade Alexander Berkman offers a moving first-person account of his own conversion from antihomosexual prejudice through conversations and personal bonds of affection with other men in his *Prison Memoirs of an Anarchist* (1912), selection in Jonathan Katz, *Gay American History* (New York: Crowell, 1976), 530–38.

124. Jonathan Katz, *Gay/Lesbian Almanac* (New York: Harper and Row, 1983), 359–66; Anderson, *Thirty Years' War*, 4, 13, 43.

125. Elizabeth Craigin, *Either Is Love* (1937; repr., New York: Lion Books, 1952), 86; Frederics, *Diana*, 58, 62. Gale Wilhelm's novel *We Too Are Drifting* (New York: Random House, 1935) is more melancholy about the inability to assert lesbian love against the demands of the biological family, but the book shares the depiction of lesbian desire and love that make claims simply by their undeniable existence.

126. Mary Casal, *The Stone Wall: An Autobiography* (Chicago: Eyncourt Press, 1930), 18, 29–39, 70, 79, 131; Frederics, *Diana*, 143; Hull, *Labyrinth*, 59, 104, 149; Anderson, *Thirty Years' War*, 4.

127. Craigin, *Either Is Love*, 119–20, 87; Casal, *Stone Wall*, 153.

128. Douglas, *Terrible Honesty*, 97; McKay, *Home to Harlem*, 68; Robinson, *What I Believe*, 109; Robinson, *Sex, Love, and Morality*, 112; Victor Robinson, "Introduction," in Frederics, *Diana*, x.

129. Randolph Bourne, "The Vampire," *Masses* 9 (June 1917); Stansell notes the limits of Bourne's sympathy for feminists who wanted too much; *American Moderns*, 269–70. Schmalhausen, "The War between the Sexes," in *Woman's Coming of Age: A Symposium*, ed. Samuel D. Schmalhausen and V. F. Calverton (New York: Horace Liveright, 1931), 275–78; Clayton, *Floyd Dell*, 148–53; Dell, *Love in the Machine Age: A Psychological Study of the Transition from Patriarchal Society* (New York: Farrar and Rinehart, 1930), 82; Faderman, *Odd Girls*, 86–88.

130. Williams, *Marxism and Literature*, 123–27.

131. Stansell, *American Moderns*, 227.

132. On the need for marriage and fear of lesbian identity as unwomanly, see Banner, *Intertwined Lives*, 252–54.

Chapter 3: Companionate Marriage

1. *Our Dancing Daughters*, story by Josephine Lovett, dir. Harry Beaumont, Metro-Goldwyn-Mayer, 1928, Videocassette.

2. Ben B. Lindsey and Wainwright Evans, *The Companionate Marriage* (Garden City, N.Y.: Garden City Publishing, 1927). Historians have applied the term "companionate" to bourgeois marriages as early as the sixteenth century, by which they mean the incorporation of romantic love and affectionate companionship and the decline of parentally arranged marriage. But the 1920s was when the term "companionate marriage" appeared. I use it in its early twentieth-century usage to include not only affection and companionship but also the emphasis on privacy, sex, birth control, and divorce. Lawrence Stone, *The Family, Sex and Marriage: In England 1500–1800*, abridged and rev. ed. (Harmondsworth, England: Penguin, 1979), 217–24.

3. Charles Larsen, *The Good Fight: The Life and Times of Ben B. Lindsey* (Chicago: Quadrangle, 1972), 34–54, 94, 105, 151–60; Ben B. Lindsey and Wainwright Evans, *The Revolt of Modern Youth* (Garden City, N.Y.: Garden City Publishing, 1925); Lindsey and Evans, *Companionate Marriage*.

4. Nancy F. Cott, *The Grounding of Modern Feminism* (New Haven, Conn.: Yale University Press, 1987), 156.

5. Elaine May, *Great Expectations: Marriage and Divorce in Post-Victorian America* (Chicago: University of Chicago Press, 1980), 137–55; Daniel Horowitz, *The Morality of Spending: Attitudes toward the Consumer Society in America, 1875–1940* (Chicago: Dee, 1985), 134; Roland Marchand, *Advertising the American Dream: Making Way for Modernity, 1920–1940* (Berkeley: University of California Press, 1985), 118.

6. Ellen Chesler, *Woman of Valor: Margaret Sanger and the Birth Control Movement in America* (New York: Simon and Schuster, 1992), 223–42.

7. The late Susan Porter Benson argues eloquently in *Household Accounts: Working-Class Family Economies in the Interwar United States* (Ithaca, N.Y.: Cornell University Press, 2007) that most Americans could not take part in the mass consumption promoted in advertising.

8. May, *Great Expectations*, 51; Horowitz, *Morality of Spending*, xxvi–xxvii; Marchand, *Advertising the American Dream*.

9. Paula Fass, *The Damned and the Beautiful: American Youth in the 1920s* (New York: Oxford University Press, 1977), 124; John Modell, *Into One's Own: From Youth to Adulthood in the United States, 1920–1975* (Berkeley: University of California Press, 1989), 76; Gilman Ostrander, *American Civilization in the First Machine Age, 1890–1940* (New York: Harper and Row, 1970), 256.

10. Debra Campbell, "'Flannery O'Connor Is Not John Updike,'" *American Quarterly* 43 (1991): 334; Liz Cohen, "Encountering Mass Culture at the Grassroots: The Experience of Chicago Workers in the 1920s," *American Quarterly* 41 (1989): 6–33.

11. Judith Stein, "Defining the Race, 1890–1930," in *The Invention of Ethnicity*, ed. Werner Sollors (New York: Oxford University Press, 1989), 266n82.

12. Joe William Trotter Jr., *Black Milwaukee: The Making of an Industrial Prole-tariat, 1915–45* (Urbana: University of Illinois Press, 1985), 28, 234–35; Willard B. Gatewood, *Aristocrats of Color: The Black Elite, 1880–1920* (Bloomington: Indiana University Press, 1990), 333–34; E. Franklin Frazier, *The Black Bourgeoisie* (New York: Free Press. 1957), 47. Older sociologists like E. Franklin Frazier, *The Negro Family in the United States* (Chicago: University of Chicago Press, 1939), and Gunnar Myrdal, *An American Dilemma*, vol. 1, *The Negro in a White Nation* (1944; repr., New York: McGraw-Hill, 1964), distinguished between a black middle class and upper class based on the importance of culture and family heritage and not just occupation or income. Professionals and substantial businesspeople were placed in the upper class, though in terms of income and security they were more comparable to a white middle class (if that). In order to stress the economic aspect and comparability with whites, I will use "middle class" to describe both groups—Frazier and Myrdal's "upper" and "middle" classes. See Gloria Hull, ed., *Give Us Each Day: The Diary of Alice Dunbar-Nelson* (New York: Norton, 1984), 22–23, and Gatewood, *Aristocrats of Color*, ix, 9.

13. Myrdal, *American Dilemma*, 1:305, 319; Raymond Wolters, *The New Negro on Campus: Black College Rebellions of the 1920s* (Princeton, N.J.: Princeton University Press, 1975), 17.

14. Beth L. Bailey, *From Front Porch to Back Seat: Courtship in Twentieth-Century America* (Baltimore: Johns Hopkins University Press, 1988), 13–24; Joanne Meyerowitz, *Women Adrift: Independent Wage Earners in Chicago, 1880–1930* (Chicago: University of Chicago Press, 1988); John Modell, "Dating Becomes the Way of American Youth," in *Essays on the Family and Social Change*, ed. Leslie Page Moch and Gary D. Stark (College Station, Tex.: Texas A&M University Press, 1983), 91–126; Wolters, *New Negro on Campus*, 67.

15. Wolters, *New Negro on Campus*, 12–13, 17, 31, 67, 254, 37.

16. Edward Christopher Williams, *When Washington Was in Vogue: A Love Story {A Lost Novel of the Harlem Renaissance}*, introduction by Adam McKible (1925–26; repr., New York: HarperCollins, 2004), 27.

17. Deborah Gray White, *Too Heavy a Load: Black Women in Defense of Themselves, 1894–1994* (New York: Norton, 1999), 124–25.

18. Ellen K. Rothman, *Hands and Hearts: A History of Courtship in America* (New York: Basic Books, 1984), 217–23; Bailey, *From Front Porch to Back Seat*, 20.

19. Robert H. Elias, *"Entangling Alliances with None": An Essay on the Individual in the American Twenties* (New York: Norton, 1973), 42, 55, 57, 9–16, 130, 136; Ostrander, *American Civilization*, 218–20; Theodore Rosengarten, *All God's Dangers: The Life of Nate Shaw* (New York: Knopf, 1975), 191–93.

20. Eli Lederhendler, *Jewish Responses to Modernity: New Voices in America and Eastern Europe* (New York: New York University Press, 1994), 142; Carla Cappetti, "Deviant Girls and Dissatisfied Women: A Sociologist's Tale," in *The Invention of Ethnicity*, ed. Werner Sollors (New York: Oxford University Press, 1989), 125.

21. Officials prosecuting abortion deaths, for example, punished single working-class men much more than married ones, thus enforcing the expectation that they marry women they impregnated. Leslie Reagan, "'About to Meet Her Maker':

Women, Doctors, Dying Declarations, and the State's Investigation of Abortion, Chicago, 1867–1940," *Journal of American History* 77 (1991): 1244, 1261. Asian proxy marriages (with "picture brides") were prohibited, and racial intermarriage was restricted in the majority of states. Immigration laws also prohibited entry of prostitutes, mistresses, and polygamists. See Nancy F. Cott, *Public Vows: A History of Marriage and the Nation* (Cambridge, Mass.: Harvard University Press, 2000), 136–39, 148–54, 163–64.

22. The judicial development of the concept of privacy had mixed effects for women, who had always been more closely scrutinized and controlled not only by community arbiters but also by the law. Women thus had a particular interest in privacy. But in the early twentieth century the conservative judiciary interpreted privacy rights—which would ultimately become an important constitutional principle—in a distinctly patriarchal manner. When a woman attempted to sue her husband for injuries due to domestic assault, using new laws giving married women the right to act legally as separate individuals, the Supreme Court in 1911 refused to allow the suit. The Court dropped the veil of privacy over marital conflict, thereby also sustaining the operation of male dominance and aggression within the marriage. This, of course, continues to be a difficulty in policing wife battering. Cott, *Public Vows*, 157, 161–63; Linda Gordon, *Heroes of Their Own Lives: The Politics and History of Family Violence* (New York: Viking Penguin, 1988), 294.

23. Cott, *Grounding of Modern Feminism*, 165; Mari Jo Buhle, *Feminism and Its Discontents: A Century of Struggle with Psychoanalysis* (Cambridge, Mass.: Harvard University Press, 1998), 45, 80, 90; Suzanne LaFollette, *Concerning Women* (New York: Albert and Charles Boni, 1926), 55.

24. Leila Rupp, *A Desired Past* (Chicago: University of Chicago Press, 1999), 121–22.

25. "The New Negro Woman," *Messenger* 5 (July 1923): 757.

26. Lynn Y. Weiner, *From Working Girl to Working Mother: The Female Labor Force in the United States, 1820–1980* (Chapel Hill: University of North Carolina Press, 1985), 4, 6; Roderick Phillips, *Untying the Knot: A Short History of Divorce* (New York: Cambridge University Press, 1991), 229.

27. Weiner, *From Working Girl to Working Mother*, 101–6; Cott, *Grounding of Modern Feminism*, 179, 185, 183; see also Sharon Hartman Strom, *Beyond the Typewriter: Gender, Class, and the Origins of Modern American Office Work, 1900–1930* (Chicago: University of Illinois Press, 1992), 387–88.

28. Cott, *Grounding of Modern Feminism*, 204; Weiner, *From Working Girl to Working Mother*, 84–88; Lois Scharf, *To Work and to Wed: Female Employment, Feminism, and the Great Depression* (Westport, Conn.: Greenwood, 1980), 21–43.

29. Hendrik Hartog, *Man and Wife in America: A History* (Cambridge, Mass.: Harvard University Press, 2000), 115–16, 28, 12–14. Separation and divorce were more accessible in the United States than in Europe due to a culture of personal liberty and to the greater geographic mobility of Americans. Men in particular could escape marriages and move to other jurisdictions where different laws prevailed. Hartog argues that legal separations (more available than divorce)

modified the legal culture of marriage and expanded the rights of women apart from marriage.

30. Cott, *Public Vows*, 107; May, *Great Expectations*, 167; Phillips, *Untying the Knot*, 228.

31. Sherwood Eddy, *Sex and Youth* (Garden City, N.Y.: Doubleday, Doran, 1929), 43–44.

32. Chesler, *Woman of Valor*, 295–97, 540–41n13.

33. Ibid., 223, 263.

34. Nathan Hale, *Freud and the Americans: The Beginnings of Psychoanalysis in the United States, 1876–1917* (New York: Oxford University Press, 1971), 257, 357; Chesler, *Woman of Valor*, 344; obituary, *New York Times*, 10 October 1943, 49; "Rachelle Yarros," in *Notable American Women*, ed. Edward T. James (Cambridge, Mass.: Belknap Press of Harvard University Press, 1971), 3: 693–94; Ira S. Wile and Mary Day Winn, *Marriage in the Modern Manner* (New York: Century, 1929); Rachelle Yarros, *Modern Woman and Sex: A Feminist Physician Speaks* (New York: Vanguard, 1933).

35. Douglas Clayton, *Floyd Dell: The Life and Times of an American Rebel* (Chicago: Dee, 1994), 139–40, 150; Floyd Dell, *Love in the Machine Age: A Psychological Study of the Transition from Patriarchal Society* (New York: Farrar and Rinehart, 1930).

36. Eddy, *Sex and Youth*; Eddy, *Eighty Adventurous Years: An Autobiography* (New York: Harper, 1955), 28–32, 117–24, 244–45. Eddy, for example, in 1932 supported Myles Horton's plan to establish the school that became the radical Highlander Folk School. Myles Horton, *The Long Haul: An Autobiography*, with Judith Kohl and Herbert Kohl (New York: Doubleday, 1990), 61–62.

37. Michael Peplow, *George S. Schuyler* (Boston: Twayne, 1980), 25–28. In 1931, Schuyler published the humorous novel *Black No More* (1931; repr., New York: Collier Books, 1971), in which the protagonist uses a scientific formula to change black skin to white, allowing him to marry a white woman as well as make a fortune from doing the same for others. The novel satirizes the foibles of black and white dating, sex, and marriage but concludes with a happy ending and children.

38. Suzanne Ellery Greene, *Books for Pleasure: Popular Fiction, 1914–1945* (Bowling Green, Ohio: Bowling Green University, Popular Press, 1974), 5, 10, 58–59, 62. See, for example, Floyd Dell, *Janet March* (New York: Knopf, 1923); Dell, *Love without Money* (New York: Farrar and Rinehart, 1931); Meredith Nicholson, *Broken Barriers* (New York: Scribner's, 1922); Sinclair Lewis, *Main Street* (1920; New York: Signet, 1961); Lewis, *Ann Vickers* (New York: Collier, 1932); Sidney Howard, *The Silver Cord: A Comedy in Three Acts* (New York: Scribner's, 1927); Walter L. Fertig, "Meredith Nicholson," http://iwp.iweb.bse/IndianaAuthors/Pages/Nicholson,%20Meredith.html (accessed 12 July 2008); "Broken Barriers," http://www.answers.com/topic/broken-barriers-film?cat=entertainment (accessed 12 July 2008); Joanne L. Yeck, "Sidney Howard," http://www.filmreference.com/Writers-and-Production-Artists-Ha-Ja/Howard-Sidney.html (accessed 12 July 2008).

39. Thadious Davis, introduction, in Jessie Fauset, *Comedy: American Style* (1933; repr., New York: Hall,1995), xv–xxxii; Jessie Fauset, *Plum Bun* (1928; repr., Boston: Routledge and Kegan Paul, 1985); Fauset, *The Chinaberry Tree* (1931; repr., New York/ pub, 1969).

40. Edward Christopher Williams, "The Letters of Davy Carr," *Messenger* 7 (January 1925) through 8 (June 1926). The story has been reprinted as a novel under the title *When Washington Was in Vogue*; see McKible's introduction, xvi–xix.

41. Ronald L. Howard, *A Social History of American Family Sociology, 1865–1940*, ed. John Mogey (Westport, Conn.: Greenwood, 1981), 39–40; Elizabeth Lunbeck, *The Psychiatric Persuasion: Knowledge, Gender, and Power in Modern America* (Princeton, N.J.: Princeton University Press, 1994), 11–24; Donald S. Napoli, *Architects of Adjustment: The History of the Psychological Profession in the United States* (Port Washington, N.Y.: Kennikat Press, 1981), 13–14, 42–44.

42. V. F. Calverton, introduction, in Phyllis Blanchard and Carlyn Manasses, *New Girls for Old* (New York: Macauley, 1930), ix; Ernest R. Groves and Phyllis Blanchard, eds., *Readings in Mental Hygiene* (New York: Holt, 1936).

43. Ernest R. Groves, *The Marriage Crisis* (New York: Longmans, Green, 1928); Ernest R. Groves and William F. Ogburn, *American Marriage and Family Living* (1928; repr., New York: Arno, 1976); Ernest R. Groves, *The American Family* (Chicago: Lippincott, 1934); Ernest R. Groves Papers, 1917–1962, "Overview," http://www.lib.ndsu.nodak.edu/ndirs/collections/manuscripts/education/Groves/biography; 1942 Program for Annual Conference on Conservation of Marriage and the Family, Ernest R. Groves Papers, Institute for Regional Studies, North Dakota State University, Fargo, North Dakota, Box 19; Bailey, *From Front Porch to Back Seat*, 119–40.

44. Stephanie J. Shaw, *What a Woman Ought to Be and to Do: Black Professional Women Workers during the Jim Crow Era* (Chicago: University of Chicago Press, 1996), 231.

45. Bettie Esther Parham, "The Modern Family," *New York Age*, 19 October 1935; Rosalind Rosenberg, *Beyond Separate Spheres: Intellectual Roots of Modern Feminism* (New Haven, Conn.: Yale University Press, 1982), 25–26.

46. Anthony M. Platt, *E. Franklin Frazier Reconsidered* (New Brunswick, N.J.: Rutgers University Press, 1991), 3–4, 6, 13–14, 23–30, 114–26; E. Franklin Frazier, *The Negro Family in Chicago* (Chicago: University of Chicago Press, 1932); Frazier, *Negro Family in the United States*; Regina G. Kunzel, *Fallen Women, Problem Girls: Unmarried Mothers and the Professionalization of Social Work, 1890–1945* (New Haven, Conn.: Yale University Press, 1993), 57–62.

47. Howard, *Social History of American Family Sociology*, 63–64.

48. Eddy, *Eighty Adventurous Years*, 123.

49. John S. Haller and Robin M. Haller, *The Physician and Sexuality in Victorian America* (New York: Norton, 1974), 47.

50. Howard, *Silver Cord*, 187. See also Fauset, *Chinaberry Tree*, 121; and Yarros, *Modern Woman and Sex*, 117. A reformed vision of psychiatry promoted in the early twentieth century included very similar arguments to break through Victorian reticence and demand in the interests of neutral scientific truth that mental

patients reveal their sexual histories. See Lunbeck, *Psychiatric Persuasion*, 52, 72. Sharon R. Ullman, *Sex Seen: The Emergence of Modern Sexuality in America* (Berkeley: University of California Press, 1997), 7–8, shows that reporting of court cases on sex crime at the turn of the century had functioned similarly—to criticize the gap between (bad) official regulations and (normal) social practices. These critics were participating in what historian David Hollinger has called the de-Christianization of American public culture in the twentieth century, in "Jewish Intellectuals and the De-Christianization of American Public Culture in the Twentieth Century," in Hollinger, *Science, Jews, and Secular Culture* (Princeton, N.J.: Princeton University Press, 1996), 17–41.

51. E. Franklin Frazier, "Family Life of the Negro in the Small Town," *Proceedings of the National Conference of Social Work* (1926): 387; Lindsey and Evans, *Companionate Marriage*, 227–28.

52. First two quotations from Rebecca L. Davis, "'Not Marriage at All, but Simple Harlotry': The Companionate Marriage Controversy," *Journal of American History* 94 (2008): 1146–49, 1155–57. Davis provides a fascinating account of the way Lindsey, religious leaders, the media, and the public interacted and interpreted Lindsey's ideas in the 1920s and 1930s. Lindsey and Evans, *Companionate Marriage*, 300, 301–3; Larsen, *Good Fight*, 192–97.

53. Chesler, *Woman of Valor*, 234; Sanger, *My Fight for Birth Control* (1931; repr., Elmsford, N.Y.: Maxwell Reprint Co., 1969), 216–23, 348; Yarros, *Modern Woman and Sex*, 21; Lindsey and Evans, *Revolt*, 294–97; Blanchard and Manasses, *New Girls for Old*, 94.

54. Lindsey and Evans, *Companionate Marriage*, 309; see also Margaret Sanger, *Happiness in Marriage* (New York: Blue Ribbon, 1926), 106–8; Wile and Winn, *Marriage in the Modern Manner*, 213–14; Dell, *Love in the Machine Age*, 15, 61.

55. Dell, *Love in the Machine Age*, 23, 66, 199, 282.

56. Groves, *Marriage Crisis*, 49.

57. For other treatments of the growing importance of the social sciences, see Cott, *Grounding of Modern Feminism*, 152–56; Buhle, *Feminism and Its Discontents*, 22–124; Jane Gerhard, *Desiring Revolution: Second-Wave Feminism and the Rewriting of American Sexual Thought, 1920 to 1982* (New York: Columbia University Press, 2001), 1–49.

58. M. M. Knight, "The Companionate and the Family: The Unobserved Division of an Historical Institution," *JSH* 10 (1924): 257–67; Groves and Ogburn, *American Marriage and Family Relationships*, 5; *The Mortarboard 1927* (1926): 28 (personal communication, Donald Glassman, Barnard College Archivist, 14 April 2003); Clement Wood, *Bernarr Macfadden: A Study in Success* (1929; repr., New York: Beekman, 1974), 175–78.

59. "Companionate Marriage Discussed at Forum," *New York Age*, 12 May 1928, 9; Kevin K. Gaines, *Uplifting the Race: Black Leadership, Politics, and Culture in the Twentieth Century* (Chapel Hill: University of North Carolina Press, 1996), 101–2.

60. Lindsey avoided the term "trial marriage" because it reeked too much of experiment and impermanence and evoked the image of insouciant youth flouting serious social commitment.

61. Knight, "The Companionate and the Family," 264–65; Marcet Haldeman-Julius, *Why I Believe in Companionate Marriage*, Little Blue Book no. 1258, ed. E. Haldeman-Julius (Girard, Kans.: Haldeman-Julius Publications, n.d.), 7. The slight shift on male economic responsibility, however, did not mean abdication of the wife's obligation of domestic service. See Cott, *Public Vows*, 167–68; Cott, *Grounding of Modern Feminism*, 179, 185.

62. Lindsey and Evans, *Companionate Marriage*, vi–vii, 195.

63. This was "positive eugenics," as opposed to "negative eugenics," which proposed to sterilize those it defined as "unfit." Wendy Kline, *Building a Better Race: Gender, Sexuality, and Eugenics from the Turn of the Century to the Baby Boom* (Berkeley: University of California Press, 2001), 3–4; Laura L. Lovett, *Conceiving the Future: Pronatalism, Reproduction, and the Family in the United States, 1890–1938* (Chapel Hill: University of North Carolina Press, 2007), 9–10. Kline makes the reasonable point that not only the decline of organized feminism but also the eugenics movement shaped the conservatism of companionate marriage and its essential affirmation of heterosexual marriage (128). However, I would argue that companionate marriage's failure to challenge motherhood does not require eugenics as an explanation per se due to the multiplicity of other forces sustaining women's childbearing roles.

64. Lindsey and Evans, *Revolt of Modern Youth*, 356; Chesler, *Woman of Valor*, 122–23, 214–16.

65. Paul Popenoe, "Family or Companionate?" *JSH* 11 (1925): 137, 133 (quotations on "selfish absorption" and "radical change in education"); Popenoe, *Modern Marriage: A Handbook* (New York: Macmillan, 1925), ix, 1–8, 42–60, 141, 124–27 (quotation on "feminist demand," 125–26). He mentions child spacing but not birth control on pages 129–30. See Molly Ladd-Taylor, "Eugenics, Sterilisation, and Modern Marriage in the USA: The Strange Career of Paul Popenoe," *Gender and History* 13 (2001): 298–327.

66. Lindsey and Evans, *Companionate Marriage*, 249–50. Kline shows how successful Popenoe was at promoting marriage counseling in his subsequent career. In that sense he was part of the broader movement for making marriage modern; Kline, *Building a Better Race*, 143–53. However, I do not see eugenics as the primary driving force for revising marriage, even though reformers like Popenoe could adapt some companionate marriage language to their own ends.

67. Davis, " 'Not Marriage at All,' " 1160; Alvah Sulloway, *Birth Control and Catholic Doctrine* (Boston: Beacon, 1959), 101, 116–17; Chesler, *Woman of Valor*, 321.

68. Lindsey and Evans, *Companionate Marriage*, 187; Dell, *Love in the Machine Age*, 210.

69. Lindsey and Evans, *Revolt of Modern Youth*, 20–30, 47; Yarros, *Modern Woman and Sex*, 30–33; Fauset, *Chinaberry Tree*, 206, 124.

70. Fauset, *Chinaberry Tree*, 152–53; Lindsey and Evans, *Companionate Marriage*, 228; Wile and Winn, *Marriage in the Modern Manner*, 53; Sanger, *Happiness in Marriage*, 132.

71. Examining the popular novels of Elinor Glyn and the advice works of Marie Stopes, David Shumway calls the books part of a "regime of rationalization" to improve

marriage; Shumway, "Something Old, Something New: Romance and Marital Advice in the 1920s," in *An Emotional History of the United States*, ed. Peter N. Stearns and Jan Lewis (New York: New York University Press, 1998), 314.

72. W. E. B. DuBois, "Black Folk and Birth Control," and Constance Fisher, "The Negro Social Worker Evaluates Birth Control," *Birth Control Review* 16 (June 1932): 166–67 and 174–75.

73. Wile and Winn, *Marriage in the Modern Manner*, 59; Dell, *Janet March*, 192. For much more on this theme, see Sanger, *Happiness in Marriage*, 191–203; also Fauset, *Chinaberry Tree*, 159.

74. Eddy, *Sex and Youth*, 125; also Lindsey and Evans, *Revolt of Modern Youth*, 205–6.

75. Lindsey and Evans, *Companionate Marriage*, 206 and all of chap. 14.

76. Dell, *Love in the Machine Age*, 54.

77. Karen Lystra's work has suggested that a strong romanticism that included sexuality characterized many Victorian marriages, but that it was kept private (rather than being broadcast as part of public ideology about marriage). Lystra, *Searching the Heart: Women, Men, and Romantic Love in Nineteenth-Century America* (New York: Oxford University Press, 1989).

78. Howard, *Silver Cord*, 135; Dell, *Love without Money*, 364.

79. LaFollette, *Concerning Women*, 65. See also Ernest Burgess, "Introduction," in Frazier, *The Negro Family in the United States*, xiv: "More and more the American family is becoming a union of husband and wife based upon the sentiment of love and the attraction of temperamental compatibility. Less and less powerful every year are the factors of economic interdependence and community control." Also Wile and Winn, *Marriage in the Modern Manner*, 116–17.

80. Wile and Winn, *Marriage in the Modern Manner*, 203.

81. Fauset, *Chinaberry Tree*, 58, 160, 233; Lindsey and Evans, *Companionate Marriage*, 33; Eddy, *Sex and Youth*, 276.

82. Lindsey and Evans, *Revolt of Modern Youth*, 47–48. In his discussion of middle-class young women who, though sexually active, were really "good," Lindsey anticipates the attitude behind the homes for unwed mothers of the 1950s, in which young unmarried white women could recoup their virtue by having and giving up their babies. The line between "good girls" and "bad girls" was becoming blurred. See Rickie Solinger, *Wake Up, Little Susie! Single Pregnancy and Race before* Roe v. Wade (New York: Routledge, 1992), 16–17.

83. Davis, "'Not Marriage at All,'" 1137–39; Haldeman-Julius, *Why I Believe in Companionate Marriage*, 25.

84. Floyd Dell, *Homecoming: An Autobiography* (New York: Farrar and Rinehart, 1933), 164.

85. Mary Strong, "Friendly Advice to Girls," *Pittsburgh Courier*, 20 July 1929, sec. 2, 7. See also W. E. B. DuBois, "So the Girl Marries," *Crisis* 35 (June 1928): 207.

86. Howard, *Silver Cord*, 109–10.

87. Lindsey and Evans, *Companionate Marriage*, 289–99.

88. Dell, *Love in the Machine Age*, 17–27, 11, 48 (quoted text, "patriarchal customs…bec[a]me modern neuroses," is all capitalized in original text). He cites

Robert Briffault, Havelock Ellis, Edward Gibbon, James Frazer's *The Golden Bough*, and various ancient writers like Herodotus and Greek poets.

89. Dell, *Homecoming*, 159.

90. The separation of love from material interests was a pervasive theme in a variety of writings on love and romance in this period. See Pamela Haag, "In Search of 'The Real Thing': Ideologies of Love, Modern Romance, and Women's Sexual Subjectivities in the United States, 1920–40," *Journal of the History of Sexuality* 2 (1992): 554–56.

91. Fauset, *Chinaberry Tree*, 152–53.

92. Blanchard and Manasses, *New Girls for Old*, 21; Judith E. Smith, *Family Connections: A History of Italian and Jewish Immigrant Lives in Providence, Rhode Island, 1900–1940* (Albany: State University of New York Press, 1985), 114–17.

93. Charles S. Johnson, *Shadow of the Plantation* (Chicago: University of Chicago Press, 1934), 6, 47–58, 90.

94. Lindsey and Evans, *Companionate Marriage*, 261; see also Blanchard and Manasses, *New Girls for Old*, 216; Sanger, *Happiness in Marriage*, 197; Wile and Winn, *Marriage in the Modern Manner*, 147; Eddy, *Sex and Youth*, 149–50. See also Howard, *Silver Cord*, 127.

95. Dell, *Love in the Machine Age*, 139; Knight, "The Companionate and the Family," 264; Haldeman-Julius, *Why I Believe in Companionate Marriage*, 23–24.

96. Dell, *Love in the Machine Age*, 357.

97. Wile and Winn, *Marriage in the Modern Manner*, 34–35.

98. Eddy, *Sex and Youth*, 149; Bettie Esther Parham, "The Modern Family: Family Incompatibilities," *New York Age*, 1 February 1936; this is echoed by Fauset in *Plum Bun*, 145. Yarros, *Modern Woman and Sex*, 174.

99. Lystra notes that affectionate and respectful companionship was often a strong theme of the letters she studied from romantic Victorian marriages. I would argue that women's greater public presence and claims in the twentieth century expanded the range and bolstered the foundation of the companionship imagined. Lystra, *Searching the Heart*.

100. Robert L. Griswold, "Divorce and the Redefinition of Victorian Manhood," in *Meanings for Manhood: Constructions of Masculinity in Victorian America*, ed. Mark C. Carnes and Clyde Griffen (Chicago: University of Chicago Press, 1990), 96–110.

101. Lewis, *Ann Vickers*, 434–43, quotation on page 442; Fauset, *Chinaberry Tree*, 132, 209.

102. Groves and Ogburn, *American Marriage and Family Relationships*, 70; Fauset, *Chinaberry Tree*, 21.

103. Gail Bederman, *Manliness and Civilization: A Cultural History of Gender and Race in the United States, 1880–1917* (Chicago: University of Chicago Press, 1995), 25–26, 168–69; Cott, *Public Vows*, 115–16; Louise Newman, *White Women's Rights: The Racial Origins of Feminism in the United States* (New York: Oxford University Press, 1999), 7, 34.

104. Louise Newman, "Coming of Age, but Not in Samoa: Reflections on Margaret Mead's Legacy for Western Liberal Feminism," *American Quarterly* 48 (1996): 240–41, 244, 236 (quotation).

105. Dell, *Love in the Machine Age*, 6, 114, 106, 111; Sanger, *Happiness in Marriage*, 225–26; E. Franklin Frazier, "Certain Aspects of Conflict in the Negro Family," *Social Forces* 10 (1931): 83. In Fauset, *Chinaberry Tree*, 204, Dr. Denleigh makes gentle fun of a non-contracepting Italian immigrant family.

106. Sanger, *Woman and the New Race*, 4–5; Sanger, *My Fight for Birth Control*, 262; Yarros, *Modern Woman and Sex*, 20–21.

Chapter 4: Modern Marriage: Three Visions

1. Floyd Dell, *Janet March* (New York: Knopf, 1923), 53. I am grateful to the late Susan Porter Benson for conversations on the term "partnership marriage," which she uses to describe the pragmatic economic and familial bonds characterizing working-class marriages in the interwar period. My usage differs in allowing for romantic love and incorporating wives' employment. Susan Porter Benson, *Household Accounts: Working-Class Family Economies in the Interwar United States* (Ithaca, N.Y.: Cornell University Press, 2007), 17.

2. Judith E. Smith analyzes the many readers' letters received by Betty Smith, author of *A Tree Grows in Brooklyn* (1943), and shows the multiple interpretations possible for any fiction as well as the great impact the novel could have on readers, in *Visions of Belonging: Family Stories, Popular Culture, and Postwar Democracy, 1940–1960* (New York: Columbia University Press, 2004), 47–62. Thomas Laqueur, *Solitary Sex: A Cultural History of Masturbation* (New York: Zone Books, 2003), 320–22; Chris Weedon, *Feminist Practice and Poststructuralist Theory* (New York: Blackwell, 1987), 139, 148, 171–73; Pamela Haag, "In Search of 'The Real Thing': Ideologies of Love, Modern Romance, and Women's Sexual Subjectivities in the United States, 1920–40," *Journal of the History of Sexuality* 2 (1992): 552. Certainly film served the same functions as fiction in this regard.

3. James R. McGovern, "The American Woman's Pre–World War I Freedom in Manners and Morals," *Journal of American History* 55 (1968): 315–33. Though McGovern argues that the style changes began earlier, he describes the flapper well.

4. Dell, *Janet March*, 53, 408, 119, 111, 207–22, 238.

5. Ibid., 255–56, 292, 306, 430–31.

6. Ibid., 204, 431.

7. Margaret Mead and her friends at Barnard College in the 1920s distinguished themselves from flappers because they saw themselves as serious about their studies. See Lois Banner, *Intertwined Lives: Margaret Mead, Ruth Benedict, and Their Circle* (New York: Vintage, 2003), 165.

8. Dell, *Janet March*, 139, 192, 34, 111, 119, 158, 238, 456. Meredith Nicholson's *Broken Barriers* also dismisses careers by showing the wife of the male protagonist as a cold career woman whose emotional neglect justifies his affair with a young wage-earning woman who, by contrast, denies being "cursed with ambitions." Nicholson, *Broken Barriers* (New York: Scribner's, 1922), 241, 320, 76.

9. Florence Seabury, "Stereotypes," in *Our Changing Morality: A Symposium*, ed. Freda Kirchwey (1924; repr., New York: Albert and Charles Boni, 1930), 225.

10. Ben B. Lindsey and Wainwright Evans, *The Revolt of Modern Youth* (Garden City, N.Y.: Garden City Publishing, 1925), 238; Lindsey and Evans, *The Companionate Marriage* (Garden City, N.Y.: Garden City Publishing, 1927), 91–95, 122; Ernest R. Groves, *The Marriage Crisis* (New York: Longmans, Green, 1928), 99–100; Ira S. Wile and Mary Day Winn, *Marriage in the Modern Manner* (New York: Century, 1929), 54; Peter Laipson, "'Kiss without Shame, for She Desires It': Sexual Foreplay in American Marital Advice Literature, 1900–1925," *Journal of Social History* 29 (1996): 507–25.

11. Lindsey and Evans, *Revolt of Modern Youth*, 94, 325–26, 20–30. For further discussion of the recuperation of young men's animal vitality, see Gail Bederman, *Manliness and Civilization: A Cultural History of Gender and Race in the United States, 1880–1917* (Chicago: University of Chicago Press, 1995), 95–110, and Elizabeth Lunbeck, *The Psychiatric Persuasion: Knowledge, Gender, and Power in Modern America* (Princeton, N.J.: Princeton University Press, 1994), 230–36.

12. This observation accords with Haag's conclusions from a study of popular and sociological accounts of love and sex in the 1920s and 1930s; "In Search of 'The Real Thing,'" 558–59, and with Lunbeck's account of the anti-Victorian perspective of early twentieth-century psychiatrists on hysterical women, *Psychiatric Persuasion*, 211.

13. Lindsey and Evans, *Revolt of Modern Youth*, 58–59; Sidney Howard, *The Silver Cord: A Comedy in Three Acts* (New York: Scribner's, 1927), 195.

14. Haag, "In Search of 'The Real Thing,'" 549–50. Lunbeck notes that psychiatrists had the same difficulty accepting the assertion of female desire; *Psychiatric Persuasion*, 208.

15. Lindsey and Evans, *Revolt of Modern Youth*, 88; also Sherwood Eddy, *Sex and Youth* (New York: Doubleday, 1929), 137; Sinclair Lewis, *Ann Vickers* (New York: Collier, 1932), 202, 210, 461–63, 469.

16. Groves, *Marriage Crisis*, 143; Floyd Dell, *Love in the Machine Age: A Psychological Study of the Transition from Patriarchal Society* (New York: Farrar and Rinehart, 1930), 132; also 336. Mari Jo Buhle's study of twentieth-century psychoanalysis shows how long analysts relied on assumptions of motherhood as women's most basic drive, as had many twentieth-century feminists before the 1920s. Only in 1934 did Karen Horney move into a "culturalist" interpretation of women's "overvaluation" of love and motherhood, and she remained a feminist protester against the Freudian establishment. See Mari Jo Buhle, *Feminism and Its Discontents: A Century of Struggle with Psychoanalysis* (Cambridge, Mass.: Harvard University Press, 1998), 38–45, 112–14, 123–24.

17. Lindsey and Evans, *Companionate Marriage*, 295–98; also, 331–63.

18. Lewis, *Ann Vickers*, 395, 541; Lindsey and Evans, *Companionate Marriage*, 118–19, 127, 130.

19. Floyd Dell, *Love without Money* (New York: Farrar and Rinehart, 1931), 6, 159, 12; Howard, *Silver Cord*, 193.

20. Clyde Griffen, "Reconstructing Masculinity from the Evangelical Revival to the Waning of Progressivism: A Speculative Synthesis," in *Meanings for Manhood Constructions of Masculinity in Victorian America*, ed. Mark C. Carnes and Clyde Griffen (Chicago: University of Chicago Press, 1990), 201. For discussion of a similar decline of black women's authority, see Deborah Gray White, *Too Heavy a Load: Black Women in Defense of Themselves, 1894–1994* (New York: Norton, 1999), 110–41.

21. Nancy Cott, *Bonds of Womanhood: "Woman's Sphere" in New England, 1780–1835* (New Haven, Conn.: Yale University Press, 1977); Carroll Smith-Rosenberg, "The Female World of Love and Ritual: Relations between Women in Nineteenth-Century America," in Smith-Rosenberg, *Disorderly Conduct: Visions of Gender in Victorian America* (New York: Knopf, 1985), 53–76; Karen Hansen, " 'No <u>Kisses</u> Is Like Youres': An Erotic Friendship Between Two African-American Women during the mid–Nineteenth Century," *Gender and History* 7 (1995): 153–82; Lillian Faderman, *Odd Girls and Twilight Lovers: A History of Lesbian Life in Twentieth-Century America* (New York: Penguin, 1992), 62–92; George Chauncey, *Gay New York: Gender, Urban Culture, and the Making of the Gay Male World, 1890–1940* (New York: Basic Books, 1994), 227–67.

22. Eddy, *Sex and Youth*, 27; Phyllis Blanchard and Carlyn Manasses, *New Girls for Old* (New York: Macaulay, 1930), 98–101, 104, 110–11.

23. Douglas Clayton, *Floyd Dell: The Life and Times of an American Rebel* (Chicago: Dee, 1994), 142–75; Nancy Milford, *Savage Beauty: The Life of Edna St. Vincent Millay* (New York: Random House, 2002), 153–59.

24. Dell, *Love in the Machine Age*, 282, 237–38, 83; Dell, *Love without Money*, 140–44.

25. Lindsey, *Companionate Marriage*, 308–13. Ernest Groves mentions homosexuality only as part of a story illustrating the dangers of sex freedom: A woman with homosexual experience in college was driven to heterosexual experimentation because she "feared [she] was hopelessly homosexual" but knew she wanted children; *Marriage Crisis*, 147. Lewis, *Ann Vickers*, 68–71, 221–34.

26. Dell, *Love in the Machine Age*, 305, 308; Katharine B. Davis, *Factors in the Sex Life of Twenty-Two Hundred Women* (New York: Harper, 1929), 290; Faderman, *Odd Girls and Twilight Lovers*, 88–92.

27. Bettie Esther Parham, "Family Incompatibilities," *New York Age*, 1 February 1936, 5; Jessie Fauset, *Plum Bun* (1928; repr., Boston: Routledge and Kegan Paul, 1985), 350; Fauset, *The Chinaberry Tree* (1931; repr., New York: AMS Press, 1969), 146, 300–301; Edward Christopher Williams, *When Washington Was in Vogue: A Love Story {A Lost Novel of the Harlem Renaissance}*, introduction by Adam McKible (1925–26; repr., New York: HarperCollins, 2004), 170.

28. Blanchard and Manasses, *New Girls for Old*, 98–111; Margaret Sanger, *My Fight for Birth Control* (1931; repr., Elmsford, N.Y.: Maxwell Reprint Co., 1969), 27–28; see also Lorine Pruette, "The Flapper," in *The New Generation: The Intimate Problems of Modern Parents and Children*, ed. V. F. Calverton and Samuel D. Schmalhausen (New York: Macaulay, 1930), 574–75.

29. Nancy F. Cott, *The Grounding of Modern Feminism* (New Haven, Conn.: Yale University Press, 1987), 185. See especially Blanchard and Manasses, *New Girls*

for Old, 214–16; Ernest R. Groves, *The American Family* (Chicago: Lippincott, 1934), 155.

30. Lynn Y. Weiner, *From Working Girl to Working Mother: The Female Labor Force in the United States, 1820–1980* (Chapel Hill: University of North Carolina Press, 1985), 100–110.

31. Eddy, *Sex and Youth*, 151; Lindsey, *Revolt of Modern Youth*, 208.

32. Dell, *Love in the Machine Age*, 197–98, 143–44; Lindsey and Evans, *Revolt of Modern Youth*, 207–8; Groves, *American Family*, 159; Eddy, *Sex and Youth*, 151.

33. Lindsey and Evans, *Companionate Marriage*, 139. See Nancy F. Cott, *Public Vows: A History of Marriage and the Nation* (Cambridge, Mass.: Harvard University Press, 2000), 156–79, and Haag, "In Search of 'The Real Thing,'" 572.

34. In the United States at the time there was substantial political opposition even to state provision for widows and single mothers; aid to two-parent families was unthinkable in its threat to the male breadwinner system in the attitudes of social welfare thinkers in the early twentieth century. Linda Gordon, *Pitied but Not Entitled: Single Mothers and the History of Welfare, 1890–1935* (New York: Free Press, 1994), 41, 98–99.

35. Gertrude Atherton, *Black Oxen* (New York: Boni and Liveright, 1923), 126; Lindsey and Evans, *Companionate Marriage*, 127.

36. Lindsey and Evans, *Companionate Marriage*, 54.

37. Williams, *When Washington Was in Vogue*, 10. This title reprints the *Messenger* story in book form.

38. Jervis Anderson, *A. Philip Randolph: A Biographical Portrait* (New York: Harcourt, Brace, Jovanovich, 1972), 138; Williams, *When Washington Was in Vogue*, 53, 84, 5.

39. Williams, *When Washington Was in Vogue*, 25, 28, 184–86.

40. Fauset, *Chinaberry Tree*, 204, 160; Williams, *When Washington Was in Vogue*, 121, 10–11, 102–11.

41. Williams, *When Washington Was in Vogue*, 255, 132, 142.

42. Ibid., 14–15.

43. Ibid., 255, 28, 275.

44. Ibid., 168.

45. Ibid., 13–14.

46. Melville J. Herskovits, "The Negro's Americanism," in *The New Negro*, ed. Alain Locke (New York: Albert and Charles Boni, 1925), 356; Kevin Mumford, *Interzones: Black/White Sex Districts in Chicago and New York in the Early Twentieth Century* (New York: Columbia University Press, 1997), 48.

47. Williams, *When Washington Was in Vogue*, 62–63.

48. Herskovits, "Negro's Americanism," 356.

49. E. Franklin Frazier, "Three Scourges of the Negro Family," *Opportunity* 4 (July 1926): 210–11. Black Protestant churches also remained such crucial bases for African American organizational and political life that Frazier was unusual among black intellectuals in attacking religion. John Hope Franklin and Alfred A. Moss Jr., *From Slavery to Freedom*, 8th ed. (Boston: McGraw-Hill, 2000), 466–67.

50. W. E. B. DuBois "Harlem," *Crisis* 34 (September 1927): 240.

51. W. E. B. DuBois, "Reviews," *Crisis* 35 (June 1928): 202.

52. Evelyn Brooks Higginbotham, *Righteous Discontent: The Women's Movement in the Black Baptist Church, 1880–1920* (Cambridge, Mass.: Harvard University Press, 1993), 186–87.

53. Lindsey and Evans, *Revolt of Modern Youth*, for example: 54, 60, 68, 83, 106; Margaret Sanger, *Woman and the New Race* (New York: Brentano's, 1920), 182; Sanger, *Happiness in Marriage* (New York: Blue Ribbon, 1926), 21; Ellen Chesler, *Woman of Valor: Margaret Sanger and the Birth Control Movement in America* (New York: Simon and Schuster, 1992), 182–92, 244, 250–51.

54. Groves, *Marriage Crisis*, 84, 86.

55. Fauset, *Plum Bun*, 66. See also Fauset, *Chinaberry Tree*, 57–58. Stock old maid characters had already appeared in early twentieth-century films, providing images of puritanical women as comically old-fashioned figures out of touch with modern values. Sharon R. Ullman, *Sex Seen: The Emergence of Modern Sexuality in America* (Berkeley: University of California Press, 1997), 20–23.

56. Jessie Fauset, *Comedy: American Style*, introduction by Thadious M. Davis (1933; repr., New York: Hall, 1995), 27, 29, 324–25.

57. Ibid., 221, 209–13, 226.

58. Willard B. Gatewood, *Aristocrats of Color: The Black Elite, 1880–1920* (Bloomington: Indiana University Press, 1990), 28–29, 202.

59. Fauset, *Comedy: American Style*, 300–302.

60. W. E. B. DuBois, "Opinion: The Children, Marriage, Birth, Infancy, Childhood, Education, the End of It All," *Crisis* 24 (October 1922): 248; DuBois, "So the Girl Marries," *Crisis* 35 (June 1928): 208–9.

61. David Levering Lewis, *W. E. B. DuBois: The Fight for Equality and the American Century, 1919–1963* (New York: Holt, 2000), 222–28; quotation on page 227. DuBois's view also reflects the early twentieth-century understanding of male homosexual behavior as part of male sexual privilege rather than as a social identity competing with heterosexuality. See Chauncey, *Gay New York*, 65.

62. Cott, *Public Vows*, 83, 86–87.

63. Fauset, *Chinaberry Tree*, 70–71, 131–32; Fauset, *Comedy: American Style*, 298; Fauset, *Plum Bun*, 274.

64. Eddy, *Sex and Youth*, 70; Groves, *Marriage Crisis*, 5, 234.

65. Intermarriage was legal in New England, New York, New Jersey, Pennsylvania, and the old Northwest Territory (except Indiana). West of the Mississippi, only Minnesota, Iowa, Kansas, New Mexico, and Washington allowed it. See Pauli Murray, comp. and ed., *States' Laws on Race and Color* (Cincinnati: Women's Division of Christian Service, 1950), 704, 257, 351, 426, 524; Peggy Pascoe, "Race, Gender, and Intercultural Relations: The Case of Interracial Marriage," *Frontiers* 12, no. 1 (1991): 5–18.

66. Rachelle Yarros, *Modern Woman and Sex: A Feminist Physician Speaks* (New York: Vanguard, 1933), 171–72; for opposition to such marriages on eugenic grounds, see Paul Popenoe, *Modern Marriage: A Handbook* (New York: Macmillan, 1925), 47.

67. Lindsey does, however, use racially stereotyped language, referring to the black wife as "Mammy." Lindsey and Evans, *Revolt of Modern Youth*, 267–78, and *Companionate Marriage*, 289–304.
68. Groves, *Marriage Crisis*, 78; Eddy, *Sex and Youth*, 114, 116.
69. Lisa Lindquist Dorr, "Arm in Arm: Gender, Eugenics, and Virginia's Racial Integrity Acts of the 1920s," *Journal of Women's History* 11 (1999): 143–66; Mumford, *Interzones*, 166–71; David H. Fowler, *Northern Attitudes towards Interracial Marriage: Legislation and Public Opinion in the Middle Atlantic and the States of the Old Northwest, 1780–1930* (New York: Garland, 1987), 273.
70. Several factors contributed to the failure of the suit: the clear legality of intermarriage in New York; her racial indeterminacy and British immigrant parents; popular antagonism aroused by the media narrative of a wealthy playboy exploiting a decent working-class woman; the New York setting, including strict jury instructions to set aside race prejudice; and strong evidence that Leonard did know of her "colored blood" and that Alice had not deceived him. Earl Lewis and Heidi Ardizzone, *Love on Trial: An American Scandal in Black and White* (New York: Norton, 2001).
71. Fauset, *Comedy: American Style*, 292–94. Organized black women in the 1890s often addressed this abuse. See Fannie Barrier Williams, "The Accusations Are False," in *Black Women in White America: A Documentary History*, ed. Gerda Lerner (New York: Pantheon, 1972), 164–66.
72. December 1925, *Chicago Defender*, quoted in Lewis and Ardizzone, *Love on Trial*, 212.
73. W. E. B. DuBois, "The Social Equality of Whites and Blacks," *Crisis* 21 (November 1920): 18; also DuBois, "President Harding and Social Equality," *Crisis* 23 (December 1921): 56.
74. E. Franklin Frazier, "Social Equality and the Negro," *Opportunity* 3 (June 1925): 167; Frazier, *The Negro Family in the United States* (Chicago: University of Chicago Press, 1939), 488.
75. Frazier, "The Pathology of Race Prejudice," in *Negro*, ed. Nancy Cunard (London: Wishart and Co., 1934), 116.
76. Fauset, *Plum Bun*, 313; Rudolph Fisher, "High Yaller," pts. 1 and 2, *Crisis* 30 (October 1925): 281–86, and pts. 3–5, *Crisis* 30 (November 1925): 33–38.
77. "White Husband in Separation Suit," *New York Age*, 30 August 1924, 1; "Mamma Lizzie Found Life's Romance When She Met 'Papa Fat,'" 6 September 1924, 1; "Mama Lizzie Thanks *The Age* for Consideration in the Case against Papa Fat," 27 September 1924, 3.
78. "Taking the 'Color Question' Out of Marriage!" *Pittsburgh Courier*, 14 December 1929, 2. See also, for example, "Interracial Romance Has Happy Ending," *Pittsburgh Courier*, 8 June 1929, sec. 1, 2; and L. F. Coles, "Would Marry White," letter to editor, 29 April 1933, sec. 2, 2. The *Courier*, of course, may have addressed the issue more due to the influence of George Schuyler, who worked as a *Courier* columnist from 1924 on. Schuyler had married a white woman in 1928 and wrote strongly in support of intermarriage. Michael W. Peplow, *George S. Schuyler* (Boston: Twayne, 1980), 23, 25. See, for example, Schuyler, "Views and Reviews,"

Pittsburgh Courier, 27 July 1929, 12, and "New York: Utopia Deferred," in *These "Colored" United States: African-American Essays from the 1920s*, ed. Tom Lutz and Susanna Ashton (New Brunswick, N.J.: Rutgers University Press, 1996), 206.

79. Tessie Liu, "Teaching the Differences among Women from a Historical Perspective: Rethinking Race and Gender as Social Categories," in *Unequal Sisters: A Multicultural Reader in U.S. Women's History*, 2nd ed., ed. Vicki L. Ruiz and Ellen Carol DuBois (New York: Routledge, 1994), 571–83; Nancy F. Cott, "Giving Character to Our Whole Civil Polity: Marriage and the Public Order in the Late Nineteenth Century," in *U.S. History as Women's History: New Feminist Essays*, ed. Linda K. Kerber, Alice Kessler-Harris, and Kathryn Kish Sklar (Chapel Hill: University of North Carolina Press, 1995), 118–21.

80. Matthew Frye Jacobson, *Whiteness of a Different Color: European Immigrants and the Alchemy of Race* (Cambridge, Mass.: Harvard University Press, 1998), 96–100, 110–11.

81. Sarah Deutsch, *Women and the City: Gender, Space, and Power in Boston, 1870–1940* (New York: Oxford University Press, 2000), 239.

82. Frazier, *Negro Family in the United States*, 461, 475; Anthony M. Platt, *E. Franklin Frazier Reconsidered* (New Brunswick, N.J.: Rutgers University Press, 1991), 17.

83. Frazier, *Negro Family in the United States*, 439, 446; Linda Gordon, "Black and White Visions of Welfare: Women's Welfare Activism, 1890–1945," *Journal of American History* 78 (1991): 574, 582–83.

84. W. E. B. DuBois, *Darkwater: Voices from within the Veil* (1920; repr., New York: Schocken, 1969), 181; Fauset, *Comedy: American Style*, 300.

85. Bettie Esther Parham, "The Modern Family," *New York Age*, 11 January 1936, 5.

86. George Schuyler, "Views and Reviews," *Pittsburgh Courier*, 30 November 1929, 12; "Working Wives," editorial, *Pittsburgh Courier*, 1 March 1930, 10; E. Franklin Frazier, "New Role of the Negro Woman," *Ebony*, August 1960, 40.

87. Fauset, *Plum Bun*, 53, 69–70.

88. Ibid., 88.

89. Ibid., 182, 192.

90. Ibid., 127, 185.

91. Ibid., 112.

92. Ibid., 290–91. This comparison also illustrates the African American emphasis on communal loyalty: Anthony is personally independent, unlike Roger, yet at the same time strongly loyal to the black race.

93. Ibid., 145.

94. Ibid., 201–2.

95. Ibid., 319.

96. Ibid., 13, 332.

97. Ibid., 333.

98. Haag, "In Search of 'The Real Thing,'" 549.

99. Fauset, *Plum Bun*, 232; also Fauset, *Comedy: American Style*, 307–13; Yarros, *Modern Woman and Sex*, 54–55.

100. Yarros, *Modern Woman and Sex*, 65; Carroll Smith-Rosenberg, "A Richer and a Gentler Sex," *Social Research* 53 (1986): 283–309; Jesse Battan, "The 'Rights'

of Husbands and the 'Duties' of Wives: Power and Desire in the American Bedroom, 1850–1910," *Journal of Family History* 24 (1999): 165–86.

101. Fauset, *Comedy: American Style*, 317.

102. Fauset, *Chinaberry Tree*, 40, 124; also Fauset, *Plum Bun*, 145; Yarros, *Modern Woman and Sex*, 14–15.

103. Sanger, *Happiness in Marriage*, 21–22; Yarros, *Modern Woman and Sex*, 15, 25.

104. Fauset, *Comedy: American Style*, 241; also 309.

105. Lewis, *Ann Vickers*, 89–90.

106. Fauset, *Plum Bun*, 130.

107. Ibid., 204, 195.

108. Yarros, *Modern Woman and Sex*, 11–12.

109. Sanger, *Happiness in Marriage*, 21–22, 96, 100; Yarros, *Modern Woman and Sex*, 21–25, 27.

110. Wile and Winn, *Marriage in the Modern Manner*, 107–8, 34–35, 117–18; Yarros, *Modern Woman and Sex*, 42–43.

111. Sanger, *Happiness in Marriage*, 183–84, 225.

112. Bettie Esther Parham, "The Husband's New Role in the Home," *New York Age*, 31 August 1935, 5; Parham, "The Home and the Wage Earning Wife," *New York Age*, 7 September 1935, 5.

113. Wile and Winn, *Marriage in the Modern Manner*, 124–25, 126, 127, 133; Yarros, *Modern Woman and Sex*, 193; Dolores Hayden, *The Grand Domestic Revolution: A History of Feminist Designs for American Homes, Neighborhoods, and Cities* (Cambridge, Mass.: MIT Press, 1982), 185–86.

114. Eddy, *Sex and Youth*, 153–54, 163; Dell, *Love in the Machine Age*, 211.

115. Cott, *Public Vows*, 169. Cott has also noted how few feminist writers in this period attended to the inequalities of housework; *Grounding of Modern Feminism*, 192.

116. Cott, *Grounding of Modern Feminism*, 157.

117. Fauset, *Chinaberry Tree*, 125, 152–53, 238.

118. Fauset, *Comedy: American Style*, introduction by Thadious Davis, xxvii, and 238–39, 270, 300.

119. Fauset, *Plum Bun*, 274–75. See also Fauset, *Comedy: American Style*, 299; Ann duCille, *The Coupling Convention: Sex, Text, and Tradition in Black Women's Fiction* (New York: Oxford University Press, 1993), 88.

120. See also Parham, "Modern Family" and "Home and the Wage Earning Wife"; Yarros, *Modern Woman and Sex*, 188.

121. Parham, "Home and the Wage Earning Wife."

122. Yarros, *Modern Woman and Sex*, 188–89, 191.

123. Fauset, *Comedy: American Style*, 316.

124. Howard, *Silver Cord*, 139; Lewis, *Ann Vickers*, 558–59; Wile and Winn, *Marriage in the Modern Manner*, 34–35, 107–8. Eddy also briefly allows the possibility of career for a wife "if one is determined"; *Sex and Youth*, 119–20.

125. Ernest R. Groves and William F. Ogburn, *American Marriage and Family Relationships* (1928; repr., New York: Arno, 1976), 35, 43; all citations are from material written by Groves.

126. Ibid., 34–37.

127. Cott, *Public Vows*, 156–79.

128. These were small proportions even of employed women: The census categories Stricker uses as proxies for career women ("Professional, Technical, and Kindred Workers" and "Managers, Officials, and Proprietors") constituted 9.9 percent of all employed women in 1910 and 13.8 percent in 1940—not a large group. Frank Stricker, "Cookbooks and Law Books: The Hidden History of Career Women in Twentieth-Century America," in *A Heritage of Her Own*, ed. Nancy F. Cott and Elizabeth H. Pleck (New York: Simon and Schuster, 1979), 484, 486; Janet M. Hooks, *Women's Occupations through Seven Decades* (1947; repr., Washington, D.C.: Zenger, 1978), 47.

129. Lorine Pruette, *Women and Leisure: A Study of Social Waste* (New York: Dutton, 1924), xi–xii; Pruette, "Flapper," 589; see also Pruette, "Why Women Fail," in *Women's Coming of Age: A Symposium*, ed. Samuel D. Schmalhausen and V. F. Calverton (New York: Liveright, 1931), 245–57; Cott, *Grounding of Modern Feminism*, 165; Weiner, *From Working Girl to Working Mother*, 100–110. And as today, many professional women hired other women to carry on domestic tasks. See Sara Alpern, *Freda Kirchwey: A Woman of the Nation* (Cambridge, Mass.: Harvard University Press, 1987), 46, 69–72; Evelyn Nakano Glenn, "From Servitude to Service Work: Historical Continuities in the Racial Division of Paid Reproductive Labor," in *Unequal Sisters: A Multicultural Reader in U.S. Women's History*, 2nd ed., ed. Vicki L. Ruiz and Ellen Carol DuBois (New York: Routledge, 1994), 405–35.

130. Lindsey and Evans, *Revolt of Modern Youth*, 88.

131. Chesler, *Woman of Valor*, 263–64.

132. Sanger, *Happiness in Marriage*, 230.

133. Sanger, *My Fight for Birth Control*, 40, 46.

134. Sanger, *Happiness in Marriage*, 78, 200; Wile and Winn, *Marriage in the Modern Manner*, 28–35; Groves and Ogburn, *American Marriage and Family Relationships*, 59–77.

135. Sanger, *Happiness in Marriage*, 58; Chesler, *Woman of Valor*, 531n27.

136. Chesler, *Woman of Valor*, 266.

137. Sanger, *Happiness in Marriage*, 51.

Chapter 5: Sexual Advice for Modern Marriage

1. Carney Landis, *Sex in Development* (New York: Hoeber, 1940), 92, 167–68.

2. In his classic article, "From an Unfortunate Necessity to a Cult of Mutual Orgasm: Sex in American Marital Education Literature, 1830–1940," in *Studies in the Sociology of Sex*, ed. James Henslin (New York: Appleton-Century-Crofts, 1971), 53–77, Michael Gordon sketches a general outline of these works, especially the increased focus on sexual technique in the 1930s. See also M. E. Melody and Linda M. Peterson, *Teaching America about Sex: Marriage Guides and Sex Manuals from the Late Victorians to Dr. Ruth* (New York: New York University Press, 1999).

3. Gordon, "Unfortunate Necessity."

4. Linda Gordon, *Woman's Body, Woman's Right: Birth Control in America*, rev. ed. (New York: Penguin, 1990), 301–23; Andrea Tone, "Contraceptive Consumers: Gender and the Political Economy of Birth Control in the 1930s," *Journal of Social History* 29 (1996): 485–506; Ellen Chesler, *Woman of Valor: Margaret Sanger and the Birth Control Movement in America* (New York: Simon and Schuster, 1992), 342–43, 372–74.

5. Roderick Phillips, *Untying the Knot: A Short History of Divorce* (Cambridge: Cambridge University Press, 1991), 186, 190–91; Wendy Kline, *Building a Better Race: Gender, Sexuality, and Eugenics from the Turn of the Century to the Baby Boom* (Berkeley: University of California Press, 2001), 142–43.

6. Lynn Y. Weiner, *From Working Girl to Working Mother: The Female Labor Force in the United States, 1820–1980* (Chapel Hill: University of North Carolina Press, 1985), 6.

7. Dixon Wecter, *The Age of the Great Depression 1929–1941* (New York: Macmillan, 1948), 198; Winifred D. Wandersee Bolin, "The Economics of Middle-Income Family Life: Working Women during the Great Depression," *Journal of American History* 65 (1978): 61; Mirra Komarovsky, *The Unemployed Man and His Family* (1940; repr., New York: Arno, 1971), 28, 130; Warren Susman, introduction, in *Culture and Commitment, 1929–1945*, ed. Warren Susman (New York: George Braziller, 1973), 11.

8. Nancy Cott, *Public Vows: A History of Marriage and the Nation* (Cambridge, Mass.: Harvard, 2000), 172–79; Barbara Melosh, *Engendering Culture: Manhood and Womanhood in New Deal Public Art and Theatre* (Washington, D.C.: Smithsonian, 1991), 51; Lois Scharf, *To Work and to Wed: Female Employment, Feminism, and the Great Depression* (Westport, Conn.: Greenwood, 1980), 21, 43–44, 46–48, 56–58, 75–79; Carole R. McCann, *Birth Control Politics in the United States, 1916–1945* (Ithaca, N.Y.: Cornell University Press, 1994), 187–88; quotation from Susman in *Culture and Commitment*, 16.

9. Program for 1942 Conference on the Conservation of Marriage and the Family, Ernest R. Groves Papers, Institute for Regional Studies, North Dakota State University, Fargo, North Dakota, Box 19; Ernest R. Groves, ms. speech, 1941, Groves Papers, Box 22, Folder 27.

10. Jonathan Ned Katz, *The Invention of Heterosexuality* (New York: Penguin, 1995), 86–93.

11. George Chauncey, *Gay New York: Gender, Urban Culture, and the Making of the Gay Male World, 1890–1940* (New York: Basic Books, 1994), 111–26.

12. Joseph H. Pleck, "The Theory of Male Sex Role Identity: Its Rise and Fall, 1936 to the Present," in *In the Shadow of the Past: Psychology Portrays the Sexes*, ed. Miriam Lewin (New York: Columbia University Press, 1984), 210. See also Estelle Freedman, "'Uncontrolled Desires': The Response to the Sexual Psychopath, 1920–1960," in *Passion and Power: Sexuality in History*, ed. Kathy Peiss and Christina Simmons, with Robert Padgug (Philadelphia: Temple University Press, 1989), 200–201, for argument that fears about unmanly men were becoming greater than fears of impure women. Landis, *Sex in Development*, 50.

13. As Jane Gerhard puts it, the authorities on women's sexuality wanted it to be "both liberated and domesticated." Gerhard, *Desiring Revolution: Second-Wave Feminism and the Rewriting of American Sexual Thought, 1920 to 1982* (New York: Columbia University Press, 2001), 21.

14. Hendrik Hartog, *Man and Wife in America: A History* (Cambridge, Mass.: Harvard University Press, 2000), 298–99; also Cott, *Public Vows*, 160.

15. H. W. Long, M.D., *Sane Sex Life and Sane Sex Living* (New York: Eugenics, 1919), 13, 15; Joseph Collins, *The Doctor Looks at Love and Life* (New York: Doubleday, Doran, 1926), 13; Johannes Rutgers, *How to Attain and Practice the Ideal Sex Life*, trans. Norman Haire (New York: Falstaff Press, 1937), 21; Th. H. Van de Velde, M.D., *Ideal Marriage: Its Physiology and Technique*, trans. Stella Browne (New York: Random House, 1930, 1957), xxv.

16. Long, *Sane Sex Life*, 6.

17. Chesler, *Woman of Valor*, 266–67; Paul S. Boyer, *Purity in Print: The Vice Society Movement and Book Censorship in America* (New York: Scribner's, 1968), 234–35, 256; Helena Wright, *The Sex Factor in Marriage* (New York: Vanguard, 1931), 33.

18. This is not to say censorship problems disappeared. For example, the post office disallowed the mailing of Hannah and Abraham Stone's *A Marriage Manual* in 1941. Chesler, *Woman of Valor*, 545n27. Books promoting better sex appeared before 1920, but they were less explicit. Peter Laipson, " 'Kiss without Shame, for She Desires It': Sexual Foreplay in American Marital Advice Literature, 1900–1925," *Journal of Social History* 29 (1996): 508; Gordon, "Unfortunate Necessity," 68–69.

19. Quotation from *Parents' Magazine* (n.d.), included in Marjorie A. Prevost to Margaret Sanger, 20 February 1932, Margaret Sanger Papers, Library of Congress, Microfilm Reel 32.

20. Chesler, *Woman of Valor*, 304; review, *New York Times Book Review*, 6 October 1935, 12.

21. Hannah M. Stone and Abraham Stone, *A Marriage Manual: A Practical Guide-Book to Sex and Marriage* (New York: Simon and Schuster, 1937); Margaret Sanger, *Happiness in Marriage* (New York: Blue Ribbon, 1926); Marie Stopes, *Married Love: A New Contribution to the Solution of Sex Difficulties* (1918; New York: Putnam's, 1931); Rachelle Yarros, *Modern Woman and Sex: A Feminist Physician Speaks* (New York: Vanguard, 1933); William J. Robinson, *Married Life and Happiness, or Love and Comfort in Marriage*, 4th ed. (1922; repr., New York: Eugenics, 1929); Wright, *Sex Factor*; Millard S. Everett, *The Hygiene of Marriage* (New York: Vanguard, 1932); Barbara Evans, *Freedom to Choose: The Life and Work of Dr. Helena Wright, Pioneer of Contraception* (London: Bodley Head, 1984), 148.

22. Gladys Gardner Jenkins, "The Business Girl Looks at Marriage," *Woman's Press* 21 (June 1929): 406–7, 414.

23. Everett, *Hygiene of Marriage*, v–vi. Birth controller Miriam Allen DeFord wrote that Everett's was the best. DeFord, "A New World," *Birth Control Review* 17 (March 1933): 67.

24. Ernest R. Groves and Gladys H. Groves, *Sex in Marriage*, 3rd ed. (New York: Emerson, 1943); Ernest R. Groves, Gladys H. Groves, and Catherine Groves, *Sex*

Fulfillment in Marriage (New York: Emerson, 1942), ix; Gladys H. Groves and Robert A. Ross, M.D., *The Married Woman: A Practical Guide to Happy Marriage* (Cleveland, Ohio: World, 1936); Max Exner, *The Sexual Side of Marriage* (1932; New York: Eugenics, 1937).

25. Minutes of Advisory Council of Harlem Clinic, 23 March 1932, Margaret Sanger Papers, Library of Congress, Reel 33; Chesler, *Woman of Valor*, 295–97.

26. Helen Brooks Grossley, "From the President's Notebook," *Journal of the National Association of College Women* 14 (1937): 40.

27. Conference Programs, North Carolina College for Negroes Conferences on Conservation of Marriage and the Family, 1942–1951, Groves Papers, Box 20, Folders 9–17.

28. Yarros, *Modern Woman and Sex*, 134–35, reports the case of a black couple. A 1950 magazine article about sex in marriage cites the Stones' and Groveses' books and several others by whites; Ben Burns, "What Married Couples Should Know about Sex," *Ebony*, May 1950, 50–52, 54–58.

29. Van de Velde, *Ideal Marriage*, 192; Edward Brecher, *The Sex Researchers* (Boston: Little, Brown, 1969), 96.

30. Stopes, *Married Love*, xix; June Rose, *Marie Stopes and the Sexual Revolution* (London: Faber and Faber, 1992), 136, 206.

31. Words of Lambeth Conference Resolution 15, cited in Evans, *Freedom to Choose*, 141. Wright and Charles A. Clinton, M.D., also deploy clerical authority. Wright, *Sex Factor in Marriage*, 17–30; Clinton, *Sex Behavior in Marriage* (1935; New York: Pioneer Publications, 1947), viii–ix.

32. Rose, *Marie Stopes*, 22, 85–86. Isabel Emslie Hutton, M.D., *Memories of a Doctor in War and Peace* (London: Heinemann, 1960), 214; Hutton, *The Sex Technique in Marriage* (1932; New York: Emerson, 1949), xviii; Evans, *Freedom to Choose*, 151–52.

33. Van de Velde, *Ideal Marriage*, 197.

34. Brecher speculates similarly on personal experience as a source for Van de Velde, in *The Sex Researchers*, 88. Jennifer Terry notes that Dr. Robert L. Dickinson also experimented on patients. Jennifer Terry, *An American Obsession: Science, Medicine, and Homosexuality in Modern Society* (Chicago: University of Chicago Press, 1999), 146.

35. Wright, *Sex Factor in Marriage*, 82.

36. Van de Velde, *Ideal Marriage*, vii.

37. Groves and Ross, *The Married Woman*, ix.

38. Sanger, *Happiness in Marriage*, 5–6; Yarros, *Modern Woman and Sex*; Stopes, *Married Love*, 108. Hutton's autobiography makes it clear she was a feminist (in relation both to women doctors' rights and to women's right to sexual knowledge and passion), but her feminism is less explicit in the marriage manual itself; Hutton, *Memories*, 16, 60, 81–82; Hutton, *Sex Technique*, 24. See also Evans, *Freedom to Choose*, 41, 149.

39. See the appendix for a full list of books and the method of choosing them.

40. Sherwood Eddy, *Sex and Youth* (Garden City, N.Y.: Doubleday, Doran, 1929), 309–24.

41. Jean Libman Block, "Are Those Marriage Manuals Any Good?" *Cosmopolitan*, October 1948, 42. James H. Jones argues that Van de Velde's book sold more than

any other manual; see *Alfred C. Kinsey* (New York: Norton, 1997), 293. Ellen Chesler cites publisher's correspondence in 1941 that claimed the Stones' book was selling more at that time; see Chesler, *Woman of Valor*, 308.

42. "Happiness or Misery: Which?", pamphlet advertisement for *Sane Sex Life* by Dr. Long, n.d., stamped August 1977, "Marriage Manuals" Vertical File, Kinsey Institute for Research in Sex, Gender, and Reproduction, Indiana University, Bloomington, Indiana.

43. Anita Clair Fellman and Michael Fellman, "The Rule of Moderation in Late Nineteenth-Century American Sexual Ideology," *Journal of Sex Research* 17 (1981): 240; Gordon, "Unfortunate Necessity," 55–57; John S. Haller and Robin M. Haller, *The Physician and Sexuality in Victorian America* (New York: Norton, 1974), 100. Karen Lystra's work on Victorian love letters suggests private talk and behavior could be much more positive on sex (within marriage) than the majority of published advice works; Lystra, *Searching the Heart: Women, Men, and Romantic Love in Nineteenth-Century America* (New York: Oxford University Press, 1989).

44. I differ from Melody and Peterson on the question of how much these works sustained male dominance. These books were not generally attacking men's power in the direct way that second-wave feminists did, and in attempting to save marriage most were working in the context of the social, legal, and economic power men exercised over wives. However, the messages of these works were more mixed than Melody and Peterson suggest, and it is too simplistic to say that "women are allowed to demand pleasure, but the fundamental power relationship remains undisturbed." To say that women have a right to sexual pleasure does in some way "disturb" gender relations. Melody and Peterson, *Teaching America about Sex*, 235.

45. Mari Jo Buhle, *Feminism and Its Discontents: A Century of Struggle with Psychoanalysis* (Cambridge, Mass.: Harvard University Press, 1998), 124–205; Gerhard, *Desiring Revolution*, 29–48. Van de Velde was conservative compared with some U.S. authors, whose writings framed feminism positively, but he was very committed to sexual pleasure for women.

46. Wright, *Sex Factor in Marriage*, 31; also Eddy, *Sex and Youth*, 125; Exner, *Sexual Side of Marriage*, 17; Bernarr Macfadden, foreword, in Charles Clinton, M.D., *Married Sweethearts: The Role of Sex Behavior in Marriage* (New York: Macfadden, 1933), iii. Elaine May shows that sexual complaints were a significant component of divorce cases in 1920, in *Great Expectations: Marriage and Divorce in Post-Victorian America* (Chicago: University of Chicago, 1980), 103–14, 178.

47. Edward W. Said, *Orientalism* (New York: Vintage, 1978), 190; Gail Bederman, *Manliness and Civilization: A Cultural History of Gender and Race in the United States, 1880–1917* (Chicago: University of Chicago Press, 1995), 25; Buhle, *Feminism and Its Discontents*, 103–4.

48. Everett, *Hygiene of Marriage*, 22; Maurice Chideckel, M.D., *The Single, the Engaged, and the Married* (New York: Eugenics, 1936), 24; Rutgers, *Ideal Sex Life*, 81. Louise Newman shows that Margaret Mead was making exactly this move in her books *Coming of Age in Samoa* (1928) and *Sex and Temperament in*

Three Primitive Societies (1935), where she was rejecting the Victorian denigration of the "primitive" in favor of selective appreciation of the supposedly lesser shame or guilt about sex in simpler societies, presenting those sexual attitudes as a critique of sexual repression in American society. Her work surely contributed to the popularity of these ideas. Newman, "Coming of Age, but Not in Samoa: Reflections on Margaret Mead's Legacy for Western Liberal Feminism, *American Quarterly* 48 (1996): 239–45.

49. Wright, *Sex Factor in Marriage*, 83, 100.

50. Van de Velde, *Ideal Marriage*, 200.

51. Stone and Stone, *Marriage Manual*, 229, 206; Van de Velde, *Ideal Marriage*, 218, 254, 259.

52. Groves and Groves, *Sex in Marriage*, 23, also 129; see also, for example, Everett, *Hygiene of Marriage*, 19; Hutton, *Memories of a Doctor*, 215; Stone and Stone, *Marriage Manual*, 207–8.

53. Groves and Groves, *Sex in Marriage*, 159.

54. Sanger, *Happiness in Marriage*, 93; Van de Velde, *Ideal Marriage*, 145.

55. Sanger, *Happiness in Marriage*, 137; Stopes, *Married Love*, 112; Groves and Ross, *Married Woman*, 64; Clinton, *Married Sweethearts*, 186; Wright, *Sex Factor in Marriage*, introduction by Rev. Gray, 24. See also Stone and Stone, *Marriage Manual*, 223.

56. Everett, *Hygiene of Marriage*, 122. This position echoes Floyd Dell's.

57. Hutton, *Sex Technique*, 70.

58. Everett, *Hygiene of Marriage*, 121; Groves and Ross, *Married Woman*, 50. See also Van de Velde, *Ideal Marriage*, 179; Stone and Stone, *Marriage Manual*, 217.

59. Stopes, *Married Love*, 53; Yarros, *Modern Woman and Sex*, 209.

60. Groves, Groves, and Groves, *Sex Fulfillment*, 194.

61. Most important here are Katharine Bement Davis, *Factors in the Sex Life of Twenty-Two Hundred Women* (New York: Harper, 1929), for which research was done in 1920; Gilbert V. Hamilton and Kenneth MacGowan, *What Is Wrong with Marriage?* (New York: Albert and Charles Boni, 1929), for which research was done in the late 1920s; Robert Latou Dickinson and Lura Beam, *A Thousand Marriages: A Medical Study of Sex Adjustment* (Baltimore: Williams and Wilkins, 1931), based on Dickinson's nearly fifty-year gynecological practice from the mid-1880s to the 1930s; Lewis M. Terman, *Psychological Factors in Marital Happiness* (New York: McGraw-Hill, 1938), for which data were gathered in 1934 and 1935; Landis, *Sex in Development*, for which research was done in the 1930s; and Alfred C. Kinsey et al., *Sexual Behavior in the Human Female* (New York: Pocket Books, 1953), for which sexual histories began to be gathered in the late 1930s. All of these studies had a very strong bias toward the middle classes, and none but Kinsey included African Americans. Some (like Hamilton's) were exclusively focused on middle-class subjects, showing these authors' concern with the marital well-being of the dominant social group of the period. For analysis of this research, see Julia A. Ericksen with Sally A. Steffen, *Kiss and Tell: Surveying Sex in the Twentieth Century* (Cambridge, Mass.: Harvard University Press, 1999), 7–10, 36–60.

62. Davis, *Factors in the Sex Life*, 39; Hamilton and MacGowan, *What Is Wrong with Marriage?* 63.

63. Davis, *Factors in the Sex Life*, 73.

64. Hamilton, *What Is Wrong with Marriage?* 144–45.

65. Dickinson and Beam, *A Thousand Marriages*, 219, 105.

66. May, *Great Expectations*, 103–7; Landis, *Sex in Development*, 93. Sharon Ullman argues such complaints about sex in divorce cases were evident in 1900, in *Sex Seen: The Emergence of Modern Sexuality in America* (Berkeley: University of California Press, 1997), 95–100.

67. Hamilton and MacGowan, *What Is Wrong with Marriage?* 202; Dickinson and Beam, *Thousand Marriages*, 62; Terman, *Psychological Factors*, 379, 386; Kinsey et al., *Human Female*, 375. Carney Landis found 30 percent of "normal" (non-mental patient) female subjects "poor" to "inadequate" in this sexual response; Landis, *Sex in Development*, 91.

68. Ericksen, *Kiss and Tell*, 38–52.

69. Terman, *Psychological Factors*, 305; Kinsey et al., *Human Female*, 371.

70. Stone and Stone, *Marriage Manual*, 247; Van de Velde, *Ideal Marriage*; Edwin W. Hirsch, *The Power to Love: A Psychic and Physiologic Study of Regeneration* (New York: Knopf, 1935); Alfred C. Kinsey, Wardell B. Pomeroy, and Clyde E. Martin, *Sexual Behavior in the Human Male* (Philadelphia: Saunders, 1948), 237.

71. Eddy, *Sex and Youth*, 316.

72. Everett, *Hygiene of Marriage*, x; also Groves, Groves, and Groves, *Sex Fulfillment*, 30; Chideckel, *Single, Engaged, Married*, ix; Stone and Stone, *Marriage Manual*, vi.

73. Ericksen, *Kiss and Tell*, 19; Elizabeth Lunbeck, *The Psychiatric Persuasion: Knowledge, Gender, and Power in Modern America* (Princeton, N.J.: Princeton University Press, 1994), 233; Dickinson and Beam, *Thousand Marriages*, 186.

74. Stone and Stone, *Marriage Manual*, 210.

75. Cott, *Public Vows*, 66; Stopes, *Married Love*, 24; Long, *Sane Sex Life*, 62–63; also Robinson, *Married Life*, 60–63; LeMon Clark, M.D., *Emotional Adjustment in Marriage* (St. Louis: Mosby, 1937), 120–21.

76. Collins, *Doctor Looks at Love and Life*, 36; Clark, *Emotional Adjustment*, 30.

77. Wright, *Sex Factor*, 46–47; Sanger, *Happiness in Marriage*, 153–54; see also Clinton, *Married Sweethearts*, 7.

78. Groves and Groves, *Sex in Marriage*, 27; Groves, Groves, and Groves, *Sex Fulfillment*, 71.

79. Stone and Stone, *Marriage Manual*, 129.

80. Van de Velde, *Ideal Marriage*, 10–11; also Exner, *Sexual Side of Marriage*, 30–31.

81. Lindsey, *Companionate Marriage*, 117.

82. William J. Fielding, *Sex and the Love-Life* (New York: Blue Ribbon, 1927), 14.

83. Stopes, *Married Love*, 23.

84. Clark, *Emotional Adjustment*, 100; see also Groves, Groves, and Groves, *Sex Fulfillment*, 71.

85. Wright, *Sex Factor*, 46; Hutton, *Sex Technique*, 96; Eddy, *Sex and Youth*, 128.

86. Stone and Stone, *Marriage Manual*, 242; Groves and Groves, *Sex in Marriage*, 124–25.

87. Groves, Groves, and Groves, *Sex Fulfillment*, 185–86; also Clinton, *Married Sweethearts*, 218; Stone and Stone, *Marriage Manual*, 258.

88. Groves and Ross, *Married Woman*, 91.

89. Floyd Dell, *Love in the Machine Age: A Psychological Study of the Transition from Patriarchal Society* (New York: Farrar and Rinehart, 1930), 239–41.

90. Everett, *Hygiene of Marriage*, 75–76; Clark, *Emotional Adjustment*, 222; Norman Himes, *Your Marriage: A Guide to Happiness* (New York: Farrar and Rinehart, 1940), 22.

91. Rutgers, *Ideal Sex Life*, 15; Groves and Ross, *Married Woman*, 88.

92. Stone and Stone, *Marriage Manual*, 263, 271; Edward Podolsky, M.D., *The Modern Sex Manual* (New York: Cadillac, 1942), 100; Clinton, *Married Sweethearts*, 236. Though sometimes the language is gender-neutral, the context suggests they mean women, not men.

93. This analysis accords with that of Jennifer Terry, who suggests that homosexuality increasingly served as a foil for developing scientific notions of "normal" masculinity and femininity. She also argues that the growing consensus of the 1920s and 1930s, that people could be placed along a continuum of masculinity and femininity, could well have increased anxiety over the boundaries of gender identity. See Terry, *American Obsession*, especially chaps. 4 and 5 and 156–59. She uses the term "spectral presence" on page 159.

94. The edition of *Sex in Marriage* cited here was published in 1943 but is essentially the same as the 1931 version (*Sex in Marriage* [New York: Macaulay, 1931]). The 1943 version of this title includes eleven additional pages of diagrams, an index, and very minor revisions, primarily more suggestions to consult physicians, and has a smaller typeface and thus fewer total pages. *Sex Fulfillment in Marriage* (1942), however, was a very thorough revision of the 1931 book.

95. Groves, Groves, and Groves, *Sex Fulfillment*, 183.

96. Jessamyn Neuhaus has examined a larger number of manuals for a longer period and also found more blaming of women and anxiety about male fragility, especially in the postwar era; Neuhaus, "The Importance of Being Orgasmic: Sexuality, Gender, and Marital Sex Manuals in the United States, 1920–1963," *Journal of the History of Sexuality* 9 (2000): 447–73.

97. Landis, *Sex in Development*, 31.

98. Sanger, *Happiness in Marriage*, 105–15; Van de Velde, *Ideal Marriage*, 1–143; Stone and Stone, *Marriage Manual*, 30–124, 167–202.

99. Hutton, *Sex Technique*, 59–74. The books with diagrams of the clitoris are Clinton (1935); Everett; Exner; the Groveses, *Sex in Marriage* and *Sex Fulfillment in Marriage*; Hirsch; Hutton; Podolsky; William S. Sadler, M.D., and Lena K. Sadler, M.D., *Living a Sane Sex Life* (New York: Wilcox and Follett, 1944); Stone and Stone; and Wright. Lisa Jean Moore and Adele E. Clarke, "Clitoral Conventions and Transgressions: Graphic Representations in Anatomy Texts, c1900–1991," *Feminist Studies* 21 (1995): 273.

100. Timothy J. Gilfoyle, *City of Eros: New York City, Prostitution, and the Commercialization of Sex, 1790–1920* (New York: Norton, 1992), 106; Charles E. Rosenberg, "Sexuality, Class and Role in 19th-Century America," *American Quarterly* 25 (1973): 143; Bederman, *Manliness and Civilization*, 168–69, 205.

101. Writers feared prosecution under state anti–birth control laws that remained in force. Gordon, *Woman's Body, Woman's Right*, 321; Everett, *Hygiene of Marriage*, 215, 223–29; Stone and Stone, *Marriage Manual*, 125–66; see also Himes, *Your Marriage*, 349–58.

102. Chesler, *Woman of Valor*, 320–23.

103. Chideckel, *The Single, the Engaged, the Married*, 59; also Sanger, *Happiness in Marriage*, 210.

104. Clark, *Emotional Adjustment*, 191; Groves, Groves, and Groves, *Sex Fulfillment*, 246.

105. Fielding, *Sex and the Love-Life*, 224; also Stopes, *Married Love*, 78–79; Sanger, *Happiness in Marriage*, 209–10; Van de Velde, *Ideal Marriage*, 265; Exner, *Sexual Side of Marriage*, 119–20; Clark, *Emotional Adjustment*, 183; Groves, Groves, and Groves, *Sex Fulfillment*, 250; Podolsky, *Modern Sex Manual*, 49; Sadler and Sadler, *Living a Sane Sex Life*, 197.

106. Everett, *Hygiene of Marriage*, 89.

107. Thomas Laqueur, *Making Sex: Body and Gender from the Greeks to Freud* (Cambridge, Mass.: Harvard University Press, 1990), 46, 161–63; Roy Porter and Lesley Hall, *The Facts of Life: The Creation of Sexual Knowledge in Britain, 1650–1950* (New Haven, Conn.: Yale University Press, 1995), 36.

108. Long, *Sane Sex Life*, 84; also Himes, *Your Marriage*, 358; Groves, Groves, and Groves, *Sex Fulfillment*, 55; Sadler and Sadler, *Living a Sane Sex Life*, 283; Hirsch, *Power to Love*, 128.

109. Stone and Stone, *Marriage Manual*, 159; also Clark, *Emotional Adjustment*, 202.

110. Fellman and Fellman, "Rule of Moderation," 248; Vern Bullough, *Science in the Bedroom: A History of Sex Research* (New York: Basic Books, 1994), 25–26; Porter and Hall, *Facts of Life*, 44; Janice Delaney, Mary Jane Lupton, and Emily Toth, *The Curse* (New York: New American Library, 1977), 13–21.

111. Everett, *Hygiene of Marriage*, 180; also, for example, Stopes, *Married Love*, 87; Groves and Ross, *Married Woman*, 166; Van de Velde, *Ideal Marriage*, 303.

112. Clinton, *Married Sweethearts*, 208; also Long, *Sane Sex Life*, 137; Everett, *Hygiene of Marriage*, 130; Himes, *Your Marriage*, 319.

113. Wright, *Sex Factor*, 109; Clark, *Emotional Adjustment*, 144; Delaney, Lupton, and Toth, *The Curse*, 13–21.

114. Fielding, *Sex and the Love-Life*, 74. I thank Laurel Cornell, of the Institute for Sex Research, for comments on a paper I presented there that stimulated my thinking on this issue.

115. For example, the Groveses' later book, *Sex Fulfillment*, gives the twice-a-week figure on page 209; see also Hutton, *Sex Technique*, 98; Stone and Stone, *Marriage Manual*, 286; Himes (using the term "normal"), *Your Marriage*, 319.

116. Fellman and Fellman, "Rule of Moderation," 249. Some Victorian works urged lesser frequency: William Alcott, in *The Physiology of Marriage* (1866),

recommended once a month—cited in Bullough, *Science in the Bedroom*, 24. The records of intercourse kept by a nineteenth-century middle-class wife and from physician Clelia Mosher's small late nineteenth-century study of middle-class wives suggest that some people's practice may have approximated the once-per-week figure. Janet Farrell Brodie, *Contraception and Abortion in 19th-Century America* (Ithaca, N.Y.: Cornell University Press, 1994), 11; Rosalind Rosenberg, *Beyond Separate Spheres: Intellectual Roots of Modern Feminism* (New Haven, Conn.: Yale University Press, 1992), 185.

117. Rosenberg, "Sexuality, Class and Role," 144, 149; Jesse F. Battan, "The 'Rights' of Husbands and the 'Duties' of Wives: Power and Desire in the American Bedroom, 1850–1910," *Journal of Family History* 24 (1999): 165–86.

118. Rosenberg, "Sexuality, Class and Role," 139–40; Kevin White, *The First Sexual Revolution: The Emergence of Male Heterosexuality in Modern America* (New York: New York University Press, 1993), 63, 70–71.

119. Lindsey, *Companionate Marriage*, 99, 90–91.

120. Sanger, *Happiness in Marriage*, 59; Stone and Stone, *Marriage Manual*, 218; see also, for example, Eddy, *Sex and Youth*, 134; Fielding, *Sex and the Love-Life*, 47; Everett, *Hygiene of Marriage*, 121.

121. Groves and Ross, *Married Woman*, 128.

122. Wright, *Sex Factor*, 96; Hutton, *Sex Technique*, 95; see also Stone and Stone, *Marriage Manual*, 289.

123. Hartog, *Man and Wife*, 298–99.

124. Himes, *Your Marriage*, 321; Sanger, 215–18; also Eddy, *Sex and Youth*, 128, 316.

125. Stone and Stone, *Marriage Manual*, 223; also Clark, *Emotional Adjustment*, 132.

126. Chideckel, *The Single, the Engaged, the Married*, 73; Van de Velde, *Ideal Marriage*, 287.

127. Sanger, *Happiness in Marriage*, 85, 99; see also Clinton, *Married Sweethearts*, 182; Chideckel, *The Single, the Engaged, the Married*, 91, 111.

128. Rose, *Marie Stopes*, 85–86, 111; Stopes, *Married Love*, 34; Van de Velde, *Ideal Marriage*, 286.

129. Wright and Stopes both thought some men also experienced it; Stopes, *Married Love*, 40; Wright, *Sex Factor*, 107–8.

130. Stone and Stone, *Marriage Manual*, 290.

131. Stopes, *Married Love*, 38.

132. Sanger, *Happiness in Marriage*, 157; Groves, *Sex Fulfillment*, 202–3; Chideckel, *The Single, the Engaged, the Married*, 109.

133. Groves, *Sex in Marriage*, 149; Sadler and Sadler, *Living a Sane Sex Life*, 211.

134. Lesley A. Hall argues for the significance of Stopes's conception as depicting "female desire as an autonomous force" not dependent on men. See Hall, "Uniting Science and Sensibility: Marie Stopes and the Narratives of Marriage in the 1920s," in *Rediscovering Forgotten Radicals: British Women Writers, 1889–1939*, ed. Angela Ingram and Daphne Patai (Chapel Hill: University of North Carolina Press, 1993), 131.

135. Van de Velde, *Ideal Marriage*, 144–58; Stopes, *Married Love*, 48–51; Sanger, *Happiness in Marriage*, 119–46.

136. Van de Velde, *Ideal Marriage*, 8.

137. Stopes, *Married Love*, 47; see also Sanger, *Happiness in Marriage*, 221, Fielding, *Sex and the Love-Life*, 117; Wright, *Sex Factor*, 87; Van de Velde, *Ideal Marriage*, 19.

138. Wright, *Sex Factor*, 87.

139. Van de Velde, *Ideal Marriage*, 172–73, 249–50.

140. Ibid., 169; Groves and Ross, *Married Woman*, 59. Laipson offers an excellent account of the emergence of foreplay in advice literature, arguing it appeared by the mid-1910s and allowed respectable women a new way to claim sexual pleasure without the Victorian associations of pleasure with immorality; Laipson, " 'Kiss without Shame,' " 509.

141. Van de Velde, *Ideal Marriage*, 174, 169; Stone and Stone, *Marriage Manual*, 269. See also Clark, *Emotional Adjustment*, 108; Groves and Ross, *Married Woman*, 59.

142. Van de Velde, *Ideal Marriage*, 159; Long, *Sane Sex Life*, 122–27, 151.

143. Hirsch, *Power to Love*, 291–92; John D'Emilio and Estelle B. Freedman, *Intimate Matters: A History of Sexuality in America* (New York: Harper and Row, 1988), 165.

144. Long, *Sane Sex Life*, 128; Stopes, *Married Love*, 47–48.

145. Van de Velde, 203–4; also, Podolsky, *Modern Sex Manual*, 49; Sadler and Sadler, *Living a Sane Sex Life*, 198; Hirsch, *Power to Love*, 294; Clinton, *Married Sweethearts*, 209.

146. Wright, *Sex Factor*, 95, 99–102. Everett cites Wright and says to experiment; *Hygiene of Marriage*, 125. Stopes, Rutgers, Exner, the Stones, Podolsky, the Groveses, and Himes urge variety and do not directly rank the positions.

147. Van de Velde, *Ideal Marriage*, 223–24; see also Hirsch, *Power to Love*, 273.

148. Clinton, *Sex Behavior*, 127; Groves, Groves, and Groves, *Sex Fulfillment*, 180; Everett, *Hygiene of Marriage*, 126; Hutton, *Sex Technique*, 101.

149. Sigmund Freud, *Three Contributions to the Theory of Sex*, trans A. A. Brill (New York: Dutton, 1962), 78.

150. Kinsey et al., *Human Female*, 582–84; Gerhard, *Desiring Revolution*, 29–43, 53.

151. Van de Velde, *Ideal Marriage*, 179, 180; Everett, *Hygiene of Marriage*, 39. Clark believed women's capacity for multiple orgasm resulted from the inadequacy of the clitoral response; after the woman attains the vaginal orgasm, he argued, "the experience frequently becomes so much more profound, involving the whole organism, that thereafter only one orgasm is necessary"; Clark, *Emotional Adjustment*, 148; Groves, Groves, and Groves, *Sex Fulfillment*, 116.

152. Sanger, *Happiness in Marriage*, 112; Groves and Groves, *Sex in Marriage*, 91–92; Groves, Groves, and Groves, *Sex Fulfillment*, 116; Clark, *Emotional Adjustment*, 148; Wright, *Sex Factor*, 92; Hirsch, *Power to Love*, 121; Himes, *Your Marriage*, 325; Podolsky, *Modern Sex Manual*, 117; Sadler and Sadler, *Living a Sane Sex Life*, 273.

153. Van de Velde, *Ideal Marriage*, 179.

154. Gerhard, *Desiring Revolution*, 29–43.

155. Groves and Ross, *Married Woman*, 67; also 90.

156. Stone and Stone, *Marriage Manual*, 257–58.

157. Landis, *Sex in Development*, 315; Kinsey, Pomeroy, and Martin, *Human Female*, 379–80.

158. Many husbands also participated in reproductive decisions. James C. Mohr, *Abortion in America: The Origins and Evolution of National Policy, 1800–1900* (New York: Oxford University Press, 1978), 113–17.
159. Gordon, *Woman's Body, Woman's Right*, 110; Davis, *Factors in the Sex Life*, 374; Dickinson and Beam, *Thousand Marriages*, 422.
160. Stone and Stone, *Marriage Manual*, 267; Rutgers, *Ideal Sex Life*, 315; Wright, *Sex Factor*, 39.
161. Gordon, *Woman's Body, Woman's Right*, 377.
162. Dickinson and Beam, *Thousand Marriages*, 108, 191, 192; Groves, Groves, and Groves, *Sex Fulfillment*, 202; Landis, *Sex in Development*, 166, 214, 92.
163. Quotations (in order) from Carolyn J. Dean, *Sexuality and Modern Western Culture* (New York: Twayne, 1996), 53; Kevin Mumford, "'Lost Manhood' Found: Male Sexual Impotence and Victorian Culture in the United States," *Journal of the History of Sexuality* 3 (1992): 56; Pamela Haag, "In Search of 'The Real Thing': Ideologies of Love, Modern Romance, and Women's Sexual Subjectivities in the United States, 1920–40," *Journal of the History of Sexuality* 2 (1992): 549; see also Melody and Peterson, *Teaching America about Sex*, 235.
164. Hall, "Uniting Science and Sensibility," 130–31.
165. See letters to Ernest and Gladys Groves in the Correspondence Series, Groves Papers.
166. Nancy F. Cott, "Passionlessness: An Interpretation of Victorian Sexual Ideology, 1790–1850," in *A Heritage of Her Own*, ed. Nancy F. Cott and Elizabeth Pleck (New York: Simon and Schuster, 1979), 175.
167. Evans, *Freedom to Choose*, 132–44, 148–52.

Conclusion

1. Tess Slesinger, *On Being Told That Her Second Husband Has Taken His First Lover and Other Stories* (1935; repr., New York: Quadrangle/New York Times, 1971), 9–10, 16–17. See also Ursula Parrott, *Ex-Wife* (New York: Grosset and Dunlap, 1929), 66.
2. Parrott, *Ex-Wife*, 88.
3. Christine Stansell, *American Moderns: Bohemian New York and the Creation of a New Century* (New York: Holt, 2000), 299–300, 307; Elizabeth Francis, *The Secret Treachery of Words: Feminism and Modernism in America* (Minneapolis: University of Minnesota Press, 2002), xviii–xx; Lois W. Banner, *Intertwined Lives: Margaret Mead, Ruth Benedict, and Their Circle* (New York: Vintage, 2003), 429.
4. Marjorie Hillis, *Live Alone and Like It: A Guide for the Extra Woman* (Indianapolis, Ind.: Bobbs-Merrill, 1936), 25, 29, 30.
5. Hendrik Hartog, *Man and Wife in America* (Cambridge, Mass.: Harvard University Press, 2000), 192; Parrot, *Ex-Wife*, 88.
6. Edith Stern, *Men Are Clumsy Lovers* (New York: Vanguard, 1934), 91.
7. For example, see Alice Echols, *Daring to Be Bad: Radical Feminism in America, 1967–1975* (Minneapolis: University of Minnesota Press, 1989); Frances M. Beal,

"Double Jeopardy: To Be Black and Female," in *Afro-American History*, 2nd ed., ed. Thomas R. Frazier (Belmont, Calif.: Wadsworth, 1988), 427–36; Beth Bailey, *Sex in the Heartland* (Cambridge, Mass.: Harvard University Press, 1999); and Jane Gerhard, *Desiring Revolution: Second-Wave Feminism and the Rewriting of American Sexual Thought, 1920 to 1982* (New York: Columbia University Press, 2001).

8. Kenon Breazeale, "In Spite of Women: *Esquire* Magazine and the Construction of the Male Consumer," *Signs* 20 (1994): 18.

9. Ruth Feldstein discusses the turn in the 1930s to critiquing women's power within the home in *Motherhood in Black and White: Race and Sex in American Liberalism, 1930–1965* (Ithaca, N.Y.: Cornell University Press, 2000), 7.

10. Lynn Y. Weiner, *From Working Girl to Working Mother: The Female Labor Force in the United States, 1820–1980* (Chapel Hill: University of North Carolina Press, 1985), 4, 89. African American married women's labor force participation grew proportionally less than the rates for the whole population, which were dominated by whites. Thirty-two percent of black wives were in the labor force in 1940 versus 47 percent in 1960.

11. Karen Anderson, *Wartime Women: Sex Roles, Family Relations, and the Status of Women during World War II* (Westport, Conn.: Greenwood, 1981), 80–83, 91–111; Miriam Reumann, *American Sexual Character: Sex, Gender, and National Identity in the Kinsey Reports* (Berkeley: University of California Press, 2005), 20; Weiner, *Working Girl to Working Mother*, 111.

12. Roderick Phillips, *Untying the Knot: A Short History of Divorce* (New York: Cambridge University Press, 1991), 211.

13. Mari Jo Buhle, *Feminism and Its Discontents: A Century of Struggle with Psychoanalysis* (Cambridge, Mass.: Harvard University Press, 1998), 125–38, 174–79.

14. Ibid., 168; Gerhard, *Desiring Revolution*, 51.

15. Jessamyn Neuhaus, "The Importance of Being Orgasmic: Sexuality, Gender, and Marital Sex Manuals in the United States, 1920–1963," *Journal of the History of Sexuality* 9 (2000): 447–73; Alfred C. Kinsey et al., *Sexual Behavior in the Human Female* (New York: Pocket Books, 1965), 579–83; Gerhard, *Desiring Revolution*, 64–73; Buhle, *Feminism and Its Discontents*, 216.

16. Elaine Tyler May, *Homeward Bound: American Families in the Cold War Era* (New York: Basic Books, 1988), 89–91, 112–13; Reumann, *American Sexual Character*, 30, 54–85, 86–127, 136.

17. May, *Homeward Bound*, 135–61.

18. Joanne Meyerowitz, "Beyond the Feminine Mystique: A Reassessment of Postwar Mass Culture, 1946–1958," in *Not June Cleaver: Women and Gender in Postwar America, 1945–1960*, ed. Joanne Meyerowitz (Philadelphia: Temple University Press, 1994), 229–62; Weiner, *Working Girl to Working Mother*, 89–97; Jacqueline Jones, *Labor of Love, Labor of Sorrow: Black Women, Work, and the Family, from Slavery to the Present* (New York: Vintage, 1985), 268–69; "Founding the National Organization for Women, 1966," in *Modern American Women*, ed. Susan Ware (Chicago: Dorsey Press, 1989), 334–40.

19. Stephanie Coontz, *Marriage, a History: How Love Conquered Marriage* (New York: Penguin, 2005), 225; Reumann, *American Sexual Character*, 142–44,

148–49; Ben Burns, "What Married Couples Should Know about Sex," *Ebony*, May 1950, 50–52, 54–58; Rebecca L. Davis, "'The Loneliness of Lovers': Marriage Encounter, Catholicism, and Pro-marriage Politics in the 1970s" (paper presented at the Berkshire Conference on the History of Women, June 2008), in possession of author.

20. John D'Emilio and Estelle Freedman, *Intimate Matters: A History of Sexuality in America* (New York: Harper and Row, 1988), 334–36, 291–95; Julia A. Ericksen, with Sally A. Steffen, *Kiss and Tell: Surveying Sex in the Twentieth Century* (Cambridge, Mass.: Harvard University Press, 1999), 75.

21. Beal, "Double Jeopardy," 340–53.

22. See, for example, Beverly Jones, "The Dynamics of Marriage and Motherhood," and Naomi Weisstein, "'Kinder, Kuche, Kirche' as Scientific Law: Psychology Constructs the Female," in *Sisterhood Is Powerful*, ed. Robin Morgan (New York: Vintage, 1970), 46–61, 205–19; Anne Koedt, *The Myth of the Vaginal Orgasm* (Boston: New England Free Press, n.d. [1970s]); Gerhard, *Desiring Revolution*, 82, 98–99, 106–7, 142.

23. Gerhard, *Desiring Revolution*, 139.

24. Joanne Meyerowitz, *How Sex Changed: A History of Transsexuality in the United States* (Cambridge, Mass.: Harvard University Press, 2002); Janice M. Irvine, *Talk about Sex: The Battles over Sex Education in the United States* (Berkeley: University of California Press, 2002), 81–88.

25. Coontz, *Marriage*, 263–78.

26. This may have been especially important for a middle class moving out of the city to the suburbs and sometimes farther from kin networks. Margaret Marsh, *Suburban Lives* (New Brunswick, N.J.: Rutgers University Press, 1990), 129–30.

27. E. Franklin Frazier, "New Role of the Negro Woman," *Ebony*, August 1960, 40.

Index

Page numbers in *italics* refer to illustrations.

United States v. One Package of Japanese Pessaries (1936), 95, 180–81, 192, 203
University of North Carolina, 182
Unpossessed, The (Slesinger), 86, 96
Urban League, 23–24, 50, 51
U.S. Public Health Service, 26, 50
U.S. Supreme Court, 223, 260n102, 266n22

Vaginal orgasm, 211–13, 221, 224
Van de Velde, Theodoor, 184, 186, 212. See also *Ideal Marriage*
"Varietism," 83
Venereal disease, 16, 18–19, 24–27, 34, 36, 39, 51–52
    African Americans and, 19, 51–52
    association of, with prostitution, 18, 25
    elitist views on, 18–19, 39–40, 46
    and sex education, 18, 24–25, 34, 36, 39–40
Victorianism, 6–10, 94, 168, 191, 272n99
    African Americans and, 22–23, 53–54, 67, 154, 210
    marriage revisionists and, 108, 111, 119, 121, 124, 127, 134, 136–37, 169, 225
    sex radicals and, 60, 62, 66, 68–70, 80, 87, 103, 104
    sexual advice literature and, 190, 191, 192, 204, 205–6, 207
    social hygienists and, 18, 19, 20, 27–31, 35, 38, 39, 44, 53–54, 56, 57, 107
    undermining of, by social change, 11–13, 35, 57, 61, 107, 108–9, 118, 136
    see also Victorian repression, myth of
Victorian repression, myth of, 6–7, 9–10, 30–31, 58, 68–70, 154
"Voluntary motherhood," 10

Wage earning, women's. See Women's employment
Walker, A'Lelia, 67
Walker, Madame C. J., 67
War Camp Community Service (WCCS), 49

Washington, Booker T., 50, 67, 109
Waters, Ethel, 79
Weeds (Kelley), 69–70
Well of Loneliness, The (Hall), 68, 99
Wells, Ida B., 77
Wembridge, Eleanor, 47
Wicks, H. M., 65
Wilcox, Ella Wheeler, 16
Wile, Ira, 114, 165, 172. See also *Marriage in the Modern Manner* (Wile and Winn)
Williams, Edward Christopher, 116, 147, 150–53, 162
Winn, Mary Day, 114, 165. See also *Marriage in the Modern Manner* (Wile and Winn)
Woman and the New Race (Sanger), 83, 136
Woman Rebel, 64, 80–81, 82
Women's Christian Temperance Union (WCTU), 9
Women's employment, 165, 219, 222
    African Americans and, 137, 162–64, 222, 239n10
    attacks on, 221
    feminism and, 133, 165, 171–74
    growth of, 112, 174, 181, 221, 222
    and independence, 46–47, 111–12, 132–33
    and male breadwinner ideology, 174, 181
    and marriage revisionists, 132–33, 148–50
Women's equality, 11, 112, 171
    African Americans and, 137, 150–53, 162–65
    and call for shared housework, 4, 148, 170–71, 174, 176
    marriage revisionists and, 112, 122–23, 124, 132–34, 135–36, 137, 148–49, 220–21
    sex radicals and, 64, 72–73, 75–79, 97–98
    and sexuality, 75–79, 179, 192–93 (see also Female orgasm)
    social hygienists and, 41–43
    see also "Feminist marriage"
Woodhull, Victoria, 9
World War I, 16–18, 21, 26, 49–50